100 CLASSIC HIKES OREGON

100 CLASSIC HIKES

OREGON

ELI BOSCHETTO

Oregon Coast | Coast Range | Western Valleys | Columbia River Gorge
Cascade Range | Central Oregon | Wallowa Mountains | Southeast Oregon

MOUNTAINEERS
BOOKS

MOUNTAINEERS BOOKS is dedicated to the exploration, preservation, and enjoyment of outdoor and wilderness areas.

1001 SW Klickitat Way, Suite 201, Seattle, WA 98134
800-553-4453, www.mountaineersbooks.org

Printed in China

First edition, 2025

Design and layout: McKenzie Long, Cardinal Innovative
Cartographer: Bart Wright, Lohnes+Wright
All photographs by the author unless credited otherwise
Cover photograph: *Lookingglass Lake in the Eagle Cap Wilderness (Hike 97)*
Frontispiece: *Mount Thielsen, Lightning Rod of the Cascades (Hike 66)*
Last page: *Heading into the Eagle Cap Wilderness (Hike 96)*

Leave No Trace Seven Principles © Leave No Trace, www.LNT.org

The background maps for this book were produced using the online map viewer CalTopo. For more information, visit caltopo.com.

Library of Congress record is available at https://lccn.loc.gov/2025012016

Mountaineers Books titles may be purchased for corporate, educational, or other promotional sales, and our authors are available for a wide range of events. For information on special discounts or booking an author, contact our customer service at 800-553-4453 or mbooks@mountaineersbooks.org.

Printed on FSC-certified ® materials

MIX
Paper | Supporting responsible forestry
FSC www.fsc.org FSC® C188448

ISBN (paperback): 978-1-68051-624-1
ISBN (ebook): 978-1-68051-625-8

An independent nonprofit publisher since 1960

Contents

Hike Locator Map 8
Hikes at a Glance 9
Introduction 15
How to Use This Guide 33
Map Legend 34

Oregon Coast and Range

1. Fort to Sea Trail 38
2. Saddle Mountain 40
3. Clatsop Loop (Tillamook Head) 43
4. Cape Falcon 45
5. Kings Mountain 47
6. Cape Lookout 48
7. Cascade Head 50
8. The Knoll and Gods Thumb 53
9. Drift Creek Falls 54
10. Cape Perpetua 57
11. Sweet Creek Falls 59
12. Dellenback Dunes 61
13. Sunset Bay to Cape Arago 62
14. Blacklock Point 65
15. Humbug Mountain 67
16. Flora Dell Falls (Rogue River Trail) .. 68
17. Hunters Cove 70
18. Samuel H. Boardman Scenic Corridor 72

Western Valleys

19. Lower Table Rock 76
20. Spencer Butte 77
21. McDowell Creek Falls 79
22. Trail of Ten Falls (Silver Falls State Park) 81
23. Cooper Mountain 84
24. Tryon Creek 85
25. Redwood Loop (Hoyt Arboretum) ... 87
26. Wildwood Trail (Forest Park) 89
27. Balch Creek and Witch's Castle 94
28. Powell Butte 95

Columbia River Gorge

29. Latourell Falls 100
30. Angels Rest 102
31. Multnomah Falls Loop 104
32. Wahclella Falls 107
33. Eagle Creek to Tunnel Falls 108
34. Hood River Mountain 111
35. Rowena Plateau and McCall Point ...113

North Cascades

36. Chinidere Mountain 118
37. Owl Point 120
38. McNeil Point 122
39. Ramona Falls 125
40. Burnt Lake 127
41. Paradise Park 129
42. East Eliot Moraine and Cooper Spur . 132
43. Elk Meadows 135
44. Timberline Trail 137
45. High Prairie and Lookout Mountain . 142
46. Mirror Lake 144
47. Old Salmon River 146
48. Twin Lakes 148
49. Timothy Lake 149

Central Cascades

50. Hunts Cove 154
51. Duffy and Santiam Lakes 156
52. Iron Mountain 158
53. Sahalie Falls (McKenzie River) 160
54. Tamolitch Falls (Blue Pool) 162
55. Little Belknap 164
56. Three Sisters Loop 165
57. Tumalo Falls 170
58. Todd Lake 172
59. Mink Lake 174
60. Rosary Lakes 178
61. Divide Lake 179
62. Diamond Peak Loop 181

South Cascades

63. Toketee Falls 186
64. Lemolo Falls 187
65. Tipsoo Peak 189
66. Thielsen Creek 192
67. Wizard Island 194
68. Garfield Peak 196
69. Seven Lakes Basin 198
70. Mountain Lakes Loop 201
71. Pilot Rock 204

Central Oregon

72. Fort Rock 208
73. Newberry Crater 209
74. Ancient Juniper Forest 212
75. Lava River Cave 214
76. Lava Butte 216
77. Shevlin Park 218
78. Misery Ridge 220
79. Steins Pillar 222
80. Lookout Mountain 223
81. Blue Basin 226
82. Strawberry Loop 228
83. Arch Rock 231
84. Crawfish Lake 233

Wallowa Mountains

85. Nine Mile Ridge 236
86. Wenaha River Trail 238
87. Imnaha River Trail 240
88. Tenderfoot Loop 242
89. Mount Howard (Tram) 244
90. Ice Lake 246
91. Glacier Lake Loop 249
92. Francis Lake 252
93. Chimney Lake 254
94. Steamboat Loop 257
95. Echo Lake 260
96. Eagle Lake Loop 263
97. Lookingglass Lake 266

Southeast Oregon

98. Juniper Gulch 270
99. Big Indian Gorge 272
100. Wildhorse Basin 274

Acknowledgments 277
Resources and Land Managers 279
References and Recommended Reading .. 281
Index 282

HIKE LOCATOR

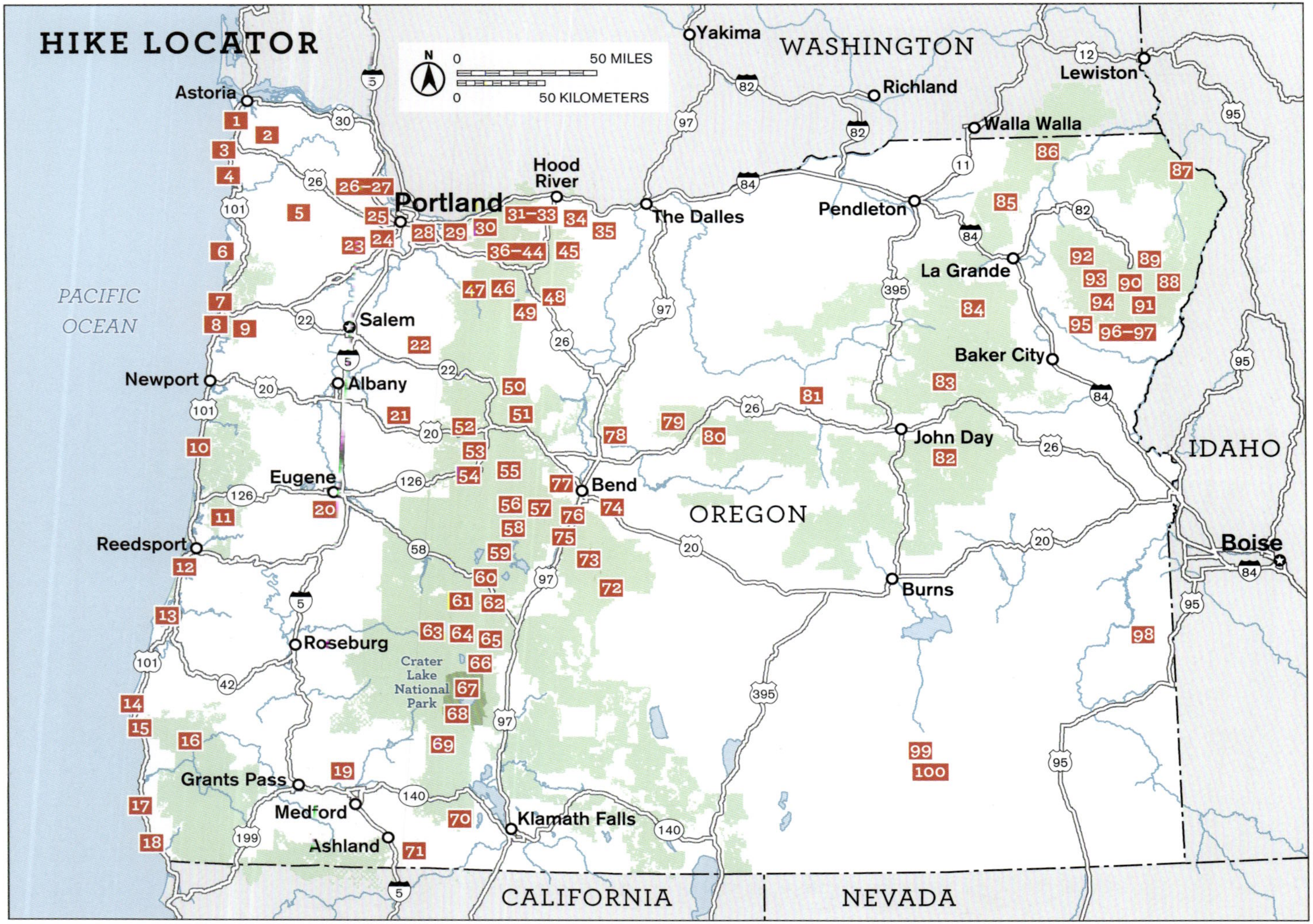

Hikes at a Glance

NO.	NAME	DISTANCE (ROUNDTRIP)	DIFFICULTY	SEASON	HIGHLIGHTS
SHORT HIKES (LESS THAN 3 HOURS)					
3	Clatsop Loop (Tillamook Head)	2.8 miles	Moderate	Year-round	Legacy trail, lighthouse view, backpacking
4	Cape Falcon	4.2 miles	Moderate	Year-round	Legacy trail, wildflowers, coast views
9	Drift Creek Falls	3 miles	Moderate	Apr–Nov	Family-friendly
10	Cape Perpetua	1.9 miles / 2.4 miles	Easy / Strenuous	Year-round	Coastal features and views, family-friendly, camping
11	Sweet Creek Falls	1.9 miles	Easy	Year-round	Waterfall, family-friendly
14	Blacklock Point	3.7 miles	Easy	Year-round	Legacy trail, coast views
17	Hunters Cove	3.3 miles	Moderate	Year-round	State park, coast views, wildflowers
20	Spencer Butte	2.2 miles	Moderate–Strenuous	Year-round	Valley views, picnic area
21	McDowell Creek Falls	1.6 miles	Easy	Year-round	Legacy trail, waterfalls, family-friendly
23	Cooper Mountain	2 miles	Moderate	Year-round	Exceptional wildflowers, historic setting
24	Tryon Creek	2.3 miles	Easy	Year-round	Legacy trail, state park, visitor center
25	Redwood Loop (Hoyt Arboretum)	0.9 mile	Easy	Year-round	Exceptional trees, visitor center, guided walks
27	Balch Creek & Witch's Castle	1.5 miles	Easy	Year-round	Witch's Castle, family-friendly
28	Powell Butte	2.5 miles	Easy	Year-round	Wildflowers, mountain views
29	Latourell Falls	2 miles	Easy	Apr–Nov	Legacy trail, partially barrier-free
32	Wahclella Falls	1.7 miles	Easy	Year-round	Waterfalls, family-friendly
34	Hood River Mountain	3 miles	Easy	Mar–Nov	Legacy trail, wildflowers, mountain views
35	Rowena Plateau & McCall Point	2.1 miles / 3.6 miles	Easy / Moderate	May–Oct	Exceptional wildflowers, gorge views
37	Owl Point	4.2 miles	Easy	Jul–Oct	Restored trail, mountain views
45	High Prairie & Lookout Mountain	2.5 miles	Easy	Jul–Oct	Legacy trail, mountain views, family-friendly
46	Mirror Lake	4.1 miles	Moderate	Jun–Oct	Lake and mountain views, backpacking

NO.	NAME	DISTANCE (ROUNDTRIP)	DIFFICULTY	SEASON	HIGHLIGHTS
53	Sahalie Falls (McKenzie River)	2.4 miles	Easy	May–Nov	Waterfalls, family-friendly
54	Tamolitch Falls (Blue Pool)	3.8 miles	Moderate	May–Nov	Unique geology, swimming hole
58	Todd Lake	1.7 miles	Easy	Jul–Oct	Legacy trail, family-friendly, camping
63	Toketee Falls	0.8 mile	Easy	Apr–Nov	Legacy trail, unique waterfall, family-friendly
64	Lemolo Falls	3.4 miles	Easy	Jul–Oct	National scenic trail, back-packing
68	Garfield Peak	3.4 miles	Moderate	Jul–Oct	Legacy trail, exceptional views, wildflowers, Crater Lake NP
72	Fort Rock	2.3 miles	Easy	Year-round	Unique geology, historical setting, family-friendly
74	Ancient Juniper Forest	3.2 miles	Easy	Year-round (weather permitting)	Unique geology, family-friendly
75	Lava River Cave	2 miles	Easy	May–Sep	Lava tube, family-friendly, flashlights required
76	Lava Butte	3.3 miles	Moderate	Year-round (weather permitting)	Fire lookout, mountain views, geology
79	Steins Pillar	3.7 miles	Easy	May–Nov	Legacy trail, unique geology, wildflowers
81	Blue Basin	4 miles	Moderate	Mar–Nov	Legacy trail, unique geology, fossils, rattlesnakes
83	Arch Rock	0.5 mile	Easy	May–Nov	Legacy trail, unique geology, family-friendly
84	Crawfish Lake	2.8 miles	Easy	Jul–Nov	Legacy trail, family-friendly, backpacking
88	Mount Howard (Tram)	2.5 miles	Easy	Jul–Oct	Gondola ride, exceptional views, family-friendly, cafe
98	Juniper Gulch	1.9 miles	Easy	Apr–Oct	Unique geology, sensitive habitat
HALF-DAY HIKES (3–5 HOURS)					
1	Fort to Sea Trail	6.2 miles (one-way)	Easy	Year-round	Historic trail, visitor center
2	Saddle Mountain	4.5 miles	Strenuous	Year-round	Legacy trail, exceptional wildflowers, views
5	Kings Mountain	4.5 miles	Brutal	Apr–Nov	Legacy trail, brutal!
6	Cape Lookout	4.7 miles	Moderate	Year-round	Whale watching

NO.	NAME	DISTANCE (ROUNDTRIP)	DIFFICULTY	SEASON	HIGHLIGHTS
7	Cascade Head	4.5 miles	Strenuous	Year-round	Wildflowers, coast views
8	The Knoll and Gods Thumb	4.5 miles	Moderate	Year-round	Wildflowers, coast views
12	Dellenback Dunes	5 miles	Strenuous	Year-round	Birding, beaches, camping
13	Sunset Bay to Cape Arago	6.5 miles	Easy	Year-round	Legacy trail, exceptional coast views, botanical garden
15	Humbug Mountain	5 miles	Strenuous	Year-round	Wildflowers, beach access, camping
19	Lower Table Rock	4.6 miles	Moderate	Year-round	Legacy trail, exceptional wildflowers
22	Trail of Ten Falls (Silver Falls State Park)	2.7–7.3 miles	Easy–Moderate	Year-round	Legacy trail, waterfalls, family-friendly, camping
26	Wildwood Trail (Forest Park)	varies	Easy–Moderate	Year-round	Legacy trail, urban forest
30	Angels Rest	4.5 miles	Moderate	May–Nov	Legacy trail, gorge views
31	Multnomah Falls Loop	4.9 miles	Strenuous	Apr–Oct	Legacy trail, waterfalls
36	Chinidere Mountain	5 miles	Moderate	Jul–Oct	Mountain views, PCT, camping
39	Ramona Falls	7 miles	Strenuous	Jun–Oct	Exceptional waterfall, river ford
40	Burnt Lake	6.6 miles	Moderate	Jul–Oct	Secluded lake, mountain views, backpacking
42	East Eliot Moraine & Cooper Spur	6.7 miles	Strenuous	Jul–Oct	Legacy trail, exceptional mountain and glacier views
43	Elk Meadows	5.5 miles	Moderate	Jul–Oct	Wildflowers, backcountry shelter, river ford
47	Old Salmon River	4.9 miles	Easy	Apr–Nov	Old-growth forest, family-friendly
48	Twin Lakes	7.3 miles	Easy	Jul–Oct	Lakes, mountain views, PCT, backpacking
52	Iron Mountain	6.8 miles	Strenuous	Jun–Oct	Mountain lookout, wildflowers, historical setting
55	Little Belknap	4.8 miles	Moderate	Jul–Oct	Lava flows, PCT
57	Tumalo Falls	6.9 miles	Moderate	Jun–Oct	Waterfalls
60	Rosary Lakes	6.8 miles	Moderate	Jul–Oct	Lakes, PCT, backpacking
61	Divide Lake	7.6 miles	Moderate	Jul–Oct	Legacy trail, huckleberries, backpacking
65	Tipsoo Peak	6.2 miles	Moderate	Jul–Oct	Legacy trail, exceptional views, PCT summit

NO.	NAME	DISTANCE (ROUNDTRIP)	DIFFICULTY	SEASON	HIGHLIGHTS
67	Wizard Island	4.3 miles	Strenuous	Jul–Sep	Legacy trail, unique geology, Crater Lake NP, boat ride
71	Pilot Rock	4.6 miles	Moderate	Jul–Oct	Unique geology, historical setting, PCT
77	Shevlin Park	4.5 miles	Easy	Year-round	Picnic area, family-friendly
78	Misery Ridge	3.7 miles	Strenuous	Apr–Nov	Legacy trail, unique geology, picnic area, state park
80	Lookout Mountain	6.9 miles	Moderate	Jun–Oct	Historical setting, backcountry shelter, wildflowers
86	Wenaha River Trail	7.5 miles	Moderate	Apr–Nov	Legacy trail, wildflowers, rattlesnakes
100	Wildhorse Lake	2.4 miles	Strenuous	Aug–Oct	Legacy trail, high elevation, wildflowers
DAY HIKES (5–8 HOURS)					
16	Flora Dell Falls (Rogue River Trail)	8 miles	Moderate	Apr–Nov	Legacy trail, waterfall, backpacking
18	Samuel H. Boardman Scenic Corridor	8 miles	Moderate	Year-round	Legacy trail, exceptional coast views
33	Eagle Creek to Tunnel Falls	11.8 miles	Moderate	Apr–Nov	Legacy trail, waterfalls, wildflowers
38	McNeil Point	9.2 miles	Strenuous	Jul–Oct	Exceptional wildflowers and views, backpacking
49	Timothy Lake	12.4 miles	Moderate	Jun–Nov	Lakes, mountain views, PCT, backpacking
50	Hunts Cove	11.8 miles	Moderate	Jul–Oct	Lakes, wildflowers, backpacking, permit required
51	Duffy & Santiam Lakes	10 miles	Moderate	Jul–Oct	Lakes, wildflowers, backpacking, permit required
66	Thielsen Creek	11.3 miles	Moderate	Jul–Oct	Legacy trail, views, wildflowers, PCT, backpacking
85	Nine Mile Ridge	7.4 miles	Strenuous	May–Nov	Legacy trail, wildflowers
87	Imnaha River Trail	9 miles	Moderate	Apr–Nov	Exceptional views, historical site
93	Chimney Lake	10 miles	Moderate	Jul–Oct	Lakes, views, backpacking
95	Echo Lake	9.8 miles	Moderate	Aug–Oct	Exceptional wilderness, mountain views, backpacking

NO.	NAME	DISTANCE (ROUNDTRIP)	DIFFICULTY	SEASON	HIGHLIGHTS
LONG DAY HIKES / BACKPACKS (MORE THAN 8 HOURS)					
41	Paradise Park	12.2 miles	Strenuous	Jul–Oct	Exceptional wildflowers and views, backpacking
44	Timberline Trail	39.4 miles	Strenuous	Jul–Oct	Legacy trail, exceptional views and wildflowers, river fords, backpacking
56	Three Sisters Loop	46 miles	Moderate	Jul–Oct	Legacy trail, exceptional views, PCT, backpacking, permit required
59	Mink Lake	20.8 miles	Moderate	Jul–Oct	Lakes, wildflowers, PCT, backpacking, permit required
62	Diamond Peak Loop	33 miles	Moderate	Jul–Oct	Exceptional wilderness, views, PCT, backpacking
69	Seven Lakes Basin	16.6 miles	Moderate	Jul–Oct	Legacy trail, exceptional wilderness, PCT, backpacking
70	Mountain Lakes Loop	16.7 miles	Strenuous	Jul–Oct	Legacy trail, remote wilderness, lakes, backpacking
73	Newberry Crater	20.8 miles	Strenuous	Jun–Oct	Exceptional views, lakes, geology, backpacking
82	Strawberry Loop	15.7 miles	Strenuous	Jul–Oct	Legacy trail, lakes, wildflowers, camping, backpacking
88	Tenderfoot Loop	14.8 miles	Strenuous	Jul–Oct	Exceptional wilderness, lakes, wildflowers, backpacking
90	Ice Lake	14.7 miles	Strenuous	Jul–Oct	Exceptional wilderness, wildflowers, backpacking
91	Glacier Lake Loop	26.5 miles	Strenuous	Jul–Oct	Exceptional wilderness, lakes, wildflowers, backpacking
92	Francis Lake	17.5 miles	Strenuous	Jul–Oct	Legacy trail, alpine lake, backpacking
94	Steamboat Loop	26.2 miles (one-way)	Strenuous	Jul–Oct	Legacy trail, exceptional wilderness, wildflowers, backpacking
96	Eagle Lake Loop	17.5 miles	Strenuous	Jul–Oct	Legacy trail, exceptional wilderness, backpacking
97	Lookingglass Lake	12.9 miles	Strenuous	Jul–Oct	Alpine lake, waterfall, views, backpacking
99	Big Indian Gorge	16 miles	Moderate	Jul–Oct	Legacy trail, exceptional views, wildflowers, backpacking

Introduction

When you think of Oregon, you likely think of green trees and rain. To be sure, it has a lot of both, and both contribute greatly to Oregon being a fantastic place to live and recreate. Of course, that's in addition to all the hipsters, donuts, microbrews, marionberries, indie music, bigfoot sightings, and *The Goonies* landmarks. But did you know that there are fantastic places in Oregon that you have probably never heard of? Places beyond the trees—places that stretch the imagination and resemble settings more akin to Hawaii, Yosemite, the Southwest, Iceland, Scotland, or even Middle Earth? And lucky for you, there are hiking trails to explore it all!

This book you're holding is your invitation and guide to fantastic hiking trails in every corner of the Beaver State—from its rugged and dramatic western coast to its otherworldly eastern borders, from its northern volcanic plateaus and river gorges to its remote southeastern mountains and high prairies. And yes, you'll also find plenty of hikes that wind through those thirty-million-plus acres of flower-, mushroom-, and faerie-filled forests. You'll be hard-pressed to name a type of terrain or landscape that you *can't* find in Oregon—along with a hiking trail to help you explore it—among its 361 state parks, 47 wilderness areas, 21 national wildlife refuges, and 11 national forests. And while this guide can't list *every* trail you'll find in Oregon, it does describe one hundred of the most amazing and unique—a collection of classic hikes that is sure to entice outdoor enthusiasts of every ability and interest. So grab yourself a refreshing kombucha and recyclable bag of organic kale chips (or other snack and beverage of your choice) and start page-turning to plan your own classic Oregon adventure!

WHAT MAKES A HIKE "CLASSIC"?

Like classic rock, classic movies, classic cars, and classic books, the concept of "classic" denotes something especially notable for its quality, style, creativity, or aesthetic, in a typically timeless fashion. That was the approach taken in selecting the destinations in this guide—to choose trails and locations that weather the seasons and the crowds, that represent the best that Oregon's diverse and unique outdoors has to offer, and that will keep you coming back again and again.

CARRYING ON AN OUTDOOR LEGACY

The original version of this guide was first published in 2004 by notable trail author Douglas Lorain, who has logged more than sixteen thousand miles on Oregon's hiking trails. His inspiration was to showcase the outstanding scenery that Oregon's outdoor places have to offer, along with all the wildflowers, old-growth forests, wildlife, and geologic features that make them especially admirable and enjoyable. In addition to publishing *100 Classic Hikes in Oregon*, Lorain has also published a number of other guides highlighting trails in both Oregon and Washington, making him one of the preeminent voices in trail knowledge and experience. Then, seeking a change of scenery and new adventures, Lorain moved east to Rocky Mountain country and published *100 Classic Hikes in Montana* in 2018.

Way back in the ancient days of 2005, when my wife and I moved from the hectic freeways and strip malls of Orange County, California, to

Opposite: Huge view from the Eliot Moraine Trail on Mount Hood

Support Your Public Lands

At the time of this book's publication, America's public lands, forests, and wilderness areas are under pressure from political and commercial interests. These lands are America's heritage and should be cherished and protected, now and into the future. If you value these public lands where you enjoy recreating, please consider joining an advocacy group or donating to one such as Oregon Wild or the Oregon Trails Coalition or, on a national level, groups like Sierra Club, Wilderness Society, and National Parks Conservation Association. Most of all, make your voice heard. Call your state and federal representatives and demand that public lands be funded and preserved.

the mellow and tree-lined suburbs of Portland, Oregon, one of the first hiking guides I picked up was Douglas Lorain's *100 Classic Hikes in Oregon*. As avid hikers, we were just itching to begin exploring our new backyard. We went on countless outings to Mount Hood and the Columbia River Gorge. Weekend trips down to the Three Sisters and out to the John Day Fossil Beds. And when we set foot into the Wallowa Mountains high country, we were certain that our move to the Northwest was for the better—a thousand times over!

Fast-forward twenty years, and I find myself following in Lorain's footsteps in more ways than one, leaving behind a career in production and marketing for trail-writing stints with *Backpacker*, Washington Trails Association, and, since 2014, Mountaineers Books. I thought I was done with guidebook writing in 2020, after the publication of my most recent book, *Day Hiking: Mount Hood*. I felt I was ready for a change of pace and was considering new ways to advocate outdoor adventure and protection. Then along came the pandemic, and everything shut down. Since going outside was really the only option at the time—and I needed a project—I pitched a few ideas to my editors at Mountaineers Books, and they came back with, "How about you take over and update *100 Classic Hikes in Oregon*?"

Admittedly, I was not eager to take on this particular project. I mean, this was a classic guide created by a legacy writer and authority on Oregon trails. It felt like they were asking me to rewrite *Star Wars* or "Bohemian Rhapsody." I had to noodle on this one for a while, considering not only the logistics of surveying and writing up descriptions for one hundred trails spanning the entire state, but also whether my style and expertise were worthy of such a lofty title by an outdoors expert of Lorain's caliber. *What the hell*, I thought. The pandemic was in full swing. I was bored out of my mind and needed an assignment. And considering the then-current state of Oregon's trails, this guide was due for an update. And maybe, by breathing some fresh air into *100 Classic Hikes*—along with some of my trademark charm, snark, and obsession with *The Lord of the Rings*—I could introduce a new generation to Oregon's amazing outdoors while still carrying on Lorain's legacy of exploration, appreciation, and advocacy.

All that romanticism aside, the development of this guide was by no means a cakewalk. I had to dodge more lightning storms and wildfires than I care to remember, experienced a few close encounters with bears, and am pretty sure I was stalked by a cougar. I was also set back for six months by a surprise heart attack (unrelated to the cougar thing). In the end, I assembled a combination of classic trails from Lorain's previous guide, some of my own favorites, and a few new additions that range from secluded lakes to volcanic slot canyons. Altogether, this updated guide offers you one hundred tried-and-true "new" classic trails that are sure to open your eyes to the scenic wonder that is Oregon—far beyond what you may have already seen or think you know.

That being said, there are some trails you will not find in this guide. Just like some of those classic eighties tunes, they've been played out (I'm talking about you, "Safety Dance"!), having become so crowded and overused that they don't need any more publicity. Others were left out because recent wildfires across the state have ravaged so much of our public lands and national forests, rendering some areas no longer worthwhile to hike or too unsafe to research during the development of this guide. Perhaps in a future update, a few of these classic classics will find their way back onto these pages. Until then, enjoy a little change of scenery with these "new" *100 Classic Hikes in Oregon*.

BEFORE YOU GO

Not so fast, eager beaver! (FYI, the beaver is Oregon's state animal.) Before you hop in your car and zip out to the nearest trailhead, take a few moments to review the following information. It will help you prepare for any permits you might need, give you the lowdown on current trail regulations and expectations, and share how you, too, can be a steward of Oregon's natural spaces.

Trailhead Permits and Fees

Like it or not, permits (and their associated fees) are becoming more of a requirement in Oregon as the state's trails and backcountry areas get more popular and crowded. And while you may bristle at the thought of having to pay to visit your public lands, a small fee can go a long way in helping to maintain roads and trails. This is especially vital in these days of ever-declining Forest Service budgets and staffing. You are most likely to find permit/fee requirements at developed trailheads and popular locations. Plenty of other trails don't require any fee or permit at all—and these are often some of the best trails where you will find the most solitude. Here are the most common types of permit and fee requirements:

A **Northwest Forest Pass** (or federal Interagency Pass) is required at many national forest trailheads. These locations are usually developed and have good parking areas, restrooms, and picnic facilities. You can purchase a one-day or annual pass at many gear shops and ranger stations; or purchase them online at discovernw.org.

Most trails in Oregon's Central Cascades region require a **Central Cascades Wilderness Permit**. These are available as single- or multi-day passes and must be reserved in advance for hikes occurring during the summer season. Permits are released in batches at the beginning of each season, with a portion held in reserve to become available seven days before each potential hike start date. Visit recreation.gov, search for "Central Cascades Wilderness," and look for the trailhead you're interested in visiting.

A handful of other locations in this guide may also require a special fee or permit for accessing trails. Some of Oregon's state parks require a **day-use fee**. These are typically paid on-site using a kiosk, cash drop box, or agency app. Oregon's only national park, Crater Lake, has its own entry fee, payable at the Mazama Village or North Entrance Road entry stations. A few trails may require a special fee for a boat or tram ride to reach a destination.

On some national forest lands, primarily in wilderness areas, visitors are asked to register and carry a **wilderness self-issue permit**. These free permits are generally found at kiosks near trailheads and wilderness boundaries, and they serve two primary purposes. The first is to register your entry into an area and your planned destination(s). This lets wilderness managers know where you're planning to go and when you're planning to exit. This information can be critical for locating you if an incident (landslide, wildfire) or emergency (injury) occurs. The second purpose is to allow land managers to monitor how many people are using trails and backcountry destinations. This helps them identify where to focus precious maintenance staff and funding to keep trails in good repair. For these important reasons, it is highly recommended that you register at every kiosk you encounter.

Road and Trail Conditions

Hiking trails throughout Oregon generally remain in good condition from one season to the next, barring any significant weather or wildfire events. Heavy rain can wash out trails. Heavy snowfall can down trees onto trails. The same can be said of roads, especially remote and/or unimproved forest roads. Wildfires—which are becoming more intense and prolific in Oregon—can devastate entire swaths of forest and accelerate damage in the form of washouts, rockfalls, landslides, and falling trees. One thing this guidebook cannot tell you is what the condition of any trail is *right now*.

When the research for this guidebook was being done, all of the featured trails were open and accessible. Some trails did show signs of damage and/or neglect, and some trails were undergoing maintenance. Many popular trails that you might expect to see in this guide were intentionally left out due to their poor condition or difficult accessibility. A handful were omitted because recent fires have rendered them no longer enjoyable. Before heading out, call the local land manager to inquire about any conditions or closures that may be affecting your trails of choice.

Trailhead Concerns

While most of us head for our favorite trails and backcountry locations for some innocent recreation and rejuvenation, not everyone has the same good intentions. Thankfully, most criminals are lazy, and committing crimes on trails is usually too much effort. That said, staying vigilant and keeping a healthy level of awareness is always a good idea. Here are a few tips to help ensure that you have a safe experience outdoors.

When arriving at the trailhead, **case the place** and look for anything or anyone that seems out of place. Criminals rely on stealth and may leave if they feel "made." Snap a casual pic of any questionable-looking vehicles (including its license plate) and make a note with a description of the person inside. When you saddle up for the trail, **never leave valuables** in your vehicle. Take (or hide) anything and everything that might look appealing. Even if it's empty, a closed sunglasses case might look like it contains an expensive pair, and a smartphone charger might make a prowler think your iPhone is still in the car.

When you're out on the trail, **trust your instincts**. If you sense that someone you meet on-trail has questionable intentions, allow yourself to be guarded and rude if necessary. Never tell anyone you meet where you're headed, especially if you're hiking alone. Be vague: "I'm just going for a while." And **never mention your party size**. If you're hiking alone, use "we" statements to baffle a potential criminal. Shouting "Hurry up, Wanda!" or "Move it, Steve!" into the bushes may deter someone who thinks you're an easy solo target.

When in the backcountry, **avoid hiking with earbuds in**. Try listening to birdsong, squeaking pikas, and babbling streams instead of blasting your favorite Metric album. Paying attention to your surroundings will help you hear someone—or something—coming.

WILDERNESS REGULATIONS AND ETHICS

In 1964, the **Wilderness Act** was authorized to protect some of the most beautiful, unique, and culturally significant natural spaces in the United States, preserving them in their primitive state for the enjoyment and recreation of the public. Wilderness areas are administered by a variety of agencies, including the US Forest Service and the Bureau of Land Management. There are currently more than eight hundred designated wilderness areas in the United States, protecting more than 111 million acres of land. Wilderness rules are often posted at trailheads and wilderness boundaries. In addition to the **Leave No Trace** principles (see below), please adhere to the following guidelines:

Know and follow the **current fire restrictions**. As Oregon's summers get hotter and drier due to climate change, wildfires are becoming more frequent and destructive. Use only approved stoves and follow all seasonal campfire bans.

Obtain and carry the proper **wilderness permits**. Some wilderness trails in Oregon have limited accessibility to protect sensitive and

Follow Leave No Trace guidelines when choosing where to camp

overused areas. Find out what permit requirements are in place for the area you'd like to visit and obtain them in advance if necessary.

Keep your **group size under twelve**. To minimize the impact of groups in wilderness areas, keep your hiking parties small, walk single file, and keep your campsites clean.

Mechanized and wheeled devices are prohibited. Leave bicycles, wagons, chainsaws, and drones at home. **Never bring fireworks** or explosive devices into wilderness areas.

Leave No Trace

When hiking anywhere, the general rule of thumb is to **Leave No Trace (LNT)**. Every hiker should take these seven LNT guidelines to heart to have the best outdoors experience, provide enjoyable experiences for others, and help maintain an attractive outdoors for future generations.

Plan ahead and prepare. You're already off to a good start with this guidebook. Use the info and resources on these pages to help you select your hikes and plan safe outings. When you can, avoid peak usage times, such as summer weekends and holidays.

Travel and camp on durable surfaces. Stick to the trails. Don't cut switchbacks, and don't tromp through flower meadows. Sensitive wilderness environments can take decades to recover from just one footprint. If you need a break, step off the trail onto a dirt or rock surface.

When it comes to camping in Oregon's forests and wilderness areas, your options are generally frontcountry campgrounds and dispersed backcountry locations. Many of the trails in this guide are located near established campgrounds, where you can take advantage of tent pads, fire rings, picnic tables, and a variety of other amenities. These locations typically have a nominal nightly fee, and some will take reservations. They make great bases for exploring several trails in a particular area.

For camping in the backcountry, first check to see if there are any restrictions. Some locations might have designated campsites or entry limits. Try to use existing campsites before creating a new one. Always choose durable surfaces (dirt, rock, snow) at least 100 feet from trails and 200 feet from water. Avoid camping in meadows or on other vegetation. When you break camp, be sure you didn't leave anything behind, and brush away any evidence of your stay.

Dispose of waste properly. Pack it in, pack it out. There's nary an eyesore as offensive as trash in the wilderness. Be extra vigilant about managing your waste—and don't be afraid to pick up any trash you may find. Nature will bless you with good juju.

For cleanup time, wash up away from camp, trails, and water sources with biodegradable soap. Never wash your dirty clothes or dishes in lakes, rivers, or streams. Dispose of your dirty wash water by scattering it over a grassy or brushy area at least 200 feet away from camps and water sources.

If you suddenly have the need to engage in the backcountry squat, find a private place at least 100 feet off-trail and 200 feet from water. Make your deposit in a hole six to eight inches deep and pack out your used toilet tissue in a

The splendor of Oregon's wilderness areas

zip-top bag. It's a good idea to pack along a little toilet kit for those just-in-case moments, even on day hikes. Use a small stuff sack to carry a lightweight trowel (for digging your hole), some toilet tissue, a zip-top bag, and some hand sanitizer for cleaning up. Animal waste bags are a terrific option for packing out used toilet tissue, as they're opaque, weigh next to nothing, and often contain a deodorizer. Toss a small roll into your kit and you'll be a happy camper.

Leave what you find. Avoid the temptation to pick wildflowers or pocket a pretty rock. Follow the hiker's motto "Take only photos, leave only footprints." This will ensure that Oregon's special and beloved outdoor spaces will continue to be enjoyed by future generations. A photo of a wildflower on your Instagram will last longer than any flower you may be tempted to pick.

Minimize campfires. Although sitting around a fire while swapping stories and roasting marshmallows is an age-old outdoor tradition, campfires can be a hassle to build and maintain—and they are also the culprits behind some of Oregon's largest and most damaging wildfires. If you feel the urge to indulge in some campfire camaraderie, build one only when and where permitted, following all seasonal rules, and only in established fire rings. Use only dead or downed wood and keep it small and under control. Be sure to monitor your campfire at all times and fully extinguish it before going to sleep or leaving the area.

Respect wildlife. When you venture out into the woods and wilderness areas in Oregon, you are a guest in the home of all the winged and furry creatures that reside in the trees, waters, and mountains. Most are mild-mannered critters that spend their days searching for food, raising their young, and keeping up their homes. When you spot wildlife on the trail, enjoy the experience from a distance to prevent the animals from getting nervous or aggressive.

While catching a glimpse of a large animal is always a thrilling experience, the critters you are most likely to see are small squirrels, chipmunks, and Canada jays. All of these, especially the latter, are more than willing to help themselves to

Mule deer

your snacks, so keep an eye on your food. And while they're cute, don't be tempted to share your trail mix with them. This conditions them to bad feeding habits and can make them aggressive, putting both you and the animal at risk.

You're less likely to see deer, elk, skunks, porcupines, bobcats, coyotes, black bears, and cougars (mountain lions)—though all of them are out there. These animals want little to do with humans, so they tend to stay away from popular camping and hiking areas. Although encounters with these intriguing and majestic animals are extremely rare, they do occasionally happen. If you find yourself in such a situation, remain silent and enjoy the experience, and know how to respond to unwanted attention if the need should arise.

Be considerate of others. Everyone deserves to have enjoyable outdoors experiences, whether they're fellow hikers, trail runners, equestrians, hunters, or mountain bikers. See the next section for suggestions about how you can exercise top-notch trail courtesy.

For more information about Leave No Trace, visit lnt.org.

Trail Etiquette

When on the trail, as in life, a little kindness goes a long way. Having a mountain lake or summit viewpoint all to yourself may be an ideal situation, but it's just not that likely—especially with the increasing number of people escaping to the forests and mountains for a little rest and relaxation time. Instead of being annoyed by others, just take a deep breath and appreciate that they're out there for the same reasons as you. After all, the more people that use and appreciate our natural spaces and public lands, the more people will take part in protecting them.

Stay on-trail when hiking. Don't be tempted to cut switchbacks or take shortcuts, as this only damages the landscape. When others follow, that damage is magnified and starts to become a blemish, reducing the beauty of a location and compromising its integrity. If you must scout around to find a safe water crossing, try to stay on durable surfaces and avoid trampling vegetation.

Stay to the right. Just like you do on roads and bike paths—unless you live in the UK—stay to the right side of the trail. This gives hikers coming the other way an easy passage without any awkward run-ins. If you're hiking with companions, try to hike single file.

Follow right-of-way guidelines. Yield to uphill hikers. Hiking uphill is a lot more work than hiking downhill and restarting an uphill slog after pausing takes much more effort. If you're joyously skipping downhill and encounter other hikers heading up, step to the side and let them pass.

Do your part to help preserve Oregon's wild spaces.

There are general rules of thumb when it comes to encountering other types of trail users. When encountering equestrians, step off the trail and let them pass. It is best to step off downslope, if possible to do so safely, so as not to spook horses. Do the same for mountain bikes. Official right-of-way rules suggest that mountain bikers should yield to hikers, but in most cases this is just not practical. As a hiker, you have more agility to move than they do, and it's easier for you to start walking again than it is for a cyclist to restart their ride. Avoid confrontations with wheeled trail users by taking the high road—just step aside to let them pass.

Take breaks off-trail. When you need to stop for a drink, catch your breath, or snap a pic, step completely off the trail (onto a durable surface) to avoid blocking other hikers. Also, make sure your pack or trekking poles aren't tripping hazards for others.

Use your quiet voice. When chatting with your hiking companions, be considerate of others. Most hikers would rather hear the soothing sounds of the wind and water than a heated debate over who was right, Captain America or Iron Man (Team Cap, all the way!).

Manage Your Dog

If you enjoy hiking with your pooch, be aware of any regulations an area or trail may have concerning dogs. This will often be posted at trailheads and/or park entrances. In this guide, look for information about dog regulations in the Notes section near the beginning of the hike descriptions. Also bear in mind that not every hiker loves dogs, and small children can often be frightened of large animals. When approaching or passing other hikers, heel your dog to your side to prevent them from encroaching on others, especially small children.

Challenging terrain that can be rough for booted feet can be doubly challenging for little doggie paws, so **choose dog-friendly trails.**

Oregon's spectacular Eagle Cap Wilderness

Avoid trails with a lot of sharp lava rock, consider the distance and elevation gain of a trail, and evaluate whether your furry friend has the stamina to complete the hike—or if you'll be carrying them back out!

You should **outfit your pooch** well for a good day on-trail. Use a pair of trail booties to protect their paws from sharp rocks, sticks, and thorns, and pack a doggy rain jacket in case the weather turns. Dogs can contract giardia from contaminated water the same way humans can. Carry enough clean water for your dog to keep them hydrated, as well as snacks and treats to keep their energy up.

Leave No Trace applies to dogs just as much as humans, so **pack out their poop**. If your dog does its business on the trail, pick it up with a disposable doggie-dropping bag and pack it out with your trash. *Do not leave dog waste bags on the side of the trail to be picked up later.* Chances are, you'll forget about it, or forget where you left it, and someone else will feel obliged to pick it up and pack it out—and no one wants to clean up after *your* dog.

SAFETY

The following information will help you stay safe and be prepared for anything you might encounter on the trail: weather conditions, water safety, cooking and food safety, river fords, and wildlife encounters. You're almost to the good stuff! Once you're fully prepared, get ready to immerse yourself in some amazing Oregon hiking experiences.

Weather

Weather on Oregon's trails is usually *somewhat* predictable. Winter is cold and snowy, spring is cool and wet, summer is warm and sunny, and fall is a mixed bag. The Northwest's volcanic Cascades can create their own weather, so conditions often change—sometimes quickly. Weather can also be quite variable from one side of the state to the other, or at different elevations. While it

Thunderstorms can build up fast over Oregon's mountains.

may be cool and rainy in the western valleys, it may be warm and sunny in the Cascades and high desert. Don't automatically discount rainy days as nonhiking days. You may just need to get around or above it. The best way to check current weather conditions and forecasts is to visit noaa.gov.

Conversely, there are good reasons *not* to go hiking if the weather or temperature looks unsavory. Hot summer days can not only be stifling and exhausting but can also produce sudden thunderstorms over the mountains that bring torrential rain, hail, snow, and lightning. Heavy rains can swell rivers and streams and make them impassable, and high winds can topple trees, especially in recently burned areas. It's a good idea to wait for storms to pass before venturing out onto the trails. And if you find yourself already out there when a storm comes through, be extra vigilant of your surroundings. Descend from high ridges and retreat from any sharp, exposed peaks.

If you observe lightning, evacuate the area as quickly and safely as possible. Just because you see lightning in the distance, that doesn't mean it can't reach you. Lightning bolts have been measured to be hundreds of miles long, so even if a storm looks far away, you have no reason to feel secure. If you need to take shelter, look for an area of low, uniform trees below the tree line. Do not shelter in a tent or under a rock overhang. And even if the day is starting off sunny, it's always a good idea to carry rain gear with you—just in case.

Water

While fresh mountain water may look clean and inviting, it takes only one gulp of contaminated

Carry a compact filter for safe drinking

water to do you in. If you're inclined to indulge in tasty mountain creeks and streams, you should only do so after filtering the water properly. Water-treatment devices range from carbon or ceramic filters that eliminate bacteria and unpleasant tastes to UV-light devices that kill bacteria and viruses. Almost all are lightweight, portable, and extremely effective. Water-treatment tablets are also available, usually made with iodine or chlorine dioxide; the latter is better because it lacks a nasty taste. When drawing water, choose a source that is clean and flowing. Avoid milky or silty water, as this often contains particles of silica (glass) that can clog filters and wreak havoc on your digestive system.

Food Storage

Whether you're out for a casual day hike or an overnight journey, you should always manage your food supply properly. Especially on overnight trips, plan to keep your food and trash in a durable bag and hang it in camp every night to keep it away from curious and hungry critters. Drybags and waterproof stuff sacks make good food bags, as they can be left outside, and their contents will be protected from rain. The alternative is to carry your food in a bear-proof canister. These are often heavy and bulky but make food management effortless. For the ultimate in lightweight and convenient food storage and protection, consider investing in a critter-proof food storage bag. *Never store your food in your tent!*

Cooking

When cooking food in the backcountry, you should do so at least 100 feet away from your tent or where you're sleeping. Use only permissible stoves (alcohol stoves are often prohibited), and make sure you have enough fuel for the length of your trip. When it's time to make dinner, place your stove on a sturdy, non-flammable surface, such as a rock or dirt, and always monitor your flame. When finished, let your stove cool completely before putting it away.

River Fording

Some of the longer and more remote trails in this guide do not have bridges for water crossings. In spring and early summer, these can be raging torrents of white water and potentially hazardous. If a waterway looks too high, too fast, or too deep to cross, it is not worth the risk. Just head back and try the trail again later in the season. If a waterway does look manageable, here are some river-fording tips:

Watch out for these hungry critters!

Look for wide, flat water when crossing rivers

Cross in the early morning hours. This is typically when snow- and glacier-fed streams are flowing at their lowest. Consider this when choosing trails that will require significant water crossings, especially if you need to cross again later in the day on your way out.

Look for straight, shallow, wide, and gentle water. If the water doesn't look safe where the trail crosses it, scout up- and downstream for a safer option. Before scouting, identify where the trail continues on the other side so you can find it once you're across.

Don't cross if the water is above your knees. If it's any higher than that, the current can easily suck you downstream. If the water is calm and flat, you may bend this rule of thumb.

Keep your boots on. Bare feet can slip on rocks and wet logs, plus you risk jamming or breaking toes or puncturing your feet on sharp rocks. Use trekking poles for balance.

Unbuckle your pack's waist belt. Your pack might shift as you slosh across, but having an easy exit strategy could save your bacon if you go for an unexpected plunge.

Hunting

Oregon's hunting seasons vary from year to year and region to region, depending on the health of the game population. If you choose to venture into a forest or wilderness during hunting season, be sure to wear highly visible, bright-colored clothing that will identify you as a human. If you hike with a dog, put them in a brightly colored vest as well, or just leave them at home. Make noise as you hike, as hunters typically avoid high-traffic areas that frighten away game. And avoid off-trail travel, where a hunter might be awaiting his next target. Hunters favor dawn and dusk, when animals are most active, so minimize risk by not hiking at these times. For complete hunting regulations and seasonal openings, visit the Oregon Department of Fish and Wildlife website.

Wildlife

The only **bears** found in Oregon are black bears (*Ursus americanus*), and they are present throughout the state. These are the smaller cousins of the mighty grizzly (or brown) bear. And while they are named "black" bears, their coloring can range from cinnamon to brown to black. These typically timid animals sustain themselves on a diet of berries, nuts, grasses, insects, and vegans (just kidding). They are extremely wary of people and prefer to be left alone to forage, feed, and raise their young. If you are fortunate enough to spot a black bear in Oregon's wilds, it is a truly magical experience. When on the trails, watch for bear signs, such as footprints, scat piles, and scratched-up trees.

So as not to startle a bear—which can make them act aggressively—it's good to make noise when hiking through overgrown brush (especially berry bushes) or when approaching blind curves. If you encounter an aggressive bear, avoid eye contact and talk calmly to identify yourself as a human—that is, not a menu item. Never turn your back on a bear and never run, just back away slowly. Occasionally, a bear will bluff charge (charge and stop short) to try to scare the holy hell out of you. Stand your ground while trying not to soil yourself. Once the bear is gone, leave the area immediately. If a black bear does attack, summon the power of Thor and fight back with all you've got.

There are estimated to be more than six thousand **cougars** (mountain lions) residing in Oregon's wild places, with the majority of those known to inhabit the northeastern Blue Mountains and southwestern Cascade Range. That said, the odds of seeing even the footprint of one of these shy, solitary animals is quite slim. Like bears, cougars tend to disappear long before you're even aware they were nearby. And while their presence may give you pause about venturing out into the woods, you can take heart in knowing that you're more likely to be struck by lightning or win the lottery than to become the next cougar victim.

In the ridiculously rare instance that you cross paths with a cougar and it gets curious about you, stand your ground and maintain eye contact. Then go nuts! Scream, yell, and wave your trekking poles. Pull your jacket up to make yourself look big and menacing. If you have children or a small dog with you, pick them up and keep them high, as cougars usually target the smallest, easiest prey. Never run from a cougar, as this may trigger the cat's instinctive urge to chase. Instead, back away slowly, never turning your back to the animal, and give it room to leave the area. Once it's gone, vacate the area immediately and notify the local land agency or Oregon Department of Fish and Wildlife. If a cougar does attack, fight back and fight dirty. Punch it in the nose, poke it in the eyes, and hit it with rocks, sticks, and whatever else you can find.

In addition to the occasional deer or elk, Oregon has a bevy of other large fauna you might possibly encounter: mountain goats, bighorn sheep, pronghorn antelope, coyotes, wolves, badgers, wolverines, bobcats, and moose. Observe and enjoy from a safe distance, savoring the experience and giving the animals plenty of space. If you ever have a threatening confrontation with any of these animals, report it to the area land manager.

Oregon is home to two varieties of **rattlesnakes**: the Western rattlesnake and the

Leaves of three, let it be

Northern Pacific rattlesnake. These snakes have a hard time living in the mild, damp Northwest, but they have found a home in the warmer southern and eastern parts of the state. Like most creatures, they're rarely aggressive unless they feel threatened. You can minimize your chances of encountering a rattlesnake by watching your footing in dry areas with low brush and tall grass, in scree fields, and on rocky outcroppings. Using trekking poles in these areas helps, as snakes are sensitive to vibrations. If you're hiking with your pup through rattlesnake country, keep them on a short leash. If you encounter a snake on the trail, back away slowly, don't make any sudden movements, and allow the snake to vacate the area first.

Oregon's wild places have plenty of little biting and stinging buggers, but unless you're allergic, simple topical treatments from your first-aid kit will relieve most bites and stings (see The Ten Essentials). The only crawlies you really need to be concerned about in Oregon are **ticks** and **mosquitoes**. Ticks typically reside in warm, grassy areas, but in recent years, with warming climates, they've become more widespread and prolific. They don't fly but rather hop aboard their intended hosts, and they can transmit various diseases, including Lyme disease. To avoid picking up these unsavory hitchhikers, wear long sleeves and pants, tuck your pants into your socks, and apply an insect repellant to any exposed skin. After your hike, do a thorough check to make sure you didn't pick up any ticks. If you find a tick attached to you, remove it with a pair of tweezers by pulling it straight out. Monitor the location of the bite, and if you notice any changes or begin feeling any unusual symptoms—headaches, fever, rash—seek medical attention.

Unfortunately, mosquitoes in the woods are just a fact of life, and they seem to get worse every year. They are most prevalent in late spring and early summer—just when Oregon's skies are clearing and you're itching (*wink, wink*) to get outdoors. By midsummer, they are usually gone—or at least significantly diminished. While reported cases of mosquito-borne West Nile virus in Oregon are extremely rare, you should still take precautions to protect yourself. It's not so much about trying to avoid getting bitten—*because you're going to get bitten*—it's about how to minimize *how much* you're bitten. If you're willing to brave the bugs to frolic in the flowers, armor up by wearing long, loose-fitting pants and sleeves, as well as a hat, and apply a good bug repellent. A head net might also help you keep your sanity. Or purchase some bug-repellent products to treat your hiking clothing (e.g., permethrin). Consider bringing treatments or balms to help soothe the bites you do get.

APPAREL AND GEAR

Day hiking does not require carrying a lot of gear. You should have comfortable and reliable footwear and clothing, and most everything else you need can fit into a small backpack. If you're going on longer or overnight journeys, you'll need to carry more. Start with a good pair of trail shoes or lightweight hiking boots. Choose footwear that comfortably fits your foot size and shape and consider going up a half size to give your feet a little room to swell once you get moving. Choose a good pair of breathable socks, preferably made of moisture-wicking wool or a synthetic material.

During the regular hiking season in Oregon (spring, summer, fall), days typically start cool and gradually warm up. This makes the layering system the best approach to planning your trail apparel. Start with breathable, moisture-wicking base layers (top and bottom). Your middle layers should consist of comfortable garments that you can get into and out of easily as you adjust to the day's changing temperatures. Lightweight pants are the best choice to protect your legs from overgrown brush, poison oak, and other scratchy things. Top it all off with a light windbreaker or rain jacket. A few other good things to pack along are a light, compressible puffy jacket, a warm beanie, and a light pair of gloves. Cotton apparel is not recommended, as it soaks easily when you sweat or get it wet—and once it gets wet, it can lead to uncomfortable chafing on warm days and potential hypothermia on cool ones.

Appropriate clothing and footwear will ensure your comfort on trail.

You should carry your essential gear in a small backpack (see The Ten Essentials). Two of the most important items you should have are a map and compass—and know how to use them! While most of the trails in this guide are relatively easy to navigate, it's still possible to lose your way if you take an unplanned detour or wander too far on an unmarked path. After all, wilderness invites exploration. Being able to identify your location on a map and find your way back to your starting point can be vital, especially if bad weather rolls in and visibility decreases.

Carrying a GPS device or smartphone with a GPS navigation app can also be beneficial for keeping track of your location as you hike. And just like with a traditional map and compass, you should know how to use them, as they won't do you any good in a pinch if you don't know which way is which. Most importantly, remember that electronic navigation devices are only helpful for as long as their batteries last. If you're going to use a GPS device or smartphone on the trail, carry extra batteries or a spare battery pack; GPS apps tend to drain smartphone batteries rapidly.

A few extra items can help ensure an enjoyable experience on-trail. Consider a small, packable camp chair or seat pad. You're likely going to be hiking to many spectacular viewpoints, so having a comfy place to sit while you eat your lunch and enjoy the view can be quite delightful. Carry a small nature guide to help you identify some of the trees, plants, flowers, and wildlife you may encounter on the trail. Some guides are available as small brochures or as apps for your smartphone. This book highlights many of the natural wonders you are likely to see, but there is so much more to discover.

The Ten Essentials

Whenever you're heading out on a hike—no matter how short or long—you should always pack the Ten Essentials, a list developed by The Mountaineers. This selection of essential items can help you out in a pinch. If you sustain a minor injury, experience a gear failure, or need to spend an unplanned night in the wilderness, you'll be glad you brought these along.

1. **Navigation (map and compass):** Download, print, or purchase a map of the trail you plan to visit. Familiarize yourself with your hiking area, including trailhead locations, connecting trails, and significant landmarks, to help keep you on track. A smartphone with a navigation app or a GPS device is good to have along too.
2. **Illumination (flashlight, headlamp):** If your hike runs late and you're caught out after dark, you'll be glad to have a light source to help you find your way back to the trailhead. Having a light or lamp can also be a source of comfort if you wind up spending an unplanned night in the wilderness.
3. **Sun protection (hat, sunscreen, sunglasses):** It's much easier to get sunburned at higher elevations, where the air is thinner and you're closer to the sun. Use a sunscreen rated at least SPF 30, and wear sunglasses and sun-protective clothing. Volcanic rocks and snow can reflect the sun back at you from all sides, so apply sunscreen even if wearing a hat.
4. **First aid:** For day hiking, carry a small kit containing bandages, antiseptic, blister-prevention supplies, tweezers, pain relievers, and perhaps a small how-to manual. For longer or overnight outings, consider adding gauze, tape, scissors, anti-inflammatory and antidiarrheal tablets, and topical antibiotics. Don't forget any important personal prescriptions. If you have allergies (e.g., pollen or bees), carry antihistamine tablets or an EpiPen, and instruct your hiking partners about what to do in case you need assistance.
5. **Repair kit and tools (including a knife):** Pack along a small kit of just-in-case items that can help you out in the event of a gear failure. Basic repair items, such as duct tape, safety pins, a length of lightweight cord, and a tube of superglue, can work wonders in a pinch. Keep a small pocketknife or multitool in your kit as well.
6. **Fire tools (matches and firestarter):** Spending a spontaneous night in the wilderness is not likely, but a campfire can provide welcome warmth in an emergency. Carry a butane lighter or waterproof matches in a zip-top bag. A small, lightweight firestarter, such as commercially prepared firestarter tabs or dryer lint soaked in petroleum jelly, can come in handy.
7. **Emergency shelter:** If a sudden storm blows in, or you have to spend the night outdoors, a lightweight shelter can help keep you warm and dry. You can carry a lightweight tarp, a heat-reflective emergency blanket, or a compact bivvy sack that doubles as a picnic blanket or seat pad.
8. **Nutrition (extra food):** Hiking burns a lot of calories, so pack along enough food to keep your energy up throughout your hike. Foods high in calories and protein, such as nuts and nut butters, energy bars, and meat jerkies, are best for sustained energy. Bring a little extra. If you wind up spending the night outdoors, you're going to get hungry.
9. **Hydration (water treatment):** Bring enough water to stay hydrated for the length of the trail you plan to hike. Keep weather and temperature factors in mind. On sweltering days at higher elevations, you will drink more than on cooler days at lower elevations. Use an electrolyte supplement to help replenish the essential minerals you'll sweat out. In addition, it's a good idea to carry a water purification method (filter,

pump, or treatment additive) in case you need more due to an extended outing.

10. **Insulation (extra clothing):** Weather and temperatures can change quickly in the mountains, so it's advisable to carry an extra insulating layer (e.g., fleece or sweater) and raingear. Pack additional layers needed to survive the night in the worst conditions that you may realistically encounter. Be sure to include a warm beanie, gloves, and extra socks.

HIKE YOUR OWN HIKE

This is the Golden Rule. Hiking is not just for überathletes and hardcore thru-hikers. Most of the destinations in this guide are all-access trails that can be hiked by just about anyone in reasonably good health. This guidebook is intended to help you discover these trails in a manner that suits your individual interests and abilities. If you're new to hiking, or to the Northwest, start with the easy trails and work your way up to more challenging ones. Enjoy each hiking experience for what it has to offer.

Many of the trails in this guide spend a lot of time in the trees—a product of all that Northwest rain that keeps Oregon so vibrant and green. Instead of getting bored with the woods, take a closer look and discover more about what's at your feet. Oregon has a fascinating natural story, much of it found in the colorful rocks and lavas on and near the trails, as well as in all the vibrant mosses, lichens, flowers, and fungi that populate the forests. Pack along a small nature guide or download a smartphone app (Oregon Wildflowers is a great one to have handy) and turn your hike into a treasure hunt. See how many species you can identify and keep a log of your finds. Give yourself bonus points if you find the elusive calypso orchid or a morel mushroom.

The elusive chocolate lily

Start flipping through this book and put some trails on your to-do list. A good place to start is the Hikes at a Glance chart at the front of the book. This will help you quickly identify trails with waterfalls, trails with wildflowers, trails with great views, or trails for kids and dogs. Put a few from each category on your list so that when you're ready to go for a hike, you'll have preselected choices ready to go. Then grab your boots and pack and head out to enjoy your own classic Oregon adventure. Happy trails!

How to Use This Guide

Congratulations on getting this far through the intro of this guide! You're almost ready to go. As you start diving into the trail selections just ahead, here are a few quick pointers to help you identify the details of each hike, and which trails you might put on your to-do list.

The **distance** of each hike is indicated in miles, to the nearest tenth of a mile. Each trail entry will indicate if the hike is a one-way trip, roundtrip, loop, or other. Mileages for side trails, alternate routes, and Extend Your Trip options are not included in this listing. Distances were determined by boots-on-the-ground surveys using a Garmin GPS, calculated with CalTopo mapping software, and compared against other reliable mapping resources. Mileages may vary slightly depending on which maps and/or devices you use.

The **difficulty** of each hike is listed as easy, moderate, strenuous, or brutal (don't worry, there's only one of those). Trails differ, so judging the difficulty of a particular hike can be tricky. A short hike with a steep climb may be strenuous, while a long hike over flat terrain may be easy. As such, these evaluations are based on a subjective approach that takes into account every potential type of user. Some of the factors taken into consideration are distance, elevation gain, type of terrain, water crossings, and exposure.

Each hike is given a **hiking time**, which represents the estimated required time for the average visitor to complete the described route. Because everyone hikes at their own pace and to their own enjoyment, these are very subjective. In general, trails are indicated as being short day hikes, which can generally be done in a few hours; regular day hikes, which can take several hours up to an entire day; overnights, which require camping in the backcountry; or multiday, for long-distance trails.

Opposite: Finding solitude in the Wallowa Mountains

The **elevation gain** indicates the *total* amount of elevation you will gain over the entire hike. This is not just the distance between the low point and the high point. There are a lot of ups and downs along the course of most trails, and all those elevation changes add up. As with distance, the figures for elevation gain were obtained using a Garmin GPS and CalTopo mapping software for the most accurate measurements possible.

The **high point** of each trail is exactly that—the elevation of the highest point you will reach along the course of your journey. It may not be at the hike's end or on top of a peak, as many trails roll up and down along the landscape. In some cases, where you descend into a valley or canyon, you may start at the high point and hike down.

With the ever-changing weather and climate, the specific hiking **season** for any particular trail in Oregon is getting more unpredictable. This listing is a general guesstimate of when each hike is *typically* accessible. Heavy snowpacks and cool springs can make trails melt out later than normal, and conversely, light snowpacks and warm springs can make them accessible earlier than normal. The same can be said when fall weather rolls in, with winter conditions arriving as early as September or October in some years. Use this information as a reference but inquire with management agencies or consult online trip reports for the most accurate accessibility information.

Each hike listing will indicate the office or agency responsible for the **management** of the trail and surrounding land. This entity will often

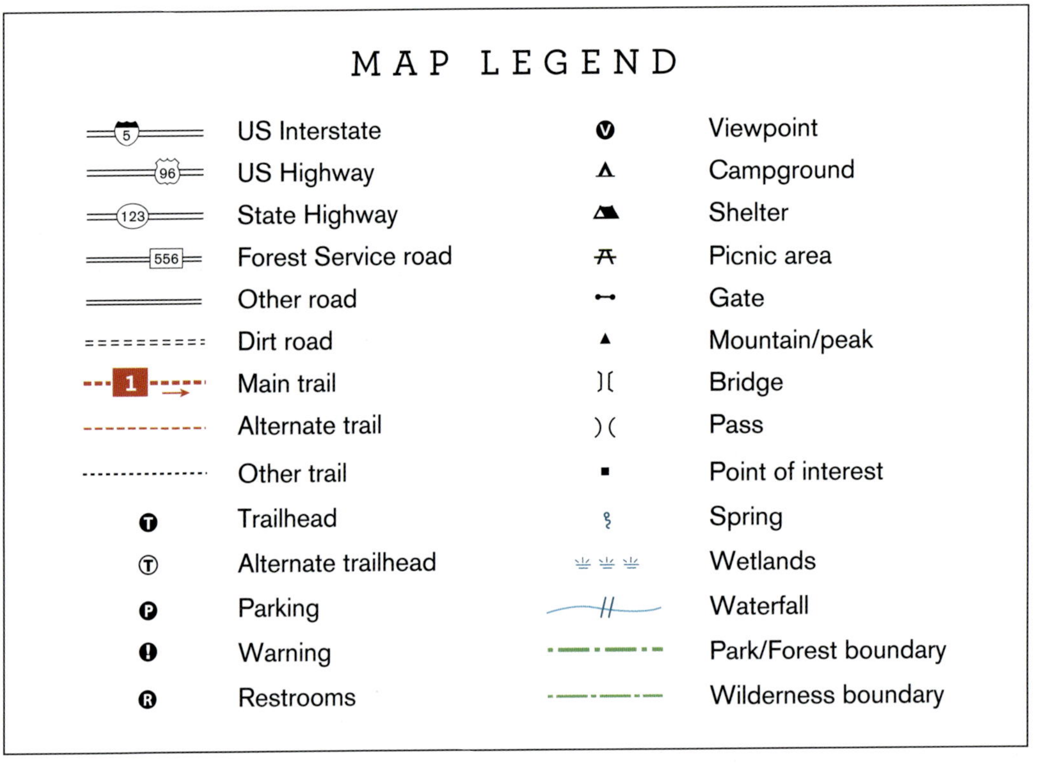

be able to provide you with up-to-date information about trail conditions and may be able to assist you in the case of an emergency. Most trails in this guide are located on national forest land and are administered by the US Forest Service. A handful of trails are managed by Oregon State Parks, the Bureau of Land Management, or other local authorities. You can find contact information for each of these in the Resources section.

If a trail has any type of **protection status**, it will be listed here. Many of Oregon's most scenic trails are in designated wilderness areas. These areas have special rules for their use and enjoyment, to preserve their natural and cultural heritage (see Wilderness Regulations and Ethics, as well as Leave No Trace). Other protected areas include state parks and national scenic areas. Whether an area is protected or not, you should always treat it as such.

The **map** listing for each hike indicates the best printed resources available for that area. In most cases, it will be published by Green Trails Maps or National Geographic Trails Illustrated, often available at outdoor gear suppliers, ranger stations, and visitor centers (see The Ten Essentials). These maps are often the most accurate and up-to-date editions available. Some trails in more remote areas might require USGS Quads, which can be downloaded for free at usgs.gov. In some cases, as with state or county parks, the best maps are the park brochures available at visitor centers or for download online. Several useful trail mapping apps are available as well, such as AllTrails and FarOut; however, these are not listed in this guide.

The **GPS coordinates** are the WGS84 degrees and decimal minutes for the starting point of each hike. These are not required to reach any of the trailheads in this guide. They are only included as a helpful reference, in case you're using a GPS device or smartphone mapping app.

Getting there provides basic driving directions to each hike's starting point. Routes are often based on driving from the nearest town or city center. Google Maps is another reliable resource and covers most of the trailheads listed in this guide; it can give you turn-by-turn directions from just about any location or direction you might be driving from. Unfortunately, due to most of these trail locations being fairly remote, public transit is not an option.

Any extra bits of pertinent info or concerns about a given location will be listed in **Notes**. For example, this entry might indicate a challenging water crossing or any wildlife or poisonous plants known to inhabit an area. This is also where you will find information about permit requirements and whether dogs are allowed.

Many of the hikes offer **Extend Your Trip** options for going farther than the described route. Suggestions for these longer and/or additional routes—along with their additional mileage and elevation gain—will be found here. Take note that not every extended route in this guide was surveyed in person. Some of this information was derived from reliable resources and conversations with managing agencies. Contact the local land manager to inquire about current conditions in these areas.

A Note about Safety

Safety is an important concern in all outdoor activities. No guidebook can alert you to every hazard or anticipate the limitations of every reader. Therefore, the descriptions of roads, trails, routes, and natural features in this book are not representations that a particular place or excursion will be safe for your party. When you follow any of the routes described in this book, you assume responsibility for your own safety. Under normal conditions, such excursions require the usual attention to traffic, road and trail conditions, weather, terrain, the capabilities of your party, and other factors. Keeping informed on current conditions and exercising common sense are the keys to a safe, enjoyable outing.

—Mountaineers Books

Opposite, top: Sunset Bay State Park

Opposite, bottom: Vibrant honeysuckle along the Oregon Coast

Oregon Coast and Range

1. Fort to Sea Trail 38

2. Saddle Mountain 40

3. Clatsop Loop (Tillamook Head) 43

4. Cape Falcon 45

5. Kings Mountain 47

6. Cape Lookout 48

7. Cascade Head 50

8. The Knoll and Gods Thumb ... 53

9. Drift Creek Falls 54

10. Cape Perpetua 57

11. Sweet Creek Falls 59

12. Dellenback Dunes 61

13. Sunset Bay to Cape Arago 62

14. Blacklock Point 65

15. Humbug Mountain 67

16. Flora Dell Falls (Rogue River Trail) 68

17. Hunters Cove 70

18. Samuel H. Boardman Scenic Corridor 72

From golden sandy beaches to volcanic cliffs and monoliths, from rainforest head- lands to coastal mountains, the trails along Oregon's Pacific Coast offer an abundance of dramatic and breathtaking scenery. Many of these destinations are steeped in cultural history, local legend, and natural wonder. Whether you're looking for a casual stroll or a serious workout, there's a place for you to enjoy here—most with views so spectacular, you'll wonder why you're not exploring the coast more often.

1 Fort to Sea Trail

Distance: 6.2 miles one-way
Difficulty: easy
Hiking time: day hike
Elevation gain: 570 feet
High point: 320 feet
Season: year-round
Management: National Park Service
Protection status: Lewis and Clark National Historical Park
Map: Lewis and Clark park brochure
GPS coordinates: N 46 13.402, W 123 88.150

Getting there: Upper trailhead: From the coastal town of Seaside, about 80 miles west of Portland, take US Highway 101 north for 10 miles to Warrenton. At the intersection just past Walmart, turn right on SE Ensign Lane and drive for 2 more miles, then turn right again on Fort Clatsop Road. After 0.6 mile, turn left into the Lewis and Clark National Historical Park visitor center parking area. Lower trailhead: From Seaside, take US 101 north for 8 miles. Just past Cullaby Lake Park, turn left on Sunset Beach Road. Continue 1 mile to the trailhead parking area on the right. ***Notes:*** Day-use fee required. The best way to hike the Fort to Sea Trail is one-way, from the Fort Clatsop visitor center to Sunset Beach. If you have two vehicles, you can leave one at the beach trailhead, then drive the other up to the visitor center to start the hike. Or use a local taxi or rideshare service. The park does not offer shuttle transportation. Dogs must be leashed.

Follow in the footsteps of Lewis and Clark's Corps of Discovery along their final stretch, from Fort Clatsop to the shore of the Pacific Ocean. You'll begin in coastal woodlands and descend through rolling farmland to the marshy, scrubby shore. The route is a mostly pleasant walk with ample views, and as you near the end you can see the roiling Pacific, just as Lewis and Clark did centuries ago.

Begin at the Fort to Sea trailhead on the southwest side of the parking area (opposite the visitor center). Walk through unimpressive upland woods for a short spell before crossing the park entrance road. Following the crossing, the well-graded trail corridor becomes more pleasant, with a lot of ferns and blackberries, making for a pleasant walk. As the trail makes its gradual ascent to the top of Clatsop Ridge at 1.6 miles, it passes several junctions with intersecting trails (see Shorten Your Trip); stick with the Fort to Sea Trail through all of these. At the top of the hill is a small shelter hut with a park map and interpretive information about some of the park's wildlife. Nearby, an open viewpoint looks westward toward the ocean over sprawling coastal woods and local farmlands.

From here, the trail transitions to rougher, narrower tread and makes a steep, switchbacking

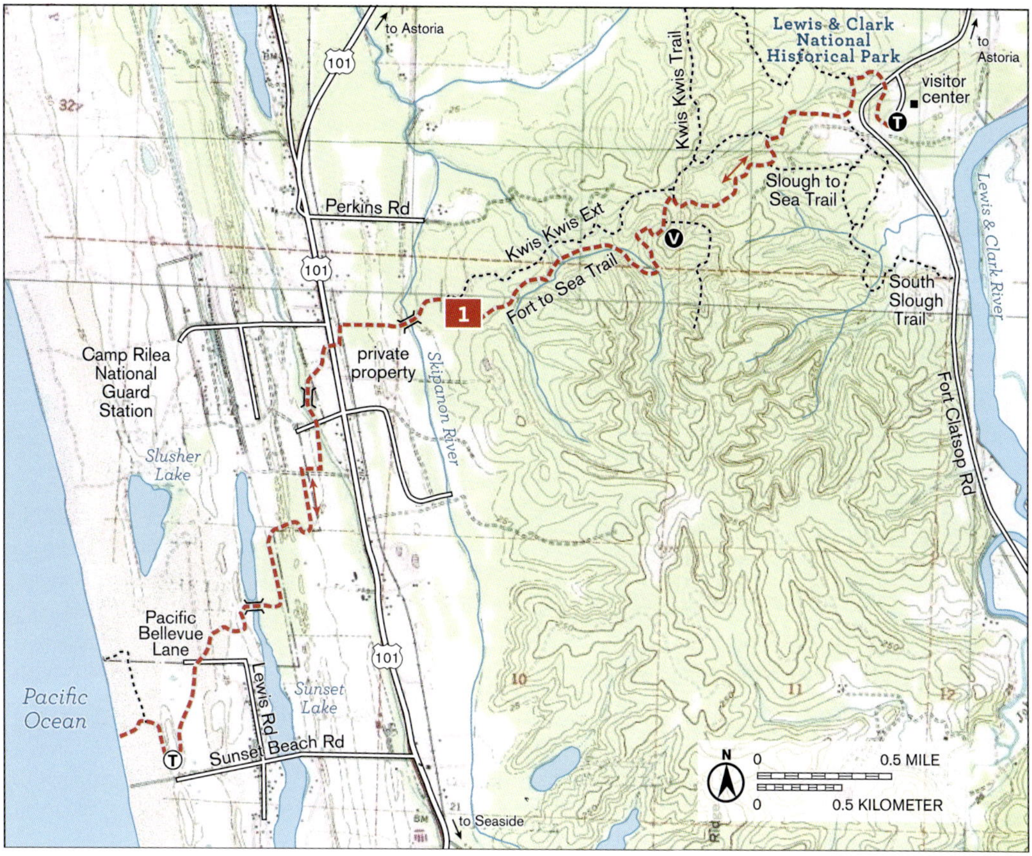

descent into a lush, boggy section of woods choked with ferns, berries, and skunk cabbage. The path crosses a trickling creek at 2 miles and proceeds to follow it down the canyon until spilling out of the woods at an old jeep road at 2.9 miles. Just right of the trail here is a vault toilet. Moving on, veer left at a junction to stick with the Fort to Sea Trail, crossing the Skipanon River, then stay on the trail westward through a narrow corridor alongside some private property. Turn left (south) right before the highway and proceed to the tunnel that passes under US 101.

The next couple miles take a winding path through rolling, coastal pastureland, skirting the boundaries of the Camp Rilea National Guard Station. The grassy hillsides through here are carpeted with seasonal daisies and hawkweed. Along the way, proceed through several cattle control gates to a wide, wooden bridge at 5 miles. This waterway is an extension of Sunset Lake and is often lined with flowering lily pads. Shortly past the bridge, veer right (west) at an unsigned junction and follow the trail as it bends south to cross Pacific Bellevue Lane at 5.3 miles. Continue southward for another 0.5 mile, through coastal boglands, to the Sunset Beach parking area and trailhead. Watch for deer among the shrubs and marshes through here, as well as for birds of prey in the trees overhead.

The last 0.4 mile of the Fort to Sea Trail heads north from the parking area into a section of coastal woods that was destroyed by a heavy storm in 2007. An interpretive sign along the way details how nature's fury was unleashed along the coast through here. At 6 miles, fork left (southwest) at the last trail junction and proceed

Grassy, windswept shores at the end of the Fort to Sea Trail

across a low dune blanketed with windswept coastal grasses and bright-yellow tansies until the trail ends on the sandy shore of the Pacific Ocean. The big headland to the south is Tillamook Head (see Hike 3). Now at the end of your journey, visualize yourself as part of the Corps of Discovery, looking out across the ocean after just completing an epic cross-country journey. Return along the same path to the Sunset Beach parking area and your waiting shuttle vehicle or return to Fort Clatsop along the same route.

Shorten Your Trip: The Kwis Kwis Trail can be used to create a 4-mile loop that returns to the visitor center parking area. This is an ideal alternative to hiking the full length of the Fort to Sea Trail, especially if you can't arrange a one-way shuttle.

2 *Saddle Mountain*

Distance: 4.5-mile roundtrip
Difficulty: strenuous
Hiking time: day hike
Elevation gain: 1750 feet
High point: 3280 feet
Season: year-round
Management: Oregon State Parks
Protection status: Saddle Mountain State Natural Area
Map: USGS Quad: Saddle Mountain, OR
GPS coordinates: N 45 96.280, W 123 68.998

Getting there: From Portland (east): Take US Highway 26 west for approximately 62 miles. Turn right (north) on Saddle Mountain State Park Road and drive this curvy, paved road for 7 miles to the trailhead at road's end. From Seaside or Cannon Beach (west): Drive south or north, respectively, to US 26 and then drive 14 miles east to Saddle Mountain State Park Road. Turn left (north) and proceed to the trailhead. ***Notes:*** Day use only; campground permanently closed. This is a very steep, strenuous trail with no running water.

When the chill and gloom of Oregon's winter and early spring finally melt away, and the sun starts warming the Northwest, the Oregon Coast Range bursts to life in spectacular fashion. Just an hour's drive from Portland, and less than that from the northern coastal cities, Saddle Mountain puts on one of the state's most stunning wildflower displays. Carpets of pink and yellow blooms paint the slopes, and rare specimens delight the senses. It's a strenuous climb to be sure, but it's guaranteed to lift your spirits as you come out of winter hibernation.

From the trailhead, plunge into dense, lush coastal woods packed with buttercups, candy flower, ferns, sorrel, and mixed berries. The trail immediately starts climbing on a moderate grade and comes to a fork at 0.2 mile. The path to the right (west) climbs to a viewpoint of Humbug Mountain. Skip this (there are better views up ahead), veering left (east) to climb a series of switchbacks as the views begin to open up. The wooded mound to the south with the cellular tower is 2452-foot Humbug Mountain. As you continue climbing, you will come across a plethora of new and brilliant wildflowers, including hedge nettle, windflower, bleeding heart, chocolate lily, and wild iris, to name but a few.

The grade increases as you near the 1-mile mark, where a wooden table beside the trail offers a place to stop and catch your breath. Continue up through a few more switchbacks to a wide view over Clatsop State Forest. At around this point, the monkey flower becomes prolific and carpets the steep slopes and trail sides in vibrant yellow. Continue up through a few more switchbacks to another impressive viewpoint, and get your first look at the Pacific, just past a ragged pinnacle jutting out of the mountainside. Beyond here, the trail makes a twisting contour of the mountainside as the wildflowers become even more prolific and views continue to improve.

The trail reaches the crest of the mountain at around 1.7 miles, where another picnic table offers a rest spot in a pocket of dense woods. Just beyond, the trail spills out into a wide-open landscape, where wild onion, wallflower, seablush, and phlox paint the hillsides in pinks and purples. Pass another viewpoint, then make a steep descent to traverse Saddle Mountain's "saddle." The final 0.3-mile climb out of the saddle to reach the summit viewpoint is a grinding ascent, with wire fencing laid across the trail for added traction and wire handrails to assist with

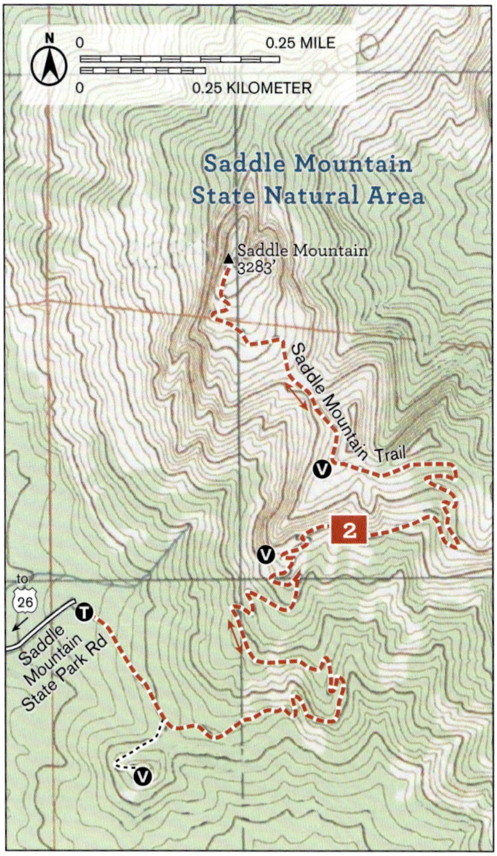

Spring wildflowers on the upper slopes of Saddle Mountain

stability. Once you're perched atop the 3283-foot summit, enjoy a sweeping, 360-degree view. Scanning clockwise from the north, take in the town of Astoria; the confluence of the Columbia River with the Pacific Ocean; Washington State's Mounts Rainier, St. Helens, and Adams; Oregon's Mounts Hood and Jefferson; Clatsop State Forest and the Oregon Coast Range; the Tillamook headlands; and finally the oceanfront hamlet of Seaside. After your well-deserved break at the top, prepare your knees for the descent back to the trailhead.

3 *Clatsop Loop (Tillamook Head)*

Distance: 2.8-mile loop
Difficulty: moderate
Hiking time: short day hike
Elevation gain: 810 feet
High point: 770 feet
Season: year-round
Management: Oregon State Parks
Protection status: Ecola State Park
Map: Ecola State Park trail map
GPS coordinates: N 45 93.111, W 123 97.839

Getting there: From Portland, drive west on US Highway 26 for approximately 75 miles to a junction with US 101. Take the ramp for US 101 South and drive 3.3 miles. Exit the highway for Cannon Beach and Ecola State Park. At the stop sign, turn right on E. 5th Street and drive for 0.1 mile, then veer right on Ecola State Park Road. Follow this road for 3.5 miles to the Indian Beach parking area and trailhead. ***Notes:*** Day use only. Parking fee required.

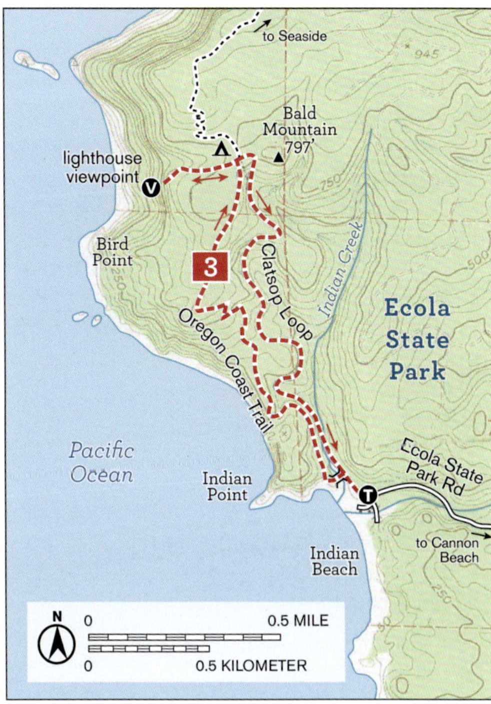

Using a short stretch of the Oregon Coast Trail, the Clatsop Loop climbs through lush coastal rainforest to a viewpoint overlooking one of Oregon's most picturesque lighthouses. Along the way, interpretive signs highlight the area's rich natural and cultural history, from the days of the Lewis and Clark Expedition to the filming of several popular movies.

Start at the trailhead beside the vault toilet building, heading uphill into the woods alongside Indian Creek. A sign near the trailhead indicates filming locations for several locally produced movies, including 1985's *The Goonies*. The trail proceeds about a hundred yards to a fork, where your loop begins. Turn left (west) and cross the creek on a footbridge, heading uphill to a view point that overlooks Indian Beach, a cluster of sea stacks, and a sea arch. Continue climbing for more views, including your first peeks of the Tillamook Rock Lighthouse, precariously perched on a large rock a little over a mile offshore.

The way climbs northwestward around a wooded hill, then through a short series of

Tillamook Rock Lighthouse—"Terrible Tilly"—from Ecola State Park

switchbacks, where elderberry and fairybells adorn the hillsides and interpretive signs provide information about significant natural and cultural features. The trail then heads up along the eastern flank of 797-foot Bald Mountain before leveling out and coming to a gravel road at 1.3 miles. Turn left (west) and follow this road past an outhouse to the hikers' camp area, where several Adirondack shelters provide a place to stay for Oregon Coast Trail hikers. A covered picnic area makes an ideal place to break for a snack or lunch, and the area also has a large fire ring. At the west end of the camp, pick up the viewpoint trail to continue your hike.

The path descends 0.2 mile through the trees on rough, rooty tread. Look to the left (south) side of the trail for an abandoned military bunker, now being reclaimed by nature. The path ends at a small viewpoint at the edge of the headland, which offers a wide panorama over the surging Pacific Ocean and the Tillamook Rock Lighthouse. Deemed "Terrible Tilly," this lighthouse has a storied history about its construction and maintenance, most notably the five hundred days it took to build. The lighthouse was first illuminated in January 1881 and stayed in operation until September 1957, even after nearly being destroyed by a furious storm in 1934. Today, the abandoned lighthouse remains on the National Register of Historic Places (see Resources).

After admiring the lighthouse and pondering the life of a Pacific Ocean lighthouse keeper, return to the hikers' camp area and proceed east along the old service road, passing the trail you came up on. Stay on this route to continue your loop as it snakes and bends southward along the slope of a wide, forested drainage. Keep your eyes peeled for owls and prey birds in the trees. The route eventually comes alongside Indian Creek once again, at around 2.5 miles. Continue downward, through the junction where you first started, and proceed a short distance back to the trailhead and parking area.

4 Cape Falcon

Distance: 4.2-mile roundtrip
Difficulty: moderate
Hiking time: short day hike
Elevation gain: 1160 feet
High point: 880 feet
Season: year-round
Management: Oregon State Parks
Protection status: Oswald West State Park
Map: Green Trails 356SX: Oregon Coast North
GPS coordinates: N 45 76.306, W 123 95.596

Getting there: From Cannon Beach, drive US Highway 101 approximately 9 miles south to the Cape Falcon trailhead on the right (west) side of the highway. From Tillamook, drive US 101 30 miles north to the trailhead. If the trailhead parking area is full, use the larger Short Sand Beach parking area 0.1 mile south. From there, you can walk the short connector trail to the Cape Falcon trailhead. ***Notes:*** This trail is open year-round, but it can be a muddy mess during winter months. Be prepared for wind and rain at any time of year.

Just a quick drive south from the oceanfront hamlet of Cannon Beach, this short stretch of the Oregon Coast Trail (OCT) contours around a wooded headland, offering stellar panoramas over the Pacific Ocean and the Cape Falcon Marine Reserve. It's an ideal spot for a nice coastal hike, without overcommitting to something longer or more challenging. It also offers fantastic bird and wildlife viewing, especially during the winter whale-migration months.

Begin at the roadside trailhead, where the often-muddy trail plunges straight into the cape's coastal woodland. In the drainage below to the left (south), Short Sand Creek makes its final run before it spills into the Pacific. The trail rises and falls on an easy grade as it contours the

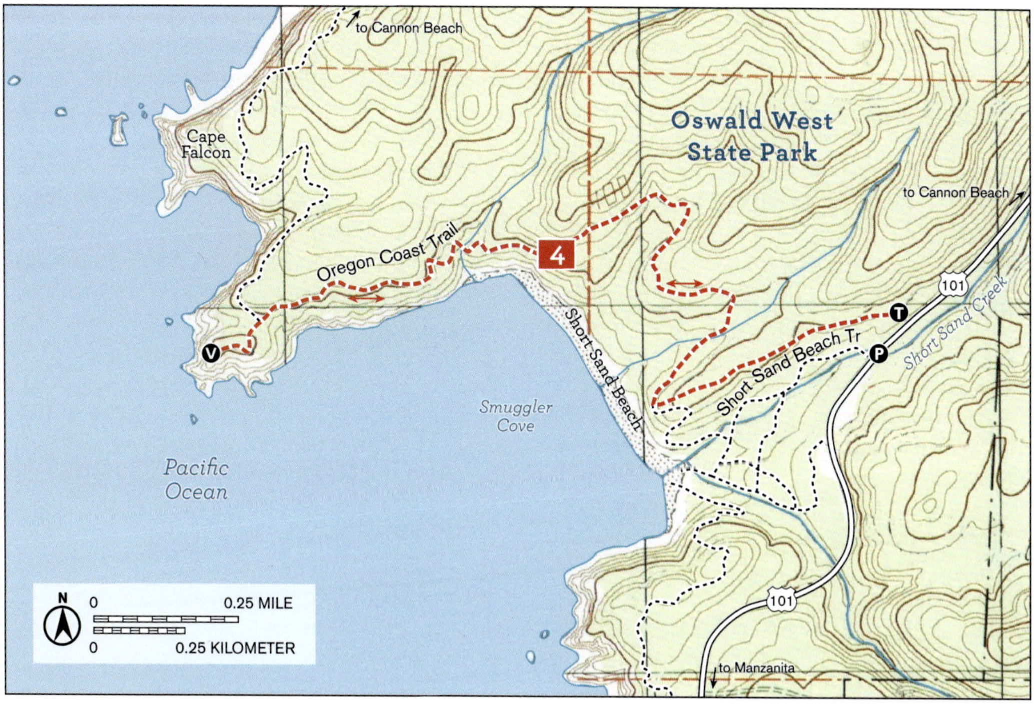

Weather rolling in at Cape Falcon

hillside, coming to a T-junction with the OCT at 0.5 mile. To the left (south), the trail drops down to Short Sand Beach and the Short Sand Beach Trail before continuing on to Neahkahnie Mountain. It's a challenging route that climbs more than 1200 feet to the OCT's highest point along the coast.

For now, turn right (north) and begin an undulating contour around the Cape Falcon headland, keeping high above Short Sand Beach. The trail dips and rises through several wooded drainages, where skunk cabbage is plentiful, and the creek crossings are usually easy hops. Views are often limited to the surrounding woods, but keep your eyes peeled for an array of wildflowers, including wood sorrel and coast manroot. At around 1.5 miles, the trail makes a big dip through one more drainage, crosses another small creek, and then begins contouring its way westward along the edge of the cape, where the Pacific Ocean surges into Smuggler Cove below.

At 2.1 miles, the trail forks again, with the OCT bending northwest to continue climbing over the headland to Arch Cape. Instead, veer left (southwest) off the main trail and through a dense thicket of head-high salal to the precipitous western edge of Cape Falcon. Here, you can take in a sweeping, 180-degree view over the Pacific Ocean from atop some impressive sea- and wind-sculpted cliffs—just exercise caution near the edge. Find a good spot to sit and enjoy a snack or picnic lunch while you watch for birds and whales. When you're ready, return to your vehicle by the same route.

Extend Your Trip: If you're up for more exploring, you can visit Short Sand Beach by taking the OCT south from the junction at the 0.5-mile mark. The trail drops down to the beach in just 0.2 mile. Then, to return to your starting point by a different route, take the Short Sand Beach Trail up the shallow creek canyon to the parking area.

5 Kings Mountain

Distance: 4.5-mile roundtrip
Difficulty: brutal
Hiking time: day hike
Elevation gain: 2540 feet
High point: 3226 feet
Season: Apr–Nov
Management: Tillamook State Forest
Protection status: none
Map: USGS Quad: Jordan Creek, OR
GPS coordinates: N 45 59.718, W 123 50.650

Getting there: From Portland, drive US Highway 26 west for approximately 20 miles. Veer left on Wilson River Highway (Oregon Route 6), following signs for Banks and Tillamook, and continue west for another 26 miles. Trailhead parking is in a shady grove on the right (north) side of the road. ***Notes:*** This is a relentlessly steep trail with no running water.

Deep in the heart of Oregon's Tillamook State Forest, Kings Mountain is a sleeping beast just waiting to test your trail mettle. The immediate view from the top of this super-steep slog is only mediocre, as you're mostly just looking out over a patchwork of Coast Range logging operations. But on bluebird days, you can see as far as Mount Hood to the east and the Pacific Ocean to the west. Just keep in mind that going up is only half the battle. Coming back down is just as—if not more—brutal on the thighs and knees. If you're a glutton for punishment, a cardio-hound, or training for a big summer trek, then give Kings Mountain a try. If you don't like to suffer while you hike, maybe skip this one.

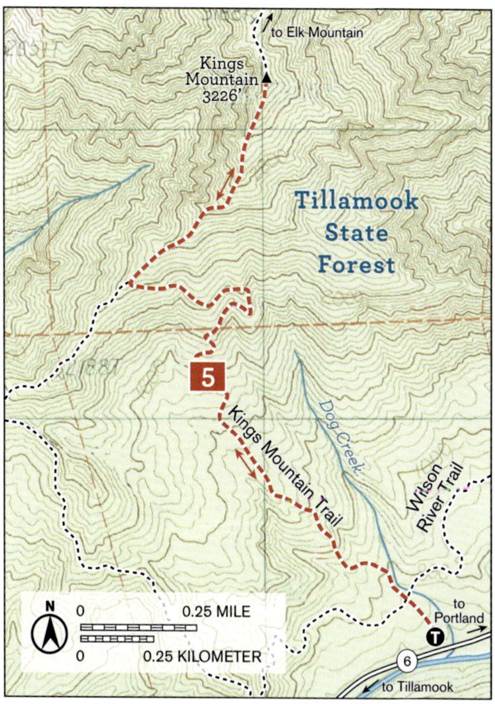

Start your trek by heading up into dense Douglas-fir and alder woods, where sword ferns carpet the shady hillside. Don't be fooled by the seemingly easy start—the pain is coming. Pass through a junction with the Wilson River Trail near 0.2 mile, skirt a brushy gully to the east containing Dog Creek, and then, as you pass through 1000 feet of elevation, start climbing. The trail twists and turns here and there but otherwise heads straight up the mountainside. At 0.6 mile, a trailside log mercifully offers a place to sit and catch your breath. For the next 0.4 mile, the grade eases a bit, and the trail is actually pleasant as it meanders through the woods among Columbia lily and blackberry. At 1 mile, another log offers a trailside break. Take advantage of it, as it gets harder from here.

The trail now starts climbing in earnest, heading up along the viewless, loose, steep tread. At 1.3 miles, the trail hooks over a shallow gully and reaches 2000 feet of elevation. Traverse the hillside for a short bit and reach the ridgeline at 1.6 miles. Now it's time to pay the piper, as the trail makes a relentless, 1000-foot ascent straight up the ridgeline. As you're cursing your way up, pass a decent viewpoint and a weathered picnic table (how the hell did they get that up here?). At 2.1

miles, pass through 3000 feet of elevation and scramble up a rocky escarpment to finally reach the 3226-foot summit. Sign the trail register to claim your victory over Kings Mountain, take a well-deserved break, and psych yourself up for the equally arduous descent. Have fun!

Extend Your Trip: Turn your Kings Mountain trek into a grand 9.6-mile loop to bag another local peak. From the summit, continue on the Kings Mountain Trail for another 1.2 miles to the Elk Mountain Trail. Turn right (east) and traipse along the ridgeline for 1.8 miles to 2788-foot Elk Mountain. From here, descend nearly 1700 feet in elevation over a little more than a mile to the Wilson River Trail. Turn right (northwest) and regain the feeling in your legs as you traverse the wooded hillsides on a lazy path back to the Kings Mountain Trail near where you started.

Huff and puff your way up the spectacularly steep Kings Mountain

6 Cape Lookout

Distance: 4.7-mile roundtrip
Difficulty: moderate
Hiking time: day hike
Elevation gain: 850 feet
High point: 850 feet
Season: year-round
Management: Oregon State Parks
Protection status: Cape Lookout State Park
Map: Cape Lookout trail guide
GPS coordinates: N 45 34.134, W 123 97.451

Getting there: From US Highway 101 in the coastal town of Tillamook, about 75 miles west of Portland, take the Netarts Highway (Oregon Route 131) west, then southwest, for 5 miles. Veer left on Whiskey Creek Road and continue south another 5.2 miles to the Cape Lookout State Park Campground. Veer left (south) onto Cape Lookout Road and wind 2.7 miles uphill to the Cape Lookout trailhead. At the crest of the hill, turn right (west) into the parking area. ***Notes:*** This trail is often rugged and muddy; sturdy trail footwear is recommended. Several sections have unprotected exposure to high, sheer cliffs; keep small children and dogs under control. Day use only.

Cape Lookout, just a short drive south of Tillamook, is a narrow spit of land that juts more than 1.5 miles out into the Pacific Ocean. It's a remnant of the sixteen-million-year-old Grande Ronde lava flow. A good, albeit often muddy, path winds out to the tip of the point, offering sweeping views up and down the Oregon Coast. The best time of year to visit Cape Lookout also happens to be the worst time of year to visit Cape Lookout. The deep winter months are ideal for eagle-eyed spectators to watch for spouting and breeching whales—always a breathtaking sight—as the cape extends out toward the gray whale migration route. Those same months, however,

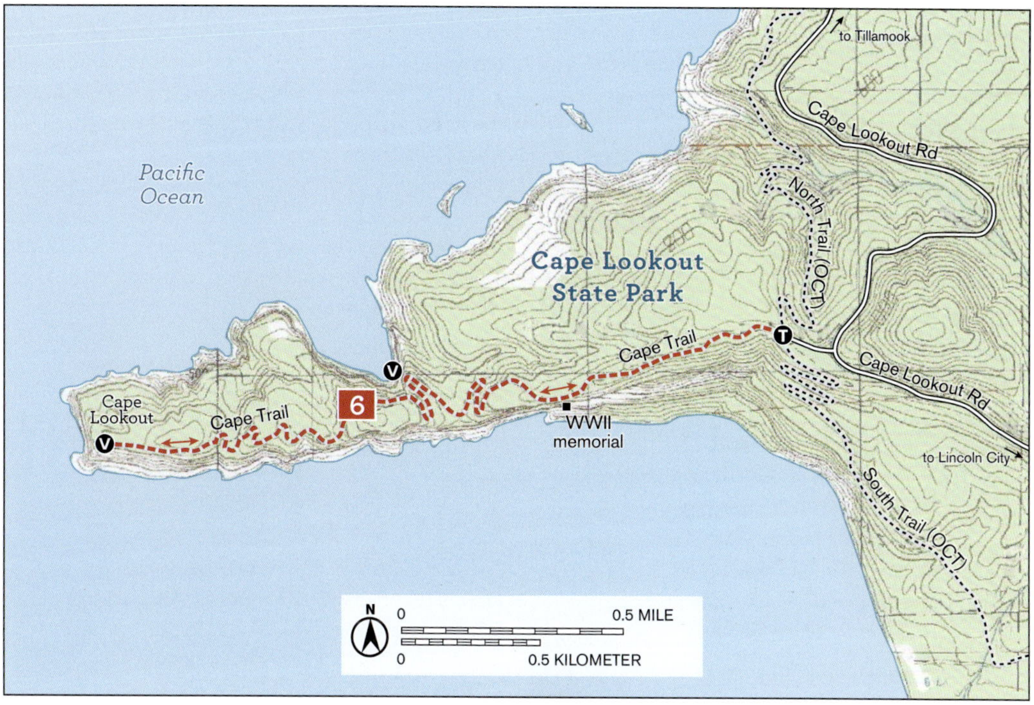

are often plagued with heavy rains and high winds, making the experience cold and soggy. If you can pick a bluebird day in the winter and have sturdy waterproof boots, then go for it. Otherwise, save this one for spring or summer when the conditions are more favorable.

Start the Cape Trail at the west end of the parking area and plunge into dense coastal woods of spruce and hemlock. Immediately to the left (south), the South Trail (part of the Oregon Coast Trail) drops away and descends to a long, sandy beach. Save this for the return trip if you still have the time and energy. The Cape Trail soon comes just alongside the cliffs, which drop steeply more than four hundred feet to the ocean below, and views open up as far as Cape Foulweather, nearly 40 miles to the south. At 0.6 mile, an easy-to-miss plaque mounted on the mossy, rocky trailside memorializes the crew of a B-17 airplane that crashed into the cape in 1943. Be sure to enjoy this first mile of trail, where the path is mostly wide and well-graded. When you reach the fenced-in viewpoint at 1.2 miles, trail conditions often deteriorate quickly.

Cape Lookout is a prime location for whale watching.

Here, on the north side of the cape, where the wind often rips across at its narrowest point, you can peer far down into the roiling Pacific Ocean below. Watch for swifts dipping and gliding on the air currents or nesting in the mossy cliffs. The path now starts heading upward into increasingly dense woods, where you just might forget you're on a narrow spit of rock barely a quarter mile wide. The trail twists and turns through several mucky, rooty sections, where countless obstacles look to trip you up—so watch your footing. By the time you start heading downward again, at around 1.7 miles, you'll be back along the southern edge, skirting more sheer cliffs. The views southward start to get bigger and more sweeping as you near the end. Finally, the trail plunges through a thicket of dense salal to the rocky point at the very tip of the cape. Enjoy the view, watch for whales and seabirds, and then return by the same route.

7 Cascade Head

Distance: 4.5-mile roundtrip
Difficulty: strenuous
Hiking time: day hike
Elevation gain: 1160 feet
High point: 1140 feet
Season: year-round
Management: Siuslaw National Forest
Protection status: The Nature Conservancy
Map: Green Trails 356SX: Oregon Coast North
GPS coordinates: N 45 04.200, W 123 99.222

Getting there: From Lincoln City, take US Highway 101 and drive approximately 6 miles north (1 mile past the Oregon Route 18 junction). Turn left (west) onto N. 3 Rocks Road and continue 2.3 miles. Where the pavement ends, turn left into the Knight Park parking area. ***Notes:*** The lower portion of this trail skirts private property; stick to the trail and don't wander off. Dogs and drones are not permitted.

If you're looking for some coastal cardio, look no further than this hearty climb to a couple of sweeping viewpoints. Designated as one of the first non-wilderness scenic areas and nature preserves, Cascade Head is jointly managed by the US Forest Service and The Nature Conservancy. This 9670-acre tract is tended similarly to the way Indigenous peoples historically maintained it to protect and preserve its coastal woods and plains. Here, stately hemlocks and spruces provide a canopy over lush fern woodlands, and berries and wildflowers thrive in sprawling slopeside meadows.

From the trailhead at the north end of the parking area, walk a short path to cross 3 Rocks Road, then dip into fern- and berry-laced woods to parallel Jas Savage Road over alternating sections of trail and boardwalk. To the right (east), through the alder and elderberry, lies a babbling creek and a sprawling meadow. Watch for deer and elk through here. Where the trail pops out of the woods at 0.4 mile, cross the road and walk along the gravel shoulder for the next 0.1 mile. Heed signs warning you to stay out of the road. Cross the road again to a well-signed trailhead marking the beginning of the Cascade Head Trail. From here, the going is all up, so take a deep breath and forge ahead.

The trail crosses a trickling stream and climbs up around a big Sikta spruce into dense woods, quickly gaining elevation over a series of manmade and natural tree-root steps. A variety of ferns and fruiting shrubs grow along the trail, including thimbleberry and salmonberry. Follow the directional signs as you head up the steady grade, making sure to stay on the trail and not wander onto private property. As you climb, peer upward at some of the massive Sitka spruces that soar toward the sky. Some of these are more than 150 years old. At around 0.7 mile,

Gobs of wildflowers and wide-open views from Cascade Head

the trail levels and winds through a grove of Sitkas, where a particularly large one lays shattered on the forest floor.

Continue weaving westward through the woods, crossing footbridges over creeks and gullies choked with ferns and skunk cabbage, while admiring the wildflowers along the way, including foxglove, hedge nettle, hawkweed, and candy flower. The shade gives way at 1.4 miles, when the trail bursts out into Cascade Head's open slopeside meadows. Continue west through thickets of goldenrod, thistle, and blackberry—watch out for thorns!—to a sweeping viewpoint at 1.7 miles. Enjoy the view over the headland and down into a secluded cove. To the south is a panoramic view of the Salmon River spilling into the Pacific Ocean; the large, rocky knob along the coast is Gods Thumb (see Hike 8). Watch for hawks, harriers, eagles, and falcons circling overhead and seals, sea lions, and otters in the surf below.

From here, the trail gets steeper, narrower, and more overgrown as it continues climbing to

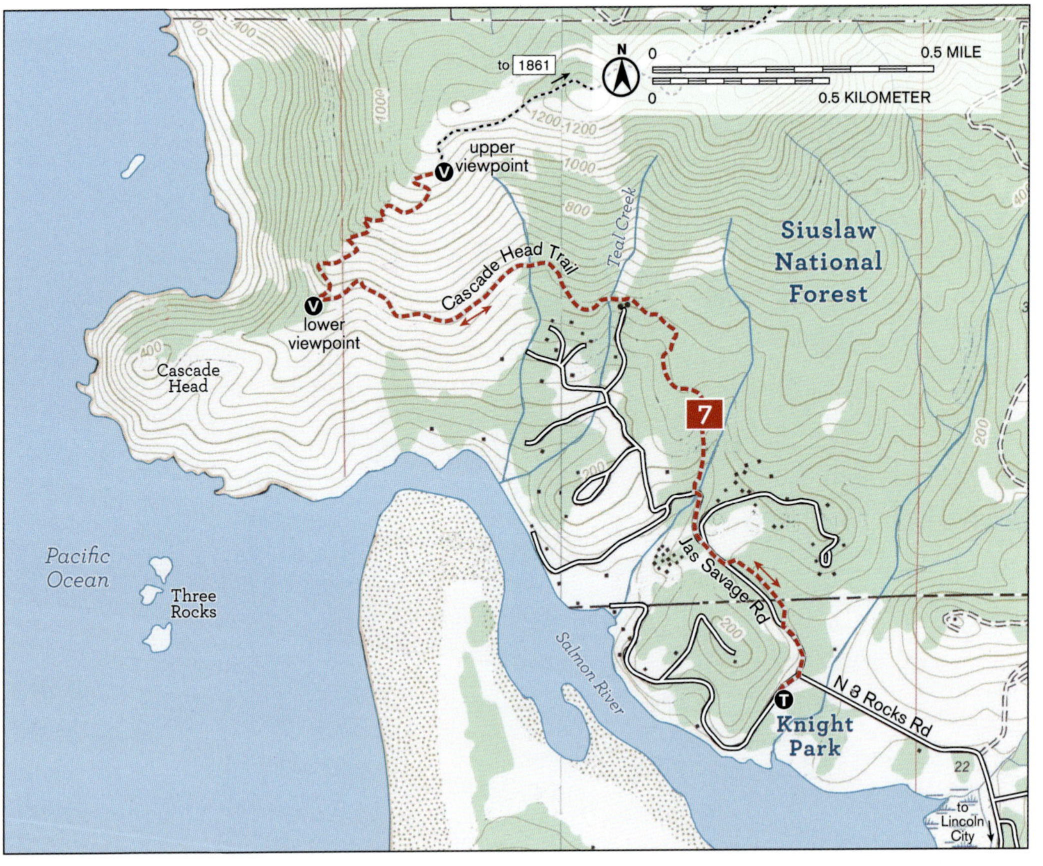

Cascade Head's upper reaches. Follow the path through stands of Queen Anne's lace, coyote brush, ragwort, and yarrow as it zigs and zags up the hillside. Be sure to adhere to the official path and avoid the shortcuts. Progress is slow as you ascend, mostly because you'll find yourself stopping to take in the view as it gets progressively wider and more impressive. Make a final ascent to reach a small plateau a little past 2.2 miles. Here you can take in a stellar view looking out over the meadows, coast, and ocean, with enough space to sit and enjoy your lunch. This makes a good turnaround spot, so when you're ready, head back down by the same route.

Extend Your Trip: At the time of this writing, the popular Harts Cove Trail was inaccessible due to a road washout. While it is still possible to get to this location, it requires hiking nearly 14 miles roundtrip. To do so, get an early start and hike the Cascade Head Trail. When you get to the upper viewpoint, continue for another 1.1 miles to Forest Road 1861. Turn left (west) and walk the road for 0.9 mile to its end. Begin the Harts Cove Trail and head steeply down into the wooded canyon of Cliff Creek, then contour the headland to cross Chitwood Creek. Make a final, short ascent over the headland to drop into the meadows above Harts Cove, enjoying the view from the trail's end.

8 *The Knoll and Gods Thumb*

Distance: 4.5-mile roundtrip
Difficulty: moderate
Hiking time: day hike
Elevation gain: 1210 feet
High point: 608 feet
Season: year-round
Management: Lincoln City Parks and Recreation
Protection status: The Knoll Open Space
Map: Green Trails 356SX: Oregon Coast North
GPS coordinates: N 45 01.069, W 123 99.793

Getting there: From US Highway 101 at the north end of Lincoln City, turn north onto NE Devils Lake Boulevard. Proceed 1.2 miles to the trailhead at the end of the road. ***Notes:*** The recommended parking area for visiting The Knoll is at the end of NE Devils Lake Boulevard. Do not use other parking areas, since this imposes on local residents.

Standing nearly 350 feet above the crashing waves along Oregon's Pacific Coast, Gods Thumb is the remnant of an ancient volcanic basalt dike. As the ocean surf continuously wears away the softer claystone and siltstone surrounding the rock, Gods Thumb will eventually become another lonely sea stack surrounded by water—but not for a hundred thousand years or so. Presently, the Thumb is accessible via a moderate trek through a coastal woodland, where you can enjoy panoramic views up and down the picturesque Oregon Coast.

Start your hike at The Knoll, just north of Lincoln City. This pleasant area, preserved as an open space in 2013, is adorned with spruce and alder woods, a couple of small creeks, and a nice assortment of seasonal wildflowers. While the obvious path heads north into the woods, begin instead with the less obvious path, on the west side of the cul-de-sac. It plunges through a dense thicket of Scotch broom then heads along a nice gravel path under shady trees. Go straight through a junction and cross a bridge over Logan Creek to the gate at NE Sal La Sea Drive, at 0.25 mile. Turn right (north) and walk up the road, being mindful of local residents. Where the road reaches a crest at the junction with NE Port Drive, at 0.5 mile, turn right (north) again and head back into The Knoll.

Gods Thumb at The Knoll Open Space

Continue climbing steeply up this old road, veering right (northeast) at a fork. The path reaches the top of the crest at around 0.9 mile at another unsigned fork. Take the left (south) fork about fifty yards to the open top of the crest for a sweeping view over Lincoln City, Devils Lake, and the Pacific Coast. Watch for elk and deer droppings in the grassy plain. After your view, return to the fork and continue northward along the wooded crest to the next junction, at 1.2 miles. Here, the Gods Thumb Trail continues straight ahead (north), while The Knoll Loop continues right (east). Continue ahead as the trail drops steeply into a wooded glen where wild irises are common.

At 1.8 miles, the trail breaks out into the open amid gobs of berry shrubs. Just 0.2 mile farther, stand at the top of the bluff overlooking the wide, blue Pacific, with Gods Thumb jutting high above the waves. Depending on the winds (which are often present here), you can continue to the top of the Thumb—just use caution along the edges of the cliffs. Otherwise, enjoy the view from the bluff. When you're ready, return to the loop trail by the same route.

Once you're back at the loop trail, turn left (east) and dip steeply off the ridge into a wooded drainage. Once the trail levels out, the walk becomes pleasant among a plethora of ferns and bright-pink foxgloves and hedge nettles. Follow this path as it snakes through the trees, over a low rise, and then reaches a junction near 4.4 miles. Turn right (west) and continue straight ahead for the last 0.1 mile back to the trailhead.

9 *Drift Creek Falls*

Distance: 3-mile roundtrip
Difficulty: moderate
Hiking time: short day hike
Elevation gain: 540 feet
High point: 960 feet
Season: Apr–Nov
Management: Siuslaw National Forest
Protection status: none
Map: Drift Creek Falls Trail 1378 (Siuslaw NF website)
GPS coordinates: N 44 93.551, W 123 85.566

Getting there: From the west (US Highway 101, about 4 miles south of Lincoln City), turn east onto Drift Creek Road and proceed 2 miles to a fork. Veer left onto Drift Creek Camp Road and continue another mile. Veer left again onto Forest Road 17 and take this narrow, winding road 9.4 miles to the trailhead on the right (east). From the east (Interstate 5 in Salem) take Oregon Route 22 west for about 26 miles toward Lincoln City. Merge onto OR 18 and drive west for another 22 miles. Turn left (south) on Bear

Drift Creek Falls pours through a gap in a wall of volcanic basalt.

Creek Road and proceed 3.3 miles to a fork. Bear left (southeast) on FR 17 and drive 5.5 winding miles to the trailhead. ***Notes:*** NW Forest Pass or Interagency Pass required for trailhead parking. Use caution and turn on your headlights on FR 17. This narrow, winding logging road is paved most of the way but has several blind corners and hairpin turns. Take it slow and use turnouts for oncoming traffic.

Located deep among the logging tracks of the Siuslaw National Forest, Drift Creek Falls is a pleasant gem of a trail. You'll visit a spectacular waterfall that jets out of a wall of columnar basalt and cross the longest backcountry suspension bridge in the Pacific Northwest. The walk is

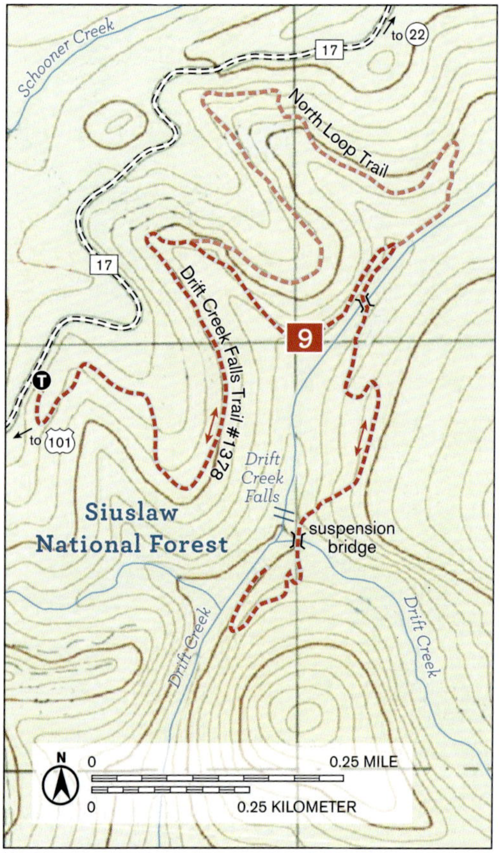

pleasant for all ages, and the view of the falls from the bridge is a unique and breathtaking sight.

Begin at the well-developed trailhead. Before you begin, snap a pic of the interpretive guide on the trailhead signboard to help you identify some of the natural features you'll see along the way. Once you set foot on the trail, it immediately descends on a moderate grade into younger fir and hemlock woods, where copious amounts of sword fern and salal carpet the forest floor. In springtime, look for the pleasant blooms of stream violets and wood sorrel adding little splashes of color.

Descend past mossy nurse logs and old cedar stumps, remnants of the logging that occurred here nearly a century ago. The trail then hooks through a small drainage at 0.6 mile and, a little farther along, comes to a fork with the North Loop Trail. For the more direct route, veer right (southeast) at the fork, staying on a wide, comfortable trail. (For a slightly longer, more secluded route, see Extend Your Trip below.) Continue descending another 0.3 mile to the next junction with the North Loop Trail, near the banks of the north fork of Drift Creek. Turn right (south) and stroll alongside the creek for a short spell, then cross on a good footbridge. The trail veers away from the creek and plunges back into mossy woods for a stretch, then comes to the brink of a narrow canyon at 1.3 miles.

Here, a 240-foot-long suspension bridge spans the canyon, nearly a hundred feet above the creek. The bridge was built in the late 1990s and has a tragic origin. The bridge's engineer, Scott Paul, was killed during construction, and the project was halted for several years. When it was finally completed in 1998—a difficult feat requiring many supplies to be flown in by helicopter—the bridge was dedicated to Paul. Step out onto the bridge to cross the canyon, taking in the aerial view of eighty-foot Drift Creek Falls spilling over a wall of twisted columnar basalt. The view is both harrowing and breathtaking.

Once across the bridge, enjoy another view of the falls from the opposite canyon wall, then proceed down the last 0.2 mile of trail to the base of the falls for another fantastic view. There's a small pool at the base of the falls but use caution if going in or near it—all waterfalls have the potential to carry rocks and debris, which can cause severe injury if you get struck. When you're ready, return to the trailhead by the same route, hiking back up and out of the canyon.

Extend Your Trip: If you're up for a slightly longer, more secluded route, hike the North Loop Trail to the falls. This narrower, more rugged path adds about a half mile to the roundtrip as it contours through another small side canyon, where it crosses a boggy tributary to Drift Creek. It's a quieter path than the main route, which can become busy on nice days and weekends.

10 Cape Perpetua

Distance: 1.9-/2.4-mile roundtrips
Difficulty: easy/strenuous
Hiking time: short day hikes
Elevation gain: 280 feet/890 feet
High point: 800 feet
Season: year-round
Management: Siuslaw National Forest
Protection status: Cape Perpetua Scenic Area
Map: Green Trails 456SX: Oregon Coast Central
GPS coordinates: N 44 28.094, W 124 10.843

Getting there: Cape Perpetua Scenic Area can be reached by driving US Highway 101 south for 26 miles from Newport (via US 20). Or drive north on US 101 for 23 miles from Florence (via Oregon Route 126). ***Notes:*** Cape Perpetua has many rugged natural features. Use extreme caution when exploring tide pools and coastal areas, and keep a safe distance from spouts, caves, and sinkholes.

Located along Oregon's rugged coastline between Florence and Newport, the Cape Perpetua Scenic Area protects 2700 acres of exceptional coastal ecosystem. With more than 26 miles of hiking trails, there is ample opportunity to explore. Marvel at the spectacular nature of the Oregon Coast—from benches of rugged lava rock pummeled by the ocean and brimming with tide pools, spouts, and sinkholes, to an old-growth temperate rainforest boasting one of the largest and oldest Sitka spruces in the state. The following suggestions are just a few of the recommended highlights. Spend a whole day here and see what else you can discover.

To visit the **Giant Spruce**, start at the trailhead between the visitor center and restrooms, dropping down a rough, paved path to the banks above Cape Creek. At 0.2 mile, the trail heads over a bridge for the steep climb to the Cape Perpetua viewpoint (more below). For now, veer right (east) and continue heading upstream. The trail climbs on an easy grade, paralleling the creek, where daisies are plentiful. At about 0.6 mile, the trail passes through a large "logout" (a walkway cut through a tree). A sign attached to the trunk indicates the tree is about two hundred years old, but this spruce is just a little baby compared to what's coming up ahead. As you proceed, you'll soon see the Cape Perpetua Campground across the creek, with a trail cutoff to the group camp coming at around 0.8 mile.

Continue heading upstream just 0.2 mile farther to the Giant Spruce. Here, at the end of the line, is a small clearing at the base of the tree with a convenient bench for viewing. Crane your neck and peer skyward to admire this ancient behemoth. Designated a Heritage Tree in 2007, it has a height of more than 185 feet and a circumference of 40 feet. It is estimated that the Giant Spruce first sprouted here at least half a century before Columbus sailed to the New World, making it nearly six hundred years old. Just let that

Cape Perpetua is home to one of the largest and oldest Sitka spruces in Oregon.

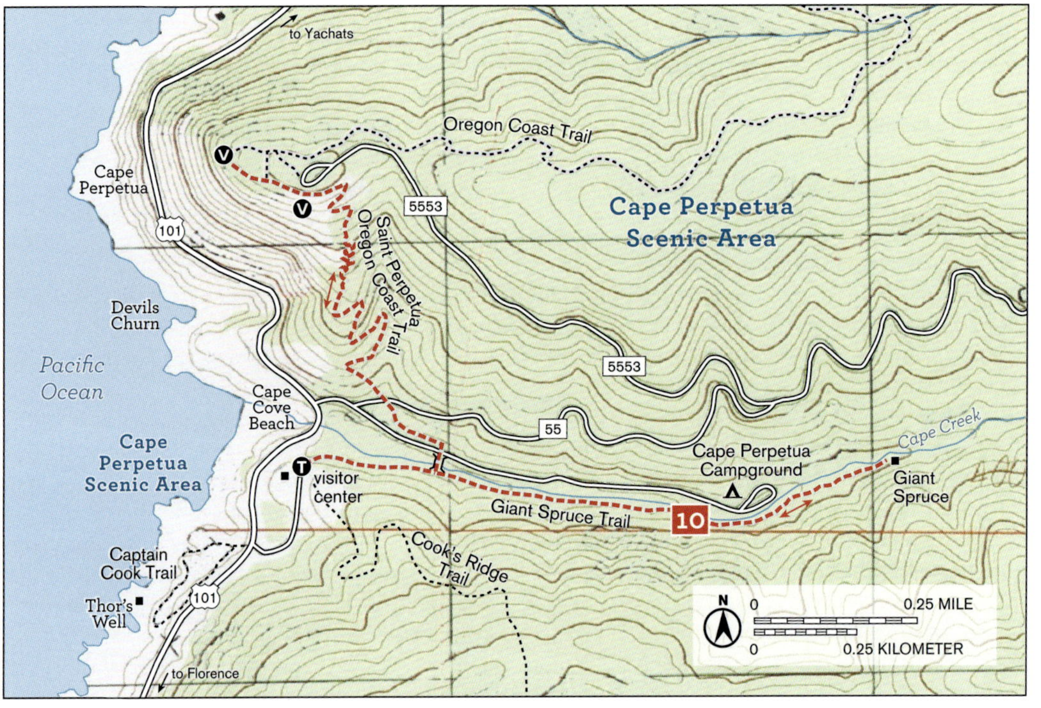

sink in for a moment. Six *hundred* years. Once your neck starts to ache from gawking and marveling at this incredible specimen, return to your starting point by heading back down along Cape Creek to the visitor center.

For a more strenuous hike with a big scenic payoff, take the **Saint Perpetua Trail** to the stone shelter at the top of the cape. Starting at the same trailhead by the visitor center, veer left (north) at the fork located at 0.2 mile and cross the bridge over Cape Creek. There's a restroom building just to the right (east). Jog left (northwest) across the campground entry road and pick up the Saint Perpetua Trail on the other side to begin the climb. Cross the viewpoint road at 0.4 mile and start switchbacking up the wooded slope under some impressively large spruce trees. At 0.8 mile, reach the lower crest and get a brief respite from the upward push as you cross a brushy powerline clearing.

From here, the trail zigs and zags up the ridgeline through more shady woods, where you're treated to a few ocean views as you get higher. The trail then bursts out into the open at around 1.1 miles, sweeping across the brushy hillside. Here, you're presented with a wide panorama over Devils Churn, Cape Cove Beach, and the wide Pacific Ocean. Climb a little farther to a viewpoint near the top, where the panorama is even better. Continue up into the summit visitor area, staying left (west) through the picnic area to reach the stone shelter at the top of the cape. Here, nearly nine hundred feet above the ocean, enjoy what's deemed the "best view on the Oregon Coast." Once you've taken it all in, return by the same route back to the visitor center.

Extend Your Trip: Reserve a little extra time to explore some of the cape's other scenic highlights. The 0.4-mile **Captain Cook Trail** below the highway leads down to a basalt bench riddled with tide pools and a close-up view of **Thor's Well**. This seemingly bottomless sinkhole is where the ocean surf surges in and out of an ancient lava tube, often creating a spectacular scene during high tides—just don't get too close!

11 *Sweet Creek Falls*

Distance: 1.9-mile roundtrip
Difficulty: easy
Hiking time: short day hike
Elevation gain: 280 feet
High point: 420 feet
Season: year-round
Management: Siuslaw National Forest
Protection status: none
Map: Sweet Creek Trails (Siuslaw NF website)
GPS coordinates: N 43 95.795, W 123 90.221

Getting there: From Eugene (east), take Oregon Route 126 west toward the coast for about 45 miles. Just before crossing the Siuslaw River in the town of Mapleton, turn left (south) on Sweet Creek Road (County Road 5036) and take this windy, paved road 10.3 miles to the lower Sweet Creek Homestead trailhead. From Florence (west), take OR 126 east for about 14 miles, cross the Siuslaw River, and turn right (south) on Sweet Creek Road. If the small trailhead lot is full, try the parking area and trailhead 0.5 mile farther up the road. ***Notes:*** During the spring high-runoff period, crossing Sweet Creek to the upper trail can be hazardous. Do not attempt if the water is too high or fast.

Tucked away in the Coast Range's Siuslaw National Forest, Sweet Creek Falls is an idyllic, family-friendly jaunt just waiting to be enjoyed. The walk is mostly effortless as the trail meanders along the creekside, crossing a series of boardwalks and showcasing nearly a dozen cascades, chutes, and small falls—all culminating at the base of the seventy-foot, multitiered Sweet Creek Falls. Spring and summer bring an abundance of delightful wildflowers to these woods, adding splashes of color to the lush green surroundings.

From the Sweet Creek Homestead trailhead (the recommended starting point), the trail winds into pleasant fir, alder, and maple woods, where fern and thimbleberry are abundant. The first small cascade appears in less than 0.1 mile, followed by another just beyond. The path then proceeds over a series of catwalks along the creekside. Some of these are secured directly into the mossy, rocky hillside, offering some delightful views of the cascades from right above the water. At about 0.6 mile, a side trail ascends through the trees to the Sweet Creek Falls trailhead, an alternative starting point if the lower trailhead parking lot is full.

Continue the pleasant walk upstream, viewing more small cascades and taking in the lush scenery. Here and there, younger trees reach skyward, growing out of old cedar stumps or mossy nurse logs. At about 0.9 mile, the trail reaches the base of Sweet Creek Falls, where a deep pool fills the head of the little canyon. A short side trail climbs up through a couple of switchbacks for a better view of the falls. Plenty of rocks along the creekside offer good spots to sit and enjoy the view as you soak it all in.

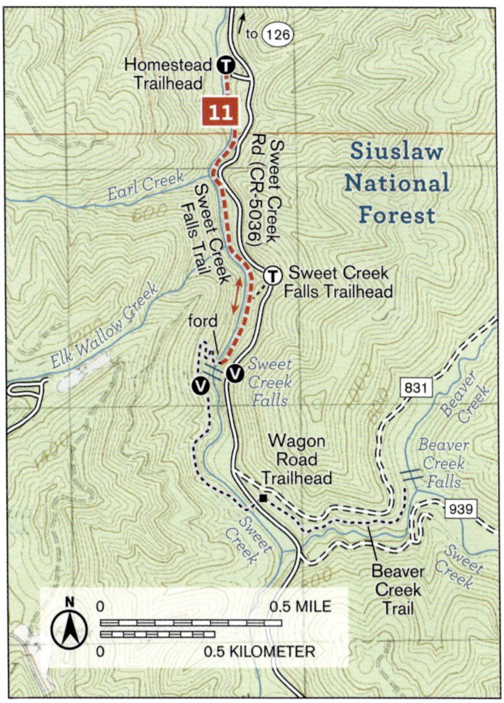

Sweet Creek features several pretty cascades.

If you're feeling adventurous—and the creek is not running too high or fast—you can continue up to a higher (and better) waterfall viewpoint. Carefully ford the creek on slippery underwater rocks and find the trail on the other side, ascending through thick shrubbery. Follow the path up a couple of steep switchbacks to a junction and turn left (south). The trail proceeds to a high viewpoint overlooking the multiple tiers of Sweet Creek Falls.

Extend Your Trip: While you're in the area, you can also check out pretty little **Beaver Creek Falls**. The hike is just an easy 0.5 mile from the Wagon Road trailhead. There's a small parking area near the trailhead, or you can extend the hike from the upper Sweet Creek Falls Trail. From the viewpoint junction mentioned above, continue up the hillside and wind your way south through more pleasant woods. When you reach Sweet Creek Road (CR-5036), jog left (north) and find the Beaver Creek Trail. The path follows another branch of Sweet Creek to its confluence with Beaver Creek, where it spills over a cluster of small slides and cascades into a clear, pretty pool.

12 Dellenback Dunes

Distance: 5-mile roundtrip
Difficulty: strenuous
Hiking time: day hike
Elevation gain: 160 feet
High point: 110 feet
Season: year-round
Management: Siuslaw National Forest
Protection status: Oregon Dunes National Recreation Area
Map: John Dellenback Dunes Trail (Siuslaw NF website)
GPS coordinates: N 43 58.433, W 124 18.516

Getting there: Get to the John Dellenback Dunes trailhead by taking US Highway 101 south from Florence for 33 miles, or north from Coos Bay for 16 miles. The trailhead parking area is on the west side of the highway. ***Notes:*** NW Forest Pass or Interagency Pass required for trailhead parking. This "trail" includes a long slog through soft, sandy dunes. Give yourself extra time, wear plenty of sun and wind protection, and carry all the water you'll need to stay hydrated. Portions of the beach are closed to protect nesting shorebirds from March through September.

Stretching for more than fifty miles along the Oregon Coast and covering more than forty thousand acres, the Oregon Dunes form one of the largest temperate dune fields in the world. Impressive sand dunes might not be first on your mind when you think about Oregon, a state that's known for its abundant rain and vast forests. It's just one more natural feature that makes this state unique. In 1972, a large portion of the area was designated as the Oregon Dunes National Recreation Area. In addition to a diverse offering of outdoor recreation opportunities—hiking,

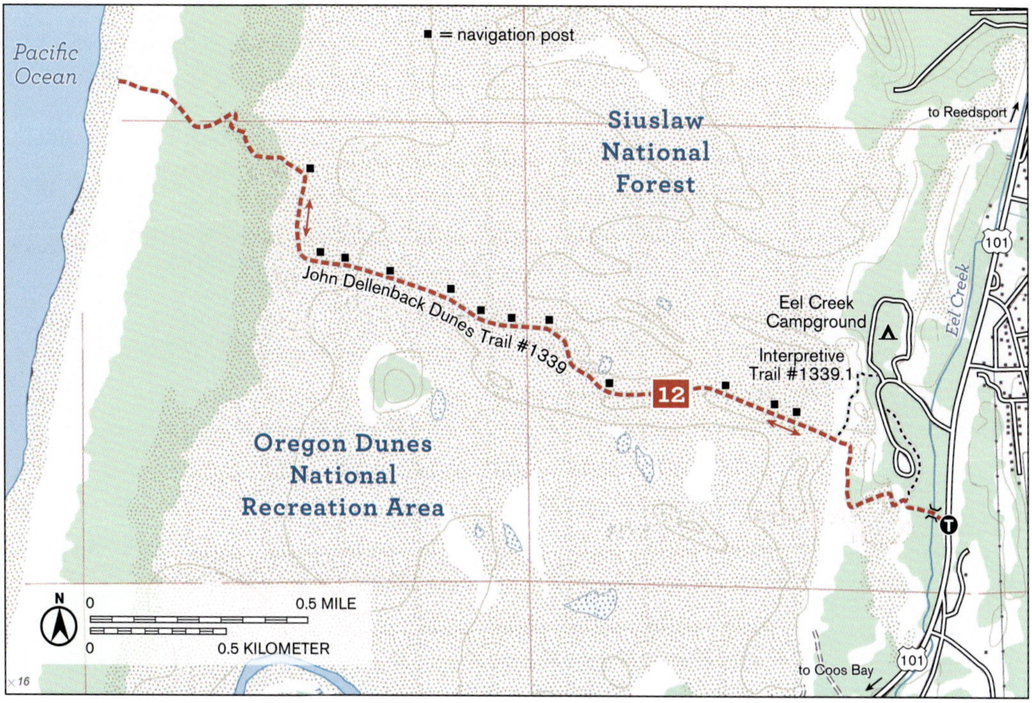

These are the dunes you're looking for.

off-road vehicles (ORV), sandboarding—the Oregon Dunes are home to a variety of wildlife, including deer, foxes, elk, porcupines, black bears, and the threatened snowy plover.

Begin your journey into this unique and desolate landscape at the John Dellenback Dunes trailhead, conveniently located right off US 101. The trail sets off on a well-graded path over Eel Creek and through coastal woods at the eastern extent of the dune field. Pass a couple of interpretive signs offering information on the area's flora and fauna, then crest a low dune for a sweeping view over the dune field. Use this as an opportunity to get your bearings as you channel your inner Luke Skywalker and peer across Tatooine. From this point forward, you're not following a trail so much as aiming for the right spot on the tree line on the opposite side of the dunes. Look for the tall posts mounted at varying distances across the field, keeping the big "tree island" on your left (south).

If you take the correct path across the dunes, you should reach the opposite tree line (N 43 59.227, W 124 21.343) at around 1.7 miles. Pick up the sandy path and head north through a corridor of head-high salal until the trail turns left (west) at 1.9 miles, plunging through a tunnel in the tangled trees. Traipse along the easy path as it winds through the woods and then over a low, grassy rise, eventually spilling out onto the sandy beach. It's not uncommon for the dunes to be sunny and sweltering while the beach is cool and foggy, all on the same day. Give yourself plenty of time for the slow trek back to your car.

13 *Sunset Bay to Cape Arago*

Distance: Up to 6.5-mile roundtrip
Difficulty: easy
Hiking time: day hike
Elevation gain: 300 feet
High point: 100 feet
Season: year-round
Management: Oregon State Parks
Protection status: Sunset Bay State Park
Map: Green Trails 456SX: Oregon Coast Central
GPS coordinates: N 43 33.123, W 124 37.398

Getting there: From Coos Bay, just south of the Mill Casino, head west on Newmark Street for 2.9 miles. Turn left (south) on Oregon Route 540 and drive for 7.2 miles. The road becomes the Cape Arago Highway and passes through Barview and Charleston before entering the park. Park in the Sunset Beach parking area and find the trailhead on the south side. ***Notes:*** There is no running water along this trail, so pack along all you need to stay hydrated for the day.

From pristine, sandy beaches to rugged, twisted coastline, the trail from Sunset Bay to Cape Arago has it all. Throw in some lush coastal woods, a clifftop observatory, botanical gardens, and a sea lion viewpoint, and you have all you need for a fantastic stroll along Oregon's dramatic southern coastline.

Starting from Sunset Beach, cross a bridge over Big Creek and climb up into shady cedar and Sitka spruce woods, where the forest floor is swathed in a variety of ferns, honeysuckle, trefoil, wood violets, and false lily-of-the-valley. The trail levels out after a quick 0.2-mile ascent and begins its pleasant, rolling course through the woods. At 0.3 mile, veer right (north) at a junction to reach the first big viewpoint. From here, you're treated to a wide panorama over Sunset Bay and a series of dramatically tilted rocks. Across the bay, look for the Cape Arago Lighthouse on Gregory Point. When you're ready, return to the junction and continue southward, skirting a wide meadow where deer and elk are common.

The trail continues its meandering path southward, dipping in and out of the woods, skirting the park road, and traversing along striking sea cliffs. The angle of these giant rock slabs showcases Mother Nature's powerful ability to twist and break the earth's surface

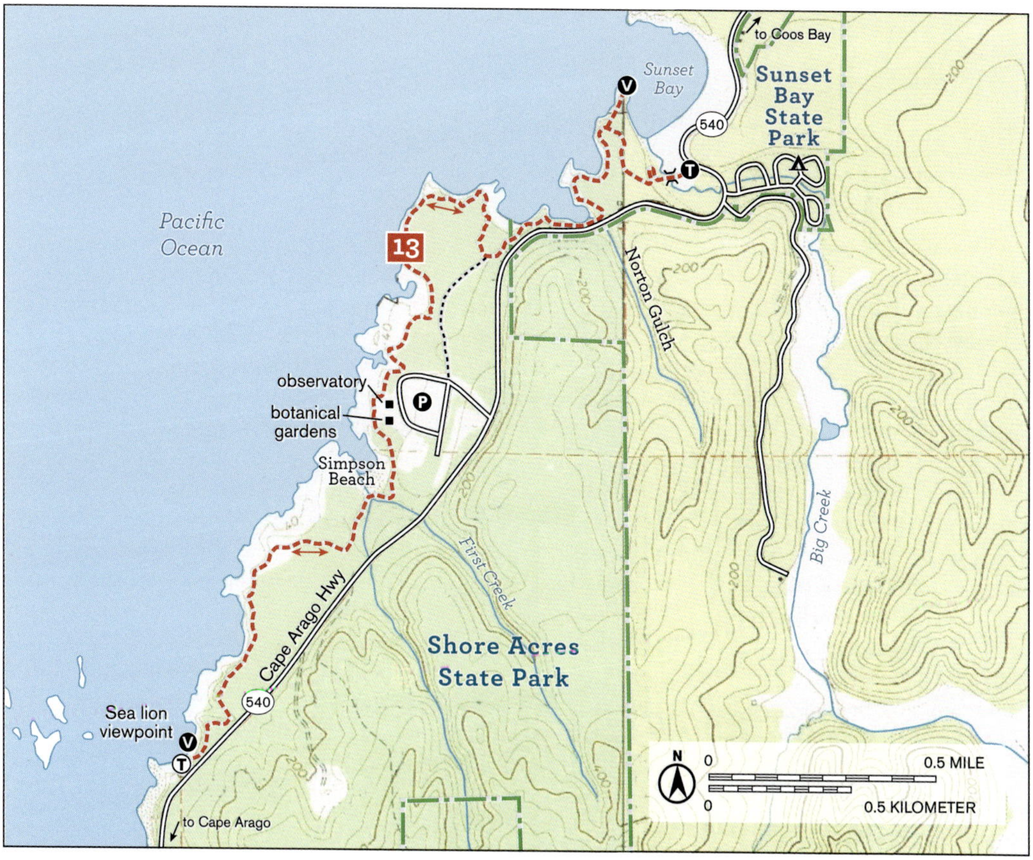

The tilted and tortured rocks at Sunset Bay

over the eons. Take advantage of any of the well-placed benches along the way to sit and ponder your tiny and insignificant place and time on the planet. Continue gawking at the scenery until you come to a grassy clearing and botanical gardens parking area at 2 miles. Here, an enclosed storm observatory stands atop the cliff, offering a wide panorama over the Pacific. Look for whales during the winter and spring migration months.

Proceed to the opposite end of the clearing and pick up the trail again near the giant, weather-beaten trunk of a downed tree. The trail passes a back gate into the botanical gardens (see below) and drops down to cross a little creek canyon at 2.3 miles, where hidden Simpson Beach lies in wait. If you packed a snack or lunch, this is an ideal spot to take a break on the warm sand and enjoy the view. From here, the trail climbs away from the beach and proceeds along the wooded clifftops, where you're presented with a few more views amid abundant fireweed, angelica, sword lily, and coast clover. At 3.2 miles, the trail pops out of the trees at a roadside viewpoint overlooking an offshore reef that often hosts sea lions. From here, the trail crosses the road and continues to Cape Arago, then inland, but this makes a good turnaround point.

Extend Your Trip: On your way back, duck into the Shore Acres State Park botanical gardens and wander among the artful and manicured displays of plants and flowers from around the world. The gardens feature a Japanese-inspired lily pond, in addition to rose, rhododendron, and azalea gardens. Admission to the gardens is free.

14 Blacklock Point

Distance: 3.7-mile roundtrip
Difficulty: easy
Hiking time: short day hike
Elevation gain: 190 feet
High point: 220 feet
Season: year-round
Management: Oregon State Parks
Protection status: Floras Lake State Natural Area
Map: Green Trails 656SX: Oregon Coast South
GPS coordinates: N 42 85.707, W 124 52.018

Getting there: From Coos Bay (north), drive US Highway 101 south for approximately 42 miles. Opposite Pacific High School, turn right (west) on Airport Road and drive 2.9 miles to its end. From Port Orford (south), drive US 101 north approximately 7 miles to Airport Road. Park in the dirt parking area opposite the airport gate.

Wildflowers abound on the Oregon Coast at Blacklock Point.

Just north of Cape Blanco State Park, Blacklock Point is an unassuming scenic highlight along Oregon's southern coastline. The trail is pleasant and fairly easy, and it's possible to find a little solitude here, away from the coast's more popular attractions and viewpoints. In summer, wildflowers often line the trail and carpet the bluff overlooking the coast, adding splashes of color to this little-used gem of a trail.

Begin with an easy walk along the fenced perimeter of the small Cape Blanco State Airport, where abundant bunchberry lines the trailside with its pretty white flowers in early summer. Where the trail forks at 0.7 mile, veer left (west) to continue to the point. The trail to the right may be your return route, depending on which way you decide to come back (see Extend Your Trip below). The path winds along through quiet, pleasant woods, descending on a gentle grade to a junction with the Oregon Coast Trail (OCT) at 1.2 miles. Turn left (south), following signs for Blacklock Point. Dip down into a shady glen and cross several small springs on a series of boardwalks.

The path then ascends to a low ridge and a junction, where the OCT veers off left (south), at 1.6 miles. Take the right (northwest) path and head out of the woods and onto the bluff overlooking Blacklock Point amid an open meadow of hawkweed and angelica. Enjoy the view of the surf pounding on the rocks below and venture as far as you're willing onto the knife-edge ridge of the point—just watch your footing. It's also possible to make a short scramble down to the beach. Looking south, you can spy the lighthouse on Cape Blanco. When you're ready to return, you can head straight back the way you came or take a longer, more roundabout route that nets you a couple more good views.

Extend Your Trip: For added views and a little more mileage, return to the signed junction at 1.6 miles and turn left (north) on the OCT. The path ahead gets a little overgrown and brushy as it works its way up the coast. Around 0.3 mile from the junction, a short path leads to a viewpoint looking back on Blacklock Point, offering another impressive view of the rugged coastline. The path then dips through a gully and crosses a creek before rising to the next viewpoint, overlooking a secluded beach beneath some layered cliffs. Just beyond, at the next junction, turn right (south) and hike for 1 mile before returning to a familiar junction. Continue left (south) for 0.7 mile, back along the airport perimeter, to return to the trailhead.

15 *Humbug Mountain*

Distance: 5-mile roundtrip
Difficulty: strenuous
Hiking time: day hike
Elevation gain: 1830 feet
High point: 1761 feet
Season: year-round
Management: Oregon State Parks
Protection status: Humbug Mountain State Park
Map: Green Trails 656SX: Oregon Coast South
GPS coordinates: N 42 68.785, W 124 43.939

Getting there: From Port Orford (north), drive US highway 101 south for 5.5 miles to Humbug Mountain State Park. The trailhead is on the right (south) side of the highway.
Notes: At the time of research, the east side loop was closed due to storm damage. Check current conditions before you go.

As you drive south from Port Orford along Oregon's striking Pacific Coast, a wooded headland vaults skyward directly ahead. Christened "Humbug" Mountain by an 1851 survey party's leader, who was upset about a navigational error, this wooded peak is one of the highest headlands along the Oregon Coast. A steep, winding trail heads up the mountain to a summit loop that culminates in a sweeping view over the coast.

Setting out from the trailhead, located across the highway from the campground, the path crosses a small creek and immediately begins climbing into shady bigleaf maple and Douglas-fir forest. Carpets of sword and maidenhair fern, wood sorrel, wild iris, and heliotrope add to the verdant setting. The first stretch is marked every quarter mile by numbered posts, allowing you to gauge the distance you've traveled. Depending on how fast you hike, this could be an *en*couraging or *dis*couraging thing. As you approach 0.7 mile, hop across the same small creek again as the trail turns though a lush drainage, then keep

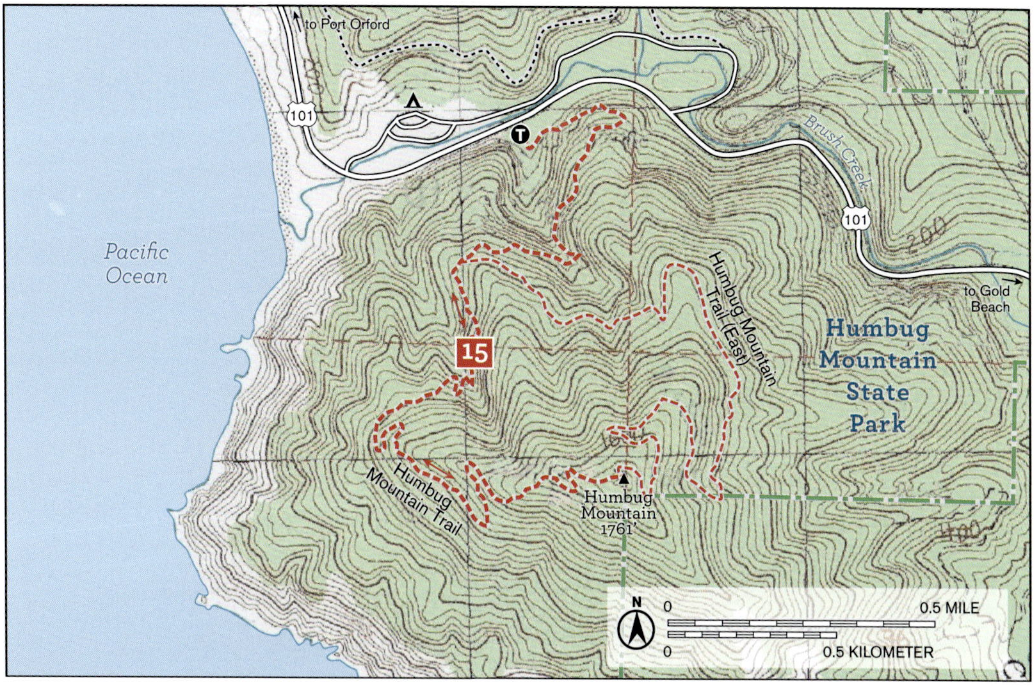

Sunset at Humbug Mountain State Park

ascending to reach the 1-mile marker. Nearby, a picnic table invites you to sit and catch your breath.

Continuing your ascent, the trail snakes around the west side of the mountain, where you get your first partial view, at around 1.4 miles. Here, you can peer northward over the Redfish Rocks Marine Preserve and out toward Port Orford. Climb through a few switchbacks, curve around the south side of the mountain, and then head up through a few more switchbacks to reach the 2-mile marker (actually at 2.2 miles). Press onward and upward through the last 0.3 mile to reach the summit, where you're rewarded with a sweeping panorama looking southward down Oregon's coastline. The pyramidal mount offshore in the distance is Lookout Rock. Plop down in the summit clearing among swaying grasses and bracken ferns and admire the view. In spring and summer, the peak is often swarming with ladybugs.

16 *Flora Dell Falls (Rogue River Trail)*

Distance: 8-mile roundtrip
Difficulty: moderate
Hiking time: day hike, overnight, or multiday
Elevation gain: 1560 feet
High point: 590 feet
Season: Apr–Nov
Management: Siskiyou National Forest
Protection status: none
Map: USFS Rogue River Trail
GPS coordinates: N 42 63.858, W 124 05.552

Getting there: At the north end of Gold Beach, just south of the bridge over the Rogue River, drive east on Jerry's Flat Road. After 9.8 miles, this road turns into Agness Road (Forest Road 33); continue for another 20.9 winding miles. When the road forks, veer right (north) onto Agness Illahe Road (County Road 375) and drive another 3.5 miles. Just past the Foster Bar Campground, veer right (northeast) and drive 0.2 mile to the Big Bend trailhead. ***Notes:*** This trail can get brutally hot in midsummer, with limited access to water. Beware of ticks, bears, rattlesnakes, and poison oak.

The entire length of the Rogue River Trail runs for more than forty miles down the spectacularly scenic river canyon, from Grave Creek to Foster Bar. The best way to tackle this epic trail is as a one-way, multiday trek, with enough time to enjoy and appreciate all the scenery, swimming holes, and backcountry camps (see Extend Your Trip). For a bite-size piece of the Rogue River Trail to whet your appetite, try this roundtrip from Big Bend to Flora Dell, culminating with a picturesque waterfall in an enchanting grotto.

Follow signs to the Rogue River Trail (#1160), ducking into shady woods and beginning with an easy stroll along the margin of a wooded slope and an open pasture. In late spring, the field is sprinkled with vibrant brodiaea and centaury. At the head of the field, near 0.5 mile, pass through a couple of gates, then cross Billings Creek on a sturdy footbridge. Just beyond, at 0.7 mile, cross an old service road and commence a rolling contour of the slope just above the river. Along the way, the trail crosses small creeks on little bridges as the path winds its way upstream.

Around the 2.4-mile mark, the trail turns to traverse the Dans Creek drainage, then commences a steady ascent up and over a high slope. The trail then dips back down to cross Hicks Creek at 3.2 miles. From here, continue on a gently descending grade, drawing closer and closer to the river, with views beginning to open up. Hop across Flea Creek on another little footbridge, then round a bend into Flora Dell at the 4-mile mark. The scene looks like it was plucked straight out of Rivendell, with a wispy waterfall plunging into a rock-ringed pool, surrounded by verdant ferns and mosses.

Flora Dell Falls is a pleasant lunch spot along the Rogue River Trail.

This spot makes an ideal destination for a pleasant day trip—especially on warm summer days when the waterfall mist fills the grotto with natural air-conditioning. Pull up a comfy rock and enjoy a poolside snack or lunch, watching for rafters passing by on the Rogue River below, where it flows lazily down a wide section of the canyon. When you're ready, head back the way you came, or venture a little farther up the canyon to see what's around the next bend.

Extend Your Trip: To get the full Rogue River Trail experience, consider using one of the river shuttle services. After you start your hike at Grave Creek, they will transport your vehicle down to the end of the line at Big Bend/Foster Bar, where you can pick it up at the end of your hike. There are numerous backcountry campsites along the river, and even a few hike-in and boat-in lodges offering meal and bedding services. The average hiker takes four to five days to complete the entire trail. Visit blm.gov/visit/rogue-river-national-recreation-trail for more information and a handy trip-planning guide.

17 *Hunters Cove*

Distance: 3.3-mile roundtrip
Difficulty: moderate
Hiking time: short day hike
Elevation gain: 860 feet
High point: 680 feet
Season: year-round
Management: Oregon State Parks
Protection status: Cape Sebastian State Scenic Corridor
Map: Green Trails 656SX: Oregon Coast South
GPS coordinates: N 42 32.887, W 124 42.600

Getting there: From Gold Beach, drive US Highway 101 south for approximately 6 miles. Turn right (west) onto Cape View Loop for Cape Sebastian State Park. After 0.2 mile, turn left (south) and proceed another 0.2 mile to the parking turnaround and trailhead. From Brookings, Cape Sebastian is 22 miles north. ***Notes:*** The very end of the trail requires a fifty-foot rappel down to the beach. A fixed rope is available to assist with the descent and climb back up.

Cape Sebastian is an often-overlooked park along the Oregon Coast Highway (US 101) between Gold Beach and Brookings. Most visitors are instead drawn to the scenic beaches along this stretch as well as the incredibly spectacular Samuel H. Boardman State Scenic Corridor (see Hike 18). But this little gem is not to be missed. Follow a pleasant trail through coastal woods and along a bench of tortured rocks before dropping—literally—to a secluded and sandy beach.

The way to the beach is almost all downhill, and the return is almost all uphill, so prepare yourself. From the trailhead, the path descends into a tunnel of ferns, thimbleberry, and Sitka spruce, bottoming out in a shady draw. Then a short ascent gains the ridgeline as the trail turns south and proceeds along a narrow path. After 0.2 mile, a window opens through the trees where a jagged pinnacle of crumbling volcanic rock juts from the hillside. From this vantage point, you can look far north up the coast, all the way past Humbug Mountain (see Hike 15) to Port Orford.

From here, the trail plunges into a steady descent, zigging and zagging its way down the ridgeline. At 0.7 mile, the forest pulls away as the

Enjoy solitude and ocean views at Hunters Cove.

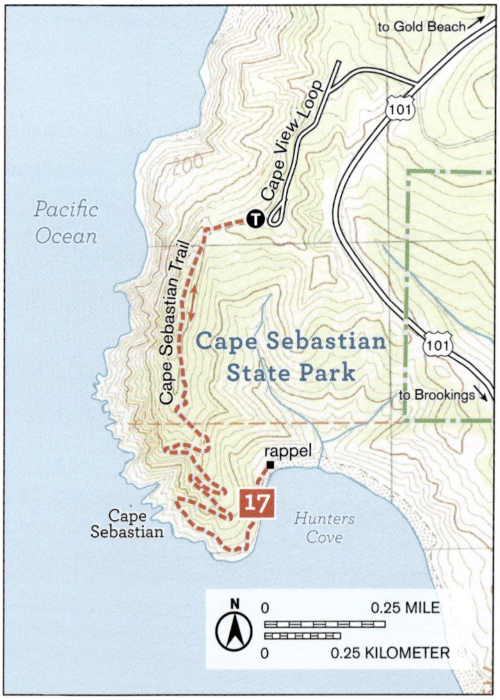

path switchbacks down a brushy, increasingly open corridor festooned with wild iris, tiger lily, Nootka rose, and camas. The path finally bottoms out at 1.2 miles and traverses the edge of a bench of twisted and tortured rock ceaselessly pummeled by the Pacific Ocean. If you venture out onto the rocks for a closer look, use extreme caution and never turn your back to the ocean.

The trail then curves around the headland and plunges back into the trees before ending abruptly at 1.7 miles. From here, you can see where the slope gave out and the trail disintegrated. The way down the loose, rocky, fifty-foot slope is via a rope secured to the hillside. If you choose to navigate it, hold the rope tightly and ease yourself down—it's a lot easier than it looks. Once your feet are planted on the sandy beach in Hunters Cove, you're more likely to be accompanied by seabirds than other people, so explore and enjoy at your leisure—and worry about the climb back out later.

18 *Samuel H. Boardman Scenic Corridor*

Distance: 8-mile roundtrip
Difficulty: moderate
Hiking time: day hike
Elevation gain: 1580 feet
High point: 480 feet
Season: year-round
Management: Oregon State Parks
Protection status: Samuel H. Boardman State Scenic Corridor
Map: Green Trails 656SX: Oregon Coast South
GPS coordinates: N 42 14.441, W 124 35.491

Getting there: From Brookings, drive north on the Oregon Coast Highway (US Highway 101) for about 8 miles to the Whaleshead Beach parking area. The rough, rocky, 0.3-mile road down to the parking area is best for high-clearance and/or 4WD vehicles. Otherwise, you can park at the top of the gravel road and walk down to the beach. ***Notes:*** The alternative to walking along Whaleshead Beach, which requires navigating steep trails from and then back to the Oregon Coast Trail (OCT), is to stay on the OCT the whole way. The OCT sets off near the parking area restroom and stays mostly atop the wooded hillside, with a couple good views as well as a wispy waterfall to enjoy.

Named for "The Father of Oregon State Parks," the Samuel H. Boardman State Scenic Corridor commemorates the man who conceived the state's park system and is perhaps the most spectacular stretch of Oregon's rugged Pacific Coast. This corridor contains eighteen view-packed miles of the Oregon Coast Trail (OCT), where you can ogle craggy sea stacks, rugged cliffs, and impressive natural arches in between secluded beaches, meadowy bluffs, and forested headlands. The following segment, between Whaleshead Beach and Cape Ferrelo, is a scenic feast for the eyes, so give yourself extra time—you will struggle to tear yourself away from each successive view. While you're hiking, don't forget to keep your eyes peeled for eagles in the trees, deer in the woods, and whales offshore.

From the parking area, drop down through the picnic area amid thickets of blackberry, horsetail, and English ivy to the beach, where you'll take in your first impressive views of Whaleshead Island. This is the larger, pointed monolith amid the cluster of rocky islets just offshore. Hop across Whaleshead Creek and head south down the beach for 1 mile. Along the way, you'll enjoy plenty of views as you hop across Coon and Bowman Creeks and wander through a mossy rock garden. Near the south end of the beach, look for a tall post marking a faint trail on the grassy hillside, right beside a jumbled creek bed. Begin a steep climb up the headland, where thistle, wild iris, and monkey flower decorate the open slopes. The trail is narrow and brushy, with steep drops to the rocks below, so step carefully. Just before the trail turns east to head upslope, take in a sweeping view of the landscape where you just walked, with Whaleshead Island now far down the beach.

Then climb steeply into dense spruce and fir forest, with abundant ferns, thimbleberry, and salal carpeting the hillsides. Step carefully as the trail twists and turns steeply upward, finally meeting the Oregon Coast Trail (OCT) at 1.4 miles. Take note of this location for your return trip, as there is no sign or trail marker here. Turn right (south) on wider, more comfortable tread, and follow the roller-coaster path through the lush woods for the next 0.9 mile to the House Rock Viewpoint at 2.3 miles. As you take in the views up and down the coast, ponder the inspiring quote on the Samuel Boardman monument: "By retaining the natural, harming as little as possible, you better serve those who are to follow."

Pick up the trail again on the other side of the parking area, continuing south on the OCT. The trail descends through a corridor of mixed berries (tasty treats in late summer), salal, and yarrow before descending into shady woods once again. At 2.6 miles, keep your eyes peeled for a side trail that branches off to the right (west). It's worth taking this 0.2-mile path through the trees to the open bluff and stunning viewpoint at its end. If you packed a picnic lunch, this is the place to enjoy it. Rocky, turquoise coves adorn either side of this abutment, with lava-rock tide

The Oregon Coast at Samuel Boardman Scenic Corridor

pools below. It's an enchanting and idyllic setting that you might possibly have all to yourself, away from the throngs of tourists crowding the beaches and viewpoints.

After your detour, continue heading south on rolling trail, marveling at the size of some of the ancient spruce and fir trees along the way. The trail suddenly bursts out of the woods for the next spectacular panorama at around 3.4 miles. The grassy headland directly ahead is your destination. You won't be able to tear your gaze away from the view as you make your way to the Cape Ferrelo Viewpoint at 3.5 miles. Cross the grassy viewpoint and find the OCT again on the south side, plunge down through a tunnel of overhanging spruce, and then head up onto the open, meadow-covered cape. Follow the trail around the head of the cape, soaking in the views up and down the coast. Choose your favorite view and plop down for a well-earned break. When you're ready, loop back to the viewpoint, then retrace your steps back to your starting point.

Extend Your Trip: Go farther on the Boardman Scenic Corridor. From Whaleshead Beach, hike the OCT north to Indian Sands (1.7 miles), Thomas Creek Bridge (the highest bridge in Oregon; 3 miles), China Beach (4.1 miles), Natural Bridges Viewpoint (5.1 miles), or Secret Beach (6.1 miles). All distances are one-way, so give yourself plenty of time for your return trip. Some highway walking may be necessary.

Opposite, top: Pleasant woods adorn the slopes of Spencer Butte.

Opposite, bottom: Stream violets are common along wooded trails.

Western Valleys

19. Lower Table Rock 76
20. Spencer Butte 77
21. McDowell Creek Falls 79
22. Trail of Ten Falls (Silver Falls State Park)........ 81
23. Cooper Mountain 84
24. Tryon Creek 85
25. Redwood Loop (Hoyt Arboretum) 87
26. Wildwood Trail (Forest Park) 89
27. Balch Creek and Witch's Castle 94
28. Powell Butte 95

You don't have to travel far from any of Oregon's western urban areas to get a quick nature fix. In fact, most of Oregon's major cities pride themselves on their outdoor offerings—from volcanic buttes and waterfall parks to nature preserves and cultural sites, to one of the largest urban forests in the United States. When you don't have time to head for the hills, head to one of your local parks or natural areas instead.

19 *Lower Table Rock*

Distance: 4.6-mile roundtrip
Difficulty: moderate
Hiking time: day hike
Elevation gain: 800 feet
High point: 2020 feet
Season: year-round
Management: Oregon BLM and The Nature Conservancy
Protection status: Area of Critical Environmental Concern
Map: Table Rocks BLM brochure
GPS coordinates: N 42 46.876, W 122 94.569

Getting there: From Interstate 5 in Gold Hill, just north of Medford, take exit 40 and turn north toward town. Turn left (west) on Oregon Route 99/2nd Avenue and drive for 0.4 mile, then go right on Dardanelles Street. Go over the train tracks, then take another right on 4th Avenue/Rogue-Umpqua Scenic Byway (OR 234). Continue for 6.1 miles, then veer right (east) on Tresham Lane. Drive for 1 mile, then turn right (south) on Wheeler Road and continue for 0.5 mile. Turn right (west) into the Lower Table Rock parking area.
Notes: Day use only. Dogs not permitted. Beware of ticks, rattlesnakes, and poison oak.

The views from Table Rock sweep over Oregon's Rogue River and southern Cascade Range.

Just a short drive north of Medford—and visible from I-5—the Table Rocks are a couple of high, volcanic mesas that harbor a thriving ecosystem of plants and animals. Named "upper" and "lower" for their relative positions to the Rogue River, both can be hiked, but the Lower Table Rock has a more developed and accessible trail system, along with a fantastic interpretive pavilion. Before starting your hike, take a few minutes to check out all the information about the rocks' natural history and native wildlife population, as well as a visual guide to some of the seventy-five varieties of wildflowers known to inhabit the area—including the endemic dwarf woolly meadowfoam, which doesn't grow anywhere else on earth.

From the pavilion, start by crossing a grassy pasture brimming with buttercups and seablush. You'll quickly pass the short, barrier-free Oak Savannah Loop, which breaks off to the right

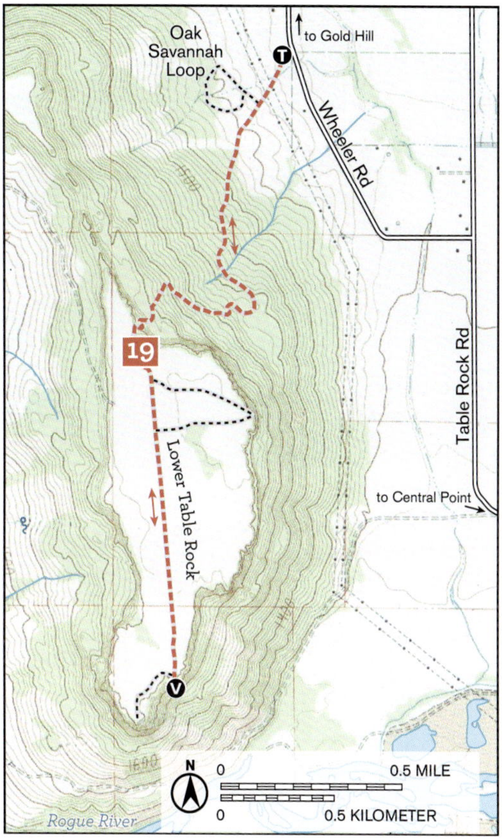

(west). This is a nice option for the mobility impaired or those with little ones in tow. From here, the trail starts gaining elevation as it heads through a grove of white oak and then through a corridor of dense buckbrush. Look for vibrant shooting stars and larkspur along the trail. Denser woods of madrone and ponderosa pine start to enclose the rock's lower slopes, and you'll be thankful for the shade if you're hiking in midsummer, when temperatures in the Rogue Valley can soar into triple digits. Stay on the trail here and keep an eye out for poison oak, as it is *everywhere*.

The path now starts gaining steady elevation as it twists and turns up the wall of the mesa. Common flowers you'll find along the way include hound's tongue, bleeding heart, and fawn lily. Keep your eyes peeled for more elusive varieties like fiddlenecks, chocolate lily, ookow, and red bells. When the trail rounds a bend at around 1.1 miles, a window through the trees offers a view eastward encompassing the Cascade Crest and 9495-foot Mount McLoughlin. This picturesque, often snow-capped peak has the distinction of being the southernmost of Oregon's big volcanic mountains and is a notable waypoint for Pacific Crest Trail hikers making their way north into Oregon.

Push through the final ascent and come to the top of the rock at 1.3 miles, where the trail flattens out and heads south across the open plateau. Stick with the obvious path, heading south, and cross a boardwalk section that protects an area of vernal ponds, home to the endangered and short-lived fairy shrimp. Be on the lookout for the dwarf woolly meadowfoam, along with mariposa lily, two-color lupine, popcorn flower, and purple-eyed grass. The trail finally ends at the southern edge of the plateau at 2.3 miles. From here, you can peer down onto the Kendall Slough on the Rogue River, and outward over Medford, the Siskiyou Summit, and Mount Ashland. A nearby cluster of rocks makes a nice perch for taking it all in. When you're fully sated, or it just starts getting too hot, turn around and retrace your steps back to the trailhead.

20 *Spencer Butte*

Distance: 2.2-mile roundtrip
Difficulty: moderate to strenuous
Hiking time: short day hike
Elevation gain: 740 feet
High point: 2054 feet
Season: year-round
Management: City of Eugene
Protection status: Eugene Parks and Open Space
Map: Ridgeline Trail System
GPS coordinates: N 43 98.035, W 123 10.178

Enjoy wide panoramas over the Willamette Valley and Central Cascades from Spencer Butte.

Getting there: From Interstate 5 in Eugene, take exit 189 for 30th Avenue. Turn west and drive toward the city for 3.1 miles, then go left (south) on Hilyard Street for 0.2 mile. At the next signal, turn right on E. 33rd Avenue and continue for 0.5 mile, then turn left on Willamette Street. Drive 2.9 miles to Spencer Butte Park on the left (east) side of the road. ***Notes:*** Beware of poison oak on the summit.

Located on the southern fringes of Eugene, Spencer Butte is a volcanic prominence and the highest point along the city's 2100-acre Ridgeline Park system. It is notable for its densely wooded lower slopes and bare summit, from which you can take in a 360-degree panorama over the Cascade Range, Coast Range, and Willamette Valley. There are contesting legends about how the butte came to be named, with one story suggesting it was christened in 1845 in honor of Secretary of War John C. Spencer, and the other claiming it was named forty years earlier after a boy named Spencer who was killed on the mount by local natives. Regardless of where the name came from, the view from the summit remains much the same as it did two centuries ago. As Dr. Elijah White wrote in his 1848 memoir, *Ten Years in Oregon*, the view from Spencer Butte is "very distinct, grand and imposing."

Two trails lead to the top of Spencer Butte. The 1.1-mile "easy" route is hard, and the 0.6-mile "hard" route is downright brutal. The following description outlines the "easy" route on the Main Trail. If you want to train for the Spartan Death Race—or just punish yourself for not eating kale this week—try the steep and rugged West Trail.

From the signed trailhead junction, head east into the woods on the well-graded gravel of the Main Trail. The path passes a picnic area at the edge of a grassy meadow, then heads under tall, shady Douglas-firs and bigleaf maples. A medley of ferns, thimbleberries, creeping thistles, and hedge nettles adorn the hills and trailside. The path hugs the slope as it gains elevation, steadily getting steeper, and then reaches a small plateau and a trail junction at 0.6 mile. Veer left (north) to stay on the Main Trail; the other path branches off right (east) to the Ridgeline Trail. As you pull away, you may be asking yourself, "Is the trail getting steeper?" Yes. Yes, it is.

Proceed up a few wooded switchbacks until the trail breaks out into the open on the butte's mostly barren upper slopes. Watch out for poison oak, as it tends to creep along the trailside. At 0.9 mile, where the trail switches back once more, you'll get a preview of the grand vistas waiting

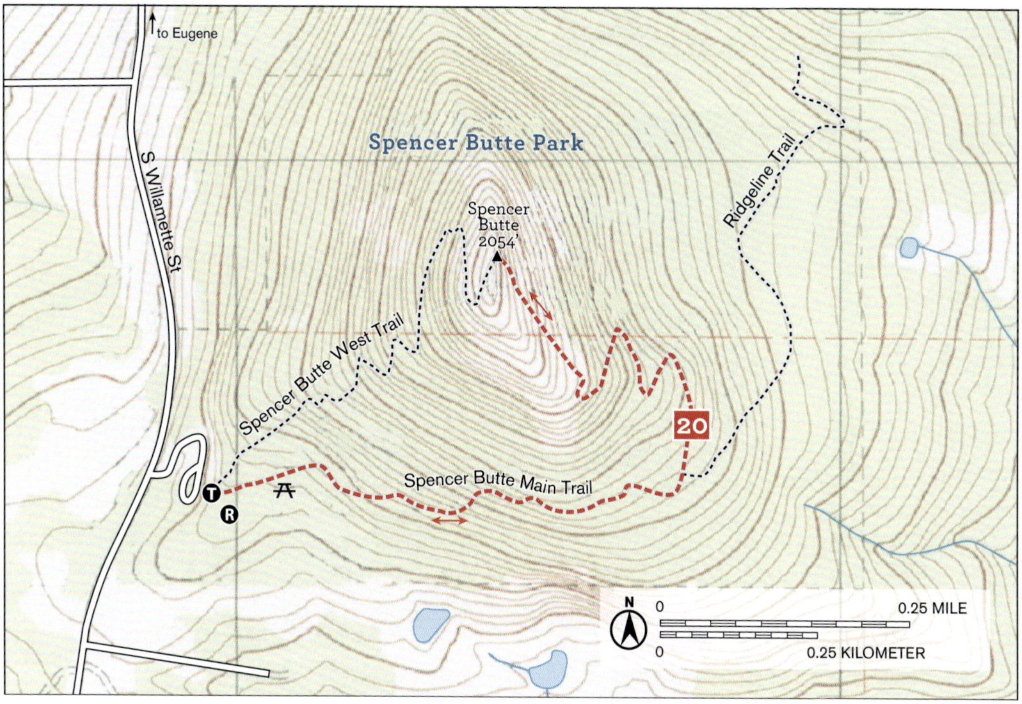

for you at the top. The next 0.2 mile to the summit is a steep stair climb—literally—on rocky steps that were installed in 2015 to help protect the butte's fragile ecosystem. Push through the last few steps and mount the summit plateau, where the view opens up in every direction. Find your own perfect perch on one of the basalt outcrops, and plop down to enjoy the scenic reward for your efforts.

21 *McDowell Creek Falls*

Distance: 1.6-mile loop
Difficulty: easy
Hiking time: short day hike
Elevation gain: 300 feet
High point: 1090 feet
Season: year-round
Management: Linn County Parks and Recreation
Protection status: none
Map: McDowell Creek Falls Park (linnparks.com)
GPS coordinates: N 44 46.430, W 122 08.228

Getting there: From Interstate 5 near Albany, drive Oregon Route 20 east for 18 miles. Turn left (north) on Old Santiam Highway, then immediately turn right (east) on Fairview Road. Drive 0.9 mile, then bend left (northeast) onto McDowell Creek Drive. Continue 7.5 miles to the park and parking area on the right (south) side of the road. If the parking area is full, you can try the upper parking area, 0.5 mile farther up the road, and start your hike from there. ***Notes:*** Day use only. Trails can be slick and muddy during the wet seasons, so wear appropriate footwear.

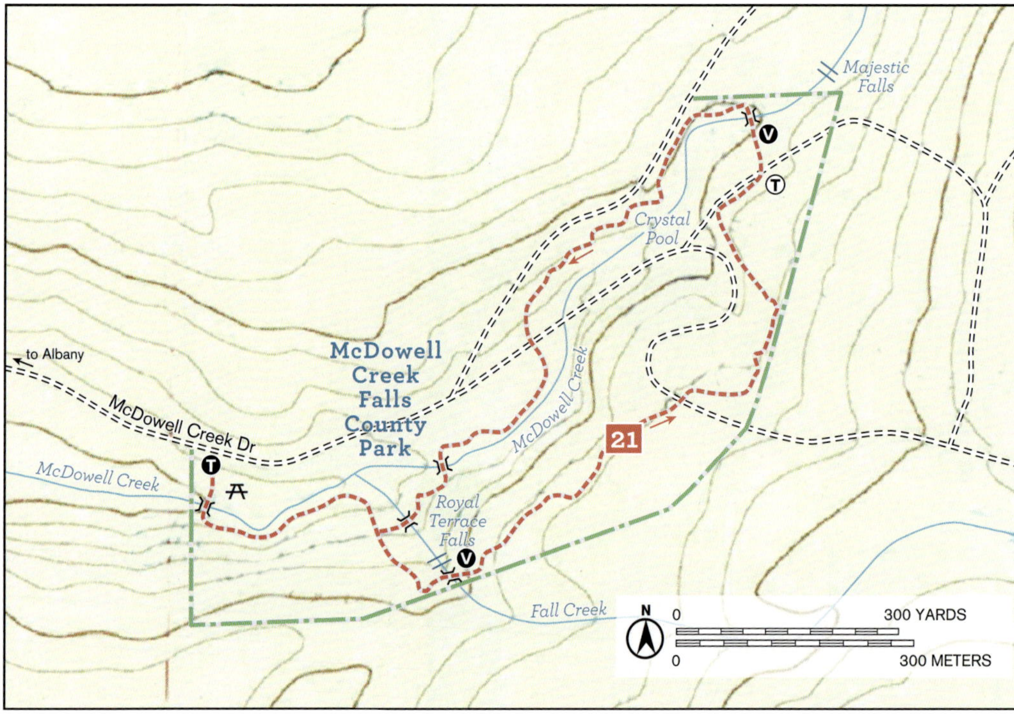

Just a short drive from Oregon's state capital, McDowell Creek Falls is a gem of a park, and it offers so much more than you would expect to find. The highlight, of course, is the two roaring waterfalls on McDowell and Fall Creeks, which fill their narrow canyons with clouds of cool mist. You will also find several pleasant picnic areas, impressive bridges and walkways, gobs of berries and wildflowers, and even a few wading and fishing opportunities, all under a canopy of lush, mossy woods. You can easily spend a whole day here.

From the lower parking and picnic area, plunge into mossy woods brimming with ferns, waterleaf, bleeding heart, trillium, and salmon- and thimbleberry. The path immediately crosses McDowell Creek on a sturdy bridge and then heads upstream, bending as it nears Fall Creek, which merges with McDowell Creek from the south. At 0.2 mile, the trail forks. To the left (east), the trail crosses the creek below multi-tiered Royal Terrace Falls. Head over to the bridge to take a peek at the falls, but save the extended gawking for later, as you'll be closing your trail loop this way.

After your peek at the falls, veer south and climb a long series of stone steps to reach the top of the 120-foot falls. A tiny viewing platform lies to the left (north) side of the trail—but the views are better from below. Just beyond, cross the creek on a small bridge and wind upward through shady cedar and fir forest, where salal and Oregon grape cover much of the hillside. Cross a trickling spring choked with skunk cabbage and come to a fork in the path at 0.5 mile. The trail to the left (north) is a steep cutoff used to shorten the loop.

Veer right (east) and cross McDowell Creek Drive, then begin traipsing downhill through copious bleeding heart and salmonberry. At 0.8 mile, cross the road again to reach the upper parking and picnic area, keeping right to stay on the trail and descend to the large viewing platform that overlooks forty-foot Majestic Falls. The view is impressive as the creek pours over a terrace of mossy basalt, filling the canyon with mist. After you've enjoyed the view, head down a remarkable wooden stairway that twists and turns into the canyon and crosses the creek.

Now enjoy a leisurely stroll downstream, passing Crystal Pool and crossing the road one more time at 1.1 miles. Bypass a couple of trails that branch off to the right; these lead to another parking and picnic area. Cross the creek on another wide bridge at 1.3 miles. As you near the close of the loop, round a bend and come to the bridge below Royal Terrace Falls. A bench here offers a fine place to sit and enjoy the view for a few moments. When you're ready, cross the bridge and connect with the trail you started on, turning right (north) to return to the parking area.

Majestic Falls is one of two waterfalls at McDowell Creek Park.

22 *Trail of Ten Falls (Silver Falls State Park)*

Distance: 2.7- to 7.3-mile loop
Difficulty: easy to moderate
Hiking time: day hike
Elevation gain: 1420 feet
High point: 1540 feet
Season: year-round
Management: Oregon State Parks
Protection status: Silver Falls State Park
Map: Silver Falls State Park brochure
GPS coordinates: N 44 87.765, W 122 65.561

Getting there: From I-5 in Salem, take exit 253 for Oregon Route 22 to Detroit Lake and Bend. Head east on OR 22 for about 8 miles to exit 9, following signs for Silver Falls State Park. Proceed north on Shaw Highway SE for 0.9 mile, head right (east) on Brownell Drive SE for 1.3 miles, and then drive 10 miles east on OR 214 to Silver Falls State Park. Turn left into the large parking area for the South Falls Day Use Area. ***Notes:*** Day use fee required. Camping available. Exercise proper right-of-way on multiuse trails. Dogs not permitted on Canyon, Winter, Maple Ridge, or Twin Falls Trails. Bears and cougars are known to inhabit the park's more remote areas—be watchful.

Silver Falls State Park is a waterfall lover's wonderland and is featured—justifiably—on more than a few Top Ten lists for Oregon destinations. Here, the merging forks of Silver Creek tumble over layers of ancient volcanic basalt in a series of dramatic and thundering displays, all nestled in a lush, wooded canyon hidden among the Willamette Valley's rolling farmlands. With more than thirty-five miles of multiuse trails, the star attraction is the Trail of Ten Falls. This 7.3-mile loop can be done whole or in part, depending on how far you want to venture. Before going, download the park's nature guide to help you identify the many colorful wildflowers, including some rarer species like fawn lilies, calypso orchids, and fairy lanterns.

Start at the South Falls Day Use Area, and proceed on a wide, paved path past the restroom, South Falls Café, and nature store, following signs for the Canyon Trail. Pause for a moment at the viewpoints overlooking 177-foot South Falls. The second-tallest (by only one foot) waterfall in the park, this dramatic horsetail plunges over the canyon rim into a wide

Journey behind South Falls at Silver Falls State Park.

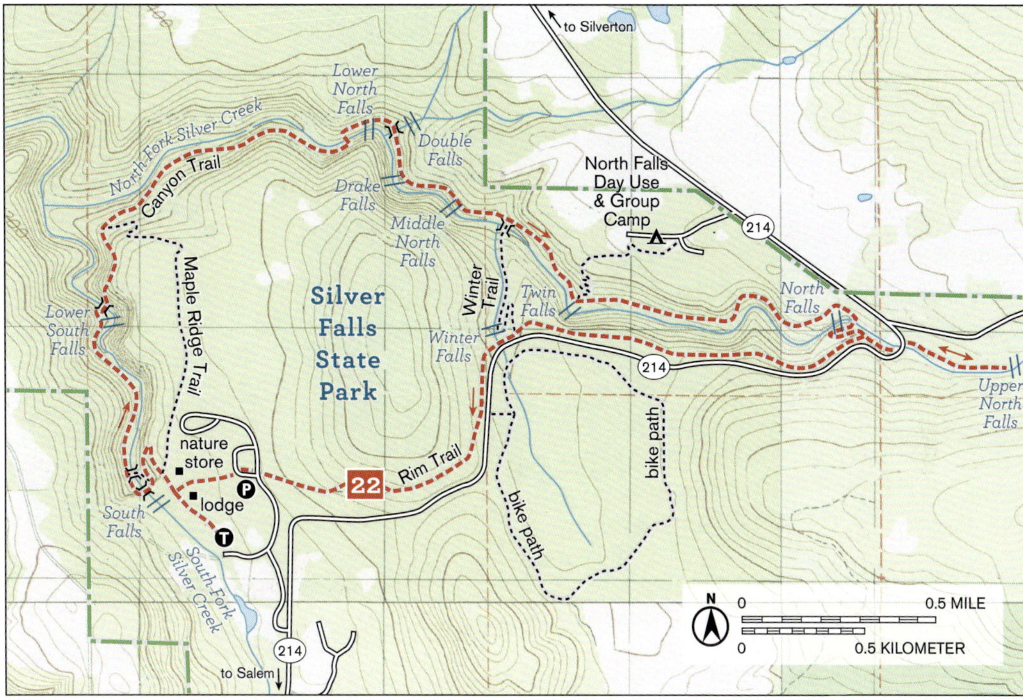

pool below, often filling the canyon with cool mist in spring and early summer. Notice the deeply undercut cavern behind the falls, where your path will soon lead you.

Head down a couple of switchbacks on a gravel path to a junction at the bottom of the canyon. Continue straight toward the thundering falls and proceed through the dripping basalt cavern behind them. Ta-da! The backside of water! Exit the cavern and continue, now on duff-covered forest trail, passing another junction and heading downstream on the Canyon Trail. The path parallels South Fork Silver Creek, descending to 93-foot Lower South Falls at 1.2 miles. Pass behind this wide curtain of water to the other side of the canyon, then continue to the next junction at 1.4 miles. For a shorter, 2.7-mile loop, you can veer right and ascend the Maple Ridge Trail to return to the parking area.

To complete the full loop, continue ahead, now heading upstream along North Fork Silver Creek. The next series of waterfalls come in rapid succession: 30-foot Lower North Falls at 2.3 miles; pretty, 178-foot Double Falls, up a short side canyon spur at 2.4 miles; 27-foot Drake Falls, partially viewable at 2.6 miles; and 106-foot Middle North Falls at 2.8 miles, which resembles something straight out of Middle Earth. The next junction comes at 2.9 miles, offering another trail cutoff. You can head right on the Winter Trail here for a more moderate, 4.8-mile loop.

Otherwise, continue southeast, staying on the Canyon Trail to reach 31-foot Twin Falls, viewable from a side trail at 3.2 miles as the cascade splits around a large rock outcrop. Bypass the Twin Falls Trail, a 0.5-mile spur that climbs steeply to the North Falls Day Use Area, and continue upstream to impressive 136-foot North Falls, which plunges into an amphitheater of mossy columnar basalt. The trail hooks around behind the falls, offering a surreal downstream view from the rocky grotto. The path then climbs a few paved switchbacks to the top of the canyon and a junction with the Rim Trail at 4.3 miles.

To see the ninth waterfall of the Ten Falls loop, you'll have to proceed east, across OR 214, and hike up a 0.3-mile spur to 65-foot Upper North Falls. This cascading curtain of falling water in a wide section of canyon is pretty enough to make the detour worthwhile. After viewing the falls, return to the Rim Trail and follow this wide, multiuse path along the canyon rim and back to the parking area. Along the way, pass another junction with the Winter Trail and a view of wispy, 134-foot Winter Falls (the tenth and last waterfall) at 6 miles. With all ten falls checked off your list, continue along the rim to return to the trailhead.

23 *Cooper Mountain*

Distance: 2-mile loop
Difficulty: moderate
Hiking time: short day hike
Elevation gain: 390 feet
High point: 770 feet
Season: year-round
Management: Tualatin Hills Parks and Recreation and Metro
Protection status: Public nature preserve
Map: Cooper Mountain Nature Park
GPS coordinates: N 45 27.156, W 122 52.212

Getting there: From Oregon Route 217 in Tigard, take exit 4B for SW Scholls Ferry Road and Washington Square. At the bottom of the ramp, turn left (south) on Scholls Ferry and proceed 2.4 miles to SW Murray Boulevard; turn right (north) and continue 0.6 mile. Turn left (west) on SW Weir Road and drive for 1.2 miles, then go right on SW 170th Avenue and continue 0.2 mile. Turn left on SW Kemmer Road and drive 1 mile to the park entrance on the left (south). ***Notes:*** Dogs not permitted. Beware of poison oak.

Home to one of the last remaining plots of native upland prairie in the wider Portland metro area, Cooper Mountain Nature Park offers a small glimpse into yesteryear, showcasing the kind of wide oak savannas that used to cover the slopes of the Tualatin River valley. Within the park, more than two hundred species of birds, mammals, amphibians, and reptiles make their homes, and every spring, the meadows are carpeted with colorful wildflowers. Bird-watchers will find unusual varieties inhabiting the trees and grasslands throughout the year.

Common camas adds splashes of vibrant purple to the open prairies at Cooper Mountain.

Start on the Little Prairie Loop, heading down this wide, graded path along a grassy slope dotted with Queen Anne's lace and young ponderosa pines. At 0.1 mile, the path forks, with the 0.6-mile Little Prairie Loop veering left (east) and the Cooper Mountain Loop beginning to the right (west). Save the Little Prairie Loop for the return trip and continue downward to the right. The path exits the trees and curves south, opening into wide views of the Tualatin River valley; an interpretive sign nearby provides information about some of the area's natural features and wildlife. Veer right (west) through the next two forks to stay on the Cooper Mountain Loop.

Alongside the path, tall shrubs of checker mallow and Oregon grape explode with pink and yellow blooms in early spring.

The path heads back into the trees, where you'll find snowberry, blackberry, trillium, and violets along the trailside. Cross a wide bridge over a small creek and come to another fork at 0.4 mile. Veer left (south) onto the Overlook Trail and descend out of the trees to the edge of the prairie and another interpretive sign. Here, enjoy more wide views of the valley and Big Prairie amid groves of moss-draped white oaks. Try using the listening horn to discern birdsong in the trees. Continue descending the mountain, merging back onto the Cooper Mountain Loop, with woods on your right (west) and the prairie on your left (east). In the spring, the savanna is decorated with a colorful patchwork of pink and blue forget-me-nots, violet blue-eyed Marys and Oregon irises, and white rock larkspur. But watch out—there's also plenty of poison oak.

The path loops around the bottom of the hill and begins climbing the opposite side of the savanna, where it turns east and crosses the creek again. Just beyond, take a peek at the quarry pond and try to spot red-legged tree frogs and salamanders. At 1.2 miles, the Larkspur Loop veers off to the right; stay left on the Cooper Mountain Loop and follow it to the next junction. Then veer right (northeast) onto Blacktail Way for a curving ascent under oak and madrone, crossing another fern-choked creek and then intersecting the Little Prairie Loop at 1.7 miles.

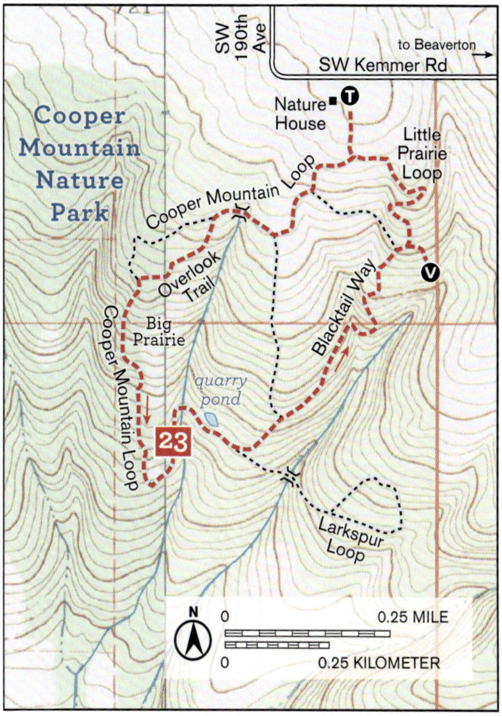

Turn right (east) for the final portion of the loop. Almost immediately, take another quick right (east) on a short side trail to the Little Prairie viewpoint. See if you can spot any of the local wildlife, then backtrack to the main trail. Veer right again (north) and ascend through a shady stand of Douglas-firs to return to the upper junction, then head right (north) one more time to complete your walk.

24 *Tryon Creek*

Distance: 2.3-mile loop
Difficulty: easy
Hiking time: short day hike
Elevation gain: 330 feet
High point: 330 feet
Season: year-round
Management: Oregon State Parks
Protection status: Tryon Creek State Natural Area
Map: Tryon Creek trail guide
GPS coordinates: N 45 44.130, W 122 67.600

Getting there: From Interstate 5, a little south of Portland, take exit 297 for SW Terwilliger Boulevard. Drive south on Terwilliger for 2.5 miles to the park entrance. ***Notes:*** Pick up a trail map and nature guide at the park's visitor center. Some barrier-free paths.

There are more than 8 miles of nature and equestrian trails at Tryon Creek State Natural Area.

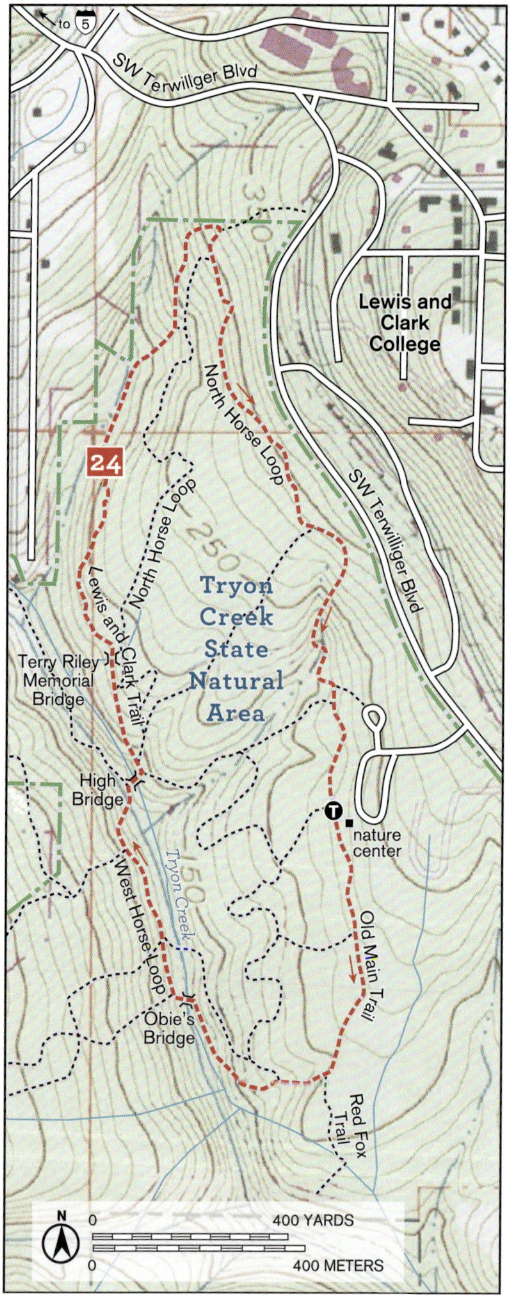

Dedicated in 1970, Tryon Creek State Natural Area preserves 635 acres of recovered woodland and creek bottom, an area that was logged in the late 1800s to support a local iron-smelting operation. It was named for Socrates Tryon, who made the original claim on the land in 1850. Today, the park offers more than eight miles of easy to moderate walking paths and hiking trails, where you can spend anywhere from a half hour to an entire day roaming under shady Douglas-firs and western red cedars. You can also admire an abundance of native shrubs and wildflowers around the park's namesake waterway. The following 2.3-mile route loops around the creek and the park's central area.

Start at the nature center and head south on the Old Main Trail for 0.3 mile. This wide, flat path ambles among dense patches of salmonberry, thimbleberry, lady fern, wood violets, and Oregon grape. In springtime, look for a profusion of big white trillium; the shiny little yellow flowers that adorn the trail almost year-round are buttercups. At the junction with the Red Fox Trail, stay right (west) to continue on the Old Main Trail, and descend to Obie's Bridge above Tryon Creek at a little over 0.6 mile. Once you've crossed the creek, veer right (north) onto the West Horse Loop and traipse beside the creek for 0.4 mile to High Bridge.

Cross the bridge and veer left (northwest) onto the Lewis and Clark Trail, proceeding on a narrower path and then crossing the Terry Riley Memorial Bridge at 1.2 miles. Just across the bridge, turn right (north) and begin a moderate ascent. Pass a spur connector to the North Horse Loop, then reach the top of the Lewis and Clark Trail at 1.6 miles. Curve right (south) for just a short distance, then veer left (southeast) onto the North Horse Loop. Now back on a wide, level trail, follow the path south, paralleling the paved bike path. At the next junction, turn left (east), then at the following junction, go right (south) to continue toward the nature center. Finally, veer right (south) onto the Old Main Trail to complete your hike with a last short ramble through the trees before returning to your starting point.

25 *Redwood Loop (Hoyt Arboretum)*

Distance: 0.9-mile loop
Difficulty: easy
Hiking time: short day hike
Elevation gain: 140 feet
High point: 800 feet
Season: year-round
Management: Hoyt Arboretum
Protection status: Nature preserve
Map: Hoyt Arboretum trail map
GPS coordinates: N 45 51.569, W 122 71.591

Getting there: From downtown Portland, drive US Highway 26 west for approximately 1.5 miles to exit 72 for the Zoo and Forestry Center. Veer right onto SW Knights Boulevard and continue 0.8 mile into Washington Park, following signs for Hoyt Arboretum. Turn right on SW Fairview Boulevard and proceed 0.1 mile to the arboretum parking area and visitor center. ***Notes:*** Parking fee required via Parking Kitty app. Dogs permitted but must be leashed. Visit the arboretum website for park hours and interpretive tours.

With more than twelve miles of walking paths and hiking trails, there's an outdoor amble waiting just for you at the Hoyt Arboretum. Founded in 1928 as a "living museum" for the recreation and education of Portland's residents, the arboretum showcases more than two thousand species of trees and plants from around the world. Many of these have identification tags to help you discern what is what. Choose one path, or link together several, and wander among deciduous maples, oaks, beeches, and walnuts and look skyward at towering evergreen redwoods, pines, firs, and spruces. Springtime is especially vibrant, with groves of flowering magnolias, cherries, and dogwoods.

For a good introduction to the arboretum, try this short, family-friendly loop that visits some of its star attractions. Begin in front of the arboretum visitor center, where you can pick up a park map, nature guide, and free activity map for kids. Cross SW Fairview Boulevard to the

Wander through a valley of giants on the Redwood Trail at Hoyt Arboretum.

Stevens Pavilion picnic shelter and turn right (north) onto the Fir Trail. Pass a junction with the Spruce Trail and continue ahead to cross SW Fischer Lane at 0.1 mile. Immediately after, veer left (northwest) at the fork and descend through the Fairy Forest. Can you find their homes? The trail then passes a giant Douglas-fir that was struck by lightning.

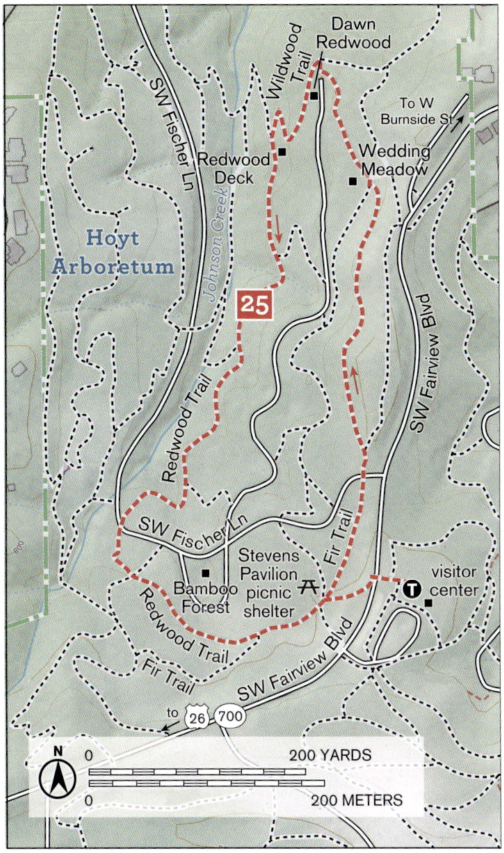

At the next junction with the Spruce Trail, at the edge of the Wedding Meadow, turn right (north) and continue to the Dawn Redwood, at a little past 0.3 mile. This "living fossil" is the park's most famous tree, and one of the few *Metasequoia* trees in the Western Hemisphere. Learn more about the Dawn Redwood, and many more of the park's unique trees on the arboretum's website (see Resources). Just past the Dawn Redwood, turn left (southwest) onto the Wildwood Trail and descend to the Redwood Deck. Here, you can admire a grove of skyscraping sequoias and coast redwoods that were planted in the 1930s. Still in their infancy, these trees could live up to two thousand years. Continue descending on a couple of easy switchbacks to the next junction at 0.4 mile and turn left onto the Redwood Trail.

Now amble southwestward, passing spur connectors that branch off to other roads or trails. At 0.7 mile, cross SW Fischer Lane once more, ascending an open slope above the Bamboo Forest. If time allows, take the short side trail down to check it out. When the Redwood Trail ends at the Fir Trail, at 0.8 mile, turn left (east) and climb the last short stretch back to the visitor center where you started.

26 *Wildwood Trail (Forest Park)*

Distance: varies; see trail description
Difficulty: easy to moderate
Hiking time: short to long day hikes
Elevation gain: varies; see trail description
High point: 330 feet
Season: year-round
Management: Portland Parks and Recreation
Protection status: none
Map: Green Trails 426S: Forest Park
GPS coordinates: N 45 30.762, W 122 43.014

Getting there: **Washington Park trailhead:** From Portland, take US Highway 26 west to exit 72 for the Zoo and Forestry Center; turn north into Washington Park. Veer left on SW Knights Boulevard and proceed past the Forestry Center and Vietnam Veterans Memorial. Park near the corner of SW Kingston Drive. Find the Marquam/Wildwood trailhead on the west side of the road. **Cornell Road trailhead:** From Portland's Pearl District, drive west on NW Lovejoy Street for about 1 mile. Veer right (northwest) at the fork onto NW Cornell Road. Proceed about 1.5 miles to the trailhead, just before the Bird Alliance

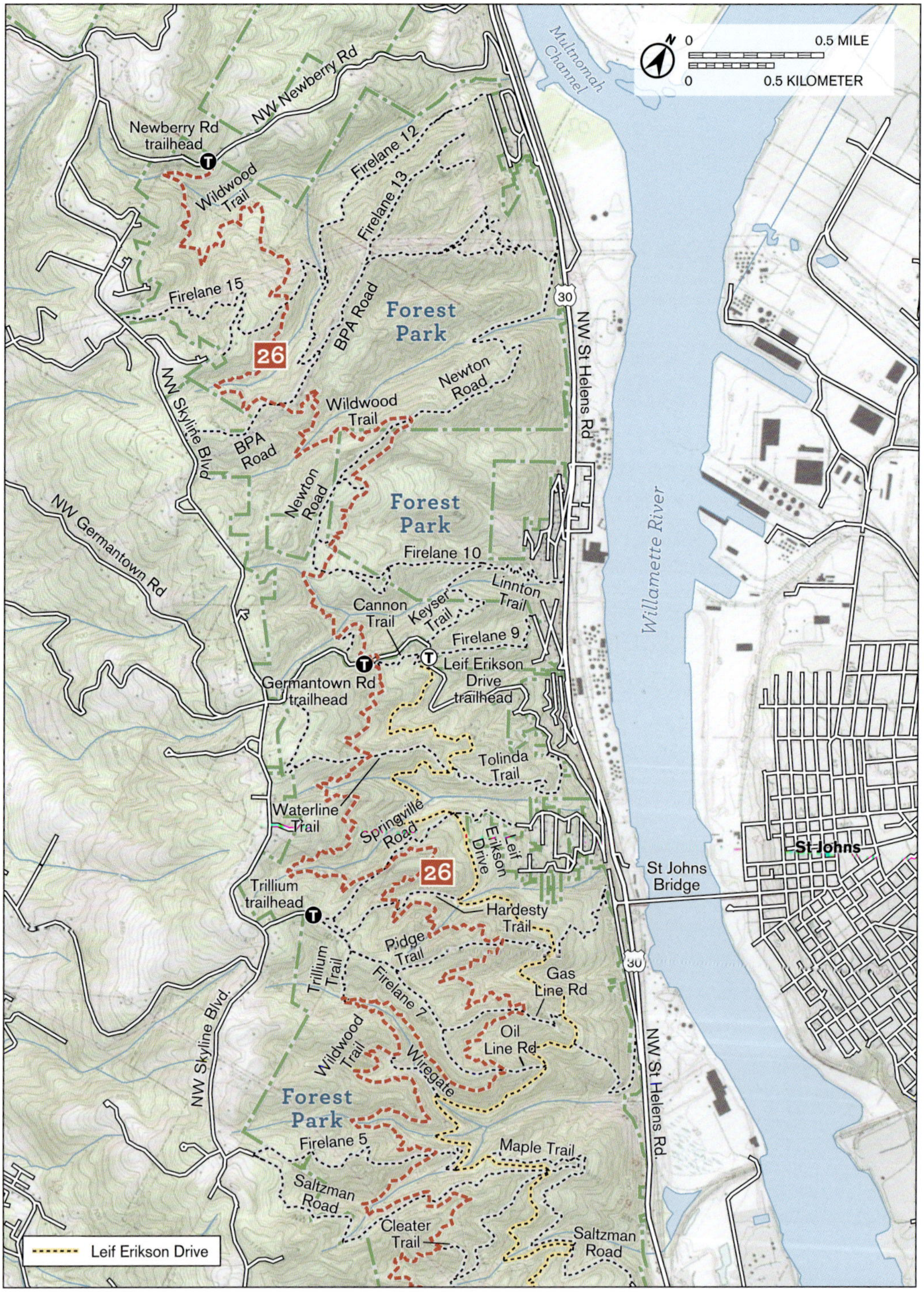
0 0.5 MILE
0 0.5 KILOMETER
Multnomah Channel
NW Newberry Rd
Newberry Rd trailhead
Wildwood Trail
Firelane 12
Firelane 13
Firelane 15
BPA Road
Forest Park
26
30
NW St Helens Rd
Newton Road
Wildwood Trail
NW Skyline Blvd
BPA Road
Newton Road
Forest Park
Willamette River
NW Germantown Rd
Firelane 10
Linnton Trail
Cannon Trail
Keyser Trail
Firelane 9
Leif Erikson Drive trailhead
Germantown Rd trailhead
Tolinda Trail
Waterline Trail
Springville Road
Leif Erikson Drive
St Johns
St Johns Bridge
Trillium trailhead
Hardesty Trail
Ridge Trail
Trillium Trail
Firelane 7
Gas Line Rd
Oil Line Rd
NW Skyline Blvd.
Wildwood Trail
Wiregate
Forest Park
Firelane 5
Maple Trail
NW St Helens Rd
Saltzman Road
Cleater Trail
Saltzman Road
Leif Erikson Drive

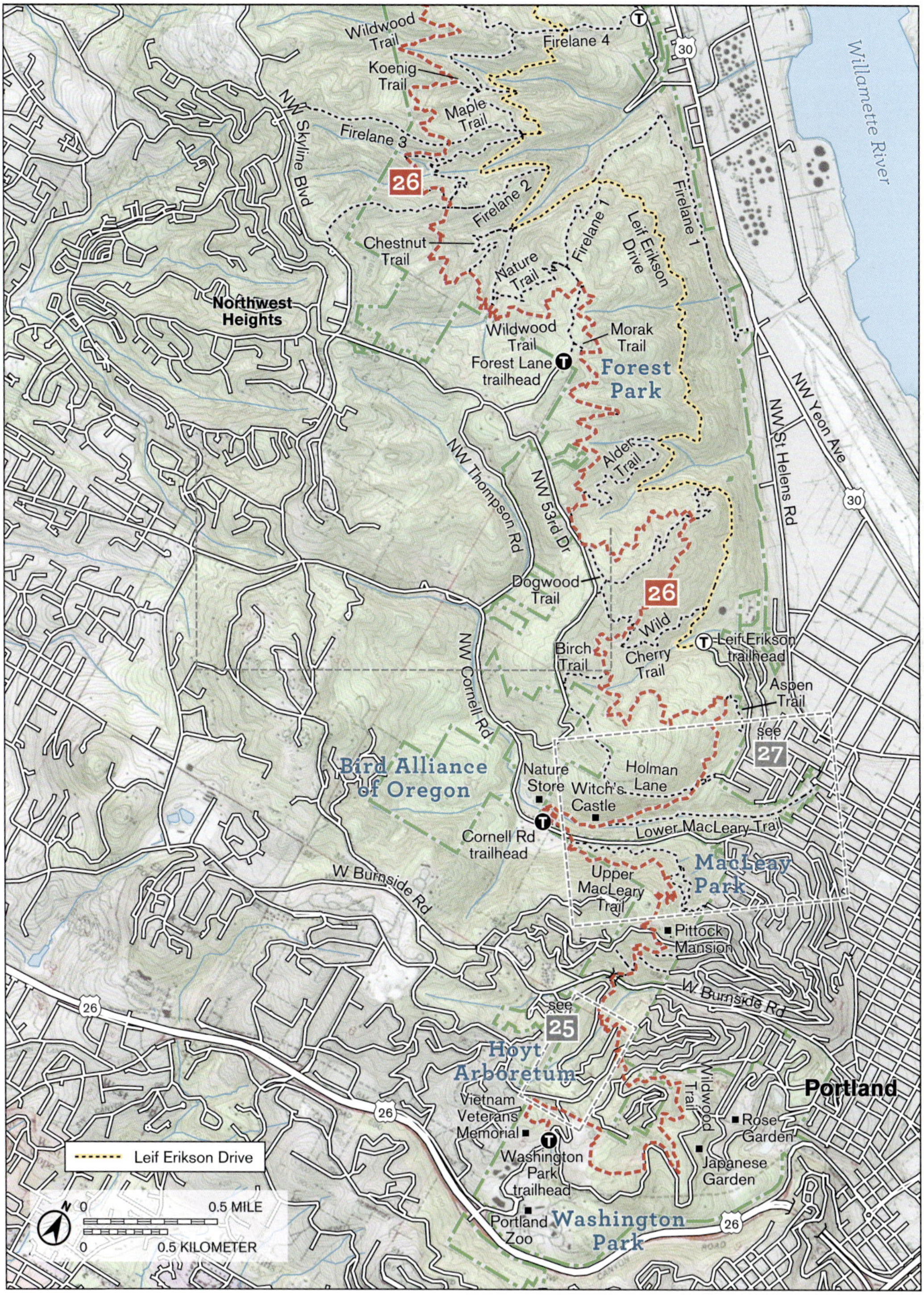

Wildwood Trail
Firelane 4
30
Willamette River
Koenig Trail
Maple Trail
NW Skyline Blvd
Firelane 3
26
Firelane 2
Chestnut Trail
Firelane 1
Leif Erikson Drive
Firelane 1
Nature Trail
Northwest Heights
Wildwood Trail
Morak Trail
Forest Lane trailhead
Forest Park
NW Yeon Ave
NW St Helens Rd
Alder Trail
NW Thompson Rd
NW 53rd Dr
30
Dogwood Trail
26
NW Cornell Rd
Wild Cherry Trail
Birch Trail
Leif Erikson trailhead
Aspen Trail
see 27
Bird Alliance of Oregon
Nature Store
Holman Lane
Witch's Castle
Lower MacLeary Trail
Cornell Rd trailhead
MacLeay Park
W Burnside Rd
Upper MacLeary Trail
Pittock Mansion
W Burnside Rd
26
see 25
Hoyt Arboretum
Wildwood Trail
Portland
26
Vietnam Veterans Memorial
Rose Garden
Washington Park trailhead
Japanese Garden
Leif Erikson Drive
0 0.5 MILE
0 0.5 KILOMETER
Portland Zoo
Washington Park
26

Tailor your own hike on Forest Park's 30-mile Wildwood Trail.

of Oregon nature preserve (formerly Portland Audubon). **Forest Lane trailhead:** From downtown, drive west on NW Lovejoy Street. Veer right (northwest) on NW Cornell Road and continue 1.9 miles. Turn right on NW 53rd Drive and go 1.7 miles to gravel Forest Lane; turn right to reach the trailhead. **Trillium trailhead:** From downtown, drive west on W. Burnside Street for about 2.5 miles. Veer right (northwest) on NW Skyline Boulevard and continue for 5.5 miles, then turn right (north) on gravel NW Springville Road to reach the trailhead. **Germantown Road trailhead:** From downtown, drive west on US 30 for 5.5 miles. Turn left (west) on NW Germantown Road and drive 1.6 miles to where the Wildwood Trail crosses the road. **Newberry Road trailhead:** From the Germantown Road trailhead, continue 0.5 mile to NW Skyline Boulevard. Turn right (north) and drive 2.6 miles to NW Newberry Road. Turn right (east) and continue 0.7 mile to the trailhead on the right (east) side of the road. ***Notes:*** Trailhead break-ins sometimes occur at the more remote locations. Do not leave anything visible or of value in your car. Dogs should be leashed. Watch for trail runners.

Forest Park is the crown jewel of Portland's urban parks system. Covering an area of more than 5100 acres and stretching for 7 miles through the eastern Tualatin Mountains, it is the largest urban forest in the United States. A 30-mile-long walking and hiking route known as the Wildwood Trail snakes through the entire east–west length of the park under a canopy of Douglas-fir, hemlock, red cedar, and bigleaf and vine maple. The trail also boasts an abundance of ferns, berry shrubs, salal, vanilla leaf, and trillium. In addition to the main trailheads, more than thirty connecting trails, spurs, and fire lanes give you practically unlimited options for creating customized hikes of any length. The following description breaks the Wildwood Trail into five segments, each a one-way day hike.

Washington Park to Balch Creek (4.7 miles, +810 feet/-1040 feet): Start at the Washington Park trailhead and meander on fairly gentle grades through the maze of trails in the Hoyt Arboretum (see Hike 25); check out a few of the park's flora features, like the sequoia and coast redwood grove. Cross the new pedestrian bridge over Burnside Road and climb to the top of Pittock Hill, with its namesake historic mansion; stop to enjoy the views and botanical garden. From here, make a steady descent through shady woods to the trailhead at NW Cornell Road, ending your hike at the Bird Alliance of Oregon.

Balch Creek to Firelane 1 (5.8 miles, +1000/-530 feet): Start at the NW Cornell Road trailhead, near the Bird Alliance of Oregon, and descend to Balch Creek. Follow the creek downstream to the Stone House, also known as the Witch's Castle (see Hike 27), and take the obligatory photo. Veer onto the Wildwood Trail to make a moderate, winding ascent before the trail levels into a pleasant walk under shady mixed forest; the way passes the Wild Cherry, Dogwood, and Alder Trails. Finish with a gentle ascent high on the hillside; veer onto the Morak Trail spur to Firelane 1 and walk the old road to end at the Forest Lane trailhead.

Firelane 1 to NW Springville Road (8.3 miles, +1240/-1150 feet): This longer section proceeds through numerous ups, downs, and creek drainages in the park's central section. Start at the Forest Lane trailhead, descend Firelane 1 and the Morak Trail to the Wildwood Trail, and proceed past the Maple Trail. Cross Rocking Chair, Saltzman, and Doane Creeks. Veer off the Wildwood after crossing the small bridge over Doane Creek, then make a hearty ascent on the narrow Trillium Trail to Firelane 7. Turn left (west) and finish at the Trillium trailhead at the gate on NW Springville Road.

NW Springville Road to NW Germantown Road (6.4 miles, +660/-970 feet): From the Trillium trailhead, head out on Firelane 7 to the Trillium Trail and then down to the Wildwood Trail. Turn left and proceed along a fairly level grade under shady woods through most of the segment. Wind through several drainage canyons and pass the Ridge and Hardesty Trails, as well as Hardesty Creek; the path also passes a lower portion of the Springville Road Trail. Hook through two more small canyons that feed Springville Creek, then begin a gentle descent that crosses the Waterline Trail and ends at NW Germantown Road.

NW Germantown Road to NW Newberry Road (5.1 miles, +700/-830 feet): This final segment of the Wildwood is also the most remote; instead of fellow hikers, you're more likely to encounter mountain bikers as they crisscross the trail on a handful of bike-friendly routes. Continue west from the NW Germantown Road trailhead, where the path rises and falls over moderate terrain to cross South Fork Linton and Newton Creeks; following the latter, make a big ascent to the BPA Road. Finish with an even bigger descent to cross both forks of Miller Creek, then reach the end at the NW Newberry Road trailhead.

27 *Balch Creek and Witch's Castle*

Distance: 1.5-mile roundtrip
Difficulty: easy
Hiking time: short day hike
Elevation gain: 360 feet
High point: 400 feet
Season: year-round
Management: Portland Parks and Recreation
Protection status: none
Map: Green Trails 426S: Forest Park
GPS coordinates: N 45 51.569, W 122 71.591

Getting there: From W. Burnside Street in the Northwest District, drive NW 23rd Avenue north to NW Thurman Street. Turn left (west) and continue 0.5 mile to NW 28th Avenue. Turn right and drive one block, then go left on NW Upshur Street. Proceed 0.2 mile to the park at the parking turnaround. Find street parking nearby. ***Notes:*** Dogs should be leashed. Watch for trail runners. Some portions of trail are barrier-free.

For a pleasant dog- and family-friendly outing that only takes an hour or so, head for this popular trail in a sleepy corner of Northwest Portland at the foot of sprawling Forest Park. Here, the Lower MacLeay Trail along Balch Creek heads straight up a wooded canyon rich in both cultural and natural history. The creek itself is named for Danford Balch, a local homesteader who was hanged in 1859 for shooting the scoundrel who absconded with his teenage daughter. Balch has the notoriety of being the first person to receive capital punishment in Oregon. In addition to boasting one of Oregon's tallest Douglas-firs, Balch Creek's real attraction is the mysterious stone building known locally as the "Witch's Castle."

Do you dare peek into the Witch's Castle?

From the trailhead, head up the wide, paved path, passing under the NW Thurman Street bridge and then up the wooded canyon. The farther you go, the higher and steeper the canyon walls get, adorned with moss-draped Douglas-firs, western hemlocks, and western red cedars. Just below the trail, Balch Creek trickles and babbles down its rocky gully of partially exposed volcanic basalt. Springtime brings color to the streambanks with trillium, wood violets, and toothwort. About 0.5 mile up the canyon, after the path has crossed the creek and crossed back again, the pavement ends, and the trail becomes dirt and gravel. Near here, look for a particularly large tree to the left (south) of the trail. This Portland Heritage Tree is believed to be one of the city's tallest Douglas-firs. If undisturbed by fire and storms, it could live to be more than a thousand years old.

Continue up the canyon for 0.25 mile to reach Balch Creek's most notable point of interest. The Stone House—or, as it's more hauntingly known, the "Witch's Castle"—is not as romantic or fearsome as the names imply. It's just an old restroom. It was built in the 1930s by the Works

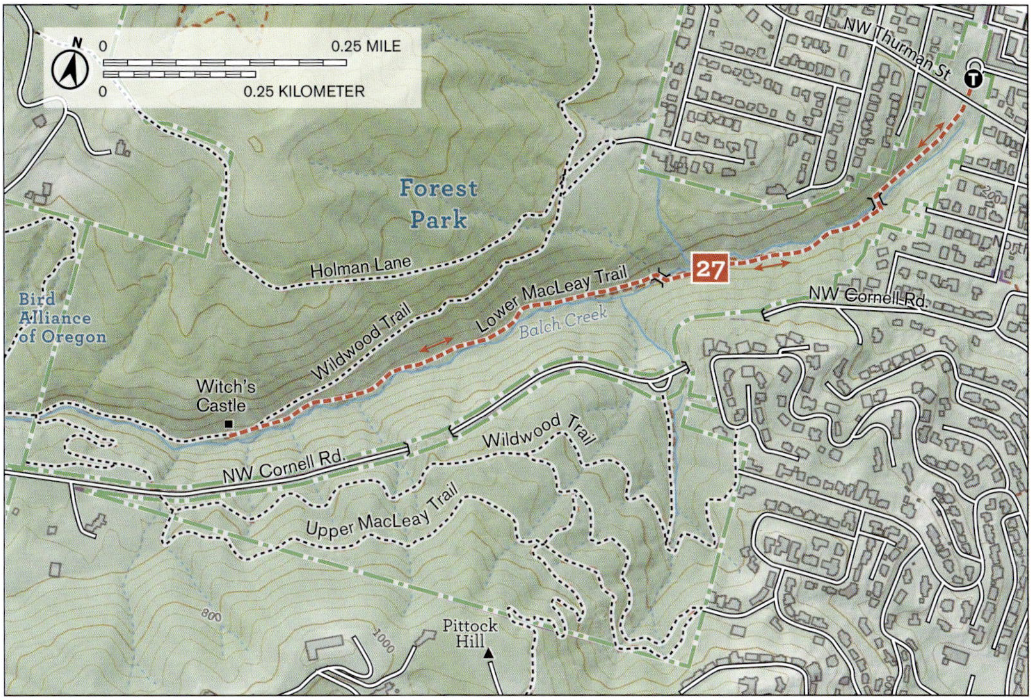

Progress Administration as a rest house for hikers. When a windstorm blew the roof off the building in 1962, it was abandoned and left for nature to reclaim. Now it's a favorite landmark, a mossy relic for kids to climb on and visitors to snap selfies with. Unfortunately, it's also a popular target for graffiti artists. Nearby, the Wildwood Trail (see Hike 26) branches off to the right. If you've gotten your fill, this makes a good turnaround point. Just do an about-face and follow the creek back down the canyon to your starting point.

Extend Your Trip: If you're up for more wandering, you have a few options from here: (1) Continue 0.6 mile up Balch Creek to NW Cornell Road and visit the Bird Alliance of Oregon (formerly Portland Audubon); (2) Walk the 0.6 mile to NW Cornell Road and then cross to the Upper MacLeay Trail for a moderate, 1-mile hike up to the historic Pittock Mansion; (3) Veer off onto the Wildwood Trail and venture into Forest Park for a continued hike, making it as short or long as you like.

28 *Powell Butte*

Distance: 2.5-mile loop
Difficulty: easy
Hiking time: short day hike
Elevation gain: 200 feet
High point: 630 feet
Season: year-round
Management: Portland Parks and Recreation
Protection status: none
Map: Powell Butte trail map
GPS coordinates: N 44 87.765, W 122 65.561

Getting there: From Interstate 205 (exit 19) in Southeast Portland, take SE Powell Boulevard 3.4 miles east. Turn right on SE 162nd Avenue and continue 0.4 mile to the

Enjoy panoramic views and wide-open skies from the trails atop Powell Butte.

visitor center and parking turnaround at the road's end. ***Notes:*** Most trails are multiuse, with some barrier-free paths. Dogs not permitted.

Situated atop and around an ancient lava dome, Powell Butte Nature Park offers year-round hiking, trail running, horseback riding, and mountain biking—as well as bird-watching, fall leaf peeping, and Cascades mountain viewing. Numerous trailheads around the butte provide access to its network of more than thirteen miles of trails and service roads, including a paved, barrier-free path to the viewpoint on the butte's summit. As you're wandering around this 612-acre natural area, you'd never guess that two fifty-million-gallon reservoirs containing most of Portland's drinking water are right beneath your feet. Check out the interpretive displays at the visitor center to discover how engineers achieved this feat.

For a pleasant outing with plenty of views, you can connect several trails for a 2.5-mile summit loop. From the visitor center, start on the paved Mountain View Trail. The path winds easily upward across the open summit plateau. In spring and summer, look for splashes of pearly everlasting and snowberry along the trail, as well as camas, lupine, and Oregon sunshine in the meadows. At the junction with the Summit Lane Loop, turn left (east) and continue to the Mountain Finder Lookout at 0.7 mile. Here, several directional plaques help you identify many of the nearby peaks, including Mount Scott, Rocky Butte, Gresham Butte, and Larch Mountain, plus a few of the farther peaks, including Mount St. Helens, Mount Adams, and Mount Jefferson.

With your elevation gain largely finished, continue hiking east, now on a gravel trail, looping around groves of walnut and white oak. Before the trail curves west at 1 mile, a short spur proceeds to a viewpoint for a look at Mount Hood. After checking out the view, return to the main trail and continue west along the preserve boundary area, with several ponds below the trail; watch for deer, coyotes, and skunks. Pass junctions with the South and Hawthorn Trails at 1.2 and 1.3 miles, respectively. At the four-way

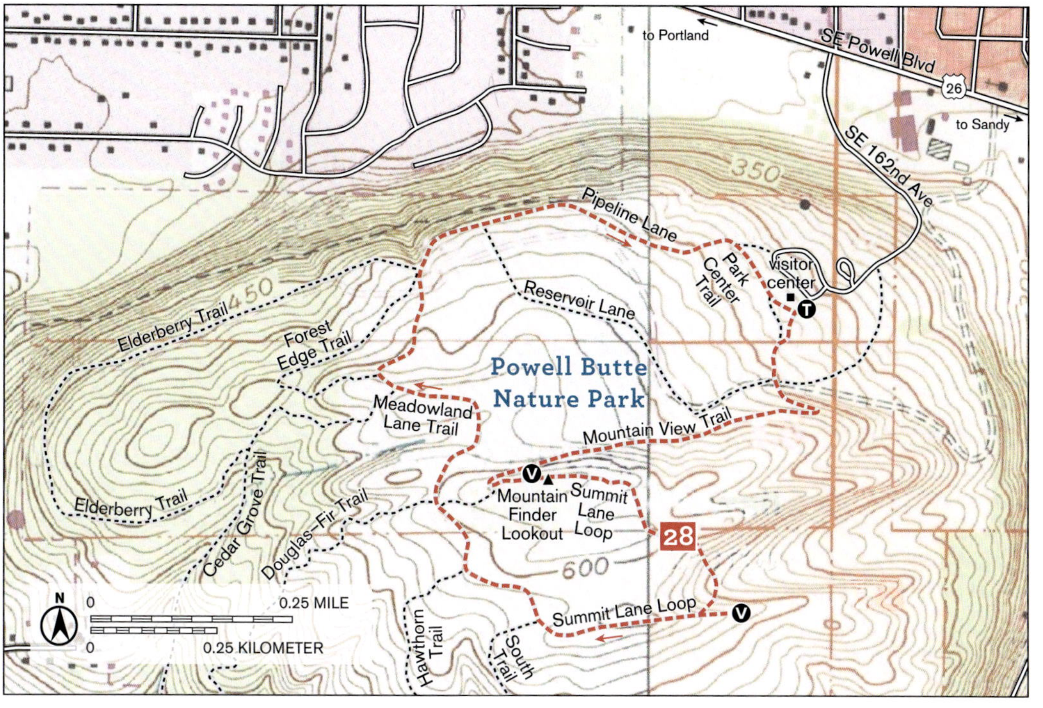

junction at 1.4 miles (where Summit Lane heads right and the Douglas-Fir Trail heads left), continue straight on the Meadowland Lane Trail. Curve through more groves of oak trees and blackberry shrubs and pass junctions with the 0.4-mile Forest Edge Trail side loop, which could be a pleasant detour if you want a change of scenery. Near 1.9 miles, the Meadowland Lane Trail ends at a T-junction with Pipeline Lane. Veer right (north) onto this dirt road and continue until the road forks beside a maintenance building. Veer left (east) onto North Access Lane for a short spell, then head right (south) onto the gravel Park Center Trail. The final stretch of the loop passes the park residence building, then ends at the visitor center.

Extend Your Trip: Opportunities for adding mileage to your hike include exploring some of the butte's forested west flanks and an almost one-hundred-year-old walnut grove. From the summit loop, veer onto the 0.9-mile South Trail or 0.7-mile Hawthorn Trail. From the Hawthorn Trail, you can use the short Fernwood Trail connector and then return via the 0.6-mile Douglas-Fir Trail. Or connect the 0.4-mile Cedar Grove Trail with the 1.4-mile Elderberry Trail for a larger, 4.3-mile loop. Or just mix and match a variety of trails to enjoy an entire day of wandering.

Opposite, top: Fairy Falls on the Wahkeena-Multomah Loop

Opposite, bottom: Tiger lilies are abundant along many Columbia Gorge trails.

Columbia River Gorge

29. Latourell Falls 100

30. Angels Rest 102

31. Multnomah Falls Loop 104

32. Wahclella Falls 107

33. Eagle Creek to Tunnel Falls .. 108

34. Hood River Mountain 111

35. Rowena Plateau and McCall Point 113

Scoured and sculpted by the ancient, glacial Missoula Floods, the Columbia River Gorge is a natural gem shared between Oregon and Washington. Due to its lush and rugged beauty, chock-full of volcanic spires and plateaus, deep slot canyons, and—most notably—an abundance of roaring waterfalls, it was designated a National Scenic Area in 1986. In 2017, a devastating wildfire swept across the Oregon side of the gorge, laying waste to fifty thousand acres and charring forest, structures, bridges, and trails. Nature is resilient, however, and the gorge has been recovering. Trails reopened a few years after the fire, beckoning visitors back to this fantastical wonderland of rock, water, mosses, and flowers.

29 *Latourell Falls*

Distance: 2-mile loop
Difficulty: easy
Hiking time: short day hike
Elevation gain: 1040 feet
High point: 650 feet
Season: Apr–Nov

Management: Mount Hood NF, Columbia River Gorge NSA
Protection status: National Scenic Area, Oregon State Parks
Map: Green Trails 428S: Columbia Gorge West
GPS coordinates: N 45 32.328, W 122 13.086

Getting there: From Interstate 205 (north or south) in East Portland, merge onto I-84, heading east toward The Dalles. Continue 18 miles into the Columbia River Gorge National Scenic Area. Take exit 28 onto Bridal Veil Road for the Historic Columbia River Highway. At the stop sign, turn right on the historic highway and drive 2.8 miles west to Guy W. Talbot State Park. Find parking on both sides of the road. ***Notes:*** High traffic and crowded parking on summer weekends.

When touring the Historic Columbia River Highway (eastbound), one of the first scenic stops is Guy W. Talbot State Park. Talbot made his name in the early 1900s as a prominent official with the local railway and power companies. In 1929, Talbot donated 220 acres of his estate to the State of Oregon for preservation as a public park. Within the park, 224-foot Latourell Falls cascades over a high basalt cliff into a rocky amphitheater of maple and cedar trees, vine maple, thimbleberry, and lady fern. Here, visitors can take paved paths up to a nice viewpoint or down to the creek below the falls. An often-overlooked path continues to a nice picnic area, then up into the canyon above the falls to Latourell's hidden upper falls, an equally pretty—and much less crowded—sight to enjoy.

Begin the 2-mile loop by descending a few paved switchbacks to the bridge that crosses the creek below the lower falls. Pause to take an obligatory photo of the falls, then leave the crowds behind by continuing down the path. The way proceeds under a high trestle, which is the historic highway, then meanders northwest to a clearing where you'll find a grassy picnic area at the edge of NE Latourell Road. At the junction at the edge of the picnic area, turn left (south) and begin ascending back into the forest. When the trail comes to an unsigned fork, veer right (southwest) and climb a few paved steps to the highway at 0.4 mile. Carefully

Get a peek behind the curtain at upper Latourell Falls.

cross the highway and then proceed on the trail signed "To Upper Falls."

The path ascends on a moderate grade under tall, shady trees; it starts out paved but eventually transitions to duff-covered forest tread. Views are spare, but a pleasant mix of maidenhair fern, wood sorrel, trillium, thimbleberry, salmonberry, and hedge nettle lines the trail. Where a large, double-trunked maple overhangs the trail in an arch-like formation, the trail takes a sharp turn left (east) and continues its moderate ascent. The prehistoric-looking plant with huge, spiny leaves that grows through this stretch is devils club—beware its needlelike thorns. As the trail passes a huge Douglas-fir, the grade eases and from this point on stays fairly gentle. Look for a viewpoint just left (north) of the trail; a bench gives you the opportunity to sit and enjoy a view of the Columbia River and Cape Horn, on the opposite side of the gorge.

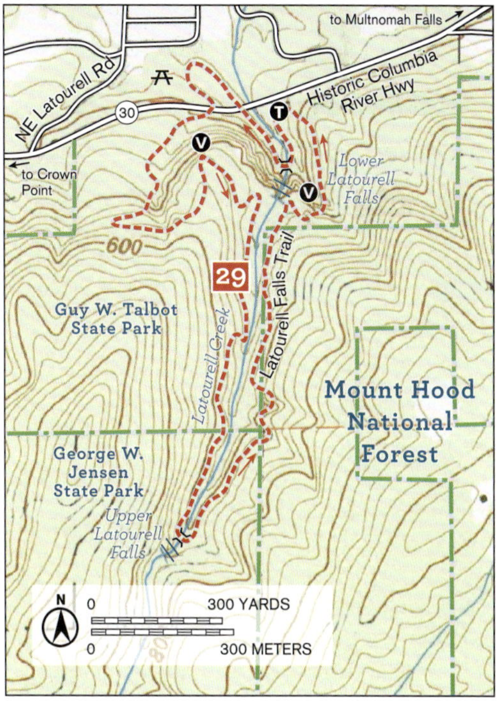

The trail then turns south and contours into the canyon, now above Latourell Creek. In early spring, look for coast manroot's little white flowers and stalks of purple hairy vetch. Continue past a couple of unmarked side trails that descend left (east) to cross the creek and head up some switchbacks to continue deeper into the canyon. The grade eases again, proceeding through a stretch dense with mossy firs and vine maple. The trail pops out into the open at 1.3 miles, where two-tiered Upper Latourell Falls pours out of the back of the canyon. The upper portion spills over a wide, fan-shaped slide, then gets funneled through a narrow cleft in the basalt wall, where it gushes out in a 120-foot plunge and fills the canyon with cool mist.

Once you've enjoyed the view, proceed across the bridge near the base of the falls and start heading down-canyon, crossing several small bridges over trickling tributaries. Skip a couple of unmarked trails to the left (west) that descend to the creek, and start making the wide, curving descent into the lower falls basin. You'll find another bench that offers a splendid view of the lower falls; this is a nice spot to sit for a snack and just enjoy. The final stretch involves a significant descent. The path eventually becomes paved again, passes another viewpoint, and then returns to the parking area.

30 *Angels Rest*

Distance: 4.5-mile roundtrip
Difficulty: moderate
Hiking time: day hike
Elevation gain: 2200 feet
High point: 1600 feet
Season: May–Nov
Management: Mount Hood NF, Columbia River Gorge NSA
Protection status: National Scenic Area
Map: Green Trails 428S: Columbia Gorge West
GPS coordinates: N 45 32.328, W 122 13.086

Getting there: From the town of Troutdale, east of Portland, drive east on Interstate 84 for about 11 miles. Take exit 28 onto E. Bridal Veil Road and drive for 0.5 mile. Trailhead parking is at the junction of E. Bridal Veil Road and the Historic Columbia River Highway. Turn right (west) onto the highway, then immediately turn into the parking area. Overflow parking is on Palmer Mill Road, 0.1 mile farther west. The trailhead is on the south side of the highway. Observe "no parking" signs. ***Notes:*** This trail was damaged in the 2017 Eagle Creek Fire. Be aware of possible falling trees, trail debris, landslides, and flooding. May not be suitable for small children or dogs. Not recommended during periods of heavy wind and rain.

Despite sustaining significant damage during the 2017 Eagle Creek Fire, the trail to this popular Columbia River Gorge viewpoint has remained mostly intact, and burned areas are recovering quickly. Ferns, flowers, and berry shrubs still blanket much of the terrain under a singed canopy of mixed conifers and deciduous trees. The silver lining following the fire is that there are now a few more open viewpoints to enjoy. Crowds typically flock to this trail on any sunny day, especially weekends, so it's best enjoyed midweek—unless you like to hike feeling like you're in an amusement park queue.

From the trailhead on the south side of the Historic Columbia River Highway, head up the Angels Rest Trail (#415) into a stately forest of tall Douglas-fir, hemlock, and alder, with an abundance of sword and licorice fern, vine maple, and salmonberry filling the understory. Watch out for patches of poison oak. In about fifty yards, come

Watch for birds of prey from Angels Rest.

to a T-junction and turn left (east) for Angels Rest. Stroll along rough and rocky tread on a gentle incline, heading into the woods. In spring and summer, look for bright-white trillium, daisies, and Columbia windflowers, as well as wood violets, hawksbeard, and sticky geraniums. Evidence of the 2017 Eagle Creek Fire begins to appear in the form of singed trees and burned snags, but the groundcover remains mostly green and lively.

The trail soon comes to the foot of a high rock slope covered with mosses and ferns, where you're given your first look out over the Columbia River. The wall of columnar basalt on the Washington side of the river is Cape Horn; the prominent peak in the distance is Silver Star Mountain. After a little more ascending, at 0.4 mile, the trail turns into the narrow canyon containing Coopey Creek. A peek through the trees and shrubs reveals the lower portion of Coopey Falls, plunging into the ravine far below. Just beyond, at an unsigned T-junction, turn right (south) to continue upward. The path left (north) proceeds to the edge of a bluff with a partial view of the upper falls. For a better view of the upper falls, take a spur trail left at the 0.5-mile mark. This short, often muddy side trail dips along the hillside to a decent viewpoint. At 0.6 mile, the trail crosses the creek on an old footbridge spared from the fire.

Now the climbing begins in earnest as you follow a series of twisting, turning switchbacks. Along the way, the trail gets a little smoother, with fewer rocks and roots to stumble over, and Oregon grape, snowberry, and ocean spray begin appearing on the hillsides. Pass through a grove of bigleaf maple then contour a ridgeline. On the other side, you'll get a peek at your destination: Angels Rest, a high, rocky prominence that looks deceptively far away. Continuing upward, enjoy another view of the Columbia River at 1.4 miles. Then continue upward, passing through another portion of charred forest. With much of the canopy burned away, more wide-open views look out over the Columbia River.

The trail then curves to contour the slope high above Coopey Creek. Cross a wide slope of slabby, andesite talus, then proceed through one more switchback to an unmarked fork at 2.1 miles, at the crest of a spiny ridge. Here, a couple of large pillars resemble a ruined stone

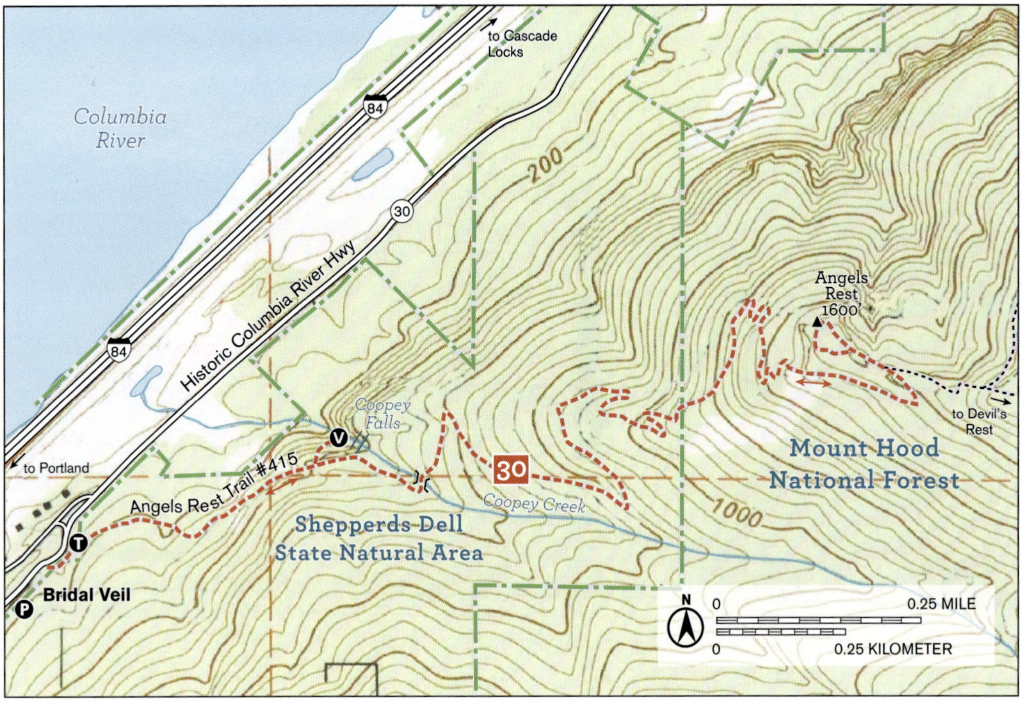

wall—they look like the crumbling ramparts of Amon Sûl, the fortress from *The Lord of the Rings*. To the right, the Angels Rest Trail continues east to many other gorge destinations; to the left (northwest), a spur trail proceeds out onto Angels Rest. Take this spur along the rocky ridgeline and through overgrown alder shrubs. Use caution, as there are precipitous cliffs in the gaps between the rocks. The final stretch is a short scramble up about twenty feet of rocky steps. Head out onto the east side of the plateau, where the panorama stretches far and wide over the Columbia River Gorge. If it's not too windy (or crowded), this is a spectacular spot for a picnic lunch. When you're ready, return to the parking area by the same route.

31 *Multnomah Falls Loop*

Distance: 4.9 miles
Difficulty: strenuous
Hiking time: day hike
Elevation gain: 1640 feet
High point: 1510 feet
Season: Apr–Oct
Management: Mount Hood NF, Columbia River Gorge NSA
Protection status: National Scenic Area
Map: Green Trails 428S: Columbia Gorge West
GPS coordinates: N 45 57.735, W 122 11.986

Getting there: From Portland, drive east on Interstate 84 for about 26 miles to the Multnomah Falls parking area at exit 31. Parking here typically requires a timed permit between Memorial Day and Labor Day, available at recreation.gov. The alternative is to attempt to find free parking along the Historic Columbia River Highway (US Highway 30), accessible via exit 22 through Corbett. Or use one of the available rideshare services, such as the Columbia Gorge Express or Sasquatch Shuttle. ***Notes:*** In spring and summer, this area is *very* busy. Be prepared for heavy crowds in the parking areas and around the lodge. Portions of the trail travel through recently burned forest, so exercise caution.

At 620 feet tall, Multnomah Falls is the highest waterfall in Oregon and the second-highest year-round waterfall in the United States. Because of its easy access, right off the Historic Columbia River Highway, it justifiably draws throngs of visitors from near and far. Don't let the crowds deter you, though. This loop hike nets you not one, but *five* fantastic and photogenic waterfalls amid a lush and stately forest, only some of which was marred by the 2017 Eagle Creek Fire. Once you get past the lower viewpoints, the crowds will fade away, and you'll get to enjoy some peaceful trail time as you explore the area's upper reaches.

Break away from the crowds surrounding the lodge and waterfall viewpoint by walking the Historic Columbia River Highway westward for 0.1 mile. Find the Wahkeena connector trail (Return Trail #442) and stroll alongside the highway for another 0.5 mile to the Wahkeena Falls viewpoint. From here, jump on the Wahkeena Trail (#420) and begin a steady ascent of the lush hillside, where maidenhair ferns, thimbleberry, fringecup, and valerian are plentiful under a canopy of conifers. At 0.8 mile, the trail crosses Wahkeena Creek on an old stone bridge and the upper falls gushes out of a slot in the basalt wall. Pass through the wall of cool mist and continue climbing through a series of switchbacks into a narrow canyon. The trail then hops back and forth across the creek a couple of times on small footbridges, coming to pretty little Fairy Falls at 1.5 miles. A bench beside the trail here is the perfect spot to sit and admire this delightful setting.

Cross the base of the falls and climb up through a few more switchbacks to a junction at 1.6 miles. Here, the Vista Point Trail (#419) climbs steeply up to an old viewpoint amid badly burned woods. Skip this trail and continue heading up the canyon to the Angels Rest Trail (#415) junction at 1.8 miles; turn left (east) to stay on the Wahkeena Trail. Continue ascending through mostly pleasant woods on comfortable trail tread. Seasonal wildflowers are abundant, including Scouler's fumewort, fairybells, and windflowers. A few pockets of burned trees show evidence of the 2017 wildfire that ripped through here. The trail finally reaches its crest in a wooded clearing at 2.1 miles, at the upper junction of the Vista Point Trail. Although viewless, this is a good spot to pause for a breather.

Wisendanger Falls is one of five idyllic waterfalls along the Wahkeena–Multnomah Loop.

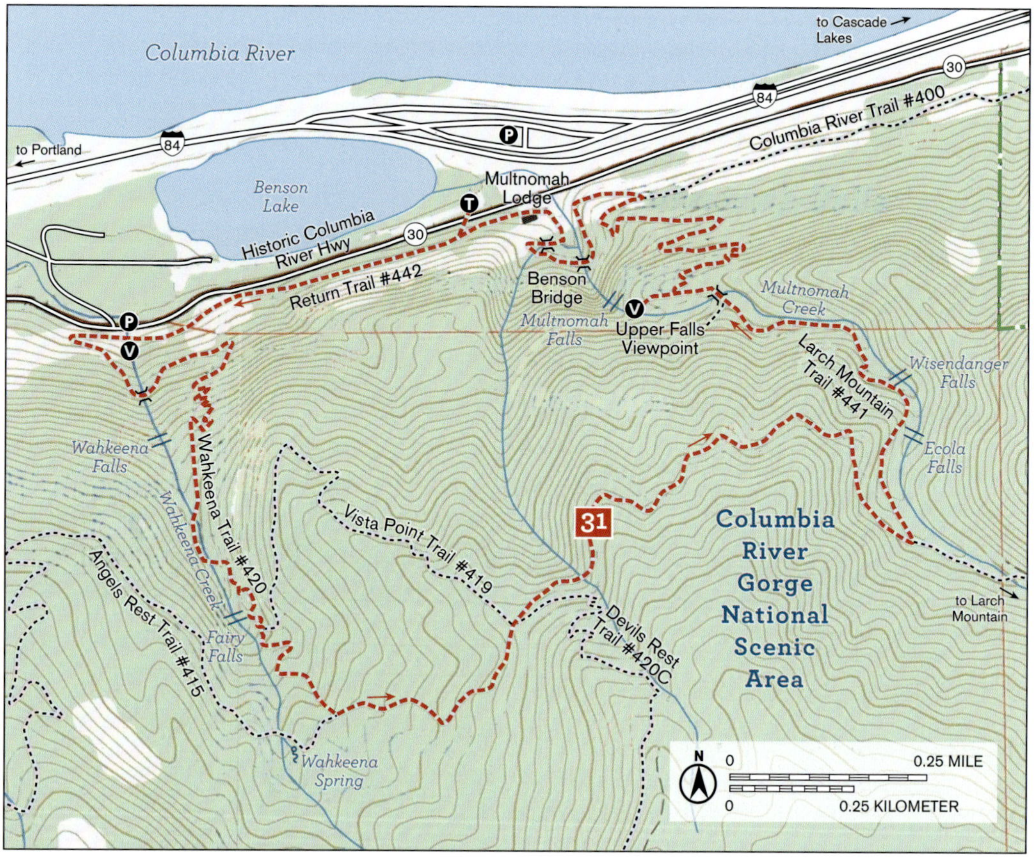

When you're ready to move on, it's (mostly) all downhill from here. Veer left (northeast) to bypass the Devils Rest Trail (#420C) and descend into Multnomah Creek's canyon. The trail winds in and out of smaller drainages and through more burned woods before meeting the Larch Mountain Trail (#441) at 2.9 miles. Turn left (north) and begin following Multnomah Creek downstream. A short distance farther, at 3.1 miles, you'll be peering over the brink of fifty-five-foot-tall Ecola Falls. Just 0.1 mile farther, pretty Wisendanger Falls spills fifty-five feet into a wide pool surrounded by mossy basalt walls. A short side trail heads upstream for a closer look.

Continue your march downstream, ogling pretty cascades, impressive basalt outcrops, and clusters of vibrant larkspur and columbine, then cross the creek on another footbridge at 3.5 miles. Just beyond, the side trail to the Multnomah Falls upper viewpoint branches off to the left (west). Descend this 0.2-mile spur to a wooden platform that presents a dizzying view straight down over the upper tier of Multnomah Falls. After your look, return to the main trail and begin the final descent. The crowds will start to pick up again as you approach the Benson Bridge at 4.6 miles. Constructed in 1914, this stone archway spanning the divide between the upper and lower falls is famous not only for its views but also for framing enchanting photos. From the bridge, head down the wide, paved path to the base of the falls and the lodge to finish your journey.

Extend Your Trip: Most of the options for adding more mileage, elevation, and views to the Multnomah Falls loop are quite long and/or strenuous. One option is to branch off for a trip to Angels Rest (see Hike 30), adding a 5.2-mile roundtrip to your day. Or for fewer miles but more climbing, you could opt for a trip up to Devils Rest. This trail gains almost a thousand feet in a little over 1.5 miles (one-way) to a viewless summit, but you can enjoy a couple of nice panoramas along the way. The longest option is to make the long climb to the top of Larch Mountain. From the junction at Multnomah Creek, this route adds a whopping 10 miles (roundtrip) and 2900 feet of elevation gain as you hike to a high, rocky perch with fantastic views.

32 *Wahclella Falls*

Distance: 1.7-mile lollipop loop
Difficulty: easy
Hiking time: short day hike
Elevation gain: 340 feet
High point: 270 feet
Season: year-round
Management: Mount Hood NF, Columbia River Gorge NSA
Protection status: National Scenic Area, Mark O. Hatfield Wilderness
Map: Green Trails 428S: Columbia Gorge West
GPS coordinates: N 45 63.040, W 121 95.392

Getting there: From Portland, take Interstate 84 approximately 36 miles east to the Bonneville Fish Hatchery at exit 40. Turn right and drive for 0.1 mile to the trailhead parking area. ***Notes:*** NW Forest Pass or Interagency Pass required for trailhead parking. Wilderness rules apply. Portions of this trail travel through recently burned forest, so exercise caution.

When you're looking for a fantastic Columbia River Gorge waterfall trail—but don't want to commit to any of the bigger and busier locations—this is the gem for you. While this trail was near the epicenter of the 2017 Eagle Creek Fire, and received considerable burn damage, it has been recovering nicely and is steadily returning to its former glory. There are still plenty of lush ferns

Wahclella Falls is a photographer's dream setting.

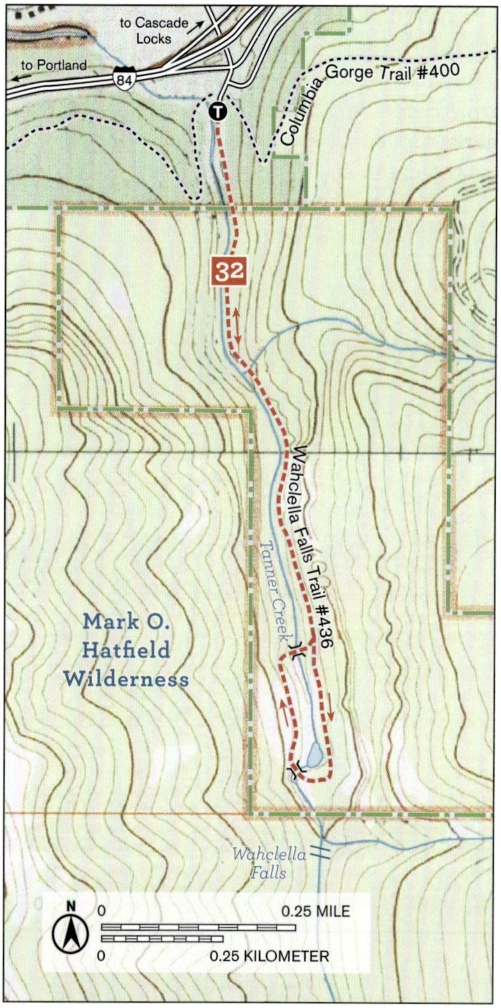

and wildflowers to be enjoyed among the vine maple and alder, and Tanner Creek sings down the canyon after gushing down a multi-tiered falls into a verdant pool at the back of the canyon.

Begin on the Wahclella Falls Trail (#436) beside a small check dam, and head upstream into the canyon, where volcanic basalt walls vault skyward and maidenhair fern, wild strawberry, and thistle line the path. After just 0.3 mile, the trail enters the Mark O. Hatfield Wilderness as a nameless cascade spills down the rocky wall right beside the boardwalk trail. From here, the trail gains most of its elevation as it climbs the slope above the creek to a junction at 0.6 mile. This begins the loop portion. Veer left (south) and mount a series of steps before descending to the creek again, right above the pool below the falls. Here, at 0.9 mile, Wahclella Falls pours out of a cleft in the rocks and fills the canyon with mist—often making clear photographs a challenge!

Drop down through the rocks and cross the creek on a wooden footbridge, then go a little farther and capture that postcard-perfect photo of the bridge right below the lower falls. Then head downstream on the other side of the creek, where maidenhair fern, thimbleberry, and oceanspray are abundant. Note the massive size of some of the boulders that have fallen into the canyon and creek bed. Cross the creek again on another footbridge and climb away from the creek to the junction where you started the loop. Turn left (north) and retrace your steps downstream and back out of the canyon.

33 *Eagle Creek to Tunnel Falls*

Distance: 11.8 miles
Difficulty: moderate
Hiking time: day hike
Elevation gain: 1420 feet
High point: 1100 feet
Season: Apr–Nov
Management: Mount Hood NF, Columbia River Gorge NSA
Protection status: National Scenic Area, Mark O. Hatfield Wilderness
Map: Green Trails 428S: Columbia Gorge West
GPS coordinates: N 45 63.671, W 121 91.953

Getting there: From Portland, take Interstate 84 approximately 37 miles east to exit 41 for the Cascade Hatchery and Day Use Area. Turn right and drive for 0.5 mile to the trailhead parking area. Heed "no parking" signs. ***Notes:*** NW Forest Pass or Interagency Pass required for trailhead parking. Wilderness rules apply. The trail can be very busy on summer weekends; consider visiting midweek. Portions of trail travel through recently burned forest, so exercise caution. Some high, narrow sections provide cable handrails for safety.

In late summer of 2017, a careless visitor tossed a smoking firework into the brush along the Eagle Creek Trail. It quickly ignited the dry brush, and the flame was fanned by high winds that were racing down the Columbia River Gorge that weekend. In no time, a raging wildfire consumed the Oregon side of the gorge, decimating wide swaths of forest, brush, and trails. In a word, it was devastating, and the entire Northwest mourned collectively. Slowly, over the following years, the area began to recover and trails reopened. When Eagle Creek Trail, at the heart of the conflagration, was finally repaired, hikers and visitors were eager to return to this beloved trail. The scene has changed, but nature has a knack for recovering from disaster. While scars remain, so do the waterfalls, and wildflowers and new trees have sprouted up in a flurry, making Eagle Creek once again a delight to experience.

Begin your journey by heading upstream on a moderate grade of rugged and rocky trail. The path is lined with bleeding heart and mixed berry shrubs, with mossy bigleaf maples offering occasional shade. Spring and summer bring a kaleidoscope of vibrant wildflowers. Look for windflowers, seablush, penstemon, and manroot, to name just a few. On wet and rocky slopes, monkey flower and stonecrop are abundant. About 1.2 miles up the canyon, the trail traverses the slope high above Metlako Falls. A viewpoint where you could look down on this plunging waterfall slid off the hillside years before the fire, so now the only view is from a distance. The trail then crosses Sorenson Creek at 1.6 miles and comes to a fork. Veer right (west) onto this 0.2-mile spur if you want to visit Lower Punchbowl Falls; otherwise, continue another 0.2 mile to the main Punchbowl Falls viewpoint. This postcard-worthy waterfall plunges thirty-five feet into an undercut basin of volcanic basalt.

Continue your journey up the canyon, turning in and out of little tributary channels, then through a burned area where the fire reached the canyon floor. The trail then narrows and clings to the hillside. At 3.2 miles, pretty Loowit Falls spills ninety feet down the opposite canyon wall into a little pool. Just beyond, cross to the other side of the creek on High Bridge as Eagle Creek is funneled through a narrow slot below. The trail then proceeds past the old Tenas Camp at 3.7 miles and recrosses the creek on the 4.5-Mile Bridge at 3.9 miles (go figure). The scene livens up as you continue upstream, with ferns and wildflowers once again adorning the slopes and trailside. At 4.6 miles, reach Wy'East Camp. Just beyond, the trail enters the Mark O. Hatfield Wilderness, where the rugged Eagle Benson

The iconic Tunnel Falls on Eagle Creek

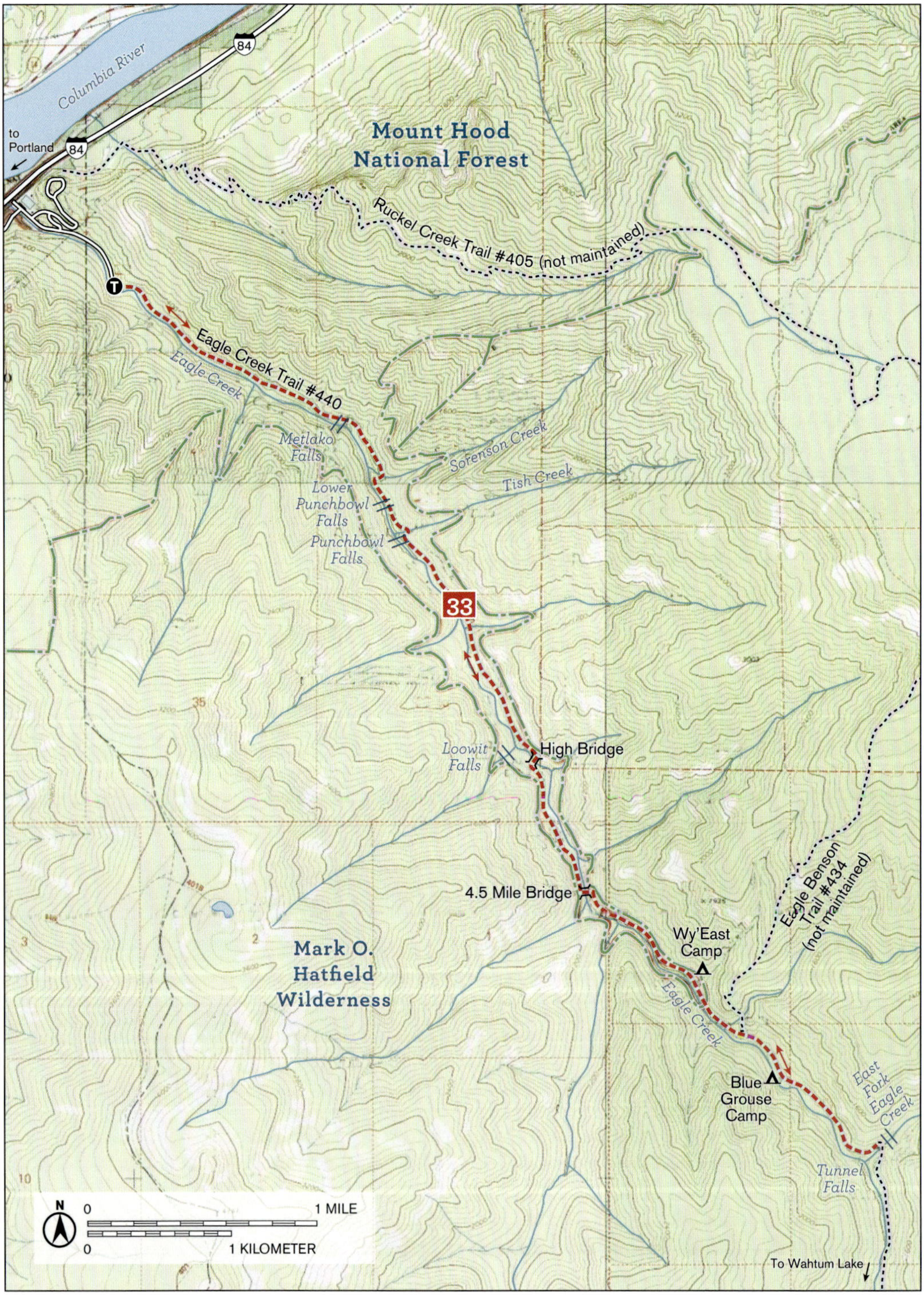

Columbia River
84
to Portland
84
Mount Hood National Forest
Ruckel Creek Trail #405 (not maintained)
Eagle Creek Trail #440
Eagle Creek
Metlako Falls
Sorenson Creek
Tish Creek
Lower Punchbowl Falls
Punchbowl Falls
33
Loowit Falls
High Bridge
4.5 Mile Bridge
Wy'East Camp
Eagle Benson Trail #434 (not maintained)
Mark O. Hatfield Wilderness
Eagle Creek
Blue Grouse Camp
East Fork Eagle Creek
Tunnel Falls
0
1 MILE
0
1 KILOMETER
To Wahtum Lake

Trail (#434) climbs steeply up the hillside to connect with the Pacific Crest Trail (PCT) on the Benson Plateau.

Enjoy a pleasant walk as the trail continues its contouring ascent up the canyon. Small cascades tumble down Eagle Creek, and columbine, larkspur, and chickweed decorate the way to Blue Grouse Camp, at 5.2 miles. When you see a larger waterfall spilling down Eagle Creek, the trail curves into a side canyon and you get your first view of roaring Tunnel Falls. Here, at 5.9 miles, the East Fork Eagle Creek plummets 170 feet down the canyon wall. The trail clings to the cliffs and passes through a tunnel in the rock behind the waterfall. It's an exhilarating sight, but use extreme caution on the narrow, slippery trail. The best views and photographs are from the opposite side, so proceed through the tunnel and ease your way along the opposite wall. From here, the trail continues another 0.5 mile to Twister Falls and destinations beyond, but this makes a good turnaround spot for a well-spent day.

Extend Your Trip: Several designated camp areas along Eagle Creek Trail offer overnight opportunities for backpacking. From Tunnel Falls, you can continue another 7 miles up the canyon to visit Wahtum Lake (see Hike 36). At the junction with the Eagle-Tanner Trail (#443), veer left (northeast) up the slope to keep following Eagle Creek Trail as it climbs high above the East Fork Eagle Creek. You can vary your return from Wahtum Lake by heading back via the PCT or Herman Creek Trail. The loop route over Tanner Butte described in the previous iteration of this guide was heavily damaged in the Eagle Creek Fire and is no longer recommended.

34 *Hood River Mountain*

Distance: 3-mile loop
Difficulty: easy
Hiking time: short day hike
Elevation gain: 590 feet
High point: 2120 feet
Season: Mar–Nov
Management: Mount Hood NF, Columbia River Gorge NSA
Protection status: National Scenic Area
Map: USGS Quad: White Salmon, OR and WA
GPS coordinates: N 45 67.614, W 121 46.194

Getting there: From the east end of Hood River (or Interstate 84, exit 64), take Oregon Route 35 south for approximately 2 miles. Turn left (east) on Whiskey Creek Drive and drive for 0.5 mile, then turn left (north) on Eastside Road. In 0.2 mile, turn right on Old Dalles Drive and proceed for 2 miles, with the last mile on good gravel. Turn right (south) into the trailhead parking area at the crest of the hill. ***Notes:*** Some of this trail is on private logging land, generously opened for public use. Stick to the established roads and trails and obey any posted closures. Beware of poison oak.

Hood River Mountain is a long ridgeline extending north–south along the east side of the Hood River Valley. This locally known (but not widely used) trail features an amazing wildflower display in mid- to late spring, making it a worthy alternative to some of the more popular and crowded locations. A bevy of brilliant wildflowers lines the way; keep an eye out for pretty little cornflowers, waterleaf, grass widows, and chocolate lilies.

From the unmarked trailhead, wind around a locked gate and start making your way up an old logging road. The path curves southwest as it gains elevation, with mixed pine and fir woods on the left (east) side and brushy, recovering clearcut on the right (west). New ponderosa pines

Wildflowers and Mount Hood views from atop Hood River Mountain

grow on the grassy slope, and colorful wooly mullein and knapweed add splashes of color. About half a mile up, as the road nears the top of the crest, views start to open to the north and west. In the near distance, you can spot Washington's Mount Adams, looking large on the other side of the gorge, with Mount Rainier's glacier-capped peak shining over the horizon.

Continue up the road another 0.3 mile to reach the summit knob alongside a stand of white oak. Now the view opens to the west and south, looking over the upper Hood River Valley, with Mount Hood taking center stage to the southwest. The old road ends here, so pick up the single-track trail as it continues southward across the open slope, descending on an easy grade. In springtime, the hillside is carpeted with vibrant balsamroot, lupine, larkspur, penstemon, and paintbrush. At 1.1 miles, pause for another view of the mountain and valley, then continue down to a clearing and one more viewpoint at 1.5 miles. Nearby is a fenced-in weather station.

A faint trail continues south along the open ridge, making a larger loop. Ignore it and turn left (east) instead, heading down a gravel service road and passing through an open meadow until you reach another gate at 1.9 miles. Turn left (north) on Elder Road and start walking up a shady, wooded corridor lined with Oregon grape. Although there are no more views, the walk is pleasant and effortless. You will pass an old cattle chute at the edge of a pasture before returning to the trailhead.

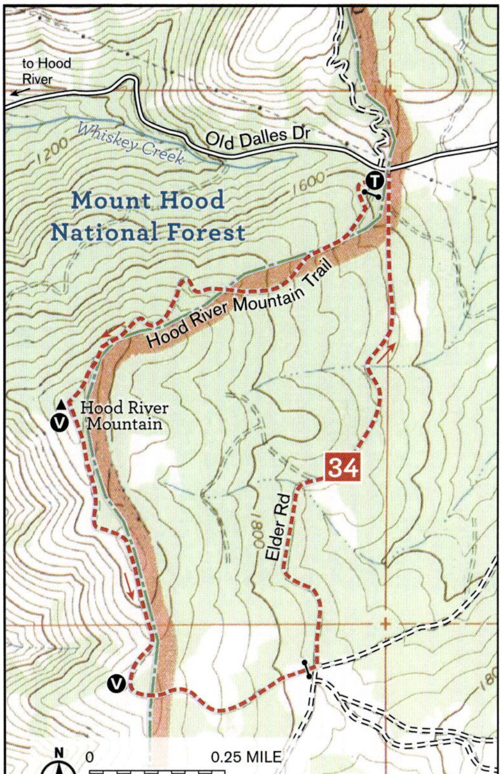

35 *Rowena Plateau and McCall Point*

Distance: 2.1-/3.6-mile roundtrips
Difficulty: easy/moderate
Hiking time: short day hikes
Elevation gain: 290 feet/1030 feet
High point: 1720 feet
Season: May–Oct
Management: Mount Hood NF, Columbia River Gorge NSA, The Nature Conservancy
Protection status: Tom McCall Preserve and Mayer State Park
Map: Green Trails 428S: Columbia Gorge West
GPS coordinates: N 45 68.265, W 121 30.032

Getting there: From Hood River, drive east on Interstate 84 for about 6 miles to exit 69 for US Highway 30. (Or from Portland, about 66 miles.) Turn right and continue east on the Historic Columbia River Highway (US 30) for another 6.6 miles. Turn right into the

Spring is the time for wildflowers on McCall Point.

Rowena Crest Viewpoint parking area. The McCall Point trailhead is on the south side of the parking area; the plateau trailhead is across the highway. ***Notes:*** Beware of ticks, rattlesnakes, and poison oak. Dogs not permitted.

The Mayer State Park and Tom McCall Preserve at Rowena Crest protect 231 acres of transition-zone prairie and wetland on a volcanic plateau in the eastern Columbia River Gorge. Managed jointly by the US Forest Service, Oregon State Parks, and The Nature Conservancy, the exact origin of this landscape of hummocky terrain continues to baffle researchers. To the casual observer, the preserve—encompassing the Rowena Plateau and McCall Point—is a wonderland of flatland and hillside wildflower meadows that come to life in midspring. Here, you can tally up the number of different blooms you find, while also enjoying birding, wildlife watching, and fantastic Columbia River Gorge views.

The hike to **Rowena Plateau** is an easy stroll through grassy wetlands and hummocky meadows, where wildflowers thrive on the ground and birds of prey soar overhead. The trip culminates at the edge of a volcanic plateau, offering views over Rowena Dell and the Columbia River. Start at the trailhead opposite the parking area and take the wide, graded path down into the preserve. After just 0.3 mile, veer right (north) to trace the edge of the plateau around two large ponds. Their brushy shores are lined with monkey flower and Nootka rose—and poison oak, so be watchful. Stay right through a couple of junctions and meet the main trail again at 0.9 mile; turn right (northwest) to descend to the viewpoint at the end. For the return trip, stick with the main trail all the way back, veering right through groves of white oak on the west side of the ponds. Then make the short ascent back to the trailhead.

The **Tom McCall Point Trail** begins with a pleasant stroll across an open prairie on a wide, graded path. Look for pretty wild hyacinth, bachelor's buttons, and desert parsley sprinkled among the shrubs and grasses. Before long, the trail begins gaining elevation as it enters a grove of ponderosa pine, ascending the ridgeline above the curving historic highway. A mix of buckwheat, biscuitroot, and stalks of vibrant-purple hairy vetch lace the sides of the trail. There is also plenty of poison oak through here, so be watchful. Around 0.6 mile, the trail quickly switchbacks to pull away from the edge and makes a wide contour through an upper meadow to gain more elevation. Here, among carpets of springtime balsamroot, lupine, and paintbrush, the views open northward, taking in the Columbia River Gorge and offering a peek at Mount Adams.

Continue climbing, entering white oak and fir woods again at just past 1 mile. The trail gets a bit steeper and the groundcover transitions to Oregon grape and honeysuckle—and more poison oak. After another 0.4 mile, the trail exits the trees as it nears the summit, twisting through wide, lazy switchbacks with wider views over the gorge and plateau. Look for the next round of flowers to join the party, including penstemon and collomia, before the trail sweeps around the south side of the mountain to gain the summit at 1.8 miles. The view from the top is wide and impressive, with Mount Hood taking center stage to the southwest. Just below the summit, a fainter trail heads southeast to a second summit, but the path gets overgrown with poison oak, so this makes a good turnaround spot.

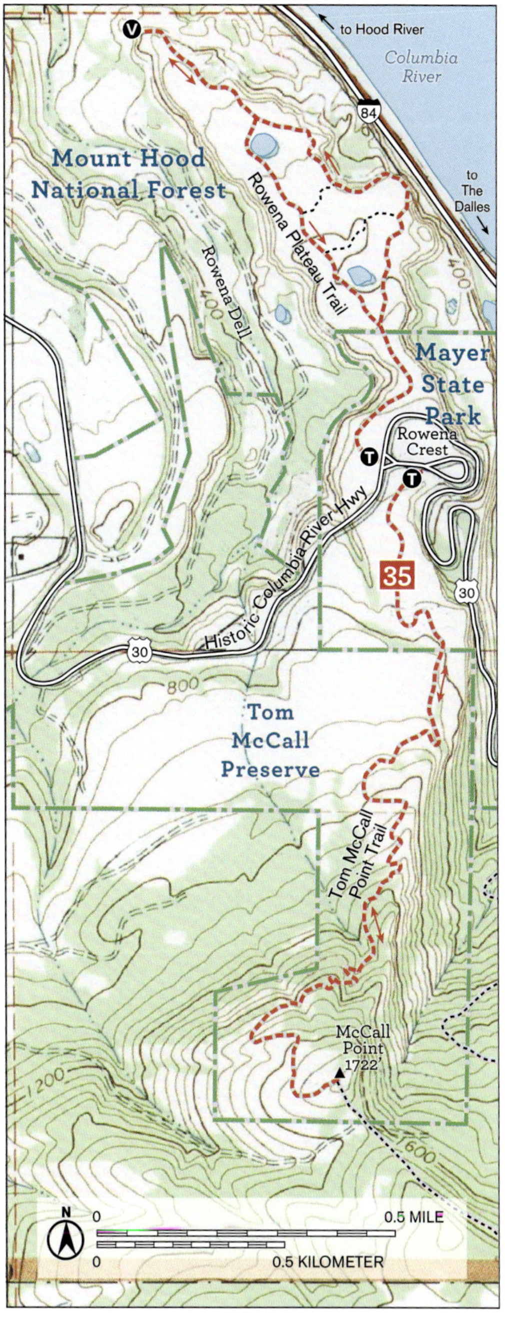

Opposite, top: Camping in Paradise Park

Opposite, bottom: Heather meadows on McNeil Point

North Cascades

36. Chinidere Mountain 118

37. Owl Point 120

38. McNeil Point 122

39. Ramona Falls 125

40. Burnt Lake 127

41. Paradise Park 129

42. East Eliot Moraine and Cooper Spur 132

43. Elk Meadows 135

44. Timberline Trail 137

45. High Prairie and Lookout Mountain 142

46. Mirror Lake 144

47. Old Salmon River 146

48. Twin Lakes 148

49. Timothy Lake 149

Like a shining beacon along Oregon's northern Cascade Crest, Mount Hood is Oregon's tallest peak. Soaring more than eleven thousand feet above the nearby Columbia River and located a little more than an hour's drive from Portland, Mount Hood is the state's premier outdoor playground. Here you can spend a summer day skiing in the morning, hiking in the afternoon, and kicking back with a microbrew and an alpenglow view in the evening—all in the same place! The following section offers a fresh and fun perspective on many of Mount Hood's classic trails, as well as a few lesser-known routes. Get outside and enjoy your own brand of solitude, discovery, and adventure in a rich and dynamic landscape of old-growth forests, enchanting lakes, volcanic ridges, and sparkling glaciers.

36 *Chinidere Mountain*

Distance: 5-mile roundtrip
Difficulty: moderate
Hiking time: day hike
Elevation gain: 1370 feet
High point: 4673 feet
Season: Jul–Oct
Management: Mount Hood NF (Hood River)
Protection status: Mark O. Hatfield Wilderness
Map: Trails Illustrated 821: Columbia River Gorge
GPS coordinates: N 45 57.725, W 121 79.279

Getting there: From Interstate 84 in Hood River, take exit 62 for US Highway 30. Turn east on Cascade Avenue, right on Mount Adams Avenue, and then right again on Wine Country Avenue, which becomes Country Club Road. Continue 2.8 miles, then turn left (east) on Barrett Drive and proceed another 1.2 miles. At the stop, turn right (south) on Tucker Road (Oregon Route 281) and drive for 2 miles, then veer right onto Dee Highway (OR 281) and go for another 6.3 miles. Make a slight right across the railroad tracks, then veer left on Lost Lake Road (Forest Road 13). Follow this road for 5.1 miles, veer right (west) onto FR 13 and go for another 4.3 miles, then veer right again onto FR 1310. Drive 6 more miles to the Wahtum Lake Campground and trailhead.
Notes: Day-use fee required for trailhead parking. Self-issue wilderness permit required. Wilderness rules apply.

Wahtum Lake is one of Oregon's more laughable geographic place-names. Designated in 1901 by a USGS survey party, Wahtum Lake was named for the last chief of the Wasco Indians. The party members were obviously unaware that *wahtum* is the Sahaptin word for "lake." Save your visit to Lake Lake for a bluebird day, when views from the summit go on forever, and Cascade peaks in both Oregon and Washington dominate in all directions.

From the trailhead below the Wahtum Lake Campground, begin with a 0.4-mile descent via a couple of switchbacks to a junction with the Pacific Crest Trail (PCT). Turn right (east) and start an easy ramble around the lakeshore, where tall, mossy hemlocks and firs, ferns, and berry shrubs keep the trail mostly cool and shady. Views remain limited as the path circuits the lake, staying away from the water on the slope above the brushy shoreline. A few user paths

Go for the views, and sweet solitude, on Chinidere Mountain.

lead to day-use spaces and primitive campsites. Curving around the east end of the lake, push your way through overgrown hedge nettle and bleeding heart, and begin a contouring ascent around the north side of the basin. As the trail climbs, bear grass carpets the hillside and lake views are obstructed by dense forest.

The trail eventually turns away from the lake basin to a junction with the Herman Creek Trail (#406) at 2 miles. Turn left (southwest) and continue another 0.1 mile to the next junction, where the Chinidere Cutoff (#406M) drops steeply to the left (south). Just beyond, the Chinidere Mountain Trail (#445) climbs away to the right (north). Take the Chinidere Mountain Trail and start climbing a series of short, steep switchbacks. The way stays mostly under the cover of trees until it reaches the upper eastern flank of the mountain, where it crosses a wide slope of shale-like talus. Continue upward, traversing the base of the rocks until the trail swings up and across the jumble, and then proceed up the spine of the mountain to its 4673-foot summit, at about 2.5 miles.

The view from the top is all-encompassing. In the near distance, take in a 360-degree sweep of Tomlike Mountain, Benson Plateau, Tanner Butte, and Indian Mountain. In the distance, Mounts St. Helens, Rainier, and Adams dominate the northern horizon in Washington, while Mounts Hood and Jefferson tower above the southern horizon in Oregon. Below, wildflowers fill the meadows on Chinidere's western slope; even farther below, Wahtum Lake sparkles in its tree-ringed basin. When you've absorbed all the views you can handle—or the wind picks up, whichever comes first—return to your starting point by the same route.

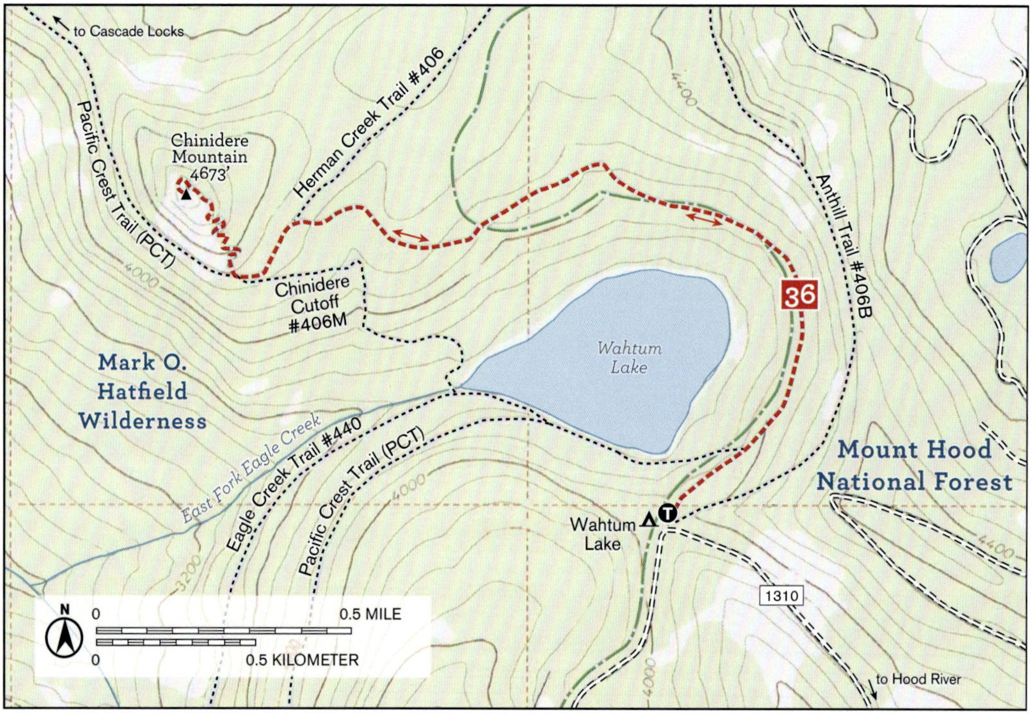

Extend Your Trip: While you're in the neighborhood, you can also bag 4555-foot Tomlike Mountain via a lesser-used route that may require a little bushwhacking and routefinding. On your return from Chinidere Mountain, veer left (northeast) onto the Herman Creek Trail and hike 1 mile to the unsigned Tomlike Mountain Trail, just north of the Anthill Trail junction. Follow this rugged path through the woods and then along the open, narrow ridgetop. The views are expansive amid some interesting, layered rock outcrops. Bagging the summit requires a moderate scramble up a pile of slabby rocks. The view from the top takes in the entire Herman Creek Canyon, as well as neighboring canyons and distant peaks.

37 *Owl Point*

Distance: 4.2-mile roundtrip
Difficulty: easy
Hiking time: short day hike
Elevation gain: 970 feet
High point: 4940 feet
Season: Jul–Oct
Management: Mount Hood NF (Hood River)
Protection status: Mount Hood Wilderness
Map: Trails Illustrated 321: Mount Hood Wilderness
GPS coordinates: N 45 44.291, W 121 72.919

Getting there: From the small town of Welches, west of Mount Hood, drive north on East Lolo Pass Road for 10.5 miles to Lolo Pass. Turn right (southeast) on Forest Road 1810 and drive for 10.5 miles; the first 5.5 miles are on good gravel, then the road becomes pavement again. Make a sharp U-turn, heading right (south) onto paved FR 16, and zigzag up the hillside for 5.4 miles. Then make another sharp U-turn right (south) onto gravel FR

1650. Drive for 3.6 miles, veering left at an unsigned fork about a mile before reaching the trailhead. FR 18 and the trailhead can also be accessed from the north via Lost Lake Road. ***Notes:*** Self-issue wilderness permit required. Wilderness rules apply. Exercise caution in burned areas.

Abandoned by the Forest Service in the 1960s, the lower portion of the Vista Ridge Trail spent decades in disrepair. And then much of the upper portion burned in the 2011 Dollar Lake Fire. It wasn't until volunteers from Trailkeepers of Oregon restored the lower portion of this old ridgetop route that it was formally recognized again, in 2018. The upside is that hikers now have another trail with good views to enjoy on the quieter north side of Mount Hood. The downside is that this route originates from the most remote trailhead on the mountain, requiring a little more time and effort to get to it.

Start on the Vista Ridge Trail (#626) with a gentle, 0.4-mile ascent through young hemlock and silver fir woods. Trillium, violets, and glacier lilies are mixed into the mountain carpet of bear grass and huckleberry. The trail eventually enters shady, more mature woods. Enjoy a pleasant ramble on duff-covered tread and then reach a T-junction. To the right (south), the Vista Ridge Trail continues, steadily climbing 2.4 miles through charred forest to the Timberline Trail; to the left (north), the Old Vista Ridge Trail (#626A) makes a rolling ascent to Owl Point. Turn left (north) onto the old ridge trail and walk briefly along the edge of the burn area before diving into greener woods. From here, the trail begins a steady and winding ascent.

The trail eventually levels along the ridgetop near the 1-mile mark, and the hiking becomes almost effortless as you pass abundant huckleberry and wild strawberry. A few well-worn user paths break off to the right (east) to viewpoints overlooking the upper Clear Branch valley. From these windows along the ridge, it's easy to pick out Pinnacle Ridge, a fin of rock resembling an old ship among a stormy sea of silvery forest. At 1.3 miles, the trail crests beside a rocky prominence, then dips into a wide huckleberry-filled meadow. Unseen to the east is 4930-foot Red Hill. Continue across the meadow. The trail ducks back into the trees and begins a gentle ascent, bending eastward to a junction at 1.9 miles.

From this point, the main route turns left (east); however, if you're up for a short detour, the path straight ahead (south) proceeds through another heather and huckleberry meadow to an impressive viewpoint atop a wide scree slope. This rock pile is a good place to watch and listen for pikas. To continue to Owl Point, veer left and ascend another 0.1 mile to the next junction, then turn right (south). Briefly follow this path through the trees, then out into the open as it curves around the slope of Owl Point at about 2.1 miles. Here, you're presented with a wide panorama, with Mount Hood to the north and the Clear Branch valley—all the way to Laurance Lake—to the east. The large ridge on

Traipse through wildflowers and huckleberries to Owl Point.

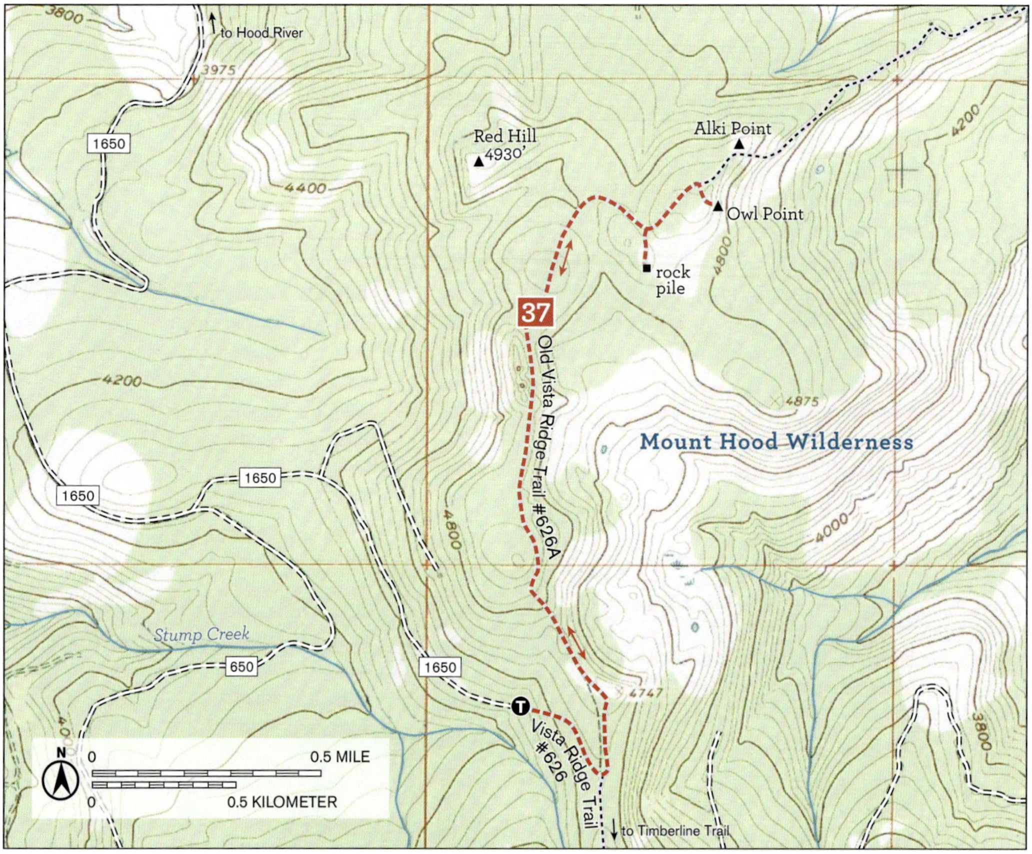

the mountain, above the tree line, is Barrett Spur. The glaciers to either side of the spur are Ladd (right/west) and Coe (left/east). The Owl Point register is in an old ammo can; if you can find it, sign your autograph before heading back the way you came.

38 *McNeil Point*

Distance: 9.2-mile roundtrip
Difficulty: strenuous
Hiking time: day hike or overnight
Elevation gain: 3210 feet
High point: 6180 feet
Season: Jul–Oct
Management: Mount Hood NF (Hood River)
Protection status: Mount Hood Wilderness
Map: Green Trails 462S: Mount Hood
GPS coordinates: N 45 22.338, W 121 49.356

Getting there: From Sandy, take Mount Hood Highway (US Highway 26) east for about 17 miles to Welches. Turn left (north) on East Lolo Pass Road and proceed 4.2 miles, then veer right (east) onto Muddy Fork Road (Forest Road 1828) and drive 0.7 mile. At the next fork, continue straight (north) on FR 1828 and drive another 5.6 miles. When

The stone shelter at McNeil Point

the road forks again, veer right (southeast) onto gravel FR 118 and drive 1.5 miles to the trailhead. ***Notes:*** NW Forest Pass or Interagency Pass required for trailhead parking. Self-issue wilderness permit required. Wilderness rules apply.

Several old stone and log shelters are scattered across the middle flanks of Mount Hood, romantic relics of a bygone era. Built in the 1930s by the Civilian Conservation Corps, a handful of these backcountry shelters still stand, while some have disappeared altogether. The McNeil Point Shelter is one of these relics. Perched high above the Timberline Trail on a meadow-covered plateau, it has stood the test of time, defying nature and gravity. Today, it still offers a bit of comforting cover when the weather goes awry. And as you sit at its doorstep, admiring the vast panorama before you, you'll have the perfect opportunity to ponder your little place on this big, magnificent mountain.

Begin your hike with a quick 0.5-mile trip up the Top Spur Trail (#785). This short connector climbs steadily on rocky, rooty ground under dense conifer forest, surrounded by berry shrubs, lady fern, and wildflowers. At the top of the trail, where it connects with the Pacific Crest Trail (PCT), turn right (east) and proceed about fifty yards to a large trail junction with a Mount Hood map board and wilderness permit kiosk. Obtain your free, self-issue wilderness permit here, then veer left (east) onto the Timberline Trail. The route forward contours the wooded north slope of Bald Mountain, high above the head of Elk Creek, and passes the Bald Mountain Cutoff at 0.9 mile. (This short spur hops over to the south side of the ridge and connects with another portion of the Timberline Trail.) Just beyond, at 1 mile, pass the McGee Creek Trail (#627), which climbs steeply from a trailhead off Lolo Pass Road.

Continue ascending through a viewless tree tunnel until the trail pops out into the open

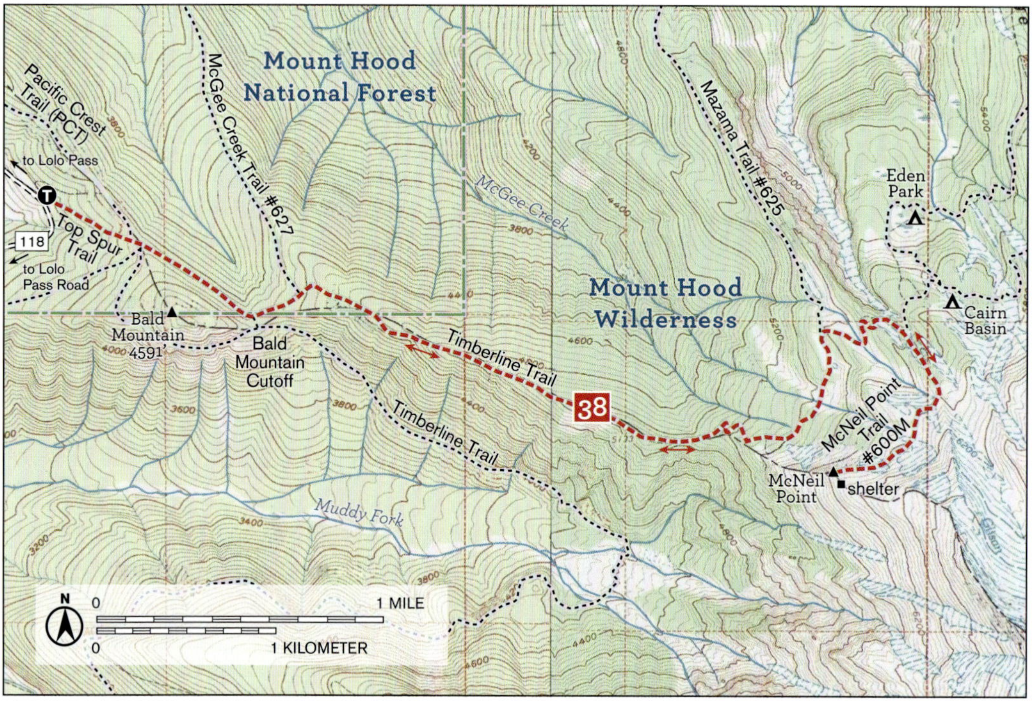

amid a ridgetop flower garden at 2.1 miles. Here, swaths of paintbrush, penstemon, Columbia lily, and mariposa lily present a colorful foreground for an impressive view of Mount Hood, Sandy Glacier, and the jagged head of the Muddy Fork Canyon. The ridgeline extending left (north) of the mountain is where you're headed. Continue on the trail as it leads back into the trees. Bear grass, lupine, and corn lily are abundant, and summer brings Columbia windflowers to the trailside. The path dips to traverse a shallow saddle then commences climbing more earnestly through a few switchbacks to an unmarked trail junction at 2.8 miles.

Veer left (northeast) to continue on the Timberline Trail, contouring the forested northwest flank of Mount Hood, where avalanche lilies are profuse in early summer. Proceed across a few small creeks at around 2.9 miles, then cross larger McGee Creek at 3 miles. All of these water crossings are easy rock-hops and are often decorated with spiraea, aster, monkey flower, and bog gentian. Cross an open meadow carpeted with pink heather at the base of a high talus slope, then climb through a couple of switchbacks to a large pond in a grassy basin. When the bear grass is blooming and the sun is shining, this meadow looks like it's illuminated with millions of flowery bulbs. Just beyond the pond, at 3.2 miles, keep right at an unmarked junction; the trail left goes to another small pond and a few campsites, then connects with the Mazama Trail (#625). Just a little farther, at 3.4 miles, the top of the Mazama Trail connects directly with the Timberline Trail.

Continue east across another meadow with more flowers and views, then arrive at the McNeil Point Trail (#600M) at 3.7 miles. Veer right (south) off the Timberline and begin ascending a heather- and paintbrush-covered ridgeline. The higher you go, the more impressive the views become. Look for Washington's big peaks behind you. The path then turns off the ridge to contour a steep talus slope, where snow often lingers into the summer months. The final stretch ascends through more meadows and flowers, then mounts the plateau of McNeil Point. Where the trail forks, at 4.4 miles, choose the high route to the left (southwest) or the rim route to the right (west) to complete your journey, reaching the McNeil Point Shelter either way at 4.6 miles. Stay and enjoy the view for a while or pitch a tent in one of the nearby clearings. When you've gotten your fill, return by the same route.

39 *Ramona Falls*

Distance: 7-mile lollipop loop
Difficulty: strenuous
Hiking time: day hike
Elevation gain: 1220 feet
High point: 3470 feet
Season: Jun–Oct
Management: Mount Hood NF (Zigzag)
Protection status: Mount Hood Wilderness
Map: Green Trails 462S: Mount Hood
GPS coordinates: N 45 23.202, W 121 49.920

Getting there: From Sandy, take US Highway 26 east for about 17 miles to the town of Welches. Turn left (north) on East Lolo Pass Road and proceed for 4.2 miles. At the fork, veer right (east) onto Muddy Fork Road (Forest Road 1828) and drive 0.7 mile, then turn right again to cross the Sandy River onto FR 1825. Drive 1.7 miles, then veer left (east) onto FR 100 and drive a bumpy 0.3 mile to the large trailhead parking area.
Notes: NW Forest Pass or Interagency Pass required for trailhead parking. Self-issue wilderness permit required. Wilderness rules apply. Requires a challenging river crossing; not recommended for small children or dogs. Road closed December 1–April 1.

Oregon is lauded for its abundant waterfalls, but Ramona Falls may be one of the most spectacular. And while it takes a little more work to enjoy this one—including a challenging river crossing—the reward far outweighs the effort. And when you stand near the base of this misty,

Leave Oregon and enter Middle Earth at Ramona Falls.

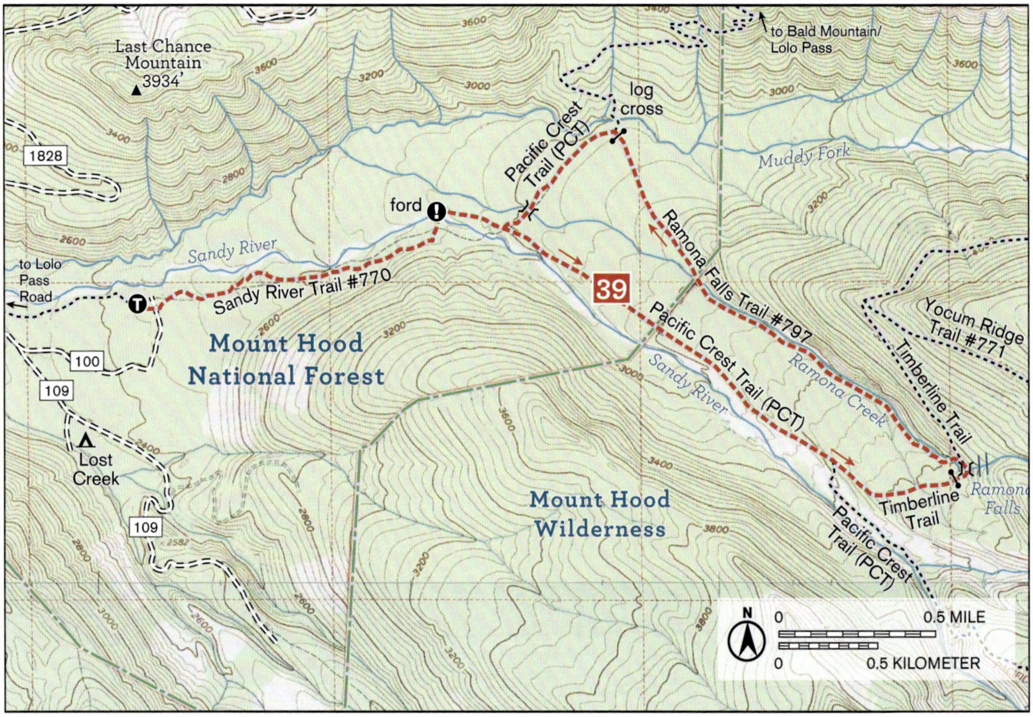

one-hundred-foot curtain of falling water hidden away in a lush, mossy grotto, you'll wonder when you left Oregon and entered Middle Earth.

Start your journey on the Sandy River Trail (#770), located in the southeast corner of the large parking area. The path heads into airy, lodgepole woods festooned with mountain rhododendron and vine maple. The way is wide and sandy and proceeds at a very slight incline. Pause at the kiosk at an old road junction to obtain your self-issue wilderness permit, then continue east and come to the bank of the Sandy River at around 0.3 mile. One of Oregon's Wild and Scenic Rivers, the Sandy flows for 56 miles—from Reid Glacier on Mount Hood to the Columbia River. Follow the trail as it parallels the river, winding through the trees; fireweed, pearly everlasting, thimbleberry, and mountain ash are plentiful.

When the trail exits the trees at 1.2 miles and drops onto the rocky floodplain of the river, start looking for a safe place to ford. There used to be a bridge here, but it washed out in 2014. The Forest Service has not replaced it, citing challenges with the river's changing course and the unstable terrain. (During peak runoff periods, the river may be too high and impassable. If it looks dangerous, it probably is—don't risk it.) Once across, ascend the bank to a sandy bench and proceed through a swath of mountain ash to what looks like an unsigned junction. Turn left (north) for the proper trail, and make a wide curve eastward, dipping through a gully and then plunging back under the cover of trees. At 1.4 miles, the path reaches a junction with the Pacific Crest Trail (PCT).

This begins the loop portion of your hike. Veer right (southeast) onto the PCT and start ascending on a steady, moderate grade, gaining good elevation above the river. The next junction comes at 2.9 miles; the PCT veers off to the right (south) and the Timberline Trail heads left (east). Take the left fork onto the Timberline Trail, and continue ascending through a stretch of dry, debris-laden woods before entering greener climes boasting more rhododendron and a lot of huckleberry. At 3.3 miles, proceed through a stock control gate, then descend into the lush, shady grotto where Ramona Falls cascades down a wall of broken columnar basalt. Take a long moment to admire the falling curtain of water, which looks like it was taken right out of the pages of a Tolkien book.

When you're ready to move on, cross the double-rail bridge below the falls and veer left (west) onto the Ramona Falls Trail (#797). Follow Ramona Creek downstream through verdant forest. The path winds along the water on soft, duff-covered tread, and the forest is brimming with ferns, berries, devil's club, and vanilla leaf. You'll cross the creek a few times on sturdy footbridges. The path then pulls away from the creek into drier lodgepole forest for a short stretch, then heads back under greener trees before reconnecting with the PCT at 5.1 miles. Turn left (southwest) on the PCT and cross Ramona Creek on a good bridge at 5.4 miles. Just 0.2 mile farther, return to the junction where you started the loop. Turn right (west), back onto the Sandy River Trail, and backtrack the way you came.

40 *Burnt Lake*

Distance: 6.6-mile roundtrip
Difficulty: moderate
Hiking time: day hike
Elevation gain: 1560 feet
High point: 4140 feet
Season: Jul–Oct
Management: Mount Hood NF (Zigzag)
Protection status: Mount Hood Wilderness
Map: Green Trails 426S: Mount Hood
GPS coordinates: N 45 22.338, W 121 49.356

Getting there: From Sandy, take US Highway 26 east for about 17 miles to the small town of Welches. Turn left (north) on East Lolo Pass Road and drive 4.2 miles. At the fork, veer right (east) onto Muddy Fork Road (Forest Road 1828) and drive 0.7 mile, then turn right again to cross the Sandy River onto FR 1825. Proceed for 2 miles. Just opposite the Lost Creek Campground entrance, veer left (southeast) onto narrow FR 109 and drive 1.4 miles on good gravel to the trailhead at the end of the road. ***Notes:*** NW Forest Pass or Interagency Pass required for trailhead parking. Self-issue wilderness permit required. Wilderness rules apply. Road closed December 1–April 1.

Nestled in a tranquil, forested basin between Zigzag Mountain and Mount Hood, Burnt Lake is a pleasant backcountry setting for picnics, paddling, and camping. And while summer weekends are popular here, this hike is just long enough to keep the larger crowds at bay,

Burnt Lake is a fantastic destination for a day hike or overnight backpack.

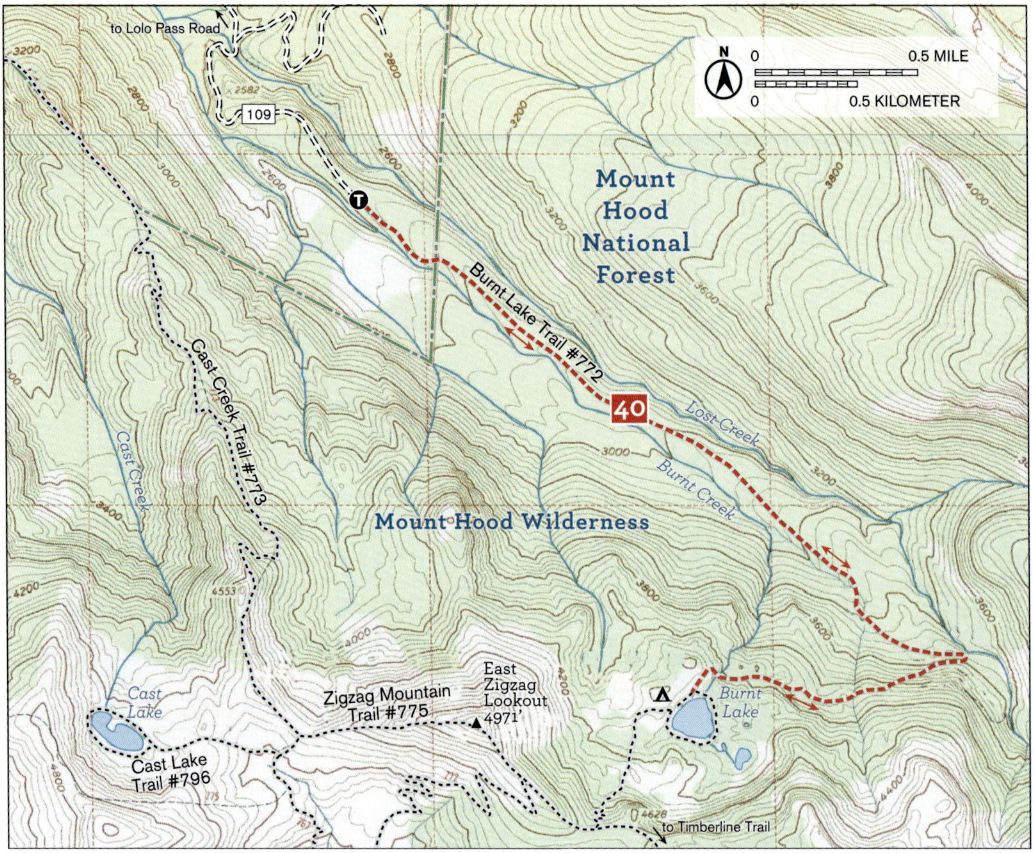

allowing for a pleasant day or overnight outing. On the hike to get to Burnt Lake, you'll see the ghosts of an ancient cedar forest that occupied the area prior to the early 1900s, when a wildfire gave the area its haunting name.

Start your hike on the Burnt Lake Trail (#772) under a canopy of vine maple, hemlock, and fir. Bunchberry, wild strawberry, mixed ferns, sorrel, and Oregon grape carpet the forest floor. In season, look for tasty thimbleberries along the trail. About a hundred yards up the trail, collect your self-issue wilderness permit at the kiosk and then continue up the wide, duff-covered path as it parallels Burnt Creek to the right (west). You'll soon begin to see the moss-covered remains of charred old-growth cedars in the forest mix. These are the enduring remains of the wildfire that scorched this area more than a century ago.

Around the 0.6-mile mark, a short path left (north) leads to a view over the wooded Lost Creek Canyon; just beyond, a short path right (south) descends to the side of Burnt Creek. The way forward is lush and pleasant, with the trail remaining mostly wide and even, making for effortless walking through the faerie-like woodland. The trail crosses a wide, shallow creek in a rocky bed at 1.9 miles, then switches back and crosses it again; the water pours across the trail here among thickets of fern, salmonberry, and devil's club—watch out for thorns! Contour up the hillside on a moderate grade, proceed through a couple more switchbacks, then traverse an open slope where several springs spill across the path. Here, you can catch a view of Mount Hood to the east before ducking back into the trees.

The ascent finally eases as you reach the 3-mile mark. Hop across the lake's outlet on large rocks, then follow the path as it levels out in dense rhododendron, reaching a fork at 3.3 miles. A map board nearby shows designated sites around the lake for picnics and day use (lettered) and overnight camping (numbered). For the best views of Mount Hood across the deep-blue, tree-ringed pool, head right and follow the trail to the sites on the west side of the lake. Once you've finished your visit to the lake, return by the same route.

Extend Your Trip: You can explore the brushy shore of Burnt Lake on a 0.4-mile loop. Or if you're up for a healthy climb to a great viewpoint, you can continue up the Burnt Lake Trail to Zigzag East Lookout. From the west side of the lake, veer right (west) and proceed past a few campsites. The trail crosses a small creek, then proceeds up a series of switchbacks to a trail junction atop the ridge, 0.7 mile from the lake. To the left (east), the Zigzag Mountain Trail (#775) goes for 2.8 miles along the viewless ridgetop to the Paradise Park Trail (#778; see Hike 41). To the right (west), the trail climbs 0.5 mile to the 4971-foot crown of Zigzag East. About halfway up, veer right (northwest) at the fork with the Burnt Lake Trail. The lookout tower is long gone, but the panoramic views of Mount Hood remain.

41 *Paradise Park*

Distance: 12.2-mile lollipop loop
Difficulty: strenuous
Hiking time: long day hike or overnight
Elevation gain: 3470 feet
High point: 6090 feet
Season: Jul–Oct
Management: Mount Hood NF (Zigzag)
Protection status: Mount Hood Wilderness
Map: Green Trails 462S: Mount Hood
GPS coordinates: N 45 19.842, W 121 42.630

Getting there: From Sandy, take US Highway 26 east for about 29 miles, past the village of Government Camp. Turn left (north) on Timberline Highway and head 6 miles up the mountain to the Timberline Lodge and ski area; park in the main parking area. ***Notes:*** Self-issue wilderness permit required. Wilderness rules apply. Requires a challenging river crossing.

The hike up to Paradise Park is arguably one of the best on Mount Hood. It is also one of the most strenuous, as there is no easy way to get there. Although there are three approaches you can take to reach these sprawling wildflower meadows, cascading streams, and in-your-face views of Mount Hood, all of them are long and involve a significant amount of elevation gain. But once you get there, all the effort is more than worth it.

Starting on the east side of Timberline Lodge, walk up the service road to the Pacific Crest Trail (PCT)–Timberline Trail junction; turn left (west) and get underway. Ramble through the ski area among plenty of summer wildflowers, passing the Mountaineer Trail (#798) at 0.9 mile. Just beyond, collect your wilderness permit at the backcountry kiosk, then drop into a rocky gully to cross Little Zigzag River. Once you crest the other side, continue downward into mixed forest, where huckleberries are abundant. Pass the Hidden Lake Trail (#779) at 1.6 miles, then follow an easy contour through a wide, flower-laden basin. The trail then curves up to the brink of Zigzag Canyon at 2.3 miles. Here, take in the impressive view of the Zigzag River—nearly seven hundred feet below—cascading down from Mississippi Head and Zigzag Glacier. Cast your gaze across the canyon to the high meadows beyond—that's where you're headed.

Paradise Park. What else do you need?

Start switchbacking down the flourishing, forested south wall, where several springs tumble down the hillside and across the trail, and shrubs, berries, and wildflowers are abundant. When you reach the rocky floor of the canyon at 3.3 miles, find a safe place to ford the roiling Zigzag River. Depending on the season and amount of runoff, this could be a challenging crossing. Use your best judgment, saving it for another day if it looks too risky. Otherwise, hop, skip, or splash across and pick up the trail on the other side.

The route now starts steadily climbing the canyon's drier north side, where you may notice a difference in the flowers and shrubbery. After a few switchbacks, veer right (northeast) off the PCT and onto the Paradise Park Loop (#757) at 3.7 miles. Continue climbing as the forest peels away and you enter a narrow drainage. Hop across a pretty creek at 4.1 miles, where wildflowers are everywhere, and make a circuiting ascent of the opposite ridge. When the trail turns back, cross the creek again and make a final ascent into the lower reaches of Paradise Park. Now that you've done the work, it's time to play.

Proceed to a four-way junction with the Paradise Park Trail (#778; different from the Paradise Park Loop) at 4.8 miles, an alternate method for reaching your destination. If you have the time and energy, turn right (northeast) and ascend another mile through sprawling wildflower meadows to a ridgetop viewpoint for an unparalleled look at Mount Hood. Otherwise, continue on the loop trail as it gently meanders along a contour of Mount Hood's western flank. Wildflowers carpet the slopes in a rainbow of colors, and you'll find numerous campsites along the way. Splash across Lost Creek at 5 miles, then

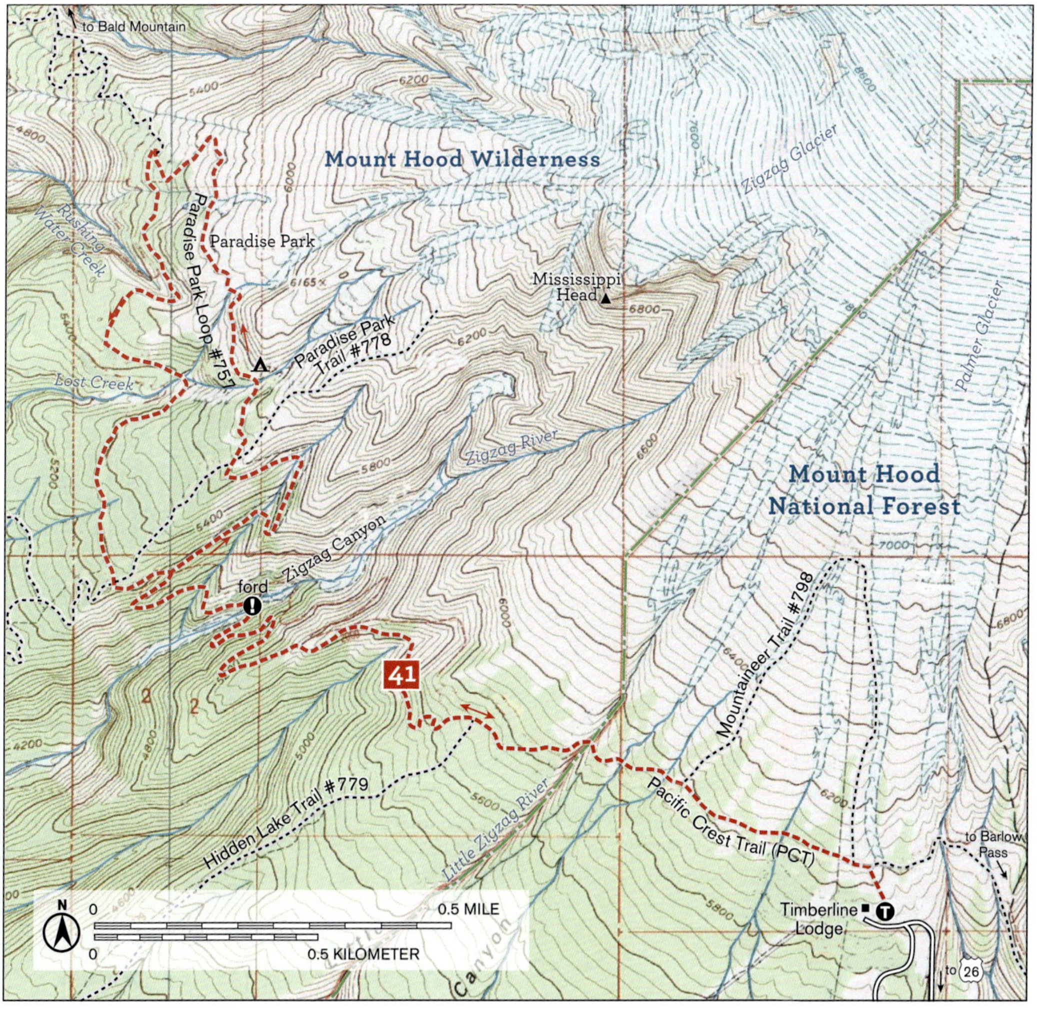

pass a boulder as big as a house just off-trail—you can't help but wonder how it came to its curious resting place.

Just when you're about to go into scenery overload, the trail turns west and descends out of the meadows and back into the trees. Drop through a few switchbacks and connect with the PCT again at 6.2 miles. Turn left (south) to begin your return journey, descending into the barren canyon of Rushing Water Creek, where you get to splash across the base of a wispy waterfall before climbing back out the other side. From here, continue through the woods, cross Lost Creek again, and proceed straight (south) through the lower junction with the Paradise Park Trail at 8 miles. When you reach the junction where you started the Paradise Park Loop, at 8.5 miles, veer right to backtrack to the parking lot. When you get back to Timberline Lodge, reward yourself with a refreshing beverage or tasty snack.

42 East Eliot Moraine and Cooper Spur

Distance: 6.7-mile roundtrip
Difficulty: strenuous
Hiking time: day hike or overnight
Elevation gain: 2680 feet
High point: 8500 feet
Season: Jul–Oct
Management: Mount Hood NF (Hood River)
Protection status: Mount Hood Wilderness
Map: Green Trails 462S: Mount Hood
GPS coordinates: N 45 40.250, W 121 65.482

Getting there: From Hood River, take Oregon Route 35 south toward Government Camp for about 22 miles. Turn right (west) onto Cooper Spur Road and continue 2.4 miles to Cloud Cap Road (NF 3512). Turn left (south) and follow this winding road uphill. The first mile to the Cooper Spur ski area is paved, then it becomes rough and rocky for the remaining 9 miles. Take it slow through the many ruts and potholes. When you reach a fork near the top, make a sharp right turn and drive the last 0.7 mile to the campground and trailhead. A high-clearance vehicle is recommended for this road; for an alternate route, see Other Options below. ***Notes:*** NW Forest Pass or Interagency Pass required for trailhead parking. Self-issue wilderness permit required. Wilderness rules apply. The trail follows a narrow ridge on loose and rocky terrain with steep drops; not recommended for small children or dogs.

Named in the 1880s for David Rose Cooper, who maintained a favorite campsite nearby, the Cooper Spur Trail tops out at nearly 8500 feet. This is the highest established trail on Mount Hood, reaching far into the alpine zone, where there is little shelter from the elements. It's a strenuous slog up loose, sandy switchbacks, where snow may remain long into the summer, but the payoff is one of the most spectacular views you can get without being a technical mountain climber. The following route takes advantage of an alternate trail that parallels the more popular Timberline Trail, and it offers more gobsmacking views than you can count.

Begin your hike at the Cloud Cap trailhead. In the near distance, you can see the old Cloud Cap Inn perched at the edge of the bluff. Constructed in 1889, it was the first resort on the mountain, and it now serves as a base for search and rescue operations. At the signed junction for the Timberline (#600) and Tilly Jane (#600A) Trails, fill out your self-issue wilderness permit and drop the slip in the slot. It's all up from here, so charge forward and head straight (south) up the Timberline Trail into the Mount Hood Wilderness under a canopy of old-growth hemlock, Douglas-fir, and silver fir, with sparse vegetation growing in the sandy soil.

The moonscape of Eliot Glacier basin

The trail quickly comes to a signed fork with the Eliot East Moraine Trail at 0.1 mile. Veer right (southwest) off the Timberline and onto this parallel trail, ascending for 0.2 mile on a fairly steep, sandy tread through increasingly open and exposed terrain. Patches of vibrant lupine and penstemon add splashes of color to the rocky, sandy slope. Before you know it, you've crested the moraine and can enjoy a bird's-eye view over the vast Eliot Glacier basin. Looking to the north, Washington's Mount St. Helens, Mount Rainier, and Mount Adams shine like beacons on the horizon. Below, the Cloud Cap Inn already appears to be far in the distance.

Make your way up the spine of the moraine, following a narrow, sandy path along the knife-edge ridge, marveling at the scene before you. Just try to imagine the view a few centuries ago, when a river of dense ice filled this entire valley. The USGS estimates that the Eliot Glacier once stretched for more than nine miles down the flank of Mount Hood. Even today, it is the largest glacier on the mountain, covering an area of more than 1.6 square kilometers, with a thickness of up to 90 meters. As you gawk at this imposing wall of ice pouring down the mountain, watch your footing on the loose rocks and sand. A slip down either side could be long and injurious.

Follow this catwalk for about 0.8 mile until the path veers to the left (east), heading down into a gully strewn with vibrant buckwheat blooms. Climb back out on the opposite side and traipse along an easy path through a rock garden of lupine and scrubby white pines, arriving at the Cooper Spur Shelter at 1.3 miles. Perched at an elevation of 6800 feet, the shelter was constructed in the 1930s by the Civilian Conservation Corps. It is one of the few remaining relics of Mount Hood's early mountaineering era. With its newer metal roof and heavy door flap, it can provide decent shelter to hikers caught out in the elements. For day hikers, it makes a nice scenic spot for a lunch stop.

From the shelter, the trail to the spur is an unyielding climb up the upper portion of the Eliot Moraine. Heading southeast from the shelter, the grade is only moderate, but the elevation and exposure will make it seem tougher as the path zigs and zags upward. The views continue improving, getting bigger with each switchback you gain, until you reach a bend at 3.1 miles. Here, you're presented with a new panorama.

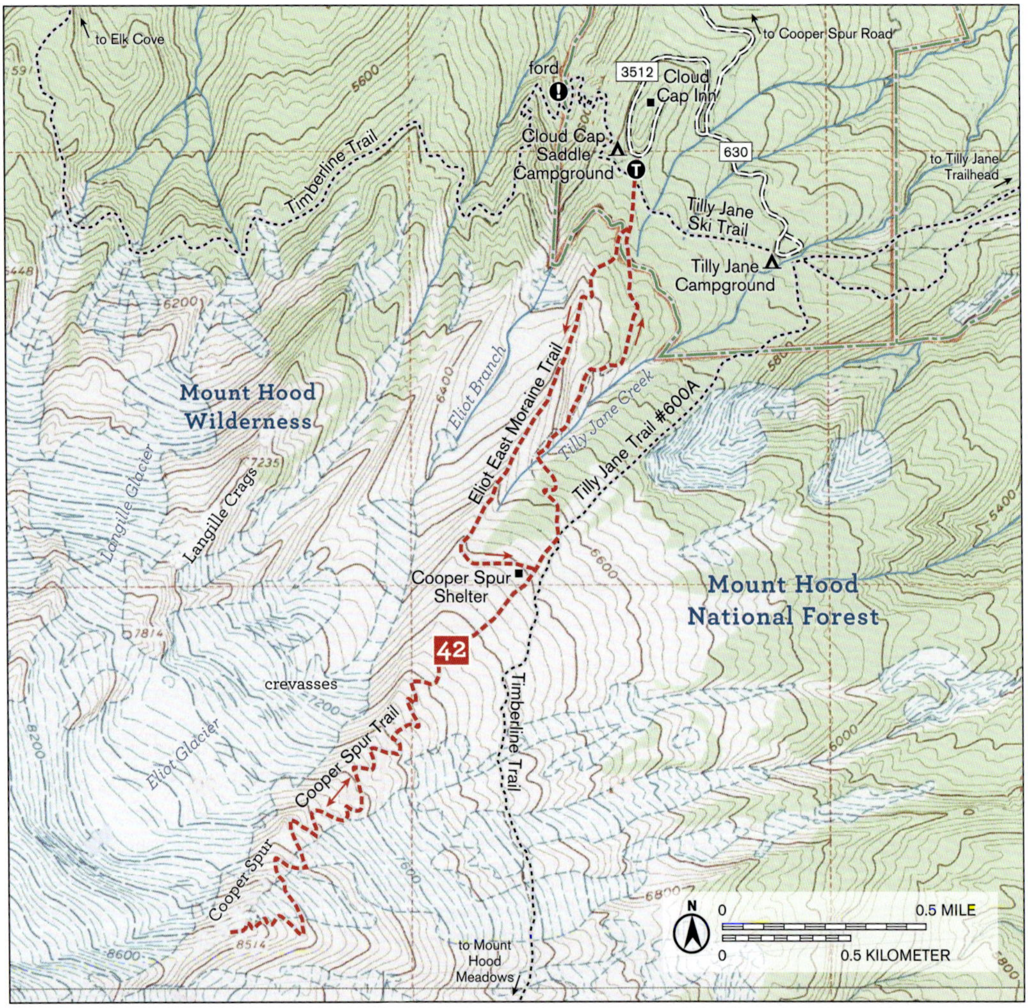

Looking southward, take in a view of the massive Newton Clark Glacier, which dominates Hood's eastern face. In the distance, Mount Jefferson, the Three Sisters, and Diamond Peak come into view. Although the view is jaw-dropping, resist the urge to call it a day here. Proceed upward just a little farther on increasingly tighter, rocky switchbacks to crest the spur at 3.3 miles.

Take your time absorbing the expansive panoramas in every direction and stare up at the east face of the mountain. The path forward turns into a narrow and treacherous climbers' route; traveling farther is not recommended. When you're ready to leave, return to the shelter, pass the moraine trail you came up on, and continue downward to a junction with the Timberline Trail for an easier return route. Turn left (north) onto the Timberline, heading through a swath of white pines and dropping into the rocky, sandy, and likely dry Tilly Jane Creek channel. Look for cairns and posts marking the route as the path weaves its way down the channel. Cross a seasonal spring, then duck into shady hemlock woods at 6.2 miles. Complete your journey with an easy downhill stroll for the last 0.5 mile to your starting point.

Other Options: If you don't want to risk damaging your expensive hybrid vehicle on the tortuous road up to the Cloud Cap trailhead, you can begin your hike farther down the mountain. Where Cloud Cap Road changes to gravel, find the trailhead for the Tilly Jane Ski Trail (#643). This route climbs 2830 feet over 3.5 miles to the Tilly Jane Trail (left; southeast), then upward to the Timberline-Cooper Spur junction. It's a steep and strenuous endeavor through partially burned woods, but it can spare your car if you're willing to make your legs do the work instead.

43 *Elk Meadows*

Distance: 5.5-mile lollipop loop
Difficulty: moderate
Hiking time: day hike
Elevation gain: 1200 feet
High point: 5270 feet
Season: Jul–Oct
Management: Mount Hood NF (Hood River)
Protection status: Mount Hood Wilderness
Map: Trails Illustrated 321: Mount Hood Wilderness
GPS coordinates: N 45 19.332, W 121 37.998

Getting there: From Hood River, drive south on Oregon Route 35 for about 30 miles. Turn right into the Hood River Meadows ski area and proceed 0.3 mile to the trailhead parking area. From Portland, you can reach the trailhead via US Highway 26 and OR 35. ***Notes:*** NW Forest Pass or Interagency Pass required for trailhead parking. Self-issue wilderness permit required. Wilderness rules apply. This hike requires a potentially challenging river crossing. Avoid trampling the meadows.

Perched on the edge of a sprawling meadow choked with summer aster, lupine, and gentian, the Elk Meadows backcountry shelter sits quietly under a grove of shady conifers, gazing upward at the east face of Mount Hood. Built in the 1930s by the Civilian Conservation Corps, it still stands—albeit a bit off-kilter—defiant against the forces of nature and gravity. It makes a delightful destination for a mountain picnic. Here, you can kick back at the edge of a sprawling meadow and watch the clouds drift by Oregon's highest peak.

Fields of aster near Elk Meadows

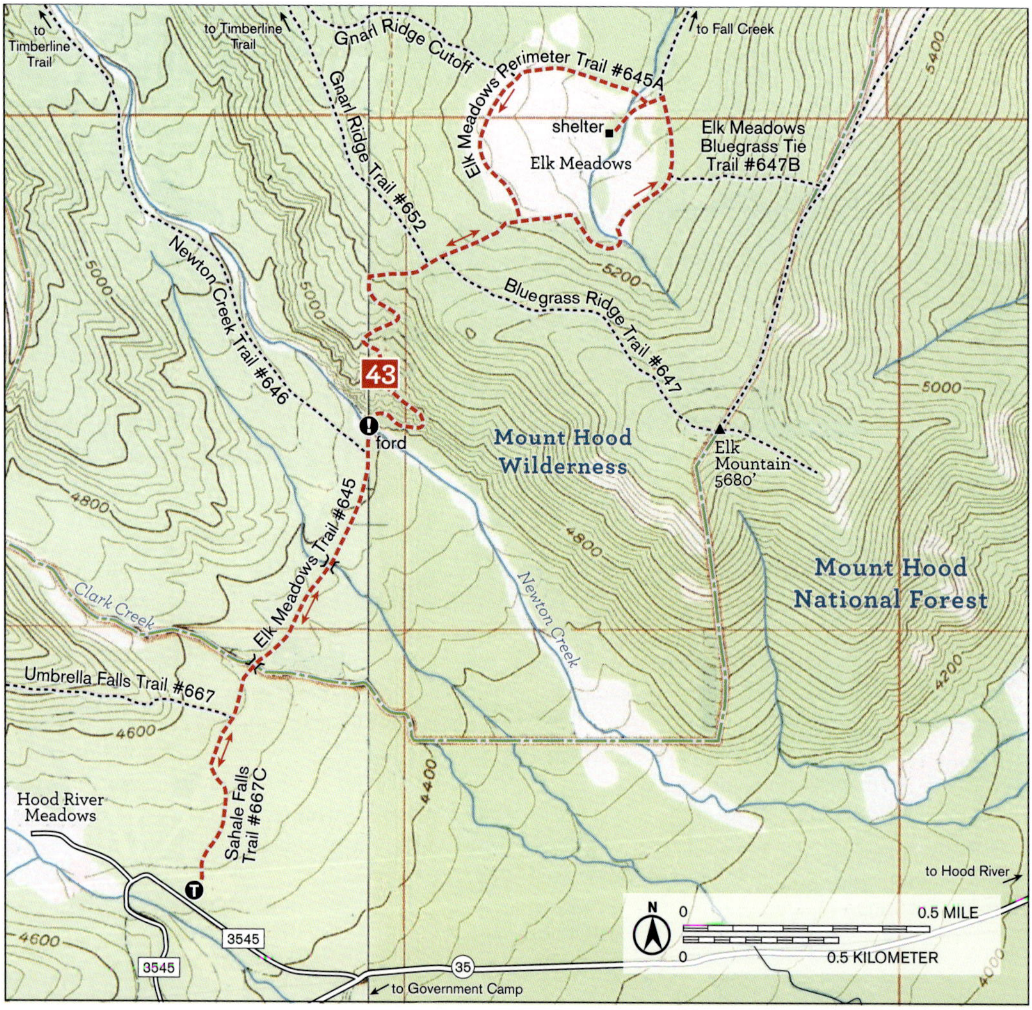

Begin on the Sahale Falls Trail (#667C) by heading north into mossy forest, where huckleberry, lupine, and bear grass are abundant. The trail crosses several Nordic ski paths that are filled with wildflowers in midsummer, then forks off to the left at 0.4 mile. Continue straight ahead (north) at this junction, now on the Elk Meadows Trail (#645). Continue to Clark Creek at 0.5 mile, where a sturdy footbridge spans the drainage. Obtain your self-issue wilderness permit here. Cross the bridge and meander through the forest, circuiting a shallow spring gully choked with wildflowers, until you reach a junction with the Newton Creek Trail (#646) at 1 mile. Just beyond is Newton Creek, where the trail drops into the rocky drainage, requiring you to find a safe passage across. In early summer, with heavy runoff, this may be more challenging. Scan upstream and downstream for a safe place to cross. Once on the other side, pick up the trail again and get ready to gain some elevation.

Start up a series of sweeping switchbacks along the forested valley wall. In many places, the trail will be narrow and slick; seeping springs spill down the slope and across the path, nourishing an abundance of wildflowers. The grade finally eases near the top, and the trail turns east to meet a wide junction at 2 miles. Here, the Gnarl Ridge Trail (#652) branches off to the left (west), and the Bluegrass Ridge Trail (#647) branches off to the right. Continue straight ahead (northeast) to the next junction, at 2.2 miles, and then turn right (east) to start a counterclockwise loop around Elk Meadows. As you circuit the meadows, you'll find a couple of nice campsites along the way. Veer left through the next two junctions to stay on the Elk Meadows loop. Reach a fork at 2.8 miles (unsigned but obvious), and veer left one more time to cross a cool creek, then proceed 0.1 mile to the backcountry shelter at the edge of the meadows. Find a comfy place to drop your gear, get out your lunch, and enjoy the view.

When it's time to get moving again, backtrack to the unsigned junction and turn left (northwest) to continue the loop around the meadows, now on the Elk Meadows Perimeter Trail (#645A). Back in the trees, a few side trails entice you to visit the edge of the meadows for more looks. In late summer, they will often be filled with blue bog gentians. At 3 miles, pass the Gnarl Ridge Cutoff (see Extend Your Trip below) as you continue curving around the west side of the meadow through berry-filled forest. Reach a familiar junction, where you began your loop around the meadows, and turn right (west) to begin your return trip. Retrace your steps down the wall, across Newton and Clark Creeks, and back to your starting point.

Extend Your Trip: For more miles, more elevation, and more views, consider these options for extending your hike through some of Mount Hood's spectacular eastside canyons. For a bigger, 7.8-mile loop that traverses the upper canyon of Newton Creek, veer off the Elk Meadows loop at 3 miles, heading up the Gnarl Ridge Cutoff to the Timberline Trail. Then turn left (west) and dip into the wide, rocky floodplain. Find your way across the braided river and climb the next ridge to a junction with the Newton Creek Trail. Turn left (southeast) and walk the view-packed, knife-edge trail before dropping into the forest again. At 6.8 miles, meet the Elk Meadows Trail again and turn right (south) for the last mile back to the trailhead.

For an even bigger 12-mile loop that you could stretch into an overnight, keep going on the Timberline, passing the junction with the Newton Creek Trail. Circuit the next big ridge before dropping down into the wide and picturesque Heather Canyon. At 6.1 miles, hop across the falls at the top of Clark Creek. Climb out of the canyon for a 2-mile rolling jaunt across the Mount Hood Meadows ski area, then veer left (south) onto the Umbrella Falls Trail (#667) at 8.5 miles. Follow this path down, pass the waterfall, and then veer right (south) onto the Sahale Falls Trail (#667C) at 10.3 miles. This trail steadily descends, paralleling the East Fork Hood River for a spell, as it brings you back to the parking area.

44 *Timberline Trail*

Distance: 39.4 miles
Difficulty: strenuous
Hiking time: multiday
Elevation gain: 9630 feet
High point: 7330 feet
Season: Jul–Oct
Management: Mount Hood NF (Zigzag, Hood River)
Protection status: Mount Hood Wilderness
Map: Green Trails 262S: Mount Hood
GPS coordinates: N 45 33.289, W 121 71.125

Getting there: From Portland, drive east on US Highway 26 for 39 miles to Government Camp. At the east end of town, turn left (north) on Timberline Highway and continue 6 miles to the Timberline Lodge parking area. From the east, Timberline Lodge is about 100 miles north of Bend, via US 97 and US 26. ***Notes:*** NW Forest Pass or Interagency Pass required at some trailheads for parking. Wilderness rules apply. Complete a self-issue

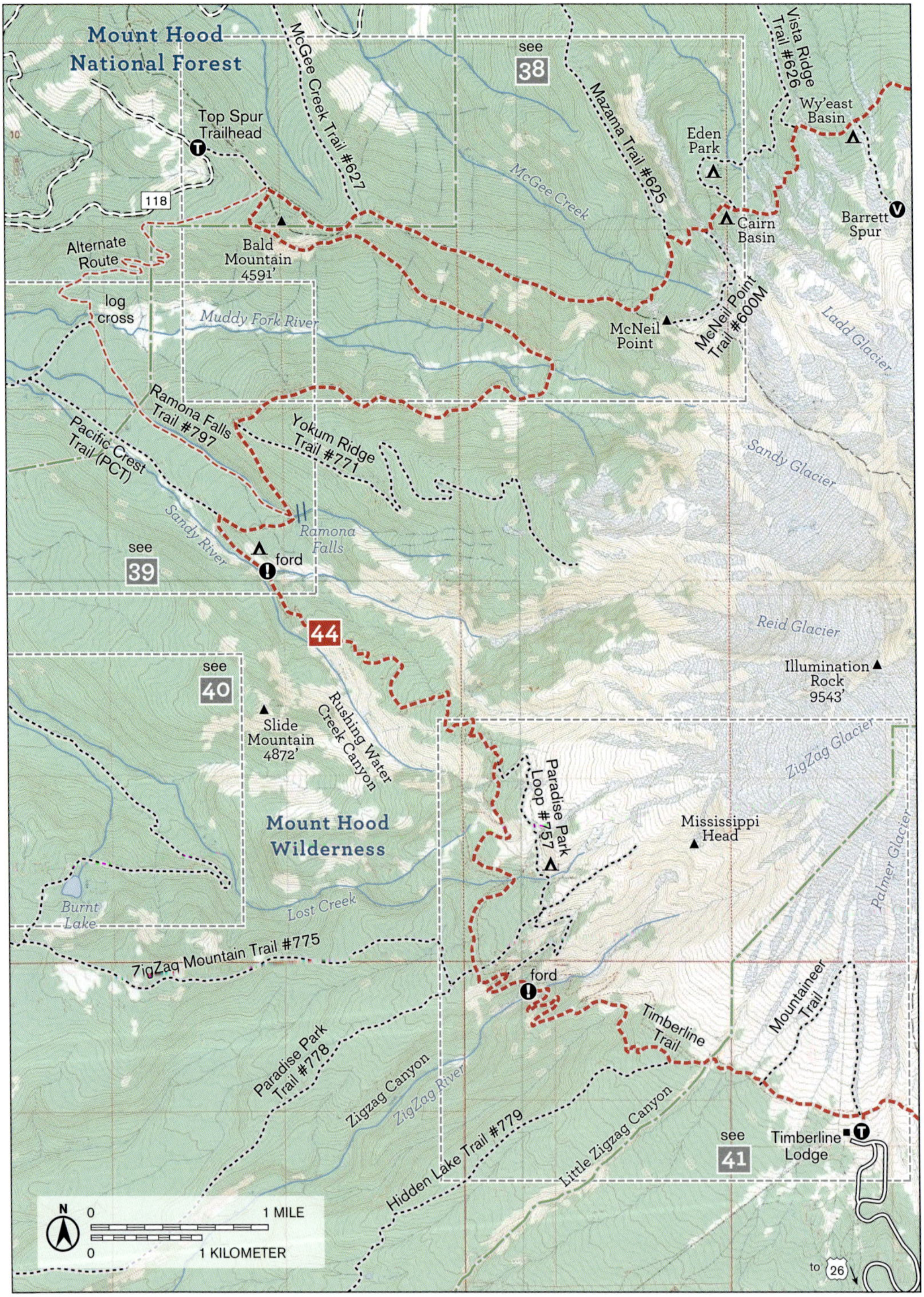
Mount Hood National Forest
see 38
McGee Creek Trail #627
Mazama Trail #625
Vista Ridge Trail #626
Wy'east Basin
Top Spur Trailhead
Eden Park
McGee Creek
118
Cairn Basin
Barrett Spur
Alternate Route
Bald Mountain 4591'
log cross
Muddy Fork River
McNeil Point
McNeil Point Trail #600M
Ladd Glacier
Ramona Falls Trail #797
Yokum Ridge Trail #771
Pacific Crest Trail (PCT)
Sandy Glacier
Sandy River
Ramona Falls
see 39
ford
44
Reid Glacier
see 40
Illumination Rock 9543'
Slide Mountain 4872'
Rushing Water Creek Canyon
Paradise Park Loop #757
ZigZag Glacier
Mississippi Head
Mount Hood Wilderness
Palmer Glacier
Burnt Lake
Lost Creek
ZigZag Mountain Trail #775
ford
Mountaineer Trail
Timberline Trail
Paradise Park Trail #778
Zigzag Canyon
ZigZag River
Hidden Lake Trail #779
Little Zigzag Canyon
see 41
Timberline Lodge
0 1 MILE
0 1 KILOMETER
to 26

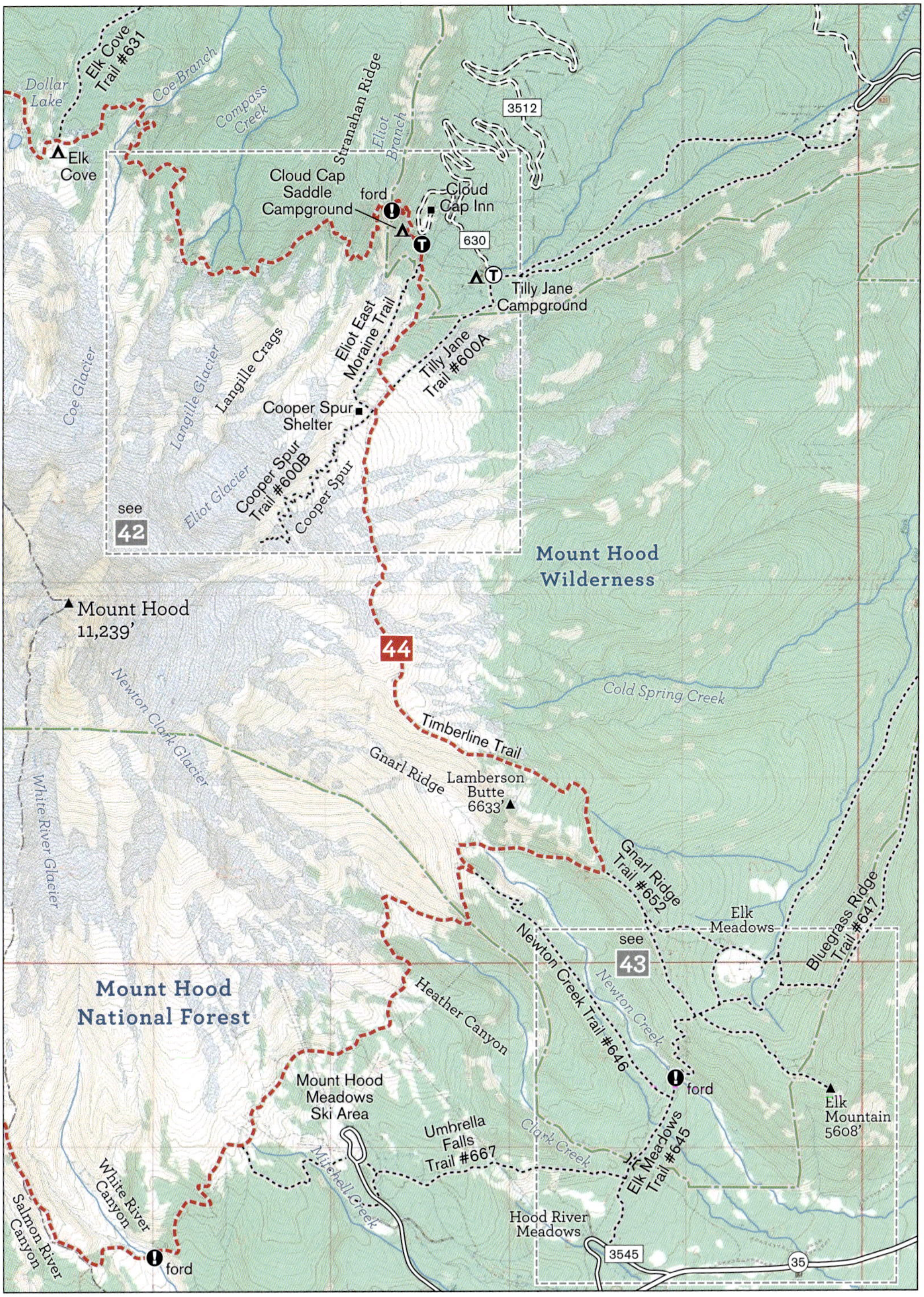
Dollar Lake
Elk Cove Trail #631
Coe Branch
Compass Creek
Elk Cove
Stranahan Ridge
Eliot Branch
3512
Cloud Cap Saddle Campground
ford
Cloud Cap Inn
630
Tilly Jane Campground
Eliot East Moraine Trail
Tilly Jane Trail #600A
Langille Crags
Coe Glacier
Langille Glacier
Cooper Spur Shelter
Cooper Spur Trail #600B
Cooper Spur
Eliot Glacier
see 42
Mount Hood Wilderness
Mount Hood 11,239'
44
Newton Clark Glacier
Cold Spring Creek
Timberline Trail
Gnarl Ridge
Lamberson Butte 6633'
White River Glacier
Gnarl Ridge Trail #652
Elk Meadows
Bluegrass Ridge Trail #647
see 43
Newton Creek Trail #646
Newton Creek
Mount Hood National Forest
Heather Canyon
ford
Elk Mountain 5608'
Mount Hood Meadows Ski Area
Umbrella Falls Trail #667
Clark Creek
Elk Meadows Trail #645
Mitchell Creek
White River Canyon
Salmon River Canyon
Hood River Meadows
3545
35
ford

wilderness permit at the appropriate kiosk. Some sections traverse loose, steep slopes and/or require river fords, which can be challenging during high runoff periods. Dogs should be leashed.

The Timberline is Oregon's signature round-the-mountain hiking trail. With a circumference of nearly forty miles—and involving nearly ten thousand feet of elevation gain—it's a challenging and exhilarating adventure that tests even the most capable of hikers. The traditional way to hike the Timberline (as described here) starts at the historic Timberline Lodge and proceeds clockwise around the mountain. However, you can start the Timberline Trail from any number of trailheads around the mountain and/or hike it in reverse. These additional options allow you to enjoy the Timberline in a variety of ways, in whole or in part, depending on your personal interests, time, and ability.

From the Timberline Lodge, walk the service road on the east side of the building up to the Timberline/Pacific Crest Trail (PCT) crossing. This marks the 0-mile point. Head west, strolling through the ski area and enjoying the rainbow of wildflowers decorating the barren ski slopes. Pass a few side trails that head up and down the mountain. At the 1-mile mark, reach the boundary of the Mount Hood Wilderness; fill out your self-issue wilderness permit at the kiosk. Then dip through Little Zigzag Canyon and head into woods of mixed fir and hemlock on a generally downward slope. At 2.3 miles, arrive at the brink of the impressive Zigzag Canyon. Take in the expansive view up the canyon to Mississippi Head and Mount Hood's summit, and down the canyon toward the Zigzag River's convergence with the Sandy River.

Switchback down to the river and find a safe crossing. This is the first of many unbridged rivers that you will need to ford. Once across, switchback up the other side to a junction with the Paradise Park Loop Trail (#757; see Hike 41) at 3.6 miles. This worthwhile alternate route parallels the Timberline for a few miles, offering sprawling wildflower meadows and in-your-face views of Mount Hood's western face, along with plenty of great campsite options. For now, continue on the Timberline, passing through a junction with the Paradise Park Trail (#778), and meandering through shady woods along the western flank of the mountain. Views are scarce for a while, until you contour through the Rushing Water Creek Canyon at 5.3 miles, where the trail crosses the base of a wispy waterfall. After another 0.5 mile, meet the other end of the Paradise Park Loop Trail and begin a long, steady descent to the Sandy River, which you'll reach at 8.6 miles.

This river crossing is the lowest point along the Timberline. Find a safe spot to cross and pick up the trail on the other side. At 9 miles, arrive at the next junction. Here, the PCT splits off left (northwest), while the Timberline veers right (east). Stick with the Timberline and proceed another 0.5 mile to spectacular Ramona Falls (see Hike 39)—arguably the prettiest waterfall on Mount Hood. Just across the bridge below the falls, the Timberline branches up to the right (northwest), around Yocum Ridge, while the Ramona Falls Trail (#797) continues west. The next stretch can be challenging, with a long traverse of a steep, loose slope and then several potentially confusing crossings of the upper Muddy Fork River. The alternative is to proceed down the Ramona Falls Trail and reconnect with the PCT, then hike up the PCT to reconnect with the Timberline at the Bald Mountain junction at 14.8 miles.

Once you reach the wide, signed Bald Mountain junction, the PCT heads off northwest to Lolo Pass, while the Timberline hooks around Bald Mountain and heads east to ascend a long ridgeline as it contours the northern flanks of Mount Hood. The trail meanders through pocket meadows of beargrass and pasque flower, passing the Mazama Trail (#625) at 17.7 miles. Just beyond, the McNeil Point Trail (#600M; see Hike 38) forks right (southeast) for a 0.9-mile ascent to an old stone shelter perched high on the mountain. The Timberline then continues through Cairn

Get above it all on Mount Hood's Timberline Trail

Basin at 18.4 miles, which used to be more pleasant before the area burned, but there are still a few worthwhile campsites on the fringes. As you continue, the trail dips in and out of many miles of burned woods, all charred by the 2011 Dollar Lake Fire.

The Timberline then meets the Vista Ridge Trail (#626; see Hike 37) at 19.4 miles. Just beyond is the spectacularly pretty Wy'east Basin, mercifully spared from the fire. A climbers' path veers off the Timberline here to ascend Barret Spur, offering impressive views of the Ladd and Coe Glaciers. There are also some choice campsites in the area. Speed on by a junction with the truly terrible Pinnacle Ridge Trail (#630) to another easy-to-miss user path at 20 miles. This route branches right (south) to ascend to little Dollar Lake, with a few decent campsites. The Timberline then dips into Elk Cove at 20.7 miles. This picturesque basin has a few good campsites south of the Timberline along the Elk Cove Trail (#631). Enjoy this while you can, because the next handful of miles to Cloud Cap are the most unimpressive of the whole loop—a lot of burned forest, numerous challenging creek crossings, and a grueling descent and ascent of the Eliot Branch Canyon. The Eliot is the most treacherous water crossing on the Timberline Trail. Use extreme caution when crossing, following proper fording techniques. If the water level looks too high or fast, consider turning around.

Once you reach the small campground at Cloud Cap, at 26 miles, you can breathe easy—at least for a little while. Use the campground's faucet to replenish your containers, as water sources are scarce for many miles. The Timberline now turns south to traverse the high, exposed east slope of Mount Hood, where the views get increasingly expansive. At 27.1 miles, pass the Tilly Jane Trail (#600A), which comes up from the east, and the Cooper Spur Trail (#600B; see Hike 42), which climbs west toward the Cooper

Spur shelter and viewpoint. This is the highest developed trail on Mount Hood, offering gob-smacking panoramas of the Eliot and Newton Clark Glaciers. It's a 4.4-mile roundtrip with 1830 feet of elevation gain, but it's definitely worth the extra time and effort.

Continue south, reaching the highest point on the Timberline at 28.5 miles. The scenery is a vast moonscape of volcanic rock and lingering snow-fields, with big views in every direction. There are few campsites on this side of the mountain, with little running water. As the trail starts descending, it reaches the top of Gnarl Ridge and another stunning viewpoint at 29.2 miles. From here, the trail bends eastward and makes a long, steady descent of Lamberson Butte to reach Newton Creek at 32 miles. Find a safe crossing, then head up and over another long ridge to traverse the wide, scenic Heather Canyon. Hop across the top of the Clark Creek waterfall and ascend the next ridge into the Mount Hood Meadows Ski Area. Here the trail meanders for several miles, crossing numerous ski slopes filled with wildflowers.

Just beyond a service road on the south side of the ski area, at 35.7 miles, the Umbrella Falls Trail (#667) splits off to the left (south). Continue on the Timberline, beginning a long descent to the wide White River Canyon. Follow cairn markers up the floodplain to cross several branches of the braided river; crossing can be tricky during high runoff seasons. Once safely across, climb out of the canyon to connect with the PCT once more at 38 miles. The Timberline/PCT now makes a steady northwestward ascent up a long, sandy ridgeline between the White and Salmon River Canyons. The trail bends westward for the last 0.5 mile before entering the Timberline Lodge Ski Area and ending at the service road where you began. Once you've finished, reward yourself with a refreshing beverage while reclining in a big, cushy chair at the Ramshead Bar in the historic lodge.

45 *High Prairie and Lookout Mountain*

Distance: 2.5-mile loop
Difficulty: easy
Hiking time: short day hike or overnight
Elevation gain: 530 feet
High point: 6525 feet
Season: Jul–Oct
Management: Mount Hood NF (Hood River)
Protection status: Badger Creek Wilderness
Map: Trails Illustrated 321: Mount Hood Wilderness
GPS coordinates: N 45 21.120, W 121 31.866

Getting there: From Hood River, drive south on Mount Hood Highway (Oregon Route 35) for about 25 miles. Turn left (east) on Brooks Meadow Road (Forest Road 44) and drive for 3.8 miles, then go right (south) on Lookout Mountain Road (FR 4410). Take this good gravel road 4.6 miles to a fork, then turn left to reach the trailhead and parking area.
Notes: NW Forest Pass or Interagency Pass required for trailhead parking. Wilderness rules apply.

There are two ways to reach the fantastic Mount Hood views on top of Lookout Mountain. One is a grueling, 3100-foot ascent from a trailhead on OR 35, via the Gumjuwac (#480) and Divide (#458) Trails. The other route, described here, is a much gentler loop trail that starts at a high, remote trailhead and makes a casual ascent through flower-laden meadows. You'll hike through pleasant hemlock and fir forest to reach the 6525-foot summit, which stares across the Hood River Valley to Mount Hood and out over the Badger Creek Wilderness. Since the trail is not long or difficult, pack a picnic and plan to hang out for a while.

Start the High Prairie Trail (#493) on the south side of FR 4420, opposite the trailhead

The High Prairie Loop offers a lot of bang for its buck.

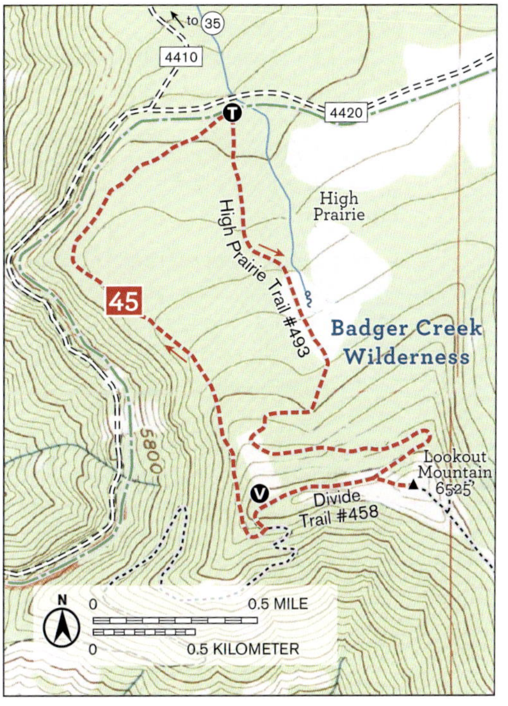

parking area. Stroll into the Badger Creek Wilderness and quickly reach a junction. To the right is your return route; for now, continue straight ahead (south) on a wide, old roadbed that gently ascends through open meadows of aster, arnica, camas, shooting star, and marsh marigold. Silver and noble firs line the trailside as you continue. At 0.5 mile, the trail curves to enter shady hemlock and fir woodlands and begins making a winding ascent of Lookout Mountain's north flank. Still on a fairly gentle grade, look for columbine, lupine, and wild strawberry alongside the trail.

As you approach 0.8 mile, exit the trees into a wide clearing, where the trail makes a U-turn to continue upward to another U-turn, just below Lookout Mountain's summit. At 1.2 miles, arrive at another junction. To bag the summit, turn left (east) on the Divide Trail (#458) and proceed 0.1 mile to the tippy-top, where a fire lookout stood until the late 1960s. To continue the loop and score equally impressive views without a detour, turn right (west) on the Divide Trail and walk the ridgeline 0.2 mile through a rock garden of Jacob's ladder, paintbrush, lupine, penstemon, and stonecrop to a rocky mound with a grand panorama that sweeps across the horizon. Enjoy stellar views of central Oregon peaks to the south, Washington peaks to the north, and Mount Hood, directly west.

After a long break at the viewpoint, head a few paces down the south side of the ridge to reconnect with the High Prairie Trail. Turn right (west) to continue the loop, which contours around the west side of the mountain. The path bends north and traverses a gravelly slope of red cinders, where a craggy volcanic pinnacle juts out of the hillside—another spot with a nice view. Then it's back into the trees, where you'll pass a truck-size lava boulder sitting beside the trail at 1.6 miles. Commence a steady descent under viewless woods filled with Oregon grape and ferns. The grade eventually eases, turning northeast to cross several pocket meadows adorned with colorful summer wildflowers. When you reach the junction at the end of the loop, turn left (north) to exit back to the parking area.

46 *Mirror Lake*

Distance: 4.1-mile roundtrip
Difficulty: moderate
Hiking time: short day hike or overnight
Elevation gain: 970 feet
High point: 4140 feet
Season: Jun–Oct
Management: Mount Hood NF (Zigzag)
Protection status: Salmon-Huckleberry Wilderness
Map: Trails Illustrated 321: Mount Hood Wilderness
GPS coordinates: N 45 18.156, W 121 46.638

Getting there: From Portland, drive east on Mount Hood Highway (US Highway 26) for approximately 55 miles to the Mirror Lake trailhead, at the west end of Government Camp.
Notes: NW Forest Pass or Interagency Pass required for trailhead parking. Very popular and crowded on summer weekends. Do not park in the Skibowl West parking lot or on the side of the highway.

If there's one hike on Mount Hood that draws locals and visitors alike, it's Mirror Lake. Since the opening of the rerouted trail in the fall of 2018, access is safer and easier, even though it's a little bit longer. The new route meanders under a canopy of mixed conifers and over a series of rustic footbridges to connect with the old trail about halfway up the hillside. Once at the lakeshore, the payoff is huge: a postcard-perfect view of Mount Hood from across the far side of the lake, which (in the right conditions) perfectly mirrors Oregon's highest peak. Of course, you will likely be sharing the trail and the views with a lot of other visitors, so put on your smiley face.

Begin from the west end of the parking area, near the restroom and information board. The trail begins as a paved, barrier-free path that snakes down toward Camp Creek into fir, hemlock, and cedar woods. Look for bunches of rhododendrons, bear grass, and lady fern along the

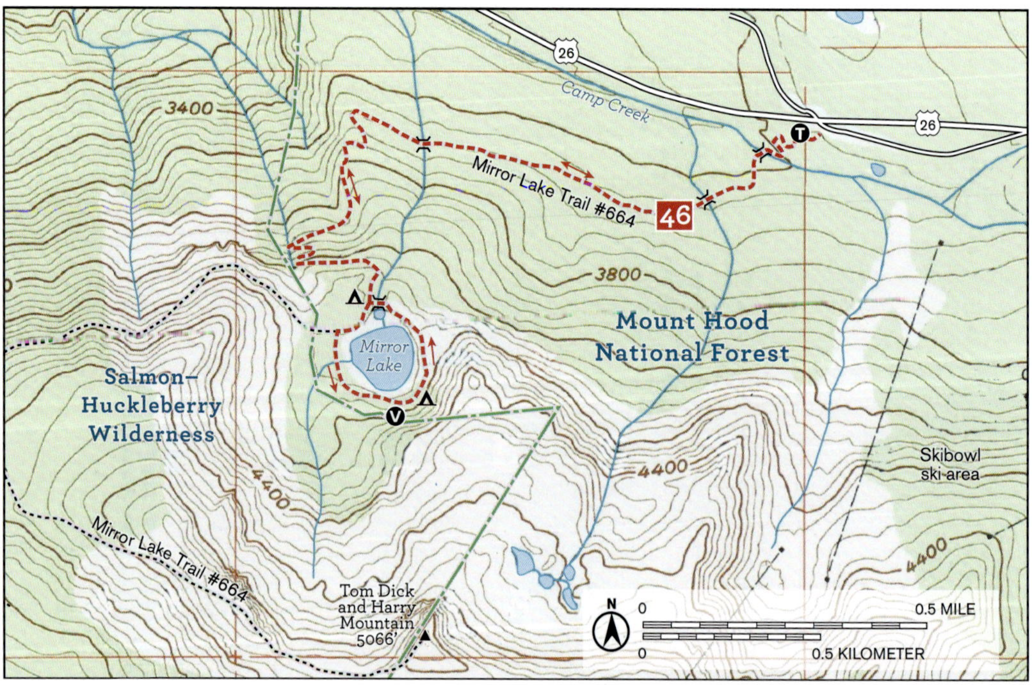

Get your own postcard-worthy shot of Mirror Lake.

trailside. At 0.2 mile, the paved section ends, and the path crosses the creek on a nice footbridge. Now on wide, duff-covered tread, meander westward on an undulating course, crossing numerous bridges over small gullies and dribbling creeks. More shrubbery begins to occupy the trailside, mostly in the form of mountain rhododendron, which blooms with vibrant clusters of pink and white flowers in early summer.

At 0.9 mile, cross another rustic bridge, this one over Mirror Lake's outlet stream, where the water cascades down the hill in a series of steps. Here, you may find patches of inside-out flower (duckfoot), wild ginger, and snowberry along the trail. Now the easy walking is over and it's time to head up, beginning with a fairly steep, curving ascent to connect with the original Mirror Lake Trail at 1.2 miles. Climb into denser woods through a series of short switchbacks that eventually ease alongside the outlet creek. At 1.8 miles, the trail forks at the beginning of the 0.5-mile lake loop. Veer right (southwest) and continue a short distance through the trees to the lake, which fills a wide, tree-ringed basin. The high, rocky ridgeline above the lake is 5066-foot Tom Dick and Harry Mountain.

Spend some time exploring the lake area, beginning with the small beach to the left (east), which grants access to the lake for wading; a few short side trails right (west) lead to secluded campsites. The lakeside loop reaches a junction at 1.9 miles, where the trail to Tom Dick and Harry Mountain branches off to the right (see Extend Your Trip). The trail then loops around the backside of the lake on planked boardwalk through boggy rose spiraea and fireweed. Look for the walkway leading left (north) to the water's edge. This is where you'll get the view that you came for: Mount Hood reflected in Mirror Lake. Photographers, if you're looking for that prize-winning shot, plan your visit for early morning or evening, when the lake water is at its calmest and the golden hour lights up the mountainside.

The trail continues around the lake and back under the cover of trees, where a few more campsites can be found. Views are then limited to the forested surroundings, with just the slightest view of the lake through the trees. Along the way, look for salmonberries, monkey flowers, and big Washington lilies, with their notably white, freckled petals. Close the lake loop by crossing the outlet on a log bridge, where thorny devil's club fills the gully. In a few more paces, return to the junction where you started the loop. Turn right (north) and make quick work of the return trip, retracing your route back to the parking area.

Extend Your Trip: For an even bigger view, consider adding a side trip to the top of Tom Dick and Harry Mountain. This roundtrip on a moderate grade adds 3.1 miles and 850 feet of elevation gain to your hike—but the additional work is worth it. Start by veering off the lake loop into the Salmon-Huckleberry Wilderness to contour an open slope of paintbrush, penstemon, pokeweed, lupine, thimbleberry, and Columbia lily. About 1 mile up, the trail makes an abrupt U-turn at a large rock pile and continues through scrubby pine forest. After winding upward over increasingly rocky terrain, mount the ridgetop at 1.6 miles. From this high perch, the view is all-encompassing in every direction. To the north, the wide profile of Mount Hood takes center stage; Mirror Lake is far below. To the south, look for central Oregon's Cascade peaks lined up on the horizon.

47 *Old Salmon River*

Distance: 4.9-mile roundtrip
Difficulty: easy
Hiking time: day hike
Elevation gain: 470 feet
High point: 1600 feet
Season: Apr–Nov
Management: Mount Hood NF (Zigzag)
Protection status: Salmon-Huckleberry Wilderness
Map: Trails Illustrated 321: Mount Hood Wilderness
GPS coordinates: N 45 18.504, W 121 56.580

Getting there: From Sandy, drive east on US Highway 26 for about 40 miles to Welches. Turn right (south) on East Salmon River Road and proceed 2.6 miles to the north trailhead or 5 miles to the south trailhead. ***Notes:*** NW Forest Pass or Interagency Pass required for trailhead parking. There's a lot to discover on this trail; bring a nature guide to help you identify the plants, birds, and animals. If the north trailhead parking area is full, proceed to the south trailhead and hike it in reverse.

Roam the Forests of Fangorn on the Old Salmon River Trail.

The Old Salmon River Trail (#742A) is a pleasant, family-friendly hike that's easy to get to, and it's often accessible earlier in the season than many other trails near Mount Hood due to its lower elevation. Enjoy a pleasant adventure through a primeval river bottom, replete with towering old-growth forest and abundant wildflowers, mosses, and fungi. The only thing missing is the dinosaurs—for those, you'll just have to use your imagination.

Start by descending into a mossy jungle of giant hemlock, cedar, fir, and big-leaf maple, with abundant vine maple filling the understory. Sword ferns, thimbleberry, sorrel, fairybells, and fringe cup carpet the forest floor. Following rain showers, when everything is damp and dripping, the scene is positively primordial; on bluebird days, scant sunlight is filtered through curtains of witch's hair, which gives the forest an illuminated, enchanted appearance. After the quick descent, cross a footbridge over a feeder creek and traipse along the riverside, where the trail is nearly flat and mostly duffy. It's easy walking, allowing you to leisurely admire the multiple layers of lush forest around you.

Near the half-mile mark, cross another creek and proceed up a winding series of steps to the side of a massive Douglas-fir that had its base blown out by a lightning strike. The trail then undulates forward, crosses yet another creek, and enters a wide area on the riverbank. Here, at around 0.8 mile, a side trail climbs left (east) to the road, and an old camp area can be found to the right (west). Camping on the river is not permitted within a quarter mile of the road, but this location makes for a nice picnic spot with good river access. If you're interested in a chilly dip, there's a deep, calm spot in the river here, between two riffles.

Continue strolling along upstream, where another side trail breaks off left (east) to the road at 1 mile. Just beyond, the trail crosses a wide, rocky creek bed. If there's water flowing, you can hop across on the many large rocks. The path then bends upward through copious berry shrubs and pops out of the trees to meet East Salmon River Road at 1.3 miles; on the opposite side of the road is a large parking area and outhouse. Carefully walk the shoulder of the road, right beside the river, for the next 0.1 mile, then pick up the trail again by veering right (southeast) back into the woods. At 1.5 miles, notice the giant, moss-covered nurse log that's been cut through. This is a signature feature of ancient forests—fallen trees nurturing new saplings.

The trail crosses another bridged creek at 1.8 miles, after which the tread gets more rugged, with frequent rocks and roots to trip you up—so watch your footing. It then skirts the Green Canyon Campground, sticking to the riverside through

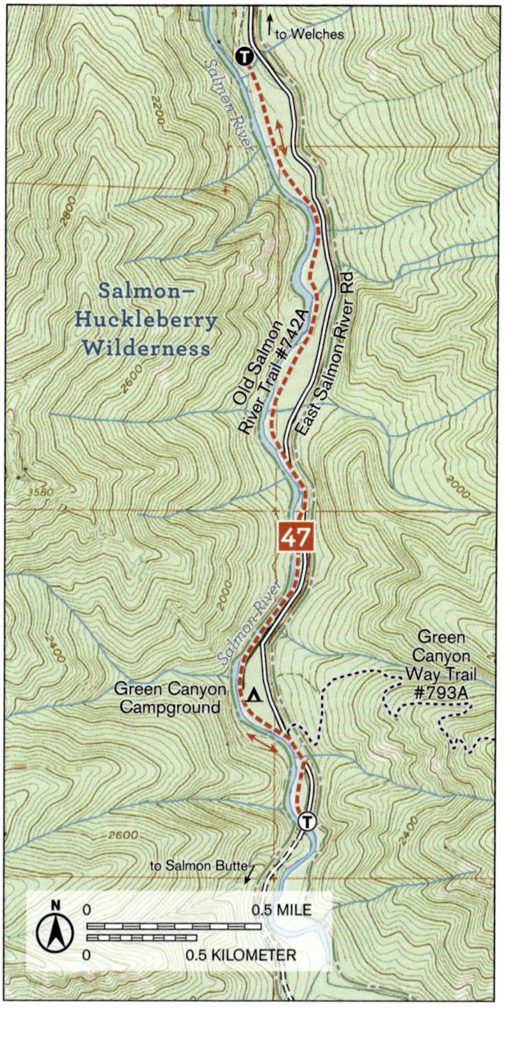

abundant mixed ferns, blackberry, salmonberry, and salal. The final stretch pops out onto the roadside once again to hug a bend in the river, then ducks back into the trees for the last 0.2 mile. Arrive at the south trailhead by the Salmon River bridge at 2.4 miles. Now all you have to do is walk back the way you came, enjoying it all over again.

48 Twin Lakes

Distance: 7.3-mile lollipop loop
Difficulty: easy
Hiking time: day hike or overnight
Elevation gain: 1160 feet
High point: 4520 feet
Season: Jul–Oct
Management: Mount Hood NF (Clackamas River)
Protection status: Mount Hood Wilderness
Map: Trails Illustrated 321: Mount Hood Wilderness
GPS coordinates: N 45 16.974, W 121 41.008

Getting there: From Sandy, take US Highway 26 east for about 35 miles; stay left at the Oregon Route 35 junction to continue south toward Bend. At the top of Wapinitia Pass, turn left (east) into the Frog Lake Sno-Park. ***Notes:*** NW Forest Pass or Interagency Pass required for trailhead parking; Sno-Park permit required November 1–April 30. Wilderness rules apply.

Just a little south of Mount Hood, the forest-ringed pools of Twin Lakes are a pleasant summer destination for a swim, picnic lunch, or easy overnight in the backcountry. In fall, the lakes are one of the better places to admire autumn color, when seasonal huckleberry and vine maple set the forest aflame with hues of red, orange, and yellow. You can even snowshoe to the lower lake in winter and spring, thanks to the wide, well-marked trail and fairly easy grades.

Begin at the trailhead on the north end of the large parking area and walk about twenty yards to a well-signed junction with the Pacific Crest Trail (PCT). Turn right (east) and commence a comfortable stroll on wide, duff-covered trail under mossy hemlocks. Look for huckleberry, rhododendron, and mountain strawberry carpeting the forest floor. After a few minutes of easy walking, the trail starts gaining elevation on a moderate grade. Take note of the blue diamond markers high up on the trees; these indicate the route for winter snow travel. The grade finally eases at 1.4 miles, when the trail comes to a wide junction at the boundary of the Mount Hood Wilderness.

Pack a picnic for a day, or your tent for an overnight, at the Twin Lakes.

From this point, turn right (east) onto the Twin Lakes Trail (#495) and proceed through a viewless saddle before making a gentle, curving descent into the lower lake basin. Catch a few peeks of the lake on the way down and cross a seasonal spring at around 1.9 miles. Just beyond, as the trail levels out for nice, easy walking, look for a side trail on the right (south) at 2.1 miles. Turn onto this short spur and proceed to the shore of Lower Twin Lake. Nearby, you'll find several campsites and plenty of lakeshore logs where you can sit to admire the scene. If you feel like taking a refreshing dip, lake access is easy. A 0.7-mile path circuits the lake for more exploring, and the Frog Lake Butte Trail (#484) starts here as well.

When you're ready for the next lake, return to the main trail, turn right (south) and begin a short, curving ascent to reach the southern shore of Upper Twin Lake at 2.7 miles. From here, you'll get a nice view across the lake, with Mount Hood peeking above the trees. A few hidden campsites can be found in the trees around the lake. Proceed along the east side of the lake through copious huckleberry and bear grass, passing the Palmateer Trail (#482) and then veering left past a spur to the Palmateer Trail. Now snake upward through the woods, curving around the north flank of 4767-foot Bird Butte, and reconnect with the PCT at 4.3 miles. For the home stretch, turn left (south) on the PCT and commence a gradual ascent, now along the west slope of Bird Butte. The trail is wide and duff-covered, making for comfortable walking back to the Twin Lakes Trail junction at 5.9 miles. From here, continue south on the PCT to retrace your steps back to your starting point.

49 *Timothy Lake*

Distance: 12.4-mile loop
Difficulty: moderate
Hiking time: long day hike or overnight
Elevation gain: 660 feet
High point: 3340 feet
Season: Jun–Nov
Management: Mount Hood NF (Zigzag) and Portland General Electric (PGE)
Protection status: none
Map: Trails Illustrated 321: Mount Hood Wilderness
GPS coordinates: N 45 08.868, W 121 44.862

Getting there: From Sandy, take US Highway 26 east for about 39 miles; stay left at the Oregon Route 35 junction to continue south toward Bend. Turn right on Oregon Skyline

Summer at Timothy Lake. Serenity now.

Road (Forest Road 42) and drive for 4.1 miles. Then go right on Abbott Road (FR 58) and drive for 2.4 miles to Little Crater Lake, staying right at a fork at 0.9 mile. Turn left on FR 230 into Little Crater Lake Campground, and drive around the camp loop to the parking area and trailhead. ***Notes:*** NW Forest Pass or Interagency Pass required for trailhead parking. A portion of this loop is open for multiuse; be courteous and share the trails. Visit the PGE website for information about camping and nightly fees. The best campsites for backpacking are at the Meditation Point peninsula on the west side of the lake or dispersed sites on the east side of the lake.

Timothy Lake is the largest lake in the Mount Hood area and offers plenty of outdoor opportunities for hikers, backpackers, campers, mountain bikers, paddlers, and more. This loop, which utilizes a stretch of the Pacific Crest Trail (PCT), can be started from several other trailheads nearer the lake, but the backdoor approach described here helps you avoid some of the busy summer crowds. With both primitive campsites and developed campgrounds all around the lake, this is a great entry-level backpacking hike for stretching your trail legs.

Start at the Little Crater Meadow trailhead and head west on a paved path for 800 feet to the Little Crater Lake viewpoint. Take in the sight of the deep sapphire pool, then continue to a wide junction with the Pacific Crest Trail (PCT) at 0.3 mile. Turn left (south) and amble along wide, duff-covered trail under shady Douglas-firs and ponderosa pines, with a medley of huckleberry, Oregon grape, vanilla leaf, and bunchberry at your feet. At 0.6 mile, the trail forks at a well-signed junction, with the PCT veering off to the left (south) and the Timothy Lake Trail (#528) heading off to the right (west). For a counterclockwise loop, take the right fork, saving the PCT for the return.

Proceed over a short boardwalk through a boggy stretch, then cross a footbridge over Cooper Creek. Just beyond, a short side trail branches off left (south) to a view over a sprawling wetlands meadow. Continue hiking and enter the North Arm Campground at 1.4 miles. Pass a vault toilet and a few campsites to contour the slope above the North Arm of Timothy Lake, where you can access water and views at a narrow, rocky beach. The trail merges with an old lakeside route at 2.1 miles and proceeds along the west shore of the main body of Timothy Lake.

Enjoy a pleasant walk on gently rolling trail under a mix of hemlock, fir, and vine maple. Numerous side trails branch off to designated campsites, many with nice lake views. At 3.6 miles, pass the side trail to Meditation Point, a small, wooded peninsula with a handful of secluded campsites. After this, contour the wooded slopeside to cross Dinger Creek on a good footbridge at 4.3 miles. The lake comes into view again, and the trail levels out for easy walking past several more campsites. Arrive at the West Shore Day Use Area at 4.8 miles. From here, walk the paved shoreline path south to FR 57, reaching it at 5 miles, and cross the dam.

On the other side of the dam, veer left (east) onto the Southshore Trail (#529). This is the trail where you're likely to have the most company, as it passes the many large, developed campgrounds and day-use areas along the lake's south shore—but it also offers plenty of nice beaches with lake views. Through this segment, you'll also have access to picnic tables, restrooms, water, and trash receptacles. Stick with the Southshore Trail through all of the campgrounds, then pass one more nice beach at 7.9 miles before turning into the inlet of the Oak Grove Fork Clackamas River. Cross the river on a footbridge, then climb a rocky slope to connect with the PCT again at 8.3 miles.

Turn left (north) to leave the crowds behind, heading into dense fir and hemlock woods, where numerous side trails break off the PCT to secluded campsites near the lakeshore. At 10.2 miles, pass a small, half-moon-shaped bay with a large camp area, then climb away from the lakeshore to proceed along the east side of the North Arm. The trail then crosses several springs and skirts the wide, wet meadow at the head of Timothy Lake before passing the Old 1916 Trail (#537; a mountain biking route). Cross Crater Creek on a wide bridge at 11.7 miles, then continue 0.1 mile to close the loop at the big junction where you started. Turn right (northeast) to backtrack the last 0.6 mile to your starting point at Little Crater Meadow.

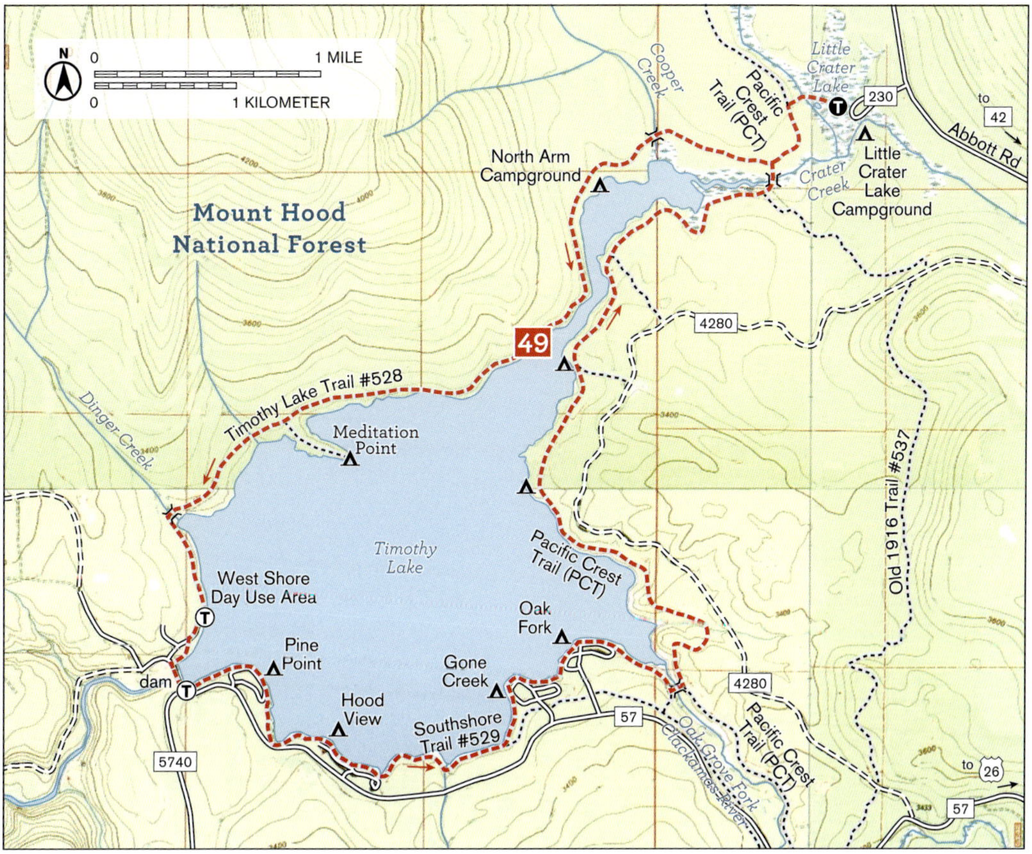

Opposite, top: Blue skies and Broken Top over Todd Lake

Opposite, bottom: Sahalie Falls on the McKenzie River

Central Cascades

50. Hunts Cove 154

51. Duffy and Santiam Lakes 156

52. Iron Mountain 158

53. Sahalie Falls (McKenzie River) 160

54. Tamolitch Falls (Blue Pool) ... 162

55. Little Belknap 164

56. Three Sisters Loop 165

57. Tumalo Falls 170

58. Todd Lake 172

59. Mink Lake 174

60. Rosary Lakes 178

61. Divide Lake 179

62. Diamond Peak Loop 181

The central section of Oregon's Cascade Range is a scenic wonderland of glacier-capped peaks, sprawling wildflower meadows, and sparkling lakes, contrasted with rugged lava flows and volcanic cones and spires. With hundreds of miles of trails spread across four distinct wilderness areas, there is no shortage of hiking options—from short waterfall hikes to multiweek treks through one of the most scenically diverse portions of Oregon, there's something for everyone. Here are just a few to get you started.

50 *Hunts Cove*

Distance: 11.8-mile roundtrip
Difficulty: moderate
Hiking time: day hike or overnight
Elevation gain: 2340 feet
High point: 5260 feet
Season: Jul–Oct
Management: Willamette NF (Detroit)
Protection status: Mount Jefferson Wilderness
Map: Green Trails 557: Mount Jefferson
GPS coordinates: N 44 65.961, W 121 89.123

Getting there: From Interstate 5 in Salem, take exit 253 for Oregon Route 22 East to Detroit Lake; drive 61 miles east, going through Detroit and Idanha. Turn left (east) on Pamelia Road (Forest Road 2246) and follow this narrow road for 3.7 miles—first on bumpy pavement and then on good gravel—to the trailhead. From Sisters, take US Highway 20 west for 25 miles, then OR 22 west for 19.4 miles to Pamelia Road. ***Notes:*** NW Forest Pass or Interagency Pass required for trailhead parking; Central Cascades Wilderness Permit required for day and overnight use (see Trailhead Permits and Fees in the Introduction). Wilderness rules apply. No camping within 100 feet of water; no campfires above 5700 feet.

The Mount Jefferson area was one of the crown jewels along Oregon's Cascade Crest, until it was hit by a double whammy—the 2017 Whitewater Fire, swiftly followed by the 2020 Lionshead Fire. The forest is bouncing back, as nature is resilient, but it will take decades for it to return to its former glory. Thankfully, a few areas were spared from the destruction, allowing hikers and backpackers to enjoy a portion of this fantastic wilderness, where the berries and wildflowers still thrive, and the creeks still flow down verdant mountainsides.

Start at the Pamelia Lake Trailhead (#3439) and head up through fir, hemlock, and cedar woods laden with bunchberry, vanilla leaf, and huckleberry. The trail is wide and the walking effortless on an easy grade, allowing you to admire your surroundings while Pamelia Creek sings down the slope nearby. Cross a small footbridge over a branch of the creek, continuing your way uphill through more berries and rhododendron, until you come to a three-way fork near the shore of Pamelia Lake at 2.1 miles. Take the middle fork into the camp area and follow the narrow user path around the lakeshore. This stretch of trail has plenty of views, easy lake access, and an abundance of secluded campsites.

When you reach the end of the camp area at 2.6 miles, turn right (south) onto the Hunts Creek Trail (#3440). The way now contours a verdant slope alongside Hunts Creek, where countless small side creeks and streams spill down the hillside, feeding a plethora of berries, ferns, and wildflowers. Bridges cross the larger cataracts,

Cascade crossing en route to Hunts Cove

and the others you can easily rock-hop to get across. The trail then turns into the creek's wide, rocky floodplain at 3.4 miles, where you'll need to make two crossings. The first is a hop across an often-muddy section of stream, and the second is a balance-beam-style log crossing over the creek's main channel. Once you're on the other side, the grade increases—but not severely—to head higher up the canyon.

Commence a contouring ascent of the wooded hillside as berries, hedge nettle, and devil's club encroach on the trail—watch out for thorns! As it gains elevation, the trail twists through a few switchbacks and turns through a few rocky chutes, crossing numerous streams and springs until it reaches the next junction at 5.1 miles. Turn left (northeast) onto the Hunts Cove Trail and proceed into the upper lake basin. A clearing in the trees offers a wide view over the meadowy basin, with Mount Jefferson's 10,497-foot peak rising over the opposite ridge. The forest thins as you near Hanks Lake; hop across its outlet at 5.5 miles, then come to a small camp area near the grassy lakeshore.

You can drop your gear here and enjoy your lunch, set up camp, or continue on to Hunts Lake. Find the trail fork on the north side of the camp area and head slightly uphill for 0.4 mile. The view from Hunts Lake is better, looking up the valley toward the Cathedral Rocks, but camping here is more limited around the brushy lakeshore. A couple of small, grassy areas near the water are nice for lunching or fishing. When you've gotten your fill of this pleasant wilderness wonderland, return by the same route. Or you can bypass the camp area around Pamelia Lake by continuing straight (northwest) on the Hunts Creek Trail to the upper junction of the Pamelia Lake Trail. Then just turn left (southwest) and head back down to the trailhead.

Extend Your Trip: For an even longer day hike, or an overnight trip, turn this into a 16-mile loop with a jaunt along the Pacific Crest Trail (PCT). To do so, continue up the Old Hunts Cove Trail for another 1.4 miles, gaining 900 feet of elevation, to reach its junction with the PCT. Turn left (north) and traipse

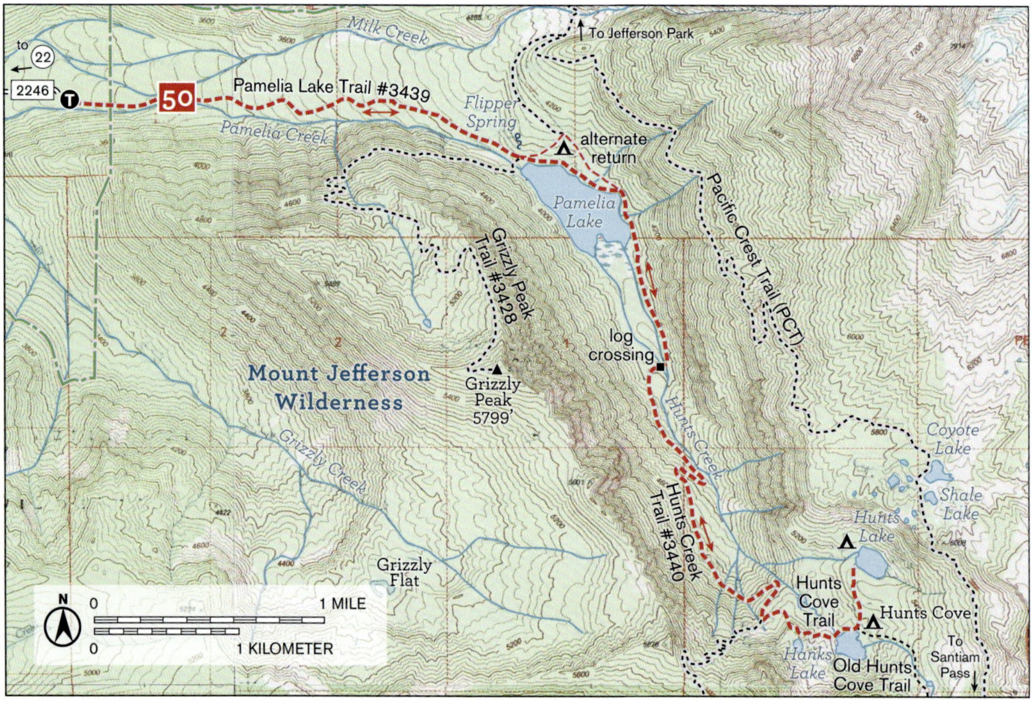

along the PCT under the Cathedral Rocks for 1.6 miles to Shale and Coyote Lakes. You can find a few campsites nearby but pay heed to the camping restrictions. From here, begin a steady descent of the wooded lower flank of Mount Jefferson, coming to a junction at around 13 miles, south of Milk Creek. Close the loop by veering left (west) off the PCT to a spur that connects you to the Pamelia Lake Trail for the home stretch.

51 *Duffy and Santiam Lakes*

Distance: 10-mile roundtrip
Difficulty: moderate
Hiking time: day hike or overnight
Elevation gain: 1410 feet
High point: 5190 feet
Season: Jul–Oct
Management: Willamette NF (Detroit)
Protection status: Mount Jefferson Wilderness
Map: Green Trails 589: Three Fingered Jack
GPS coordinates: N 44 49.119, W 121 94.999

Getting there: From Salem, drive east on Oregon Route 22 toward Detroit Lake for about 74 miles. Continue through Detroit and Idanha, then turn left (east) on Forest Road 2267 and drive for 2.9 miles to the trailhead. From Sisters, drive west on US Highway 20 for 25 miles, then take OR 22 west for 5.8 miles to FR 2267. ***Notes:*** NW Forest Pass or Interagency Pass required for trailhead parking; Central Cascades Wilderness Permit required for day and overnight use (see Trailhead Permits and Fees in the Introduction). Wilderness rules apply. Mosquitoes can be voracious here in early summer—be prepared!

The Mount Jefferson Wilderness is pocked with myriad sparkling pools, wildflower meadows, and rugged volcanic peaks and ridges, all inviting exploration and relaxation. Its network of trails offers plenty of opportunities for hiking and backcountry camping. Unfortunately, much of the region has burned over the last generation, leaving wide swaths of forest dry and unappealing, with many trails in poor condition. Thankfully, this route to two pretty lakes with fantastic mountain views is still mostly pleasant—just be prepared to share it with others.

From the quiet Duffy Lake Trailhead (#3427), head into green and lively woods as you quickly enter the Mount Jefferson Wilderness. The walking is pleasant and mostly effortless under mossy Douglas-firs and hemlocks as the trail contours the slope above the North Santiam River. Just before reaching the Turpentine Trail (#3490) at 1.5 miles, check out the "wave" of volcanic rock just upslope of the trail. Veer right (southeast) at the fork, continuing toward Duffy Lake, with the grade increasing just enough to feel like you're starting to get a workout. The trail snakes eastward through the woods and eventually crosses the North Santiam River at 2.6 miles. Depending on the season, this could be a wet or dry crossing.

Continue to the next junction, at 3 miles, and veer left (north) past the Lava Lakes Trail (#3433). Then proceed just 0.3 mile farther to another junction, near the shores of Duffy Lake. To the right, the Santiam Lake Trail (#3491) heads southeast toward Santiam Lake, your ultimate destination. For now, continue left (east) along the shores of pleasant Duffy Lake as ragged, 5849-foot Duffy Butte rises beyond. Some primitive backcountry campsites near the shore offer opportunities for a fairly easy overnight outing. The scene is pleasant and peaceful, even with portions of the butte still displaying singed snags and trees, reminders of the wildfire that swept through here in the early 2000s.

To continue to Santiam Lake, proceed to the next junction, at 3.6 miles, and make a quick right (south) on the Blue Lake Trail (#3422) to connect to the Santiam Lake Trail. Turn left (east) and follow this path on a steadily increasing grade, passing the Dixie Lakes Trail (#3494) at 4.1 miles, and ascend to the next fork at 4.5 miles. Veer right (southwest) to begin the traverse around the west side of Santiam Lake, where a user path at 4.7 miles breaks off left (east) to a couple of nice campsites near the lake's outlet. Continue across an open meadow to the next fork, at 4.9 miles, and descend to the upper end of the lake, where you'll find more campsites, as well as impressive views of 7841-foot Three Fingered Jack, a ragged and heavily glaciated shield volcano. When you're ready, return by the same route, or try one of the alternatives below.

Enjoy fishing and swimming at quiet Duffy Lake.

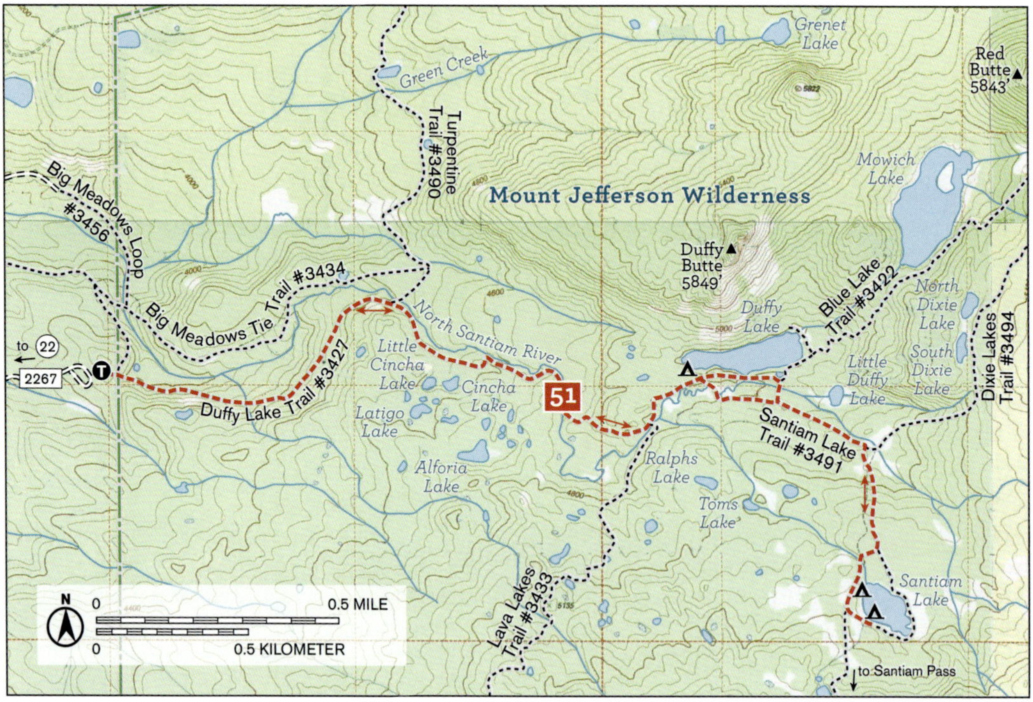

Extend Your Trip: From Santiam Lake, you can follow the user path around the lakeshore, although it gets brushy and overgrown in places. Or you can continue wandering south on the Santiam Lake Trail for 4.2 miles to the Berley Lakes and beyond to the Pacific Crest Trail. Another alternative is to start back toward Duffy Lake but then veer right onto the Dixie Lakes Trail to loop up and around to Mowich Lake. This route is not maintained well and traverses a wide burn area, but you're sure to find plenty of solitude if you don't mind a little scrambling and bushwhacking. When you reach the Blue Lake Trail, turn left (west) to descend to Mowich Lake and then continue down to Duffy Lake, for a total of 3.5 additional miles.

52 *Iron Mountain*

Distance: 6.8-mile loop
Difficulty: strenuous
Hiking time: day hike
Elevation gain: 1900 feet
High point: 5455 feet
Season: Jun–Oct
Management: Willamette NF (Sweet Home)
Protection status: none
Map: USGS Quad: Harter Mountain, OR
GPS coordinates: N 44 39.522, W 122 14.081

Getting there: From Albany, take US Highway 20 east for approximately 62 miles to the Tombstone Sno-Park and trailhead. ***Notes:*** NW Forest Pass or Interagency Pass required for trailhead parking.

Once the site of one of Oregon's many renowned fire lookouts, Iron Mountain is a 5455-foot, red-rock prominence that offers commanding views from its summit perch. The lookout is long gone, but in its place is a public viewing platform with a mountain-finder map to help you pinpoint more than a dozen Cascades peaks and affords views in every direction. And when you're not casting your gaze to the distant horizon, you can enjoy closer-in delights, such as an abundance of wildflowers, shrubs, and berries (more than three hundred varieties), as well as a short jaunt on the historic Santiam Wagon Road Trail.

Begin your hike at the Tombstone Pass trailhead by heading up the road at the back of the parking area. Just past the restroom, turn left (east) onto the Tombstone Nature Trail (#3419) and drop down into mixed woods crowded with copious amounts of thimbleberry and bunchberry. Enjoy this pretty path as it traces the edge of a sprawling meadow bursting with summer flowers and berries. An interpretive sign provides information about the significance of this meadow to both Native peoples and early settlers, who used this location as a place to hunt, gather, and take shelter as they passed through this section of the Cascade Range. An optional 0.3-mile side loop circuits the meadow.

As you pull away from the meadow, carefully cross the highway at 0.5 mile and start up the Cone Peak Trail (#3408). The path contours eastward under more pleasant woods until you reach the 1-mile mark and begin switchbacking up the side of the mountain. Although there are no views yet, the abundance of flowers and berries keeps the climb pleasant and interesting. The trail then bursts out of the trees at 2 miles and crosses an open plateau with impressive views of 5646-foot Cone Peak. Summer brings plenty of color in the form of flowering stonecrop, buckwheat, and paintbrush. From here, the trail turns west and begins twisting and turning around large rock outcrops and over small creeks, making a circuit around the back (north) side of Iron Mountain.

At 3.7 miles, reach the west side of the mountain and veer left (east) onto the Iron Mountain Trail (#3389). The way climbs steeply as it switchbacks up an open slope festooned

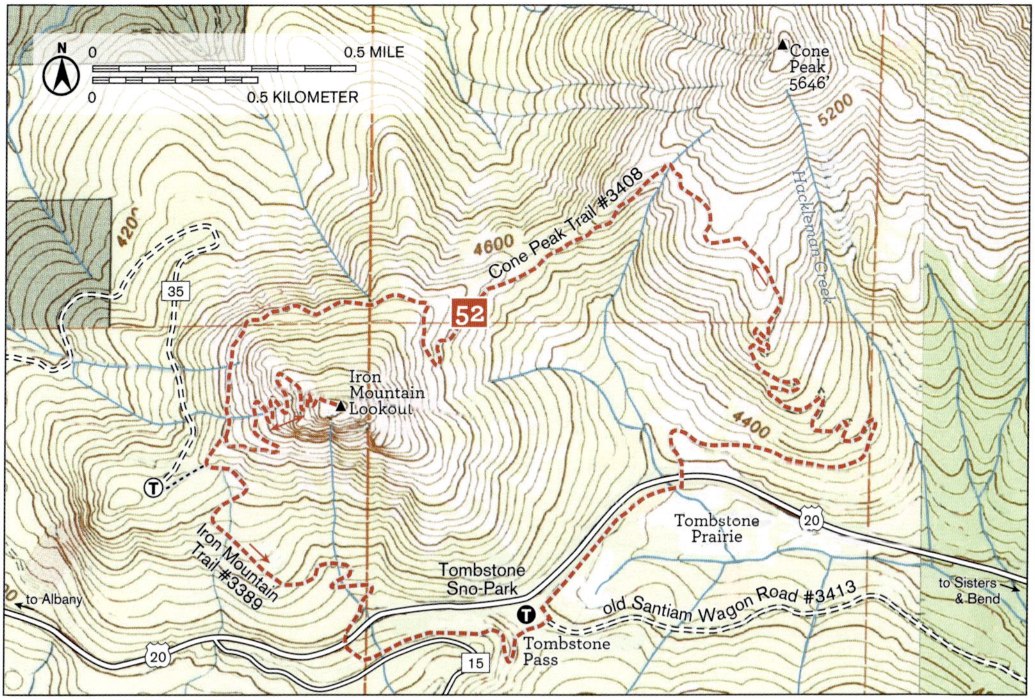

Cone Peak on the way to Iron Mountain

with outcrops of red rock and tufts of colorful buckwheat. About halfway up, a trailside bench offers a place to stop and catch your breath. Step onto the summit platform at 4.5 miles, where the 360-degee view is all-encompassing. Use the mountain-finder map to pinpoint Mount Jefferson, the Three Sisters, and more than a dozen other peaks. After your look, descend back to the junction to continue your loop, turning left (south) and proceeding to another trail fork at 5.3 miles. Here, a short spur trail breaks off right (southwest) to an alternate trailhead and restroom at the end of Forest Road 035.

Begin a steady descent as the trail drops into dense, lush forest, where the thimbleberry is copious, and ferns and wildflowers blanket a meadowy slope. As you near the bottom, pass through what resembles a rock gate at 5.8 miles, then reach the highway just 0.2 mile farther. Make a slight jog right (west) as you quickly and carefully cross the highway, then drop down a short spur trail to the old Santiam Wagon Road Trail (#3413). Turn left (east) and follow the old road as it contours a densely wooded hillside, crossing several seasonal springs until it curves south. Then ascend a few switchbacks to reach the trailhead where you started.

53 *Sahalie Falls (McKenzie River)*

Distance: 2.4-mile loop
Difficulty: easy
Hiking time: short day hike
Elevation gain: 440 feet
High point: 3000 feet
Season: May–Nov
Management: Willamette NF (McKenzie River)
Protection status: none
Map: USFS McKenzie River National Recreation Trail
GPS coordinates: N 44 34.833, W 121 99.649

Getting there: From Springfield/Eugene, take Oregon Route 126 east for about 64 miles to the Sahalie Falls viewpoint and trailhead. ***Notes:*** These trails are often crowded on summer weekends; consider visiting midweek for fewer crowds and easier parking. The multiuse McKenzie River Trail is popular with mountain bikers; be mindful and courteous, stepping aside when they approach. Some barrier-free paths.

The McKenzie River National Scenic Trail (#3507) follows the river for 26 miles, running from its upper (eastern) trailhead near Fish Lake to its lower (western) trailhead near the small town of McKenzie Bridge. A one-way trip makes for a delightful, downhill stroll through ancient lava flows and old-growth forest brimming with wildflowers and berries, with the river churning and tumbling down its rocky channel beside you. If you don't have a few days to enjoy the entire trail, try this bite-size section that visits a couple of spectacular, thundering waterfalls.

From the well-marked trailhead just off OR 126, resist the urge to go straight to the

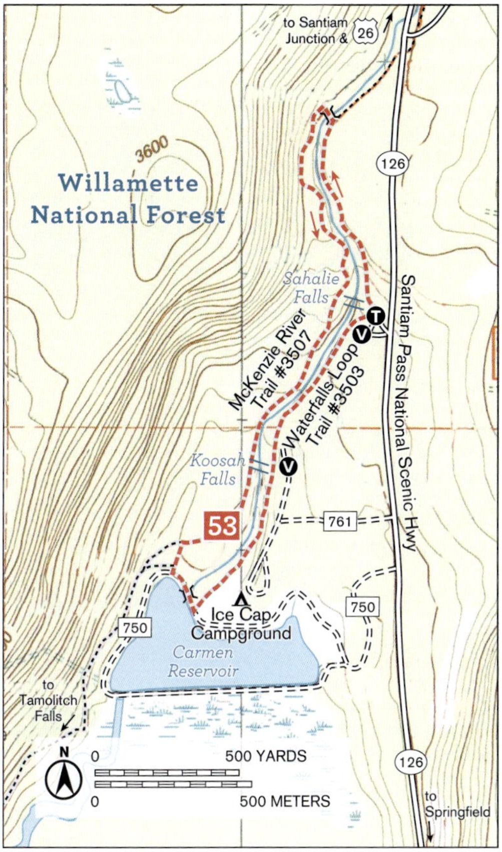

Koosah Falls on the McKenzie River

Sahalie Falls viewpoint. Instead, head north up the Waterfalls Loop Trail (#3503) for 0.1 mile to the upper viewpoint, where the McKenzie River pours over a lava dam and fills the canyon with mist. From here, continue north, winding through pleasant woods to a junction with the McKenzie River Trail at 0.4 mile. Turn left (west) and cross the wide bridge over the river, then go left again to head south on the McKenzie River Trail. The route twists and turns (mostly) downhill, now on the opposite side of the river, passing big lava outcrops and a small plunge pool. At 0.9 mile, reach the edge of a cliff and a view looking over Sahalie Falls from a new angle.

Continue winding downhill. At 1.1 miles, a whitewater cascade resembles a vortex of falling water. You'll get a better view from the other side. Just 0.1 mile farther, Koosah Falls fills the river gorge with cool mist. Below the falls, the gorge narrows into a slot and the trail skirts the edge for a short distance before reaching the next junction at 1.4 miles. Here, the McKenzie River Trail continues downstream to Tamolitch Falls (see Hike 54 and Extend Your Trip). For now, veer left (south) and take the connector spur to the shoulder of Forest Road 750, where a vault toilet is available on the shoulder. Turn left (southeast) again and walk the road over the bridge, where the river flows into the Carmen Reservoir.

Just over the bridge, pick up the Waterfalls Loop once again and head north, now uphill, into the trees. Pass a side trail that connects to the Ice Cap Campground and reach the wide viewpoint over Koosah Falls at 1.9 miles. From this location, you can enjoy a better view of the double falls. The trail follows the river upstream, skirting the vortex cascade—don't get too close to the edge! From here, it's a quick 0.3 mile with a steady stair climb to close the loop at the Sahalie Falls viewpoint. Stop to take in the big waterfall view you bypassed in the beginning. Enjoy the falls with all the other spectators, then head back up to the trailhead and your waiting vehicle.

Extend Your Trip: You can visit Tamolitch Falls and the Blue Pool (see Hike 54) by continuing 3.3 miles downstream on the McKenzie River Trail, for a total roundtrip of 9 miles. From the spur junction at the bottom of the waterfall loop, continue south, skirting the Carmen Reservoir and following the river downstream to the next junction. Turn left (east) to descend to the water or right (west) to reach the viewpoint above the pool. After your visit to the pool, retrace your steps back upstream and then follow the directions noted above for the second half of the waterfall loop.

54 *Tamolitch Falls (Blue Pool)*

Distance: 3.8-mile roundtrip
Difficulty: moderate
Hiking time: short day hike
Elevation gain: 380
High point: 2410
Season: May–Nov
Management: Willamette NF (McKenzie River)
Protection status: none
Map: USFS McKenzie River National Recreation Trail
GPS coordinates: N 44 29.067, W 122 03.563

The fantastical Blue Pool at Tamolitch Falls

Getting there: From Springfield/Eugene, take Oregon Route 126 east for about 58 miles to the Tamolitch Falls (Blue Pool) trailhead. Observe "no parking" signs. ***Notes:*** This trail is often crowded on summer weekends; consider visiting midweek for fewer crowds and easier parking. Portions of the multiuse McKenzie River Trail are popular with mountain bikers; be mindful and courteous, stepping aside when they approach.

The magical Blue Pool at Tamolitch Falls is a favored summer swimming hole on the wooded west side of the Central Cascades. Looking more like something you would find on the Hawaiian Islands, the pool is created by the McKenzie River, which disappears into an ancient, porous lava flow 3 miles upstream and then reappears here as a deep spring bubbling up out of the riverbed. Above the pool, the usually dry Tamolitch Falls serves as a reminder of how the river used to surge above ground (now only in extremely wet seasons) and spill into the basin below. Standing at the edge of the dry falls and looking down on the cerulean lagoon is a unique and otherworldly experience.

The trail to Blue Pool starts at a bend on Forest Road 655, near a small outhouse building. Look for a sign on the right indicating the hiker path for the McKenzie River Trail (#3507). Just uphill is the bike path. Head into the woods along the river under a canopy of hemlock, western red cedar, vine, and bigleaf maple. The wide, graded trail is lined with vanilla leaf and fairybells, along with a variety of ferns and berry shrubs, and the McKenzie River sings and burbles alongside. Cross a small footbridge over a feeder creek, then cross a long, curving bridge over a boggy area at 0.6 mile.

Going forward, the trail gets rough and rocky as it snakes through ancient, mossy lava flows. Watch your step on the loose lava rocks and cobbles, which seem eager to help you twist an ankle. At 1.3 miles, the trail skirts the edge of the river gorge, giving you a view far down below. Look around this area for evidence of *pahoehoe*, ropy layers of lava that once flowed down the valley in molten, liquid form. Hike just a little farther to reach the edge of a bluff overlooking the fantastical Blue Pool. At an unsigned but obvious fork, veer right (east) and cross the dry riverbed, then scramble down to the water's edge. If you dare, you can take a dip in its icy depths. Explore at your leisure and then return by the same route.

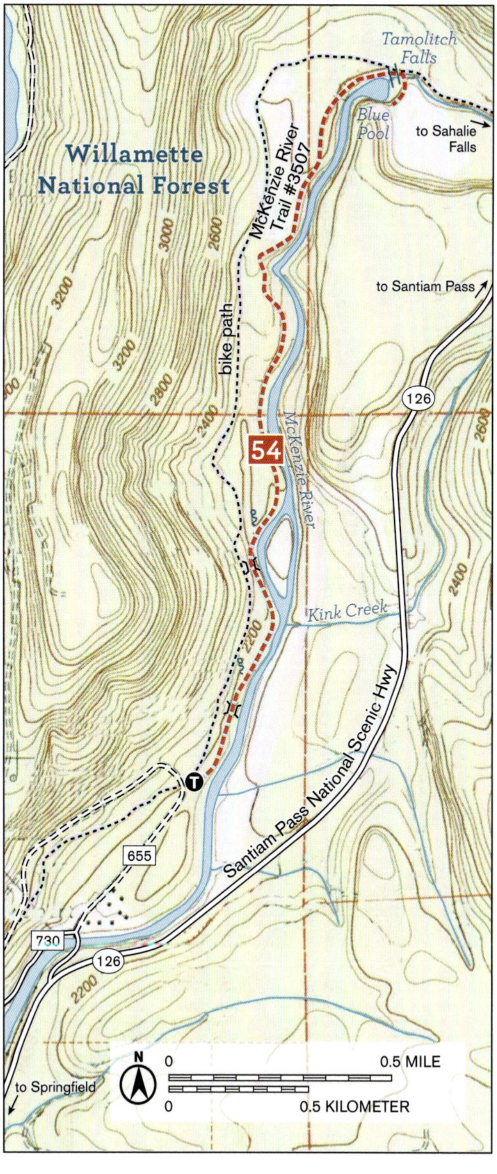

55 *Little Belknap*

Distance: 4.8-mile roundtrip
Difficulty: moderate
Hiking time: day hike
Elevation gain: 1090 feet
High point: 6305 feet
Season: Jul–Oct
Management: Deschutes NF (Sisters)
Protection status: Mount Washington Wilderness
Map: Green Trails 589SX: Three Sisters Wilderness
GPS coordinates: N 44 26.028, W 121 80.961

Getting there: From Sisters, take Oregon Route 242 approximately 15 miles west to McKenzie Pass. The trailhead is on the right (north) side of the road, just past the Dee Wright Observatory. ***Notes:*** NW Forest Pass or Interagency Pass required for trailhead parking; Central Cascades Wilderness Permit required for day or overnight use (see Trailhead Permits and Fees in the Introduction). This trail can be brutally hot in midsummer, with little shade and no water. Use sun protection and stay hydrated. Very rough lava rock trail; not recommended for dogs.

Geologically infantile, the Belknap lava flows are only 3000 to 1500 years old. Covering more than forty square miles on the eastern side of central Oregon's Cascades, most of the dense, basaltic andesite lava originates from 6872-foot Belknap Crater, a shield volcano similar to those found on the Hawaiian Islands. This lava is intermingled with more lava originating from 6305-foot Little Belknap, where the rugged terrain is marked by pressure ridges and collapsed lava tubes. The Pacific Crest Trail (PCT) cuts its path directly between the two, and a short side trail ventures to the very brink of the smaller volcano.

Start your hike on the PCT within a forested *kipuka*—a Hawaiian word that means "land surrounded by lava." This small, shady island of pine, fir, ferns, huckleberry, and penstemon will be your only shelter from the sweltering Oregon desert sun as you make your way into the black lava of Mordor. Take a moment to slather on some sunscreen before you move on. The trail ascends over the western flank of the hillock, then crosses a petrified river of stone separating the trees from another *kipuka*. Instead of crossing over the second one, the PCT circuits west around its base, in the margin between the shady forest and the jagged lava. Take a breather in the cool air under the trees—it will be the last shade you'll enjoy for a long while.

At 0.7 mile, leave the islands behind and begin ascending the southern slope of Little Belknap. The shallow grade would make the hiking easy, if it weren't for the loose and uneven lava trail surface. Take your time and watch your footing to avoid trips and ankle rolls. Despite its bleakness, the roiling, twisted terrain is evidence of the youthful origins of Oregon's Cascades. As the trail climbs, the views become wider and more

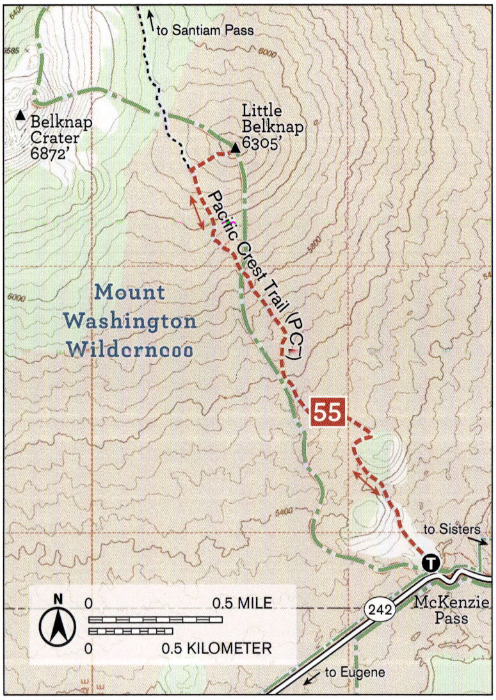

Trek across a barren lavascape to Little Belknap Crater.

fascinating. The PCT finally comes to a low crest at 2.2 miles, where a trail sign points the way to Little Belknap. Veer right (east) onto this side trail and take note of the difference in the lava's surface. The crumbly, blocky lava is called *a'a*; the smooth, ropy-looking lava is known as *pahoehoe*. Just before reaching the jagged summit, pass a small cave, which is actually a portion of an exposed lava tube.

The trail ends at a notch between a pinnacled mound and the summit proper. From this notch, take the faint boot path that wraps around the north side to a cave with multiple lava arches overhead; this is the vent of Little Belknap. Use caution as you peer down the throat of this recently active volcano, where snow and ice remain in deep shadows year-round. To claim the summit, gaining 360-degree views of central Oregon's Cascade peaks among a roiling sea of rock, carefully scramble up the crumbly side of the eastern summit cone. When you're done exploring, return by the same route.

56 *Three Sisters Loop*

Distance: 46-mile loop
Difficulty: moderate
Hiking time: multiday
Elevation gain: 7440 feet
High point: 7020 feet
Season: Jul–Sep
Management: Willamette NF (McKenzie River); Deschutes NF (Cascade Lakes, Sisters)
Protection status: Three Sisters Wilderness
Map: Green Trails 589SX: Three Sisters Wilderness
GPS coordinates: N 44 03.407, W 121 76.715

Getting there: From Bend, head west on Century Drive for about 21 miles, following signs for Mount Bachelor. Continue past the ski area onto the Cascade Lakes Scenic Byway (Oregon Route 46) for 6 miles to the Devils Lake Campground and trailhead.
Notes: NW Forest Pass or Interagency Pass required for trailhead parking; Central Cascades Wilderness Permit required for day or overnight use (see Trailhead Permits and Fees in the Introduction). Wilderness rules apply. Exercise caution in recently burned areas. Snow may linger into summer at higher elevations.

Deschutes National Forest
Willamette National Forest
Three Sisters Wilderness
Three Sisters Wilderness
Green Lakes Trail #4070
Pole Creek Trail #4072
Camp Lake Trail #4074
Trout Creek Trail #4067
Scott Pass Trail #4068
Scott Pass (6040')
PCT
North Mathieu Lakes Trail #4062
Matthieu Lakes
to 242 & McKenzie Pass
Yapoah Lake
Yapoah Crater 6737'
Opie Dilldock Pass 6890'
Collier Cone 7534'
Minnie Scott Spring
North Sister 10,085'
Middle Sister 10,047'
Little Brother 7810'
Scott Trail #3531
Glacier Creek
Glacier Way #4336
Sister Springs
Obsidian Falls
56
Pacific Crest Trail (PCT)
Linton Meadows Trail #3547
Eileen Lake
Obsidian Creek
White Branch
Obsidian Trail #3528
Soap Creek
Pole Creek
South Fork Whychus Creek
to Sisters
to Eugene
242
15
1026
1 MILE
1 KILOMETER
0
N

Park Meadow Trail #96A
Whychus Creek
Park Meadow
East Fork Park Creek
Broken Top 9175'
Todd Trail #34
Broken Top Trail #10
Golden Lake
56
7000' Pass
Green Lakes
Green Lakes Trail #17
Deschutes National Forest
Soda Creek Trail #11
Carver Lake
Three Sisters Wilderness
Moraine Lake Trail #17.1
Cascade Lakes Scenic Byway
to Bend
Devils Lake
372
Chambers Lakes
South Sister 10,358'
South Sister Climber Trail #36
Moraine Lake
Kaleetan Butte 6853'
Wikiup Plains Trail #12.1
to Willamette Pass
Separation Creek
Mesa Creek
Rock Mesa 6850'
LeConte Crater 6620'
LeConte Crater Trail #14.3
Elk Devils Trail #12
Wikiup Plains Trail #12.1
Pacific Crest Trail (PCT)
Reese Lake
Mesa Meadow
Wikiup Plain
Mirror Lakes Trail #20
Sisters Mirror Lake
Hinton Creek
The Wife 7054
James Creek Trail #3546
Eileen Lake Trail #4348
Foley Ridge Trail #3511
Three Sisters Wilderness
James Creek
Willamette National Forest
Nash Lake Trail #3527
Top Lake
Nash Lake
N
0
1 MILE
0
1 KILOMETER

The Three Sisters loop is an epic journey around Oregon's volcanic Cascades.

While the Timberline Trail makes one massive circuit around Mount Hood, this loop around the Three Sisters links more than half a dozen trails into an epic, multiday adventure. With multiple trailheads and access points, there is no one way to hike this 46-mile loop, but the following description outlines one of the most common and popular routes, with easy access from the trailhead at Devils Lake. Over the course of your journey, you will experience everything from lively woods and idyllic meadows to subalpine plains and volcanic wastelands. You can easily channel your inner Frodo as you embark on your journey through the fantastical Middle Earth of central Oregon.

Begin your hike with a steady ascent on the Elk Devils Trail (#12) into the Three Sisters Wilderness. The trail climbs under dense woods near Tyee Creek to a junction—the first of many, many trail junctions that you will need to navigate over the course of your 46-mile circuit. Turn left (southwest) to continue to the next junction at 0.9 mile. Veer right (northwest) onto the Wickiup Plains Trail (#12.1) for a quick mile around the base of 6834-foot Kaleetan Butte before veering right (north) onto the Le Conte Crater Trail (#14.3). Continue around the butte and onto the sprawling, cinder-covered Wickiup Plain to the Moraine Lake Trail (#17.1) junction at 2.3 miles. Veer left (northwest) to stay on the crater trail and traipse across the open plain dotted with buckwheat and lupine. At 3 miles, the trail crosses from the Deschutes National Forest into the Willamette National

Forest and sideswipes 6620-foot Le Conte Crater before intersecting the Pacific Crest Trail (PCT) at 3.6 miles.

Your trek now follows the PCT north for the next 18 miles as it traverses the western slopes of the Three Sisters. Turn right, crossing meadows of cinquefoil and skirting alongside the obsidian-covered Rock Mesa before descending into the Mesa Creek Meadows at 6.6 miles. Here, you'll find several campsites in the trees to the west of the trail and reliably running water flowing through the north side of the meadow. From here, the PCT climbs into blackened forest burned in the 2017 Nash Fire. Make quick work of this unsightly section, veering right (east) to bypass the James Creek Trail (#3546) and Hinton Creek. At 9 miles, arrive at pleasant Reese Lake. A couple of decent campsites sit near the lake, from which you'll have some stunning views of red-headed, 10,358-foot South Sister. Near the lake, a well-trodden path follows Separation Creek up into the Chambers Lakes basin.

Continue hiking the PCT north, dipping in and out of burn areas. Cross Linton Creek and ascend to the rocky plains on the west slope of 10,047-foot Middle Sister. The views here are expansive in every direction. At 11.9 miles, pass the Linton Meadows Trail (#3547) and commence a moderate ascent to Obsidian Falls. At 14.3 miles, a short side trail veers left (north) to the base of this wispy, twenty-foot waterfall. Above the falls, cold and delicious Obsidian Creek flows out of Sister Springs right alongside the trail. Amble through fields of obsidian and then drop down to Glacier Creek at 15.3 miles, where several campsites sit among the trees. The route then

Waterfalls and more waterfalls on the hike up Tumalo Creek

pinnacle of your trail loop, turn left (south) onto the Swampy Lakes Trail and begin the downward journey into the City of Bend's watershed. As the trail bends east, find a way across the Middle Fork and begin a long, contouring descent along the slope of an unnamed ridge. A few wide views open over Tumalo Canyon. At 5.1 miles, hop across Spring Creek. Descend a little more to the next junction, at 5.8 miles, and turn left (east) onto the Bridge Creek Trail (#24). The show's not over yet—follow this melodic brook downstream to a bluff over Bridge Creek Falls at 6.1 miles. Complete your loop by hopping across Spring Creek one more time before proceeding down through ponderosa pines and manzanita for the last 0.8 mile to your starting point.

58 *Todd Lake*

Distance: 1.7-mile loop
Difficulty: easy
Hiking time: short day hike or overnight
Elevation gain: 80 feet
High point: 6170 feet
Season: Jul–Oct
Management: Deschutes NF (Bend–Fort Rock)
Protection status: none
Map: Green Trails 589SX: Three Sisters Wilderness
GPS coordinates: N 44 02.348, W 121 68.204

Getting there: From downtown Bend, drive west on SW Century Drive for about 21 miles to the Mount Bachelor recreation area. Continue west for 2 miles on the Cascade

Lakes Scenic Byway. Turn right (north) on the unpaved road signed for Todd Lake. Slowly drive this bumpy, rocky road 0.6 mile to the trailhead. ***Notes:*** Permits not required for day use and lake access, but venturing into the Three Sisters Wilderness from Todd Lake requires a Central Cascades Wilderness Permit (see Trailhead Permits and Fees in the Introduction). Dogs must be leashed.

Start your hike at the gated road, opposite the parking area. A nearby signboard provides a map of the lake, along with some information about the surrounding forest. Follow the old road up a gentle grade as Todd Creek burbles down the shrubby drainage to your left (west). After 0.1 mile, the path forks in several directions on either side of a large interpretive sign; an outhouse is to the right (east). Read the sign to learn about the origins of Todd Lake. Although the information posted here explains that the lake was named after John Y. Todd, it was originally called "Lost Lake." It wasn't changed to Todd Lake until 1922, after local citizens claimed there were "too many Lost Lakes" in the Cascade Range.

From the sign, take the right fork onto the Todd Lake Loop (#34.1). Do not take the farther right fork onto the Todd Trail (#34). This latter route climbs away from the lake and into the Three Sisters Wilderness. It's worth taking the short spur trail on the left (west) to a nice viewpoint that looks down the length of the lake, where the ragged peaks of Broken Top are visible above the forested basin. After your view, commence your casual stroll around the scenic lakeshore. The path proceeds through shady evergreens as summer wildflowers line the

Enjoy a relaxing stroll around Todd Lake.

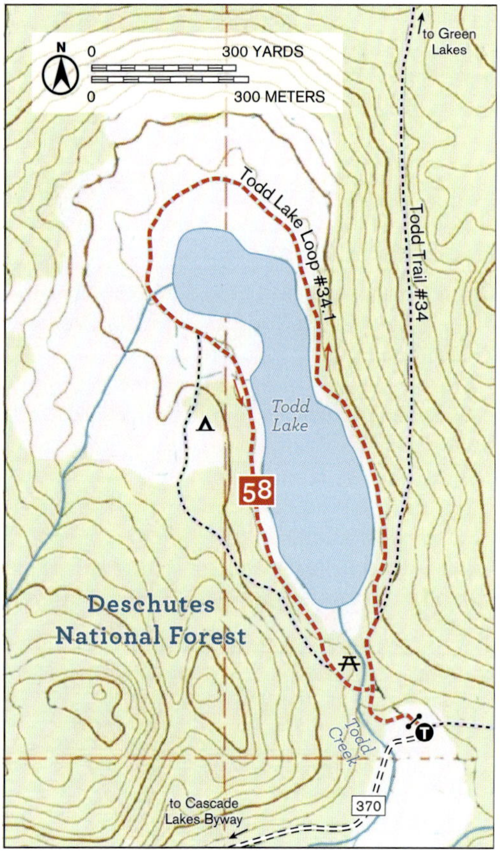

trailside. Along the way, you'll find a few grassy sections on the eastern lakeshore that invite you to spread out a blanket and enjoy a picnic.

At about 0.7 mile, the trail exits the trees and proceeds into the lake's upper wetlands. Several small footbridges span trickling creeks and springs that run down into the lake. Look for bog stars, white flowers that grow in clusters along the verdant creeksides. The path makes a wide pass through the upper meadow, where you're treated to a fine view of Todd Lake and 9065-foot Mount Bachelor. Be sure to remain on the path and boardwalks through this sensitive area. At around 1.2 miles, now on the west side of the lake, the path leaves the meadows and reenters shady woods. A side trail on the right (west) leads to the lake's few backcountry campsites.

Continue strolling along, at times right along the water's edge. At 1.4 miles, the trail opens into a wide, grassy shoreline—another location that invites you to settle in and enjoy the view. From here, it's just another 0.2 mile to complete the loop, returning to the interpretive sign. A few picnic tables are available in the area, but they are set back from the lake, with only limited views. After enjoying your day at Todd Lake, make your way back down the old road to the trailhead where you started.

59 *Mink Lake*

Distance: 20.8-mile lollipop loop
Difficulty: moderate
Hiking time: day hike or overnight
Elevation gain: 2590 feet
High point: 5750 feet
Season: Jul–Oct

Management: Willamette NF (Middle Fork); Deschutes NF (Bend–Fort Rock)
Protection status: Three Sisters Wilderness
Map: Trails Illustrated 1004: Pacific Crest Trail, Oregon North
GPS coordinates: N 43 95.326, W 121 80.274

Getting there: From downtown Bend, drive west on SW Century Drive for about 21 miles to the Mount Bachelor recreation area. Now on the Cascade Lakes Scenic Byway, continue for 13 miles, heading west and then south. Two miles past the Elk Lake Resort, turn into the Six Lakes trailhead parking area on the west side of the highway. ***Notes:*** NW Forest Pass or Interagency Pass required for trailhead parking. Wilderness rules apply. Overnight users must obtain a Central Cascades Wilderness Overnight Permit (see Trailhead Permits and Fees in the Introduction). Day hikers should complete a self-issue wilderness permit at the trailhead kiosk. Mosquitoes can be a nuisance here in early summer.

Explore the Cascade Lakes basin at Mink Lake.

The Cascade Lakes area, just south of the Three Sisters, is replete with trails that lead to dozens of secluded backcountry lakes with prime camping, fishing, and floating opportunities. This easily accessible route forgoes the more popular Elk Lake trailhead for a quiet path into the central Mink Lake basin, with access to the Pacific Crest Trail for tailoring even longer treks if you want to explore more.

The trail begins on the Six Lakes Trail (#14) with an easy westward jaunt into young lodgepole pine woods. At first, there's not much to look at on the dry forest floor. But shortly after entering the Three Sisters Wilderness, grouse whortleberry, currant, pipsissewa, lupine, and pearly everlasting start to liven things up. The diversity of the woods also improves as hemlock and Douglas-fir are added to the mix. After a pleasant first mile along a (likely) dry creek bed, the trail turns south and crosses the outlet of Blow Lake on a sturdy footbridge. The trail then wraps around the southeast shore of the lake. Views of the shallow, tree-ringed pool are scarce from the trail, but a couple of user paths veer off to secluded campsites, where views improve.

The trail continues up a gentle grade, following another drainage through cool and pleasant forest. Shortly after passing a mucky pond on the left (south), at around 2.2 miles, you'll see glimpses of Doris Lake through the trees. The trail doesn't go directly to the lake, but several user paths over the next 0.2 mile branch off to nice campsites near the lakeshore. These are ideal locations to set up camp if you had a late start or just want a shorter alternative to doing the entire loop. After Doris Lake, the trail continues its gentle ascent around a low ridge, then comes to a junction with the Senoj Lake Trail (#14.1) at 3.2 miles. Turn right (west) and continue upward a little farther to the crest of the ridge at 4 miles.

From the viewless crest, the trail begins a steady—but not too steep—descent through more stands of lodgepole pines and lush woods. After passing a few small pocket meadows, intersect

Elk Lake
Cascade Lakes Scenic Byway
to 58
to Bend
Blow Lake
Six Lakes Trail #14
Deschutes National Forest
Doris Lake
Senoj Lake Trail #14.1
Senoj Lake
Three Sisters Wilderness
Leech Lake
59
to Three Sisters
Pacific Crest Trail (PCT)
Willamette National Forest
Mink Lake Trail #3526
Cliff Lake
Cliff Lake Trail
Horseshoe Lake
Porky Lake
Porky Lake Trail #4338
Merrill Lake
Goose Lake
Goose Lake Trail #3542
Mink Lake Trail #3526
Mac Lake
Puppy Lake
S Lake
Long Lake
Upper Snowshoe Lake
Mink Lake
Lakeside Trail #3525
McBee Trail #3523
Martin Way Trail
to Diamond Peak
1 MILE
1 KILOMETER

the Pacific Crest Trail (PCT) at 5.3 miles. To the left, the PCT heads south toward Diamond Peak; to the right, it heads north toward the Three Sisters. Proceed across the PCT, going straight ahead (west) onto the Mink Lake Trail (#3526). The route continues descending through overgrown huckleberry and vanilla leaf, crossing a few small springs. At times, the trail might be hard to find—keep an eye out for the blazes carved into tree trunks marking the way. The descent finally ends at 7.4 miles, at a trail junction near the shore of grassy Goose Lake. One small camp can be found a short distance past this junction.

Opt for the left fork here, staying on the Mink Lake Trail, and make an easy ascent of another low ridge. The trail winds through the trees and berry shrubs for a spell, then arrives alongside Porky Lake at 8 miles. Keep following the trail as it contours around the lake; a large camp area with good water access can be found at 8.1 miles. Pass the Porky Lake Trail (#4338), then mildly ascend to arrive at Mink Lake at 9 miles. Turn right (northwest) on the Lakeside Trail (#3525) and begin the 2.5-mile loop around picturesque Mink Lake. Over the next mile, several nice, secluded campsites can be found along the lake's northern shoreline. Views southward look toward 6144-foot Packsaddle Mountain.

The route continues around the foot of Mink Lake, crossing the lake's swampy outlet. Just beyond, the Martin Way Trail and Starwano Trail (#3537) branch off toward Junction and Martin Lakes, respectively. Turning southeast, the trail now begins tracing the southern shore of Mink Lake. If you look closely, you might catch a peek of South Sister's snowy, 10,358-foot summit over the forested ridge across the lake. A few more decent campsites can be found near the shoreline, then better campsites at 10.5 miles on a wooded peninsula. The latter is a particularly choice spot, with nice lake views in all directions. Watch for an assortment of ducks and geese on the lake's surface, as well as hawks and ospreys diving for their evening meals.

At 11.1 miles, the Lakeside Trail ends as it reconnects with the Mink Lake Trail, at a junction a little south of where you started the loop around Mink Lake. Here, a great viewpoint looks west over the entire length of Mink Lake. Turn right (southeast) and begin climbing out of the lake basin. The trail mounts a low ridge adorned with rock gardens of manzanita and heather, then climbs a little more to meet the PCT again at 11.9 miles. Turn left (east) onto the PCT backcountry superhighway and almost immediately arrive at misty S Lake. A serviceable campsite lies near the lakeshore at 12 miles.

Continuing onward, the PCT bends northward around large Mac Lake; at around 12.3 miles, look for a side trail that descends toward the lakeshore and a large camp area. There are several tent spots here, making it suitable for groups. The next lake in the chain is Merrill Lake, at 12.8 miles. Views of this lake are scarce, with no access due to the dense brush. At 13.1 miles, the PCT enters a small burn area near the west shore of Horseshoe Lake. An old campsite can be found here among the charred trees and snags. For a better option, continue a little farther, crossing the lake's rocky outlet to reach a nice campsite at 13.3 miles. There's good water access here, and the views—despite the burned west shore—are pleasant.

From here, the PCT heads north, contouring an increasingly steep slope through thickets of huckleberry. At 14.1 miles, the Porky Lake Trail breaks off to the left (west); to the right, the unsigned Cliff Lake Trail proceeds 0.1 mile to a backcountry shelter and nice campsite near the lakeshore. Continue north on the PCT, looking and listening for pikas along a high, rocky wall. Just before closing your lakes loop, at 15.4 miles, find one more campsite along the PCT near a shallow, unnamed lake to the right (east). At 15.5 miles, when you finally reach the junction with the Six Lakes and Mink Lake Trails again, turn right (east) off the PCT and retrace your steps back to the Six Lakes trailhead.

60 Rosary Lakes

Distance: 6.8-mile roundtrip
Difficulty: moderate
Hiking time: day hike or overnight
Elevation gain: 920 feet
High point: 5850 feet
Season: Jul–Oct
Management: Deschutes NF (Crescent)
Protection status: none
Map: Trails Illustrated 1004: Pacific Crest Trail, Oregon North
GPS coordinates: N 43 59.713, W 122 03.143

Getting there: From the Eugene/Springfield area, take the Willamette Highway (Oregon Route 58) east for about 62 miles to the Willamette Pass ski area. Just beyond, turn left (north) on a gravel road signed for the Pacific Crest Trail. The trailhead is behind an ODOT maintenance building. From the Bend area (east), take US Highway 97 south and OR 58 west for about 70 miles to Willamette Pass. ***Notes:*** This route is also marked for winter snow travel.

From Willamette Pass, the Pacific Crest Trail (PCT) climbs to a cluster of pretty, forested lakes with ample camping opportunities before continuing its journey north into the Three Sisters Wilderness. It's an ideal location for a pleasant day hike or an easy overnight in the backcountry. Spend a day or two picking berries and enjoying swimming in the picturesque lakes—just be prepared to share the area with others, especially on summer weekends.

Before getting underway, be sure to fill out your self-issue wilderness permit. These help the Forest Service allocate funds for much-needed

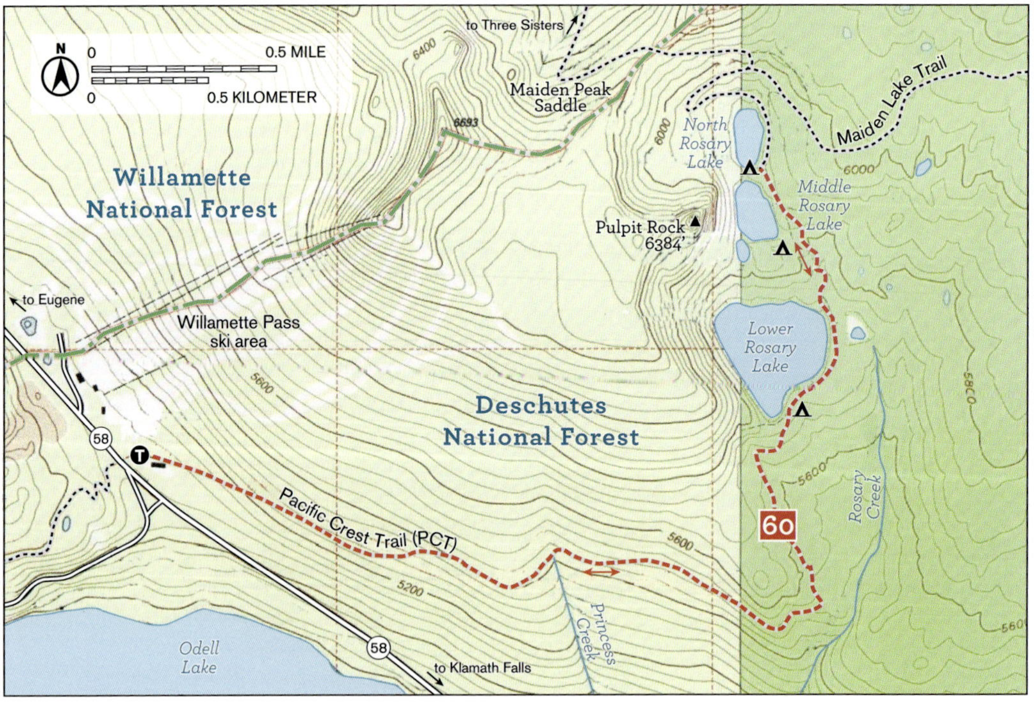

Take a hike on the PCT to the Rosary Lakes.

trail maintenance. Once you're ready to go, take the trailhead spur 100 yards north to its junction with the PCT, hang a right, and head north under the shade of fir, pine, and hemlock forest. The trail is soft and duff-covered, making the initial ascent easy and enjoyable, and the woods are lush and cool, with an abundance of maidenhair fern, mountain strawberry, currant, and huckleberry. About a mile on, the forest becomes noticeably drier, with debris and log-outs littering the wooded floor. After another mile up, the trail bends north, leveling to a pleasant walk in increasingly greener surroundings. Mount a small rise and then come to the south shore of Lower Rosary Lake at 2.6 miles. The largest and prettiest of the Rosary Lakes, this vivid blue-green pool is flanked on its west side by the ragged face of 6384-foot Pulpit Rock.

From here, the PCT curves sharply right (east) to skirt the east side of the lake, passing several idyllic campsites, then crosses the lake's rocky outlet channel. By midsummer, this crossing is usually dry. The trail then continues upward on an easy grade through copious berry shrubs, then levels again at the forested shore of Middle Rosary Lake, at 3.3 miles, with Pulpit Rock rising directly above. Listen for pikas chirping in the talus below the peak. A user path breaks off left (west) and heads around the middle lake's west shore to a couple of secluded campsites. Just a little farther, between Middle and North Rosary Lakes, a large camp area occupies the wooded space, with pleasing views over the lake basin. Pick your favorite of the lakes and enjoy a picnic lunch or an afternoon swim, or pitch your tent for a night outdoors. When you're ready to return to the trailhead, head back the way you came.

61 *Divide Lake*

Distance: 7.6-mile roundtrip
Difficulty: moderate
Hiking time: day hike or overnight
Elevation gain: 1610 feet
High point: 6450 feet
Season: Jul–Oct
Management: Willamette NF (Middle Fork)
Protection status: Diamond Peak Wilderness
Map: USGS Quad: Diamond Peak, OR
GPS coordinates: N 43 57.553, W 122 19.295

Getting there: From the Eugene/Springfield area, take the Willamette Highway (Oregon Route 58) east for about 35 miles. Pass through the small town of Oakridge and turn

Quiet Divide Lake in the Diamond Peak Wilderness

right (south) on Hills Creek/Kitson Springs Road. Follow this paved road for 11.7 miles, past Hills Creek Lake. Then continue on Forest Road 23 for 8 miles to the Vivian Lake trailhead on the left (north) side of the road. ***Notes:*** Wilderness rules apply. Mosquitoes can be relentless in early summer.

Tucked away in a forested basin at the foot of 7100-foot Mount Yoran, little Divide Lake is a quiet getaway just a stone's throw away from the Cascade superhighway of the Pacific Crest Trail (PCT). You would never guess it, however, as most PCT hikers barely cast a glance in this lake's direction, instead making a beeline for resupplies and cheesy pizzas at their next rest stop, just a few trail miles north of here. That leaves this secluded pool available for anyone seeking a little quiet relaxation, and this hike guides you there via a backdoor into the Diamond Peak Wilderness.

From the trailhead on the remote FR 23, start on the Vivian Lake Trail (#3662), heading east into the Diamond Peak Wilderness. The trail begins with a fairly easy upward grade, leading you through mossy white pines and Douglas-firs, with an abundance of tasty huckleberries. After just 0.6 mile, pass the Diamond Peak Tie Trail (#4239), which splits off to the right (south). Continue another 0.2 mile to the brushy and berry-lined shores of Notch Lake, where you'll find a couple of decent campsites around the south and east shores. Just past the lake, at 0.9 mile, veer right (southeast) at a signed fork onto the Mount Yoran Trail (#3683).

From here, the ascent becomes steeper and more earnest, crossing Pinto Creek and climbing into pleasant but mostly viewless woods. Follow the trail as it bends south and then east again, mounting a wooded ridge at 2.5 miles. This ridge is a low arête that once divided ancient glacial basins. Cruise along the ridgetop for the next mile, with windows in the trees offering glimpses of 8744-foot Diamond Peak, just to

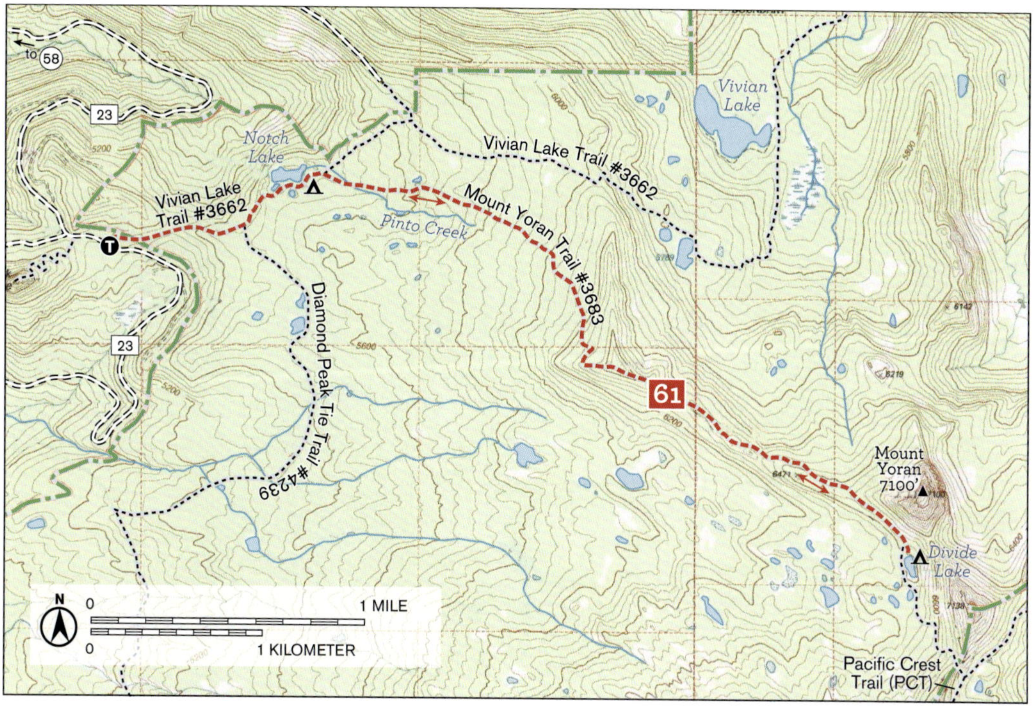

the south. The path then veers over the side of the ridge and along the flanks of Mount Yoran, descending through a field of wooded debris to the north shore of quiet little Divide Lake. Several secluded campsites are scattered in the trees around the lake, and a rugged user path scrambles steeply up to the little mountain's view-packed summit.

62 Diamond Peak Loop

Distance: 33-mile loop
Difficulty: moderate
Hiking time: multiday
Elevation gain: 3990 feet
High point: 7050 feet
Season: Jul–Oct
Management: Willamette NF (Middle Fork); Deschutes NF (Crescent)
Protection status: Diamond Peak Wilderness
Map: Trails Illustrated 1005: Pacific Crest Trail, Oregon South
GPS coordinates: N 43 57.960, W 122 04.368

Getting there: From the Eugene/Springfield area, take the Willamette Highway (Oregon Route 58) east for about 62 miles to the Willamette Pass ski area. Just beyond the pass, turn right (south) on Forest Road 5810 and proceed 2.2 miles to the Trapper Creek trailhead on the right (west) side of the road, directly across from Shelter Cove Resort. From the Bend area, take US Highway 97 south and OR 58 west for about 70 miles to Willamette Pass; turn left (south) onto FR 5810 and drive to the trailhead. ***Notes:*** Wilderness rules apply. Complete a self-issue wilderness permit at the trailhead kiosk.

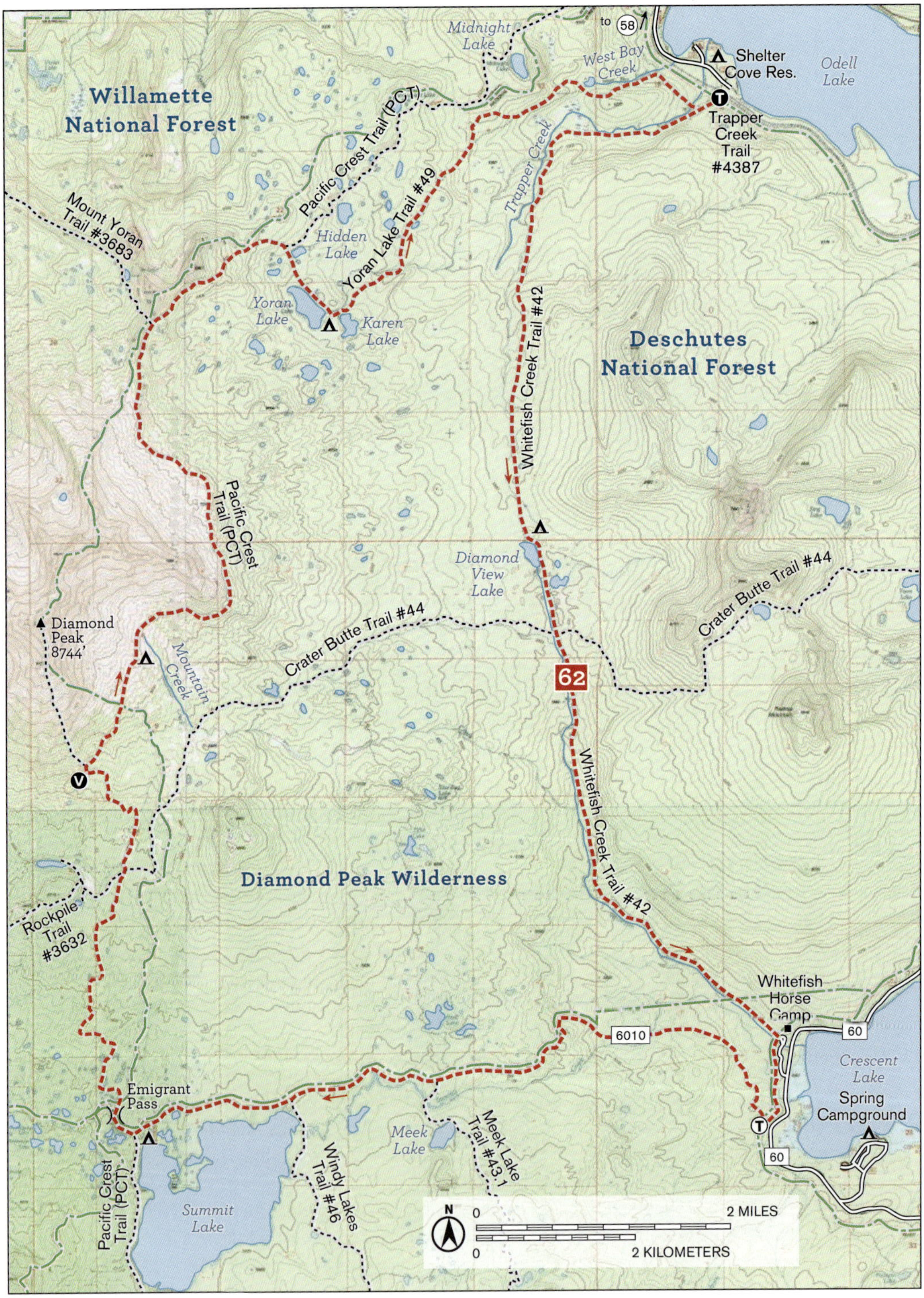

Midnight Lake
to 58
Shelter Cove Res.
Odell Lake
West Bay Creek
Willamette National Forest
Pacific Crest Trail (PCT)
Trapper Creek Trail #4387
Trapper Creek
Yoran Lake Trail #49
Mount Yoran Trail #3683
Hidden Lake
Yoran Lake
Karen Lake
Whitefish Creek Trail #42
Deschutes National Forest
Pacific Crest Trail (PCT)
Diamond View Lake
Crater Butte Trail #44
Diamond Peak 8744'
Mountain Creek
Crater Butte Trail #44
62
Whitefish Creek Trail #42
Diamond Peak Wilderness
Rockpile Trail #3632
Whitefish Horse Camp
6010
60
Crescent Lake
Spring Campground
Emigrant Pass
Meek Lake
Meek Lake Trail #43.1
Windy Lakes Trail #46
Pacific Crest Trail (PCT)
Summit Lake
60
N
0
2 MILES
0
2 KILOMETERS

The Diamond Peak Wilderness evokes images of the High Sierra.

Despite its relatively easy access and fantastic scenery—and unlike its neighboring wilderness areas—the Diamond Peak Wilderness doesn't attract crowds. That's too bad for everyone who misses out on this quiet wilderness with its abundance of alpine meadows, pocket lakes, and icy streams spilling out of high glacial cirques. Conversely, it's good for you, because you're likely to enjoy this area with limited company—and sans complicated permit requirements. If you don't have time to do the entire loop, at least get your feet wet with a day hike to Diamond View Lake, which will doubtless entice you to come back for more.

Your trek begins with an easy jog up the Trapper Creek Trail (#4387) and into the Diamond Peak Wilderness. After a quick 0.2 mile, veer left (south) onto the Whitefish Creek Trail (#42) and begin ascending under a mix of spruce and fir woods as Trapper Creek sings down its lush drainage. The trail passes several small cascades and idyllic pools as it flirts with the creekside. Begin a more earnest ascent as the path turns south and pulls away from the creek, continuing through more pleasant woods until you reach the north end of Diamond View Lake at 4.8 miles. You will immediately find several inviting campsites beckoning you to stop and drop your gear as you skirt around the east side of the lake. Enjoy a picture-perfect view of 8744-foot Diamond Peak, justifying this forested pool's enchanting name.

Continue south from the lake, passing another small trailside pool, and go straight through a crossroads with the Crater Butte Trail (#44) at 5.7 miles. Now following the Whitefish Creek drainage, the trail begins a steady descent into increasingly drier woods of lodgepole pine and crosses a small spring at 8 miles. Reach the end of the trail at 9.7 miles, near the Whitefish Horse Camp at sprawling Crescent Lake. Hang a right (south) on the campground road and proceed to a spur trail that parallels FR 60. Take advantage of the water spigots along the way to top off your containers. At 10.6 miles, when you reach FR

6010/398, hang another right (north) and start up this rough dirt road. For the next 5 miles, continue up the viewless road, keeping watch for dirt bikes and off-road vehicles tearing up and down the bumpy path.

Just when you've had enough of the road, the Meek Lake Trail (#43.1) appears at 14.2 miles. Hang in there a bit longer and continue up the road, passing a chain of swampy lakes, and reach the northeast shore of Summit Lake at 15.7 miles. You'll find a large campsite nearby, and the Windy Lakes Trail (#46) heads south from here. Stay on the road for just one more mile, still heading west, and come to a small, primitive campground at a forest road junction at Emigrant Pass. There's a handful of good campsites here, but if you want something even better, head south on the old forest road. Here, you'll find the Pacific Crest Trail (PCT) paralleling Summit Lake's west shoreline, with a few fine, secluded campsites offering fantastic views over one of the Cascade Crest's largest and prettiest lakes.

From Summit Lake, your trek continues on the PCT, heading north from Emigrant Pass. The route passes several small ponds and primitive campsites, making an easy, winding ascent through an abundance of greenery. At 19.9 miles, the PCT cuts through a four-way junction; from here, the Rockpile Trail (#3632) heads left (west) to a couple of small lakes, and the Crater Butte Trail heads right (east) to places you've already visited.

Continue straight (north), staying on the PCT as it eases to a level walk through copious huckleberries—a delightful treat if you're passing through in season. As the climbing commences, the trail makes a U-turn at an open viewpoint at 21.2 miles; the view south showcases Cowhorn Mountain, Sawtooth Mountain, Mount Thielsen, and even far-off Mount McLoughlin. Nearby, among the rabbitbrush, fireweed, and carpets of whortleberry, a large cairn marks an unsigned climbers' trail that peels off to the left (northwest).

From here, the PCT ascends onto the open, rocky plains of Diamond Peak's eastern slope. The landscape is a jumble of multicolored lava rock and pocket meadows of heather and saxifrage. Welcome to the alpine high country of the Oregon Cascades! Next, the entire sweeping extent of Diamond Peak comes into view, curving from west to north. Lofty ridges and pinnacles vault skyward above expansive talus slopes spilling from glacial cirques and moraines. As you gawk at the scenery, cross a few dry drainage gullies before coming to Mountain Creek at 22.6 miles, which runs reliably well into summer. Just below (east) of the PCT, there are a few nice campsites along the creek with good views. The trail then bends east, alternating through pockets of shady forest and open slopes, before eventually dipping under the cool shade of old-growth.

As the PCT wraps around Diamond Peak's northeastern flank, enjoy the occasional view up at the northern summit. Cross one pleasant pocket meadow after another until you arrive at a clear, pretty pond in a shallow basin at 25.4 miles. Now the descent begins. Pass the Mount Yoran Trail (#3683; see Hike 61) and then arrive at shallow Lils Lake at 27.8 miles. From here, turn right (south) off the PCT and onto the Yoran Lake Trail (#49) to complete the final stage of your journey. Loop past Yoran and Karen Lakes, where you'll find a few more pleasant campsites, then commence a long, winding descent back toward Odell Lake. As you near the bottom, hop across West Bay Creek, then turn right (southeast) onto the Whitefish Creek Trail. When you reach a familiar junction at 32.8 miles, hang a left (northeast) and return to the trailhead where you started.

Opposite, top: Rose spiraea is common near lakes and wet meadows.

Opposite, bottom: Alpenglow on Devils Peak in the Sky Lakes Wilderness

South Cascades

63. Toketee Falls 186
64. Lemolo Falls 187
65. Tipsoo Peak 189
66. Thielsen Creek 192
67. Wizard Island 194
68. Garfield Peak 196
69. Seven Lakes Basin 198
70. Mountain Lakes Loop 201
71. Pilot Rock 204

From the oak savannas near the California border, to the sharp ridgelines of the Sky Lakes Wilderness, to the surreal and captivating Crater Lake, Oregon's southern Cascades are filled with outdoor playgrounds worth exploring. Rich in both natural and cultural history, here you will find unique features that you can't see in any other part of the state, including a settler-era waypoint, a mountaintop transformed by lightning, and a volcano inside of a lake inside of a volcano!

63 *Toketee Falls*

Distance: 0.8-mile roundtrip
Difficulty: easy
Hiking time: short day hike
Elevation gain: 170 feet
High point: 2420 feet
Season: Apr–Nov
Management: Umpqua NF (Diamond Lake)
Protection status: none
Map: park map board
GPS coordinates: N 43 26.409, W 122 42.743

Getting there: From Roseburg, take North Umpqua Highway (Oregon Route 138) east for about 60 miles. Turn left (north) on Toketee-Rigdon Road (Forest Road 34) for Toketee Lake, drive 0.2 mile, and then turn left into the falls parking area. The trailhead is at the west end of the parking lot. ***Notes:*** This path, while short, requires climbing and descending more than two hundred stair steps. Stay safe and do not go beyond safety fences and rails.

Not all hikes need to be a major endeavor—sometimes a short trail is the perfect way to appreciate some natural Oregon splendor. Toketee Falls—appropriately named, as *toketee* is the Chinook word for "pretty"—epitomizes the idea that good things do indeed come in small packages. Located along the North Umpqua Highway, this short trail to a uniquely spectacular waterfall is an ideal spot to stop and stretch your legs on the way to Diamond Lake, Crater Lake National Park, or a variety of other southern Cascades destinations.

The first thing you'll notice when you pull into the parking area is the massive pipeline that runs along the back of the parking area, often spouting fountains of water from cracks in the casing. This is part of the North Umpqua Hydroelectric Project. On hot days, it's not a bad thing to cool off under one of these misty

The enchanting Toketee Falls

showers. Head for the trailhead at the end of the parking area and dip into shady woods of towering Douglas-fir, red cedar, and bigleaf maple. The walking is pleasant and easy along the river, with abundant sword fern, Oregon grape, thimbleberry, and rhododendron keeping the forest vibrant and cool.

About halfway to the waterfall viewpoint, the path ascends a series of stone steps to a small rise overlooking the river, with a view of the water plunging into a narrow chasm of churning potholes. From here, the path steeply climbs a series of stairways over a rise on the hillside, then descends to a wide viewing platform. From this high perch, you can take in the sight of two-tiered Toketee Falls; the one-hundred-foot lower falls pours through a slot in a wall of columnar basalt and tumbles into the river canyon below. It's one of the more unique and picturesque waterfalls in Oregon, making it a completely worthwhile roadside attraction. When you're done enjoying the falls, return the way you came.

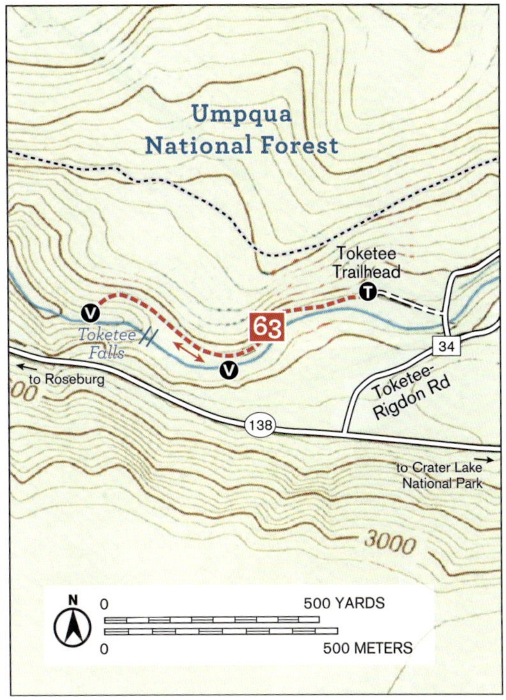

64 *Lemolo Falls*

Distance: 3.4-mile roundtrip
Difficulty: easy
Hiking time: short day hike
Elevation gain: 440 feet
High point: 4090 feet
Season: Jul–Oct
Management: Umpqua NF (Diamond Lake)
Protection status: none
Map: USGS Quad: Lemolo Lake, OR
GPS coordinates: N 43 32.916, W 122 20.273

Getting there: From Roseburg, take North Umpqua Highway (Oregon Route 138) east for about 72 miles toward Crater Lake National Park. Turn left (north) on Birds Point Road (Forest Road 2610) for Lemolo Lake, continuing another 4.3 miles. Veer right (northeast) at the fork to stay on Birds Point Road, crossing the Lemolo Lake Dam. At the next fork, veer left (northwest) on FR 2610 and proceed 0.6 mile along the viaduct, then turn left over a one-lane bridge. Park on the shoulder of the dirt road; the signed Lemolo Falls trailhead is on its south side. ***Notes:*** Do not enter the river above the waterfall! The optimal hiking season for the North Umpqua Trail varies. Sections higher in elevation (east) have a shorter season, while sections lower in elevation (west) have longer seasons. For more information about the entire trail, visit the Umpqua National Forest website (see Resources).

The North Umpqua Trail is an epic, 79-mile route that begins at Maidu Lake, near the Cascade Crest, and ends at Swiftwater Park, east of Roseburg. The trail is nearly all downhill (from its head at Maidu Lake), traveling through lush conifer woods as it follows the North Umpqua

Lemolo Falls on the North Umpqua Trail

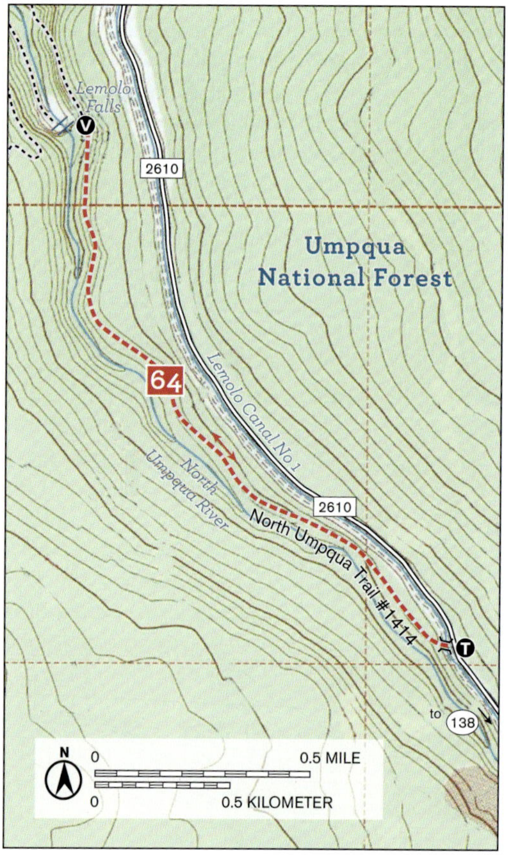

River and passes numerous picturesque lakes and roaring waterfalls. If you don't have a week or longer to enjoy the full trail, try this little slice of the North Umpqua Trail, not far from Crater Lake National Park. This hike will whet your appetite for a longer journey next time.

From the trailhead, plunge into shady fir and hemlock forest, with abundant ferns, salal, bleeding heart, and vanilla leaf along the trailside. The path heads generally downward on a gentle grade for most of the way to the falls viewpoint, meaning the return trip is all uphill—but it's not strenuous, making this a pleasant outing for all ages. The trail crosses a couple of seasonal creeks in the first 0.3 mile, then begins paralleling the North Umpqua River. A pretty cascade spills over a rock slide at 0.7 mile. Just beyond, the trail hugs a "weeping wall," where seeping springs drip down a wall of mossy volcanic rocks, and vibrant monkey flowers and trefoils are common.

A short distance farther, at 0.9 mile, look for a cluster of volcanic boulders perched on the hillside above the trail—you might think of them as Bilbo's trolls. Here, the trail crests a low rise, then continues its descent alongside the river. Cross another spring and traverse a slope dense with thimbleberry. At 1.4 miles, a giant Douglas-fir lays sprawled across the trail; a notch has been cut out of the trunk to allow for easy passage. Climb through and proceed another 0.2 mile to a high point on the trail that looks down on one-hundred-foot Lemolo Falls, roaring into the canyon below. Beyond here, the trail pulls away from the river, so this is the best view you will get. Soak in some of those refreshing ions, then begin your uphill journey back to the trailhead where you started.

Extend Your Trip: With a dozen trailheads accessing the North Umpqua Trail, you can tailor a variety of hikes to your liking, from short outings to multiday backpacks. Longer trips may require a shuttle vehicle to avoid backtracking long distances. The best way to experience the full North Umpqua Trail is to begin at Maidu Lake, just a mile west of the Pacific Crest Trail (PCT). Begin at the Miller Lake Campground and hike west on the Maidu Lake Trail for 2.7 miles. Cross the PCT and continue another mile to Maidu Lake, which has abundant camping options. Take the trail around either side of the lake, then start your North Umpqua Trail trek from the north end of the lake. From here, you can hike the entire 79 miles to Swiftwater Park or exit the trail at any of the other access points along the way.

65 *Tipsoo Peak*

Distance: 6.2-mile roundtrip
Difficulty: moderate
Hiking time: day hike
Elevation gain: 1500 feet
High point: 8034 feet
Season: Jul–Oct
Management: Umpqua NF (Diamond Lake)
Protection status: Mount Thielsen Wilderness
Map: Trails Illustrated 1005: Pacific Crest Trail Oregon South
GPS coordinates: N 43 22.379, W 122 06.741

Getting there: From Diamond Lake, take Oregon Route 138 north for about 4 miles. Turn right (east) on Forest Road 4793 and drive this washboard gravel road for 1.6 miles. Veer right at the fork onto FR 100 and continue 3.4 miles to the trailhead. The last mile of this

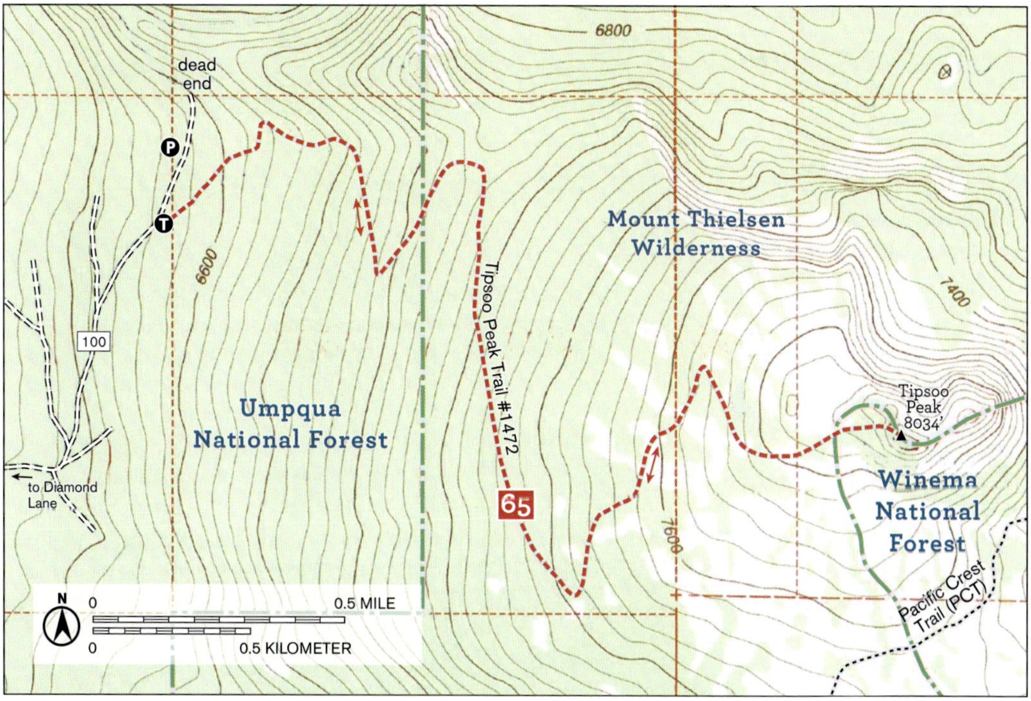

Big panorama of Howlock Mountain and Mount Thielsen from Tipsoo Peak

road is very rough and rutted, requiring a high-clearance vehicle. Find a parking pullout on the left (west) side of the road just past the trailhead. ***Notes:*** Wilderness rules apply. If you reach the summit and see thunderstorms building, retreat from the top and descend as quickly as possible.

You've likely heard the hikers' motto "The journey is the destination." Well, for the Tipsoo Peak Trail (#1472), the destination is the destination. Although this somewhat lackluster trail climbs up through uninspiring woods, Tipsoo Peak overlooks the highest point of the Pacific Crest Trail (PCT) in the Northwest, offering a huge scenic payoff. And because of its somewhat challenging entrance roads, you're likely to find plenty of solitude here, despite its proximity to the busy Diamond Lake recreation area and Crater Lake National Park.

Start from the remote and easy-to-miss trailhead on the old forest road, plunging into shady, viewless hemlock woods, where little grows on the ground—except for the occasional patch of grouse whortleberry—and baby hemlocks vie for their space in the sun. The way

heads up on a generally moderate grade, gaining elevation through long, lazy switchbacks, and enters the Mount Thielsen Wilderness at 1 mile. The path is wide and duff-covered, making for easy travel, so feel free to zone out and ponder the mysteries of the universe as you listen to the breeze in the trees and the occasional birdsong. At about 1.5 miles, take note of an especially huge hemlock that soars skyward, dwarfing everything nearby.

Things start to get more interesting as you near the peak. At 2.8 miles, the forest thins, and you're given tantalizing peeks of the grandeur to come. The trail underfoot turns to cinders as you pass through pocket meadows and lava rock gardens sprinkled with heather, penstemon, and buckwheat. Reach the edge of the crest at 3 miles. From here, the final stretch is an easy scramble up to the 8034-foot summit ridge. At the top, the entire southern and central Cascade Crest bursts into view. Howlock Mountain and Mount Thielsen take center stage looking south, while Cowhorn Mountain, Diamond Peak, the Three Sisters, and even a sliver of Mount Jefferson line up to the north. Below, to the southeast, the PCT crosses through 7560-foot Tipsoo Pass. Take some time to plop down and take it all in. When you can finally tear yourself away from the view, return to your vehicle via the same route.

66 Thielsen Creek

Distance: 11.3-mile roundtrip
Difficulty: moderate
Hiking time: day hike or overnight
Elevation gain: 1650 feet
High point: 6940 feet
Season: Jul–Oct
Management: Umpqua NF (Diamond Lake)
Protection status: Mount Thielsen Wilderness
Map: Trails Illustrated 1005: Pacific Crest Trail Oregon South
GPS coordinates: N 43 18.352, W 122 13.349

Getting there: From Roseburg, take North Umpqua Highway (Oregon Route 138) east for about 78 miles toward Crater Lake National Park. Turn right (west) for Diamond Lake Resort and Campground, curving south for 0.4 mile. Then turn left for the Howlock Mountain trailhead, directly across from the Diamond Lake gas station. ***Notes:*** NW Forest Pass or Interagency Pass required for trailhead parking. Wilderness rules apply. Exercise caution in burned areas. Equestrian use is common on these lower trails; exercise right-of-way courtesy.

Although a large portion of this trail burned in 2020, a good stretch still makes it worthwhile. Once you get through the dry and desolate burn on the lower flanks, you'll enjoy pleasant woods along a singing creek and then top out on the Pacific Crest Trail (PCT), with a fantastic view straight up the north face of imposing Mount Thielsen—the lightning rod of the Cascades! Pack a lunch for a picnic beside the wildflower-laden creek, or wander along the PCT for a mile or so northward to enjoy views over Diamond Lake and Howlock Mountain.

Start on the Howlock Mountain Trail (#1448), taking the path straight ahead (northeast) and

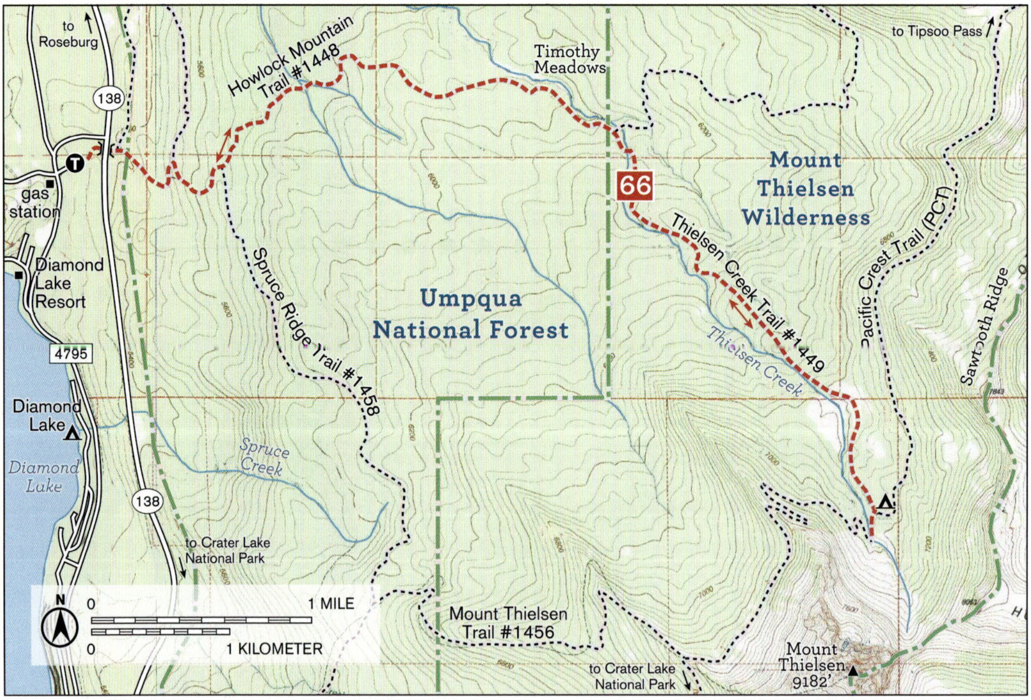

Thielsen Creek below Thielsen Peak

passing through a tunnel under the highway. You'll stick with this trail for the next 3 miles, climbing gradually through increasingly burned woods. Along the way, you'll pass several equestrian trails and a junction with the Spruce Ridge Trail (#1458). Occasional patches of manzanita and dogbane add a little greenery to the otherwise stark and charred surroundings. The path dips through a dry gully at 1.7 miles, then an island of green trees at 2.1 miles, mercifully spared from the fire. At 2.8 miles, the trail meets Thielsen Creek amid a green, swampy swath and passes what remains of the Timothy Meadows.

The scenery finally improves at around 3.1 miles, rewarding your perseverance, as the trail exits the burn zone and plunges into refreshingly green and lively woods. A little farther up, as the trail bends north, it crosses Thielsen Creek. There's no bridge, so find a safe crossing and come to the next junction on the other side. Turn right (south) on the Thielsen Creek Trail (#1449) and continue heading uphill. The ground cover starts to diminish as the surface becomes more cindery—the explosive debris of Mount Mazama's eruption some 7700 years ago. Continue snaking upward, getting your first tantalizing view of Mount Thielsen as you near the top, then reach a junction with the PCT at 5.5 miles.

If you're planning an overnight in the backcountry, you'll find several decent campsites near the junction here. For the view you came for, turn right (south) on the PCT and proceed another 0.1 mile to Thielsen Creek. Where the creek runs across the trail, turn left (south) and head upstream on a user path into a gorgeous, parklike setting. Thielsen Creek tumbles down the narrow canyon and 9182-foot Mount Thielsen towers overhead. The deep, rocky pockets and crevices on the north side of the peak—until 2020, the home of the Lathrop Glacier—can retain snow long into the summer.

Extend Your Trip: The previous edition of this guide detailed a lollipop loop trip that involved hiking 3 miles north on the PCT and then descending via the Howlock Mountain Trail, for a 15.5-mile roundtrip. The PCT section is still pleasant and accessible, with some nice views of Sawtooth Ridge, Howlock

Mountain, and Diamond Lake. However, the upper portion of the Howlock Mountain Trail was heavily damaged by storms and has not seen maintenance since 2024, so it is not currently recommended. An alternative is to hike 5 miles north from Thielsen Creek to Tipsoo Pass. At 7560 feet, this is the highest point of the PCT in Oregon. From either the Howlock junction or Tipsoo Pass, you can backtrack down the way you came.

67 *Wizard Island*

Distance: 4.3-mile roundtrip
Difficulty: strenuous
Hiking time: day hike
Elevation gain: 1390 feet
High point: 6930 feet
Season: Jul–Sep
Management: National Park Service
Protection status: Crater Lake National Park
Map: Cleetwood Cove trailhead kiosk
GPS coordinates: N 42 97.972, W 122 08.335

Getting there: From Mazama Village (south park entrance on Oregon Route 62), drive 6.7 curvy miles up Munson Valley Road toward Rim Village. Turn left (west) on Rim Drive and continue 5.9 miles around the crater to the junction at Merriam Point. Turn right (east) to stay on Rim Drive and proceed 4.5 miles to Cleetwood Cove. From Diamond Lake (north entrance on OR 138), drive 9.1 miles south to Rim Drive. Turn left (east) and proceed 4.5 miles to Cleetwood Cove. Give yourself extra time to arrive in anticipation of heavy park traffic. ***Notes:*** Requires both park entry fee and boat ride ticket. Reservations recommended (see Resources). No running water is available, and summer temperatures can get very hot. Bring all you need to stay cool and hydrated, and use sun protection. The Cleetwood Cove Trail will be closed for a major renovation beginning in the summer of 2026. During this closure, boat tours will not be available to visit Wizard Island.

Oregon's most unique hike is perhaps also its most exclusive. After all, where else in the world can you hike to the top of a volcano, within one of the world's deepest, clearest lakes, within a larger volcano?! It all began more than 7700 years ago, when ancient Mount Mazama blew her top and then collapsed into herself, creating a gaping crater. Over the centuries that followed, rain and snowmelt filled the crater, even as the mountain began rebuilding itself with a new peak. That peak eventually grew out of the lake to form Wizard Island. The only way to get to the island is via a boat ride from Cleetwood Cove, on the north side of the crater rim. Both the boat ride and the hike give you a fascinating look at the inside of an ancient volcano, showcasing the dynamic nature of Oregon's Cascade Range.

The trail begins on the rim at a large parking and visitor area. Interpretive signs and safety warnings offer information about the trails ahead. Begin a steep, steady, mile-long descent to the Cleetwood Cove boat dock under shady hemlocks, enjoying occasional views out over the lake. A few benches offer a place to sit and catch your breath. Remember, you're beginning your hike at a high elevation (nearly seven thousand feet), so pace yourself. As you descend farther into the crater, the trees peel away and the switchbacks lead down increasingly exposed, dusty slopes. If you haven't already, now is a good time to slather on your sunscreen. Once you reach the boat dock, check in with the attendant for your ride.

Enjoy a cool, breezy breather as your boat captain whisks you across Crater Lake's otherworldly azure waters to Wizard Island. The ride is

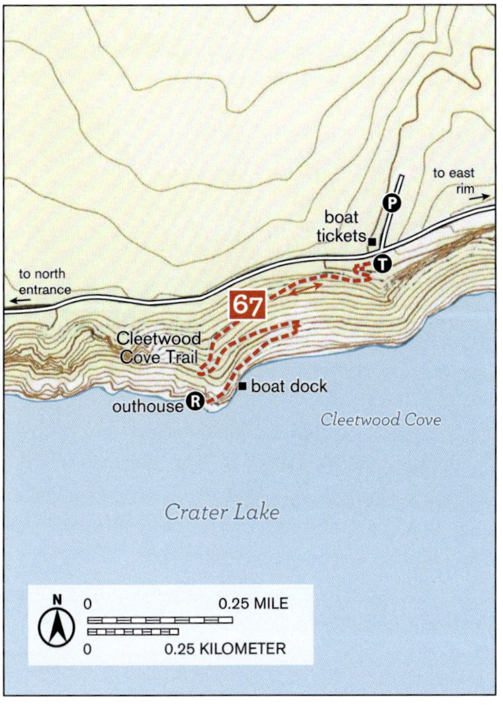

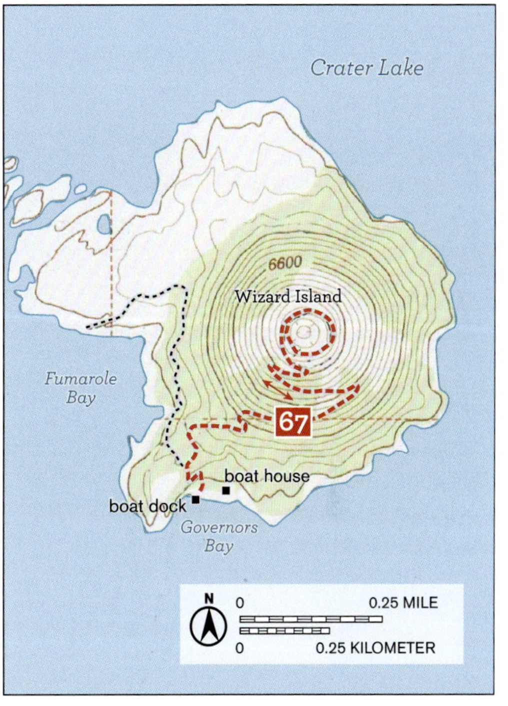

exhilarating and amazing, giving you a close-up view of the exposed bowels of Mount Mazama. Visible are millennia of volcanic deposits that formed the ancient volcano, including lava flows and pyroclastic deposits. As you cruise around the northwest wall of the crater, you'll get views of pinnacles, vents, volcanic dikes, and colorful ash deposits. Marvel at the striking Llao Rock, a 1200-foot-thick wall of dacite lava that creates the highest point on the crater wall, and note the fins of volcanic rock that make up the Devil's Backbone.

Once you reach the island and disembark, head 0.1 mile up the trail through a rocky lava flow to a junction. From here, you have two hiking choices: an easier, 0.6-mile walk along the rugged shoreline to the emerald pools at **Fumarole Bay**, or a moderate, 1-mile ascent to the rim of Wizard Island's **summit crater**. Veer right at the junction to take the summit trail, which is well graded and makes for a fairly easy ascent—just remember the elevation and pace yourself. The path twists upward through hemlock woods around the base of the crater, where patches of bleeding heart, penstemon, and manzanita eke out a rugged existence amid the porous surface. When the trail switches back at 0.8 mile, look directly west at the 8013-foot prominence of The Watchman on the crater rim, topped by a fire lookout. Once you reach the summit rim, enjoy a leisurely walk around the crater, taking in spectacular views across Crater Lake in every direction. Along the south rim, look for 8054-foot Garfield Peak (see Hike 68), and along the southeast waterline, try to spot the mysterious Phantom Ship rock formation.

With little shade to protect you from the sun, you're not likely to linger very long on the rim—and besides, you have a boat to catch. Return by the same route, descending to the boat dock, where you can rest under a mossy, shady hemlock or take a refreshing dip in the lake's crisp, clear water while you wait. Don't be late for your ride, as boat traffic to and from the island

Wizard Island rises from the azure depths of Crater Lake.

is precisely timed. Enjoy your trip back to the Cleetwood Cove dock, then finish your hike by climbing the crater rim back to the trailhead. Be sure to plan ahead for this return trip, conserving some of your water for what will likely be a hot, grueling slog. Once you reach the rim again, the nearest cold drinks are a 10.5-mile drive away in Rim Village.

68 *Garfield Peak*

Distance: 3.4-mile roundtrip
Difficulty: moderate
Hiking time: short day hike
Elevation gain: 1020 feet
High point: 8054 feet
Season: Jul–Oct
Management: National Park Service
Protection status: Crater Lake National Park
Map: Crater Lake park brochure
GPS coordinates: N 42 90.963, W 122 14.020

Getting there: Crater Lake National Park's south entrance can be accessed via Oregon Route 62 from Medford (southwest), or via US Highway 97 and OR 62 from Klamath Falls (southeast). The north entrance can be accessed via OR 138 from Roseburg (west), or via US 97 and OR 138 from Bend (northeast). Travel times range from 1 to 2.5 hours. Once in the park, follow signs to the Crater Lake Lodge in Rim Village. ***Notes:*** Park entry fee required. Summer weekends are very busy; consider an early morning or midweek visit. No water is available on this trail, and summer temperatures can be hot. Carry all the water you need to stay hydrated at high elevations.

At a little more than eight thousand feet above sea level, Garfield Peak is one of the highest points on the south rim of Crater Lake. From atop this perch, you can enjoy a stunning panorama over the cerulean waters of this volcanic spectacle, which formed when rain and snowmelt filled the caldera left behind after the eruption and collapse of Mount Mazama some 7700 years ago.

Because there is so little organic material in the crater, the lake water is some of the clearest and cleanest in the world, giving it an otherworldly appearance. The hike to the summit is not long or steep, but the full exposure and high elevation can still make you wheeze along the way. Pace yourself, stay hydrated, and take advantage of the few shaded areas to take breaks..

From wherever you manage to park in the Rim Village area—and this may be a challenge unto itself—walk the paved path eastward to the historic Crater Lake Lodge. Pass in front of the lodge, enjoying the views along the way, and find the trailhead on its east side in a wide, slopeside meadow. Head down the gravel path and savor the brief shade provided by lodgepole pine and mountain hemlock—you won't get much more after this. The trail then begins contouring upward along the south side of the rim, with the occasional switchback. Enjoy plenty of views along the way, as well as an abundance of pretty ceanothus, oceanspray, buckwheat, pasque flower, and phlox decorating the hillsides.

After a steady mile of climbing, the trail switches back again, continuing upward through a wide-open meadow. Once it reaches the rim of the crater, at 1.1 miles, you're treated to a spectacular lake view. Continue another 0.1 mile to the next viewpoint and look east to spot the Phantom Ship, a formation in the lake near the crater wall. This odd-shaped tower of volcanic rock loosely resembles a ghostly sailing ship and stands 170 feet above the surface of the lake. The remains of an ancient volcano that predates Mount Mazama, the Phantom Ship is more than four hundred thousand years old.

After a short, leisurely stroll, the trail begins climbing again, passing a couple of benches at 1.4 miles, then proceeds up through another short series of switchbacks. Another viewpoint offers a look eastward at the Eagle Crags, which adorn the north faces of Garfield Peak, Dyar Rock, and Applegate Peak. As the trail makes its final circuit around the south and east sides of Garfield Peak, just before reaching the summit, you'll find a breathtaking view eastward over the crater rim.

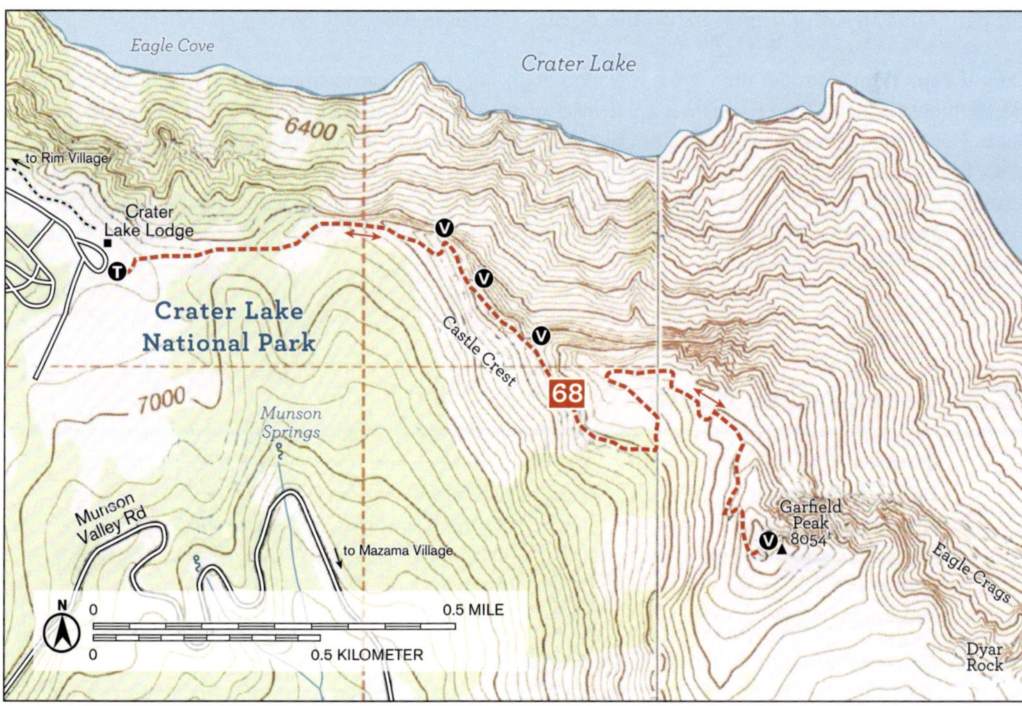

The PCT approaching Devils Peak in the Sky Lakes Wilderness

by a hikers' camp. Continue around the lake, crossing a couple of creeks, then come to the shore of Middle Lake at 5.1 miles. A lone campsite can be found near here. At 5.6 miles, reach the Cliff Lake junction. If planning an overnight outing, consider camping at Cliff Lake, which has several nice campsites with pleasant views. You can dump your gear here and day hike up and around Devils Peak, returning via the short Cliff Lake Trail spur from the PCT.

Otherwise, turn right (southwest) and head around the north side of Cliff Lake, backed by an impressive view of 7582-foot Devils Peak. The trail then heads up and around South Lake, with a campsite near the west shore at 6 miles. Continue ascending at a moderate grade through parklike settings, passing pocket meadows and crossing small creeks and springs, before mounting a rise on the flank of 7315-foot Venus. At 7 miles, continue straight (west) through a junction with the Alta Lake Trail (#979), then veer left (south) onto the Devils Peak Trail (#984). The path contours higher along the slope of Venus, then upward onto the flank of 7415-foot Jupiter. Now traverse a wide talus slope, where wide panoramas open up to the north, then make a gradual ascent through a small pass on the flank of 7474-foot Lucifer, reconnecting with the PCT at 8.5 miles.

Back on the PCT, turn left (northeast) and make a wide, contouring ascent along the upper flanks of Devils Peak to reach a pass on the east shoulder at 9.1 miles. Give yourself some time to pause here and absorb the view—one of the best on the PCT in Oregon. To the north, you can pick out the high peaks on the rim of Crater Lake; to the south, take in distant Mount McLoughlin and the southern Cascade Crest. When you're ready to continue, tip over the north side of the shoulder and start a steady, switchbacking descent. In some years, snow may linger on the trail long into summer. As you descend, cross several springs and find several campsites along the trail, at 10.1, 10.5, and 11.2 miles. During peak summer, these are typically occupied by long-distance PCT hikers, eager to take advantage of the water sources before heading into the long, dry region to the north.

The trail grade eases at 11.5 miles, where the PCT meets the Cliff Lake Trail (#983). This 0.5-mile spur connects with the Seven Lakes Trail to the west, then proceeds around the east side of the lake. For some great camping and great views—sans PCT hikers, because they typically don't want to deviate too far from the main trail—veer left (west) and pitch your tent by the lake. Otherwise, veer right (north) and continue along the PCT for another 0.7 mile to the Seven Lakes Trail junction where you started your loop. Now retrace your steps back to the Sevenmile Trail and make your exit by the same path.

Extend Your Trip: In this section of the Sky Lakes Wilderness, and along this stretch of the PCT, there are almost too many options for further exploration to list. You might consider hiking 1.8 miles (one-way) to **North Lake** and **Lake Ivern** from the Middle Lake junction. Or hike 1 mile (one-way) to **Lake Alta** from the junction west of South Lake. If you want to go even farther, you can head south on the PCT from the Lucifer junction, hiking for 11.5 miles to **Island Lake**, another picturesque setting with several good camping options.

70 *Mountain Lakes Loop*

Distance: 16.7-mile lollipop loop
Difficulty: strenuous
Hiking time: overnight
Elevation gain: 3090 feet
High point: 7570 feet
Season: Jul–Oct
Management: Fremont–Winema NF (Klamath)
Protection status: Mountain Lakes Wilderness
Maps: USGS Quads: Lake of the Woods South, OR; Aspen Lake, OR
GPS coordinates: N 42 39.971, W 122 10.108

Getting there: From Klamath Falls, head west to merge onto Falls Highway (OR 140) for Medford and continue for 15 miles. Turn left (west) on Forest Road 3637 and drive for 1.8 miles on good gravel, then turn left (south) on FR 3664. Drive 2 miles to the Varney Creek trailhead, following the signs. The road gets steep and a little bumpy but is suitable for most vehicles. ***Notes:*** Portions of this trail are unmaintained; expect to navigate a lot of blowdown. Some routefinding may be necessary. Older Forest Service maps show the trail on the south side of Whiteface Peak higher on the slope; these are no longer accurate. Mosquitoes here can be voracious in early summer—be prepared!

While Oregon hikers flock to the Cascade Crest, this small, unassuming wilderness area on the east side offers a few day and overnight trail options for those wanting to ditch the crowds and enjoy some quiet, picturesque backcountry scenery. And if you visit midweek, you're more likely to have only squirrels and gray jays for company instead of fellow hikers—even in the peak of summer.

From the trailhead, begin on the Varney Creek Trail (#3718) and plunge into a viewless forest of mixed pine and fir. It's a lackluster start, with little adorning the forest floor save for a few patches of chinquapin and pipsissewa. The trail bends south to head up the Varney Creek valley, entering the Mountain Lakes Wilderness at 1.2 miles, then crosses the creek in a boggy area tangled with debris. Now on the west side of the creek, the trail continues upstream, still viewless, until it traverses an open meadow of goldenrod, larkspur, and lupine at 2.7 miles. The peak directly east is 7979-foot Mount Harriman. Continue heading upstream, gaining steady elevation, until you come to a fork in the road at 4.4 miles. This begins the loop portion of the trail.

Take the right (southwest) fork onto the Mountain Lakes Loop Trail (#3727) and enjoy a leisurely walk to shallow Eb and Zeb Lakes, on either side of the trail. These lakes could be a good spot to break for lunch—or to set up a tent if you had a late start. Top off your water here if needed, as there is none to be found until you reach the other side of the loop. From the lakes, the trail makes a steady, switchbacking ascent through more woods, then heads up a rugged talus slope to reach a 7420-foot saddle at 5.6 miles. Just before crossing over, take in a wide panorama eastward that extends all the way out over the Klamath basin.

Tip over to the other side of the ridge and contour along the west side of Whiteface Peak. To the west, you can easily spy Brown Mountain and 9495-foot Mount McLoughlin on the Cascade Crest. As the trail descends into dry lodgepole woods, keep a sharp eye out. The trail can be hard to find through some stretches and passes through a series of junctions—some marked, some not. As a rule of thumb, stay left at every junction until you reach the lake. Pass the Mountain Lakes Trail (#3721) and Clover Creek (#3722) Trail, at 6 and 6.8 miles, respectively. Next, cross an extension of a wide talus slope at 7.3 miles, and

Charming Eb Lake makes a nice lunch spot on the Mountain Lakes Loop.

watch for a sudden left (north) turn at 7.5 miles. This turn is easy to miss, so be ready for it. From here, the trail starts zigzagging northeastward up the hillside. Watch for cairns and other markers to help lead the way. Near the top, at 7.9 miles, veer left at another junction to crest the ridge and reach a fantastic lakes viewpoint. The trail continues climbing along the ridge a little farther, reaching the loop's high point and another junction at 8.8 miles. Here, a side trail branches off right (south) to 8208-foot Aspen Butte.

It's all downhill from here. Veer left (east) and then left again (north), passing the South Pass Lake Trail (#3720) at 9.3 miles, and drop into the Lake Harriette basin. The trail down through here is rough, so watch your footing. The path bottoms out and passes a small pond at 10.4 miles, then comes to the north shore of picturesque Lake Harriette at 10.8 miles. A few nice campsites with good views can be found in the area. Nearby, the Moss Creek Trail heads off north. Follow the trail around the lakeshore to reach a couple more campsites 0.2 mile farther, on the west side of the lake. Pick your perfect spot, drop your gear, and enjoy the solitude. The next morning, proceed through a low pass, then circuit around an unnamed lake at 11.5 miles. At 11.9 miles, reach Lake Como, which has a few good campsites. Just 0.4 mile farther, return to the start of the loop. Turn right (north) and head back along the Varney Creek Trail the same way you came in.

Shorten Your Trip: Don't have time for the full loop, or want to avoid the potential hassle of routefinding? Just day hike to one of the lake basins. Head up the Varney Creek Trail and veer right (southwest) to visit Eb and Zeb Lakes for a 9.4-mile roundtrip, or veer left (southeast) to visit Lake Como and Lake Harriette for an 11.8-mile roundtrip.

71 Pilot Rock

Distance: 4.6-mile roundtrip
Difficulty: moderate
Hiking time: day hike
Elevation gain: 1250 feet
High point: 5640 feet (rock base)
Season: Jul–Oct
Management: Oregon BLM (Medford)
Protection status: Cascade-Siskiyou National Monument, Soda Mountain Wilderness
Map: Trails Illustrated 1005: Pacific Crest Trail Oregon South
GPS coordinates: N 42 04.737, W 122 58.390

Getting there: From Medford, take Interstate 5 south for about 25 miles toward California. Take exit 6 and drive south on Old Highway 99 for 2.1 miles. Turn left (east) onto 40-2E-33 and proceed 1 mile on this bumpy gravel road to a parking turnout beside a wooden gate arch; do not park in front of the gate. ***Notes:*** Beware of ticks, rattlesnakes, and poison oak. Respect seasonal closures for nesting birds.

Before street signs, Thomas Guides, Google Maps, and GPS, there were big rocks, tall trees, rivers, meadows, and mountains. These were the navigational aids used by Native Americans and the migrants who followed. For those traveling between the Shasta and Rogue River valleys, Pilot Rock was the prominent landmark indicating the way through the mountains. Originally called *Tan-ts'at-seniphtha* (stone standing up), Pilot Rock is a 570-foot-tall, 25-million-year-old volcanic plug composed of columnar andesitic lava. It is one of the tallest and oldest volcanic features in the Siskiyou Mountains, which are much older. A shorter, more direct trail leads directly to the base of the rock, but this slightly longer jaunt along the

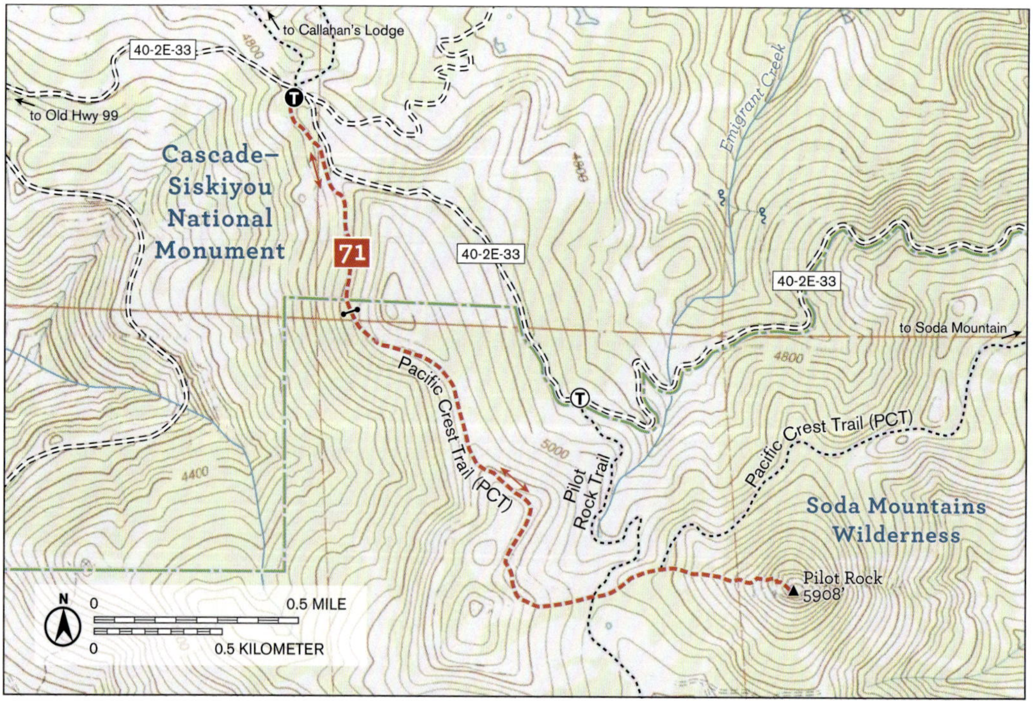

Peer straight up the columnar basalt walls of Pilot Rock.

Pacific Crest Trail (PCT) offers a pleasant hike through an oak savanna, with a few impressive views thrown in for good measure.

Find the PCT on the south side of the road, opposite the parking turnout, and plunge into mixed woods of white oak, ponderosa pine, Oregon grape, and oceanspray. Look for bright little blooms of pink dianthus dotting the trailside. After a short stretch, the woods deepen as the trail passes through a stretch of shady firs, where thimbleberry and false lily-of-the-valley carpet the forest floor. At 0.6 mile, pass through a stock control gate (be sure to close it again after you pass through), and curve eastward into a stretch of juniper woods. Get your first view of Pilot Rock looming ahead, and at 0.8 mile, you're treated to a wide panorama southward over the Siskiyou Summit and the Klamath Mountains, where 14,180-foot Mount Shasta takes center stage.

Continue contouring along the open hillside for a short spell, enjoying the views and the blossoms of colorful buckwheat that line the trailside. The path then dips back into shady forest. Cross an old logging road at 1.4 miles before descending into a wooded basin. The more direct Pilot Rock Trail meets the PCT at 1.7 miles, connecting from the left (north) side. Continue another 0.2 mile to the next junction and peel right (east) off the PCT onto the Pilot Rock Trail to begin the ascent to the rock's base. The way climbs steeply via twisting switchbacks, where views are scarce until you're near the top. Just past 2 miles, at an unmarked junction, a climbers' trail breaks off to the right (southeast); continue left (northeast) for the last 0.3 mile to the rock's base.

The view at the base of Pilot Rock is impressive, where the twisted columnar structure vaults skyward. Depending on your relationship with heights, it's possible to scramble to the top of the rock without the aid of climbing gear; however, this should only be attempted by sure-footed adventurers. For everyone else, enjoy the views from the base, then return to your starting point via the same route.

Extend Your Trip: From the Pilot Rock Trail junction, more than 2600 miles of the Pacific Crest Trail are at your immediate disposal. Explore as near or far as you like—up to 930 miles to the north and 1724 miles to the south. Some worthwhile northbound destinations include Hobart Bluff (9 miles), Soda Mountain Lookout (9.5 miles), and Hyatt Lake (19 miles).

Opposite, top: East Lake in the Newberry Crater

Opposite, bottom: Fall color along Tumalo Creek

Central Oregon

72. Fort Rock 208
73. Newberry Crater 209
74. Ancient Juniper Forest 212
75. Lava River Cave.............. 214
76. Lava Butte 216
77. Shevlin Park 218
78. Misery Ridge 220
79. Steins Pillar 222
80. Lookout Mountain 223
81. Blue Basin 226
82. Strawberry Loop 228
83. Arch Rock 231
84. Crawfish Lake 233

From volcanic craters to subterranean tunnels, ancient forests, and remote ridgelines, central Oregon is packed with outdoor wonders. In this part of the state, you can ramble through volcanic shrub steppe and admire the scenic peaks of the Ochoco and Blue Mountains. No matter which hike you choose, you're sure to be rewarded with natural beauty. Central Oregon is a scenic wonderland just waiting to be explored.

72 *Fort Rock*

Distance: 2.3-mile loop
Difficulty: easy
Hiking time: short day hike
Elevation gain: 380 feet
High point: 4540 feet
Season: year-round
Management: Oregon State Parks
Protection status: Fort Rock State Natural Area
Map: USGS Quad: Fort Rock, OR
GPS coordinates: N 43 37.282, W 121 06.646

Getting there: From Bend, take US Highway 97 south for about 30 miles to La Pine. Turn left (southeast) onto Oregon Route 31 and continue another 29 miles. When the road forks, veer left (east) onto County Road 5-10 and drive 6.4 miles. Then turn left (north) on Cabin Lake Road and proceed for 1 mile. Finally, turn left (west) on CR 5-11A and drive 0.7 mile to the visitor parking area. ***Notes:*** Day use only. Observe seasonal closures to help protect nesting birds. Fort Rock Cave is only open for reserved tours.

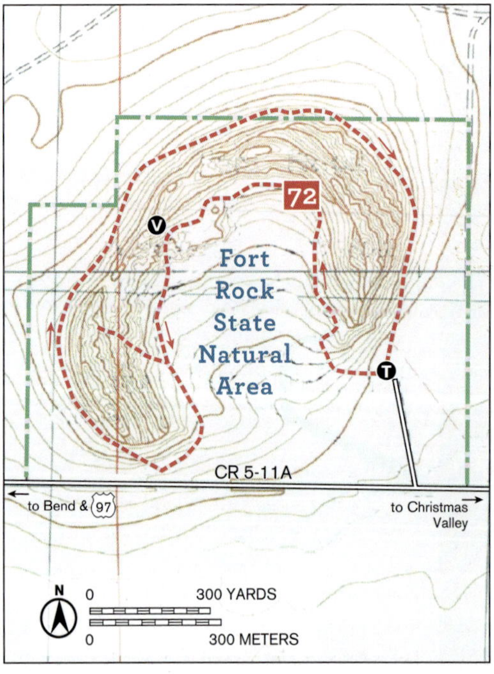

Imagine a vast, shallow inland sea filling much of central Oregon's high desert region. Now imagine an explosion of lava and ash in the middle of that sea—the result of hot magma rising to the surface and encountering the wet lake bed. Known as a maar volcano, this geological phenomenon is exactly what happened here tens of thousands of years ago, when all that material blew up and rained down into the sea, forming a near-perfect ring of volcanic tuff more than two hundred feet high. As the millennia wore on, the inland sea eroded the sides of the ring and eventually broke through, opening the southern walls. Then the sea dried up and ancient Native peoples began populating the area; some local artifacts date back more than nine thousand years. Resembling the walls of a crumbling fort—hence its name—Fort Rock is a unique and unusual landmark in Oregon's high desert that's well worth visiting.

There is no one way to hike the short trails that explore Fort Rock, making it easy to wander

Fort Rock is an ancient volcano that rose from the middle of an inland sea.

at will. The loop described here lets you examine both the interior and exterior of the formation, taking in all the unique details and features of this primeval volcano. Start at the southwest corner of the parking area and head into the crater. Follow the path as it curves north to trace the interior in a counterclockwise circuit. If you look closely at the ragged walls, you may see water lines marking the depth of the ancient sea that once filled the ring. As you approach the west side of the crater, climb onto the walls to a viewpoint that looks west over the ancient seabed—now a sea of dry sagebrush and spotty junipers—and spot a small butte where a cache of prehistoric artifacts was discovered.

Once you've completed your tour of the ring interior, you can return to the parking area or continue your exploration with a loop around the ring exterior. As you tour the exterior, the path is faint and overgrown in places, but all you really need to do is follow the walls of the crater. Look for more water lines from the ancient sea, as well as evidence of the volcanic tuff being eroded and sculpted through the ages. The overhangs of the walls are popular nesting places for a variety of birds, including several kinds of sparrows, prairie falcons, swifts, and owls. After about 2.3 miles of wandering, you'll find yourself back at the parking area where you started.

73 *Newberry Crater*

Distance: 20.8-mile loop
Difficulty: strenuous
Hiking time: overnight
Elevation gain: 3230 feet
High point: 7984 feet
Season: Jun–Oct
Management: Deschutes NF (Bend–Fort Rock)
Protection status: Newberry National Volcanic Monument
Map: Guide to Newberry National Volcanic Monument
GPS coordinates: N 43 70.093, W 121 27.276

Getting there: From Bend, take US Highway 20 south for about 20 miles. Turn left (southeast) on Forest Road 21 for Paulina Lake and continue 13 miles to the Paulina Lake Campground. Across from the campground, turn right (south) on FR 500 and proceed 0.7 mile to the large trailhead parking area on the right (west) side of the road. ***Notes:*** NW Forest Pass or Interagency Pass required for trailhead parking. This trail has no access to running water, so bring what you need. The total distance listed above includes a 0.8-mile roundtrip summit visit.

Right in the heart of Oregon, on the east side of the Cascade Range, the unassuming Newberry Caldera is the largest volcano in the Cascade volcanic arc. Covering an area of more than 1200 square miles, the caldera last erupted a mere 1300 years ago and is still considered to be active. Nestled in the center of the caldera, the Newberry Crater holds two sizable lakes—Paulina Lake and East Lake—separated by a cinder cone and lava flow. Numerous trails explore the

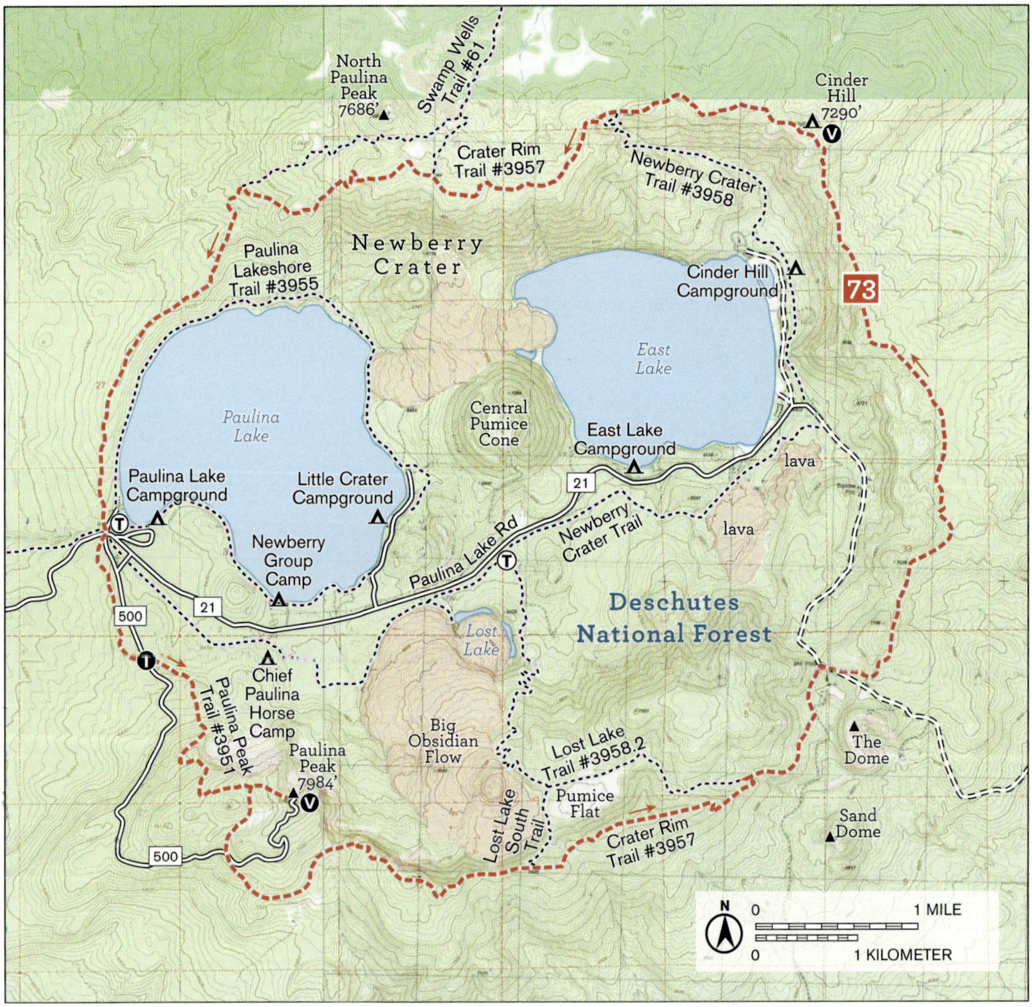

Big Obsidian Flow seen from Paulina Peak

lakes, lava flows, and peaks around the crater rim, but for the whole experience, try this 20-mile loop that offers impressive panoramas over the lakes, as well as the wider caldera area.

Start on the Paulina Peak Trail (#3951) and begin the long slog up the forested hillside. Sure, you could start at the top of the peak, but then you'd have to do the big climb at the very end of your hike. Better to tackle it first, then enjoy the cruise around the crater rim. At about 1 mile, burst out of the woods and get your first big view of Paulina Peak's north face, dominated by volcanic spires rising out of a sprawling talus slope. The trail ducks back into the woods for a stretch, then skirts along the precipitous edge of the peak, offering sweeping views over the lakes and crater. When you reach a junction with the Crater Rim Trail (#3957), at 1.6 miles, veer left (east) for the 0.4-mile detour to the summit viewpoint. The panorama from the 7984-foot summit takes in Paulina and East Lakes, the Big Obsidian Flow, the entire caldera area, and Cascades peaks that stretch for hundreds of miles. It's a "wow" view, so be prepared to spend some time here.

Once you've taken it all in, return to the Crater Rim Trail junction, and turn left (south) to begin your circuit. The path makes a steady descent to the forested south flank of Paulina Peak, crossing the peak road at 3 miles, then ambles pleasantly through grassy meadows and shady woods. Views to the south take in countless cinder cones within the wider caldera area. On clear days, you may be able to spy the snowy cap of 14,180-foot Mount Shasta, some 160 miles away in Northern California. The trail skirts the rim once more, now high above the Big Obsidian Flow, where a violent eruption spewed from the crater's south rim. At 5.5 miles, pass a junction with the Lost Lake South Trail, which descends along the east side of the Big Obsidian Flow to Paulina Lake Road.

Continue along the rim ridgeline until the trail dips over the outer edge and into a shallow canyon at 7.3 miles. Here, the Lost Lake Trail (#3958.2) breaks off to the left (west). Take the path to the right (east) to stay on the Crater Rim Trail. Traverse the crater's east slope and pass The Dome, another colorful cinder cone. A little farther along, at 8.3 miles, cross a gravel road and commence a casual ramble through viewless pine woods. The trail eventually begins gaining elevation again and reaches the exposed slope of 7290-foot Cinder Hill at 12.7 miles. This flat spot on the open crater rim offers a wide panorama over East Lake and the Central Pumice Cone, with Paulina Peak on the other side of the crater. A few good tent sites can be found in the area, making it an ideal location for camping.

From Cinder Hill, the trail begins its westward journey, dipping in and out of the woods and offering a few sparing views. Pass a junction with the Newberry Crater Trail (#3958) at 13.9 miles, then the Swamp Wells Trail (#61) at 15.5 miles. In another 0.5 mile, the trail reaches its last high point amid an open slope of red cinders. As you start descending from here, you're treated to some impressive views of Paulina Lake backed by Paulina Peak. The trail then steadily drops to cross the lake's outlet at 19.7 miles. Head up to cross Paulina Lake Road, then make a quick dogleg right (west) to continue on the Crater Rim Trail. This area is also signed for Nordic use, so follow the signs carefully. Complete your loop with a last, viewless mile through dense woods to return to the trailhead.

Other Options: **Paulina Lakeshore Trail:** This 7.3-mile, mostly flat trail skirts the shores of Paulina Lake, offering plenty of views and giving you the opportunity to take a dip in the chilly waters. Start at the trailhead in the Paulina Lake Campground, near the boat ramp, and begin a counterclockwise circuit of the lake. The trail passes through the Newberry Group Camp and Little Crater Campground before traversing the north shoreline. Near the end of the loop, drop into the Paulina Lake store for a refreshing drink or ice cream, then cross the lake's outlet to return to your starting point.

Newberry Crater Trail: For a hike that can be squeezed into a long day (or a short overnight), try this 15-mile option that loops around both Paulina and East Lakes. Park at the Big Obsidian Flow trailhead and pick up the trail heading east. Pass the East Lake and Cinder Hill Campgrounds, then climb to the north crater rim. Join the Crater Rim Trail and continue around the north rim, taking in wide views of Paulina Lake and Paulina Peak. Descend to the lake's outlet, cross the road, and proceed past the Paulina Lake Campground and Chief Paulina Horse Camp. Finish with a walk along the flanks of the Big Obsidian Flow.

74 *Ancient Juniper Forest*

Distance: 3.2-mile loop
Difficulty: easy
Hiking time: short day hike
Elevation gain: 220 feet
High point: 3780 feet
Season: year-round (weather permitting)
Management: Oregon BLM
Protection status: Oregon Badlands Wilderness
Map: BLM: Oregon Badlands Wilderness
GPS coordinates: N 43 95.759, W 121 05.158

Getting there: From Bend, take US Highway 20 east for approximately 15 miles to the Flatiron Rock trailhead. ***Notes:*** The Oregon Badlands has no water and little shade. The best times to visit are in spring and fall, when the weather is more favorable.

It may not look like it, but the rock- and juniper-covered Oregon Badlands was formed from the remnants of an ancient volcano. Designated a wilderness area in 2009, and encompassing an area of more than twenty-nine thousand acres, the Oregon Badlands Wilderness protects one of the state's most unique volcanoes. Unlike the obvious volcanoes along the Cascade Range—such as Mount Hood and Mount Jefferson—the Badlands volcano was formed when an active lava tube broke open, allowing liquid magma to cover the area and build a shield-type volcano.

Begin at the Flatiron Trailhead sign board, taking the left (north) fork for the Ancient Juniper Trail. The path dips through a shallow gully, then begins snaking on a gentle upward grade through stands of juniper trees and clusters of rabbitbrush. The junipers here are some of the oldest living trees in Oregon, with lifespans of more than a thousand years. In spring, the landscape is painted with wisps of color in the form of Oregon sunshine, mariposa lily, monkey flower, and buckwheat. Exposed outcrops and pressure ridges exhibit the two distinct kinds of lava that inundated the area: chunky, blocky formations (called *a'a*) and ropy, fluid formations (called *pahoehoe*).

The trail winds easily through the arid landscape, reaching the top of a low ridge at 0.8 mile. As you're walking, keep your eyes peeled for some of the resident wildlife, including mule deer, elk, pronghorn, coyotes, and jackrabbits. More than a hundred types of birds are also known to inhabit the area, including golden eagles, falcons, and sage grouse. The path starts twisting downward until it comes to a signed junction with the Flatiron Rock Trail at 1.9 miles. If you're just out for a short jaunt, turn right (south) and proceed 1.2 miles back to the trailhead for a nice, casual loop. If you've got the time and energy to explore more, check out the Extend Your Trip options below.

The Ancient Juniper Forest comes alive in spring and summer.

Extend Your Trip: **Flatiron Rock:** Add 3.4 miles to the Ancient Juniper loop with an out-and-back trek to an unusual lava formation, where you can wander along a narrow, moatlike crack in an exposed pressure ridge. You'll see unusual pinnacles and arches, with a few window-like openings that frame panoramic views of Cascade peaks. Get there by turning left (north) off the Ancient Juniper Trail, following the Flatiron Rock Trail northward for 1.6 miles to the next junction. Then veer left (west) and ascend a sandy path into the rock formation. Wander the 0.2-mile loop around the inside of the rock, then return to the Flatiron Rock Trail and follow it all the way back to the trailhead.

Badlands Rock: For a full day in the Badlands that visits Flatiron Rock, The Castle, and Badlands Rock, add this 7.5-mile loop to your trek for an 11-mile adventure. Start by following the directions above to Flatiron Rock. After you've looked around, return to the previous junction and head east on the Castle Trail. After a flat 0.4 mile, reach The Castle, another exposed lava formation that you can venture into and explore; find it just along the trail to your right (south). Then continue east for 0.7 mile to Badlands Rock, a colorful cinder cone that juts skyward among the surrounding junipers. Turn right (south) on the Badlands Rock Trail and amble for 2.7 miles on this wide, old roadbed to the next junction. Turn right here to join the Homestead Trail, a narrow, lesser-used track that can be overgrown in places, and continue for 2.2 miles. When you reach a familiar junction with the Flatiron Rock Trail, turn left (south) and hike the last 1.2 miles back to the trailhead.

75 *Lava River Cave*

Distance: 2-mile roundtrip
Difficulty: easy
Hiking time: short day hike
Elevation gain: 200 feet
High point: 4500 feet
Season: May–Sep
Management: Deschutes NF (Bend–Fort Rock)
Protection status: Newberry National Volcanic Monument
Map: Guide to Newberry National Volcanic Monument
GPS coordinates: N 43 89.534, W 121 36.972

Getting there: From Bend, take US Highway 97 south for about 10 miles. Take the exit for Crawford Road (Forest Road 9702), then turn left (south) on Cottonwood Road. Follow this road for 1.2 miles to the Lava River Cave parking area and entrance.
Notes: Parking reservations are required during the summer; obtain them in advance at recreation.gov. NW Forest Pass, Interagency Pass, or park entry fee required. The cave has no lighting source and is cold year-round; bring a strong flashlight or lantern and a jacket. To prevent the spread of white-nose syndrome, a fatal disease ravaging Oregon's bat population, do not wear any clothing or footwear that has been in any other cave system. Dogs prohibited.

One of the most unique and interesting hikes in Oregon is one you can't even see on the surface—instead, you'll travel nearly two hundred feet underground, following the path of an ancient lava flow. Known as "lava tubes," these underground tunnels are formed when fluid lava (*pahoehoe*) flows downhill in a channel. The surface of the flow is the first to cool and crust over, insulating the interior liquid lava and letting it continue to flow. Eventually, when the eruption ceases, the lava drains out of the passage, leaving an empty tunnel behind. These formations are often filled with a variety of unique and interesting features, all hidden from the world in a subterranean tunnel of mystery.

Enter Oregon's volcanic underworld in the Lava River Cave.

Begin your journey by descending a paved path into an open "skylight"—a section of the tube that has collapsed, creating an opening. Once you enter the cave, the temperature drops significantly, even if it's a hot day outside. Don your jacket and turn on your light, then head down into the dark. A series of grated stairs and walkways leads through the Collapsed Corridor and into Echo Hall, a wide section of tunnel where the ceiling soars more than fifty feet

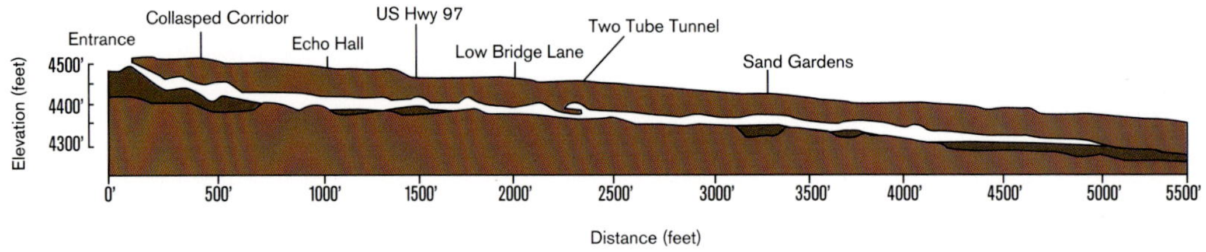

overhead and sparkles with formations of melted basalt. Lava deposits along the wall here indicate the depth of the lava flow as it passed through here. At 0.3 mile, the cave trail passes under US 97, then drops into Low Bridge Lane, where the ceiling dips to a mere 5.5 feet. Duck your head through here, as smacking your noggin on hard lava rock will likely make you see stars. The heat and gases once trapped in these narrow sections often melted and remelted the rock, making it look shiny and gooey.

The next point of interest is just beyond, at 0.4 mile, where the tube splits into two channels at the appropriately named Two Tube Tunnel. Take either path and then continue downward to the Sand Gardens, at 0.6 mile. The sand here is not a remnant of the lava flow; it comes instead from tiny bits of ash that were carried into the cave by water dripping through cracks in the ceiling. This accumulation of ash sand and dripping water created unique spires and pinnacles that have taken hundreds of years to form. Be careful not to disturb these delicate formations. From here, the tube continues for another 0.4 mile, getting narrower and shorter, since sand has filled and plugged the bottom of the tube over time. Watch your head as the ceiling closes in. When you've reached the end, turn around and retrace your steps back to the entrance.

Extend Your Trip: After your journey into the underworld of central Oregon's volcanic landscape, you can continue your explorations of the Newberry National Volcanic Monument at the Lava Lands Visitor Center and Lava Butte (see Hike 76) or various trails and interpretive sights at the Newberry Crater (see Hike 73).

76 *Lava Butte*

Distance: 3.3-mile roundtrip
Difficulty: moderate
Hiking time: short day hike
Elevation gain: 600 feet
High point: 5016 feet
Season: year-round (weather permitting)
Management: Deschutes NF (Bend–Fort Rock)
Protection status: Newberry National Volcanic Monument
Map: Guide to Newberry National Volcanic Monument
GPS coordinates: N 43 91.132, W 121 35.360

Getting there: From Bend, take US Highway 97 south for about 10 miles. Take the exit for Crawford Road (Forest Road 9702), then turn right (north) into the parking area for the Lava Lands Visitor Center. The trailhead is at the northeast end of the parking area. ***Notes:*** NW Forest Pass, Interagency Pass, or day-use fee required for parking. Visitor center hours vary by season; see website for more info. During summer, a shuttle bus runs from the visitor center to the Lava Butte summit. Do not disturb fire lookout staff.

Lava Butte has one of Oregon's few remaining staffed fire lookouts.

The central Oregon area has one of the highest concentrations of recently active volcanic features in the state. But recent means something different in geological terms; the latest volcanic event in this area occurred a mere 1300 years ago. The Newberry National Volcanic Monument, a fifty-four-thousand-acre area just south of Bend, encompasses the Newberry Caldera and showcases a plethora of natural features, including lava flows, cinder cones, pinnacles, and craters. One of these features is the five-hundred-foot-high cinder cone called Lava Butte. Open year-round, this prominence offers a stellar panorama over the central Cascade Range and is home to a working fire lookout tower, one of just a few that remain in Oregon.

This hike is simple to navigate: from the gated road/trailhead, just start hiking up the red cinder road. If hiking during peak summer, yield to the shuttle buses going up and down the road. The ascent is steady, but not steep, as the road/trail winds upward around the cone's cindery base. Along the shoulders of the road/trail, clusters of rock penstemon eke out their existence in the dry, porous surface. As you round the north side of the cone, stands of ponderosa pine adorn the cindery slopes, but they offer little respite from the midsummer sun. Once you reach the small parking area at the top, at 1.4 miles, take the short path up to the lookout tower platform and take in the expansive view. The current tower is the fourth structure to occupy this location. The original lookout was erected in 1933, with subsequent structures replacing the previous ones in 1958 and 1970. Constructed in 1998, the current lookout tower is still staffed by working fire watchers.

From the lookout tower, continue your exploration by taking the 0.3-mile trail around the summit crater rim. The views across the summit crater are impressive from every angle—especially when you consider that this volcanic area is still considered "active." The trail dips to a low point on the south side before climbing back up to the parking area. Help preserve the area by remaining on the trail and not venturing into the summit crater. Once you're back at the parking area, retrace your steps, heading back down the road/trail to your starting point.

Extend Your Trip: Don't miss some of the other short interpretive trails around the Lava Lands Visitor Center. The 1-mile, barrier-free **Trail of Molten Land** is a paved path that winds through the rugged basalt lava flows on the south side of Lava Butte. Here, you can see a moonscape of jumbled *a'a* lava, pressure ridges, and pinnacles. For a shorter, family-friendly path, follow the 0.3-mile **Whispering Pines Trail** to explore the edge of the lava flow among shady pine trees.

77 Shevlin Park

Distance: 4.5-mile loop
Difficulty: easy
Hiking time: day hike
Elevation gain: 330 feet
High point: 3850 feet
Season: year-round
Management: Bend Parks and Recreation
Protection status: Nature preserve
Map: Bend Parks and Recreation: Shevlin Park
GPS coordinates: N 44 08.167, W 121 37.862

Getting there: From central Bend near US Highway 97, take NW Newport Avenue west for approximately 4.3 miles. At the third roundabout, continue straight (west) on NW Shevlin Park Road for another 2.8 miles. Turn left (south) into the parking area. ***Notes:*** Day use only. Some trails are multiuse. Dogs must be leashed. Stay on designated trails and respect private property.

Take a walk through Oregon history at Shevlin Park.

Located on the western outskirts of Bend, Shevlin Park is a 980-acre nature preserve along a charming stretch of Tumalo Creek. The park was dedicated in 1920 in honor of the president of the local Shevlin-Hixon Lumber Company, who died at the young age of 32. Archeological finds in the area indicate that Native peoples populated the river canyon as far back as fourteen thousand years ago. The landscape along the

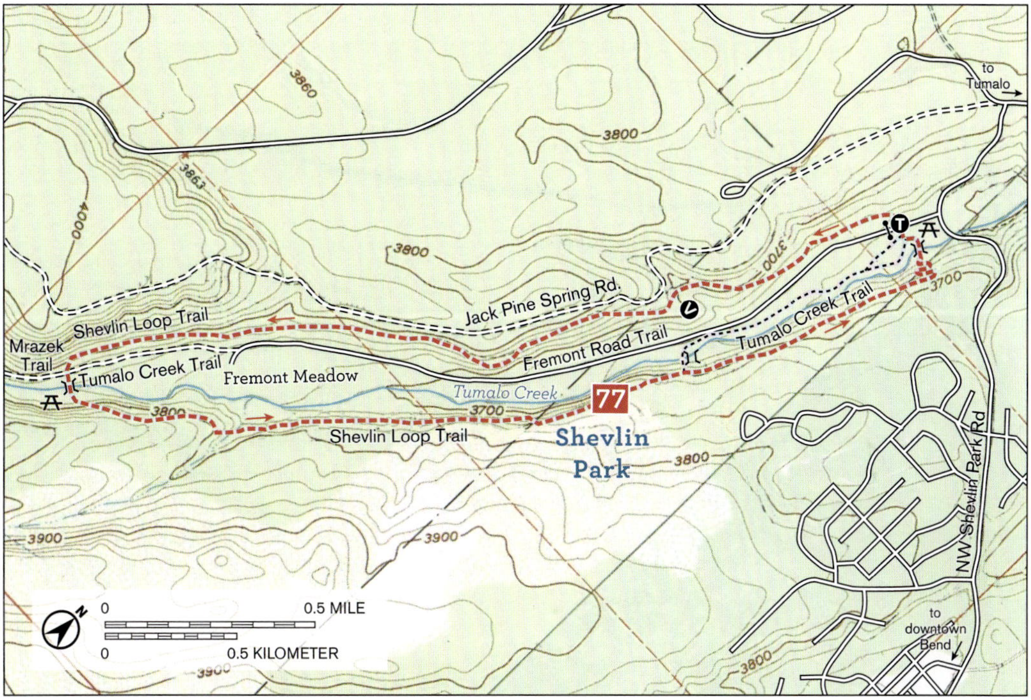

canyon walls is largely sagebrush and manzanita, set among stately old-growth ponderosa pine woods and fragrant junipers. The lush creek bottom boasts a variety of Douglas-fir, spruce, alder, aspen, and western larch. These latter specimens make Shevlin Park an attractive destination for autumn leaf-peeping.

The best way to experience Shevlin Park is with a jaunt along the 4.5-mile Shevlin Loop Trail. Begin at the trail map kiosk at the southwest corner of the parking area and head into the open ponderosa woods. Clusters of black lava boulders dot the hillside, adding an interesting contrast to the high desert flora. Proceed through several signed junctions, sticking with the loop trail, until you reach the Hixon Crossing viewpoint at 0.7 mile. From 1930 to 1957, a railroad trestle crossed the river canyon here, hauling lumber to the Brooks-Scanlon logging camp, now home to Bend's Old Mill District.

Continue hiking, passing larger lava boulders and junctions with the Mrazek, Fremont Road, and Tumalo Creek Trails. The path then dips down to cross Tumalo Creek on a rustic footbridge before arriving at a picnic area under a grove of tall, shady firs at 2.2 miles. Enjoy a pleasant break here as the creek sings down its channel nearby, then begin a short, steady ascent to the rim of the south canyon wall. Take a quick look over the creek canyon, then dip over the side of the rim through a jumble of boulders before proceeding along the canyon rim once more. Enjoy the occasional view of the creek as you draw nearer to civilization again. Continue straight through a couple more junctions at 3.6 miles, then drop down through a couple of switchbacks to the creek. At 4.4 miles, cross the creek on another bridge. Once across the bridge, it's just a quick 0.1-mile walk through the picnic area back to the parking lot and trailhead.

Extend Your Trip: If you're up for a little more exploring, veer left (south) after the last footbridge to wander up the Tumalo Creek Trail. The path follows the creek upstream through groves of aspen, then crosses the creek on another footbridge at 0.6 mile. Across the bridge, the trail climbs up to the canyon rim to meet the Shevlin Loop Trail at a familiar junction. From here, make an about-face and head back down the creek the way you came.

78 Misery Ridge

Distance: 3.7-mile loop
Difficulty: strenuous
Hiking time: day hike
Elevation gain: 960 feet
High point: 3290 feet
Season: Apr–Nov
Management: Oregon State Parks
Protection status: Smith Rock State Park
Map: Smith Rock State Park
GPS coordinates: N 44 36.630, W 121 13.746

Getting there: From US Highway 97 in the small town of Terrebonne, 22 miles north of Bend, drive east on Smith Rock Way for 1.6 miles. Turn left (north) on NE 17th Street and drive for 0.5 mile, then go right (east) on NE Wilcox Avenue. Continue for 0.5 mile, then turn left (north) on NE Crooked River Drive to enter the park. Proceed past the campground to the welcome center and trailhead parking. ***Notes:*** Day-use fee required. Most trails within the park are multiuse. Depending on how sturdy your knees are, you may want to do this loop in reverse.

Approaching the imposing Monkey Face

Smith Rock is renowned as one of the best rock-climbing formations in the United States. But you don't have to be a climber to bag the summit of this rugged, volcanic outcrop and enjoy the panoramic views from the top. The quickest non-climbing way up is via the appropriately named Misery Ridge Trail. This steep, rocky path grinds more than 650 feet up to the summit plateau and is sure to get you huffing and puffing along the way. You can lessen the misery, however, by hiking this loop trail around the back side of the rock for a more gradual ascent to the top.

Start at the paved trailhead, just north of the welcome center. Descend toward the Crooked River, first on a paved path with an interpretive viewpoint, then on wide gravel tread. Turn right onto The Chute Trail and quickly switchback down to the river's edge, at 0.2 mile. A grassy park area next to the river has a water fountain for topping off your bottles. Proceed across the river on a wide bridge to the base of towering Picnic Lunch Wall, a seven-hundred-foot-high wall of

flaky, volcanic tuff. (Tuff is a light, porous rock formed by the consolidation of volcanic ash.) On the other side of the river, start your loop by turning left (south) onto the Riverside Trail.

Enjoy a pleasant stroll alongside the Crooked River. The path skirts around Ship Rock, a towering dike of crumbly, purplish rhyolite. (A dike is an intrusion of rock into an existing formation, often volcanic or igneous in nature.) Traverse along the base of Morning Glory Wall, one of the most popular climbing walls in the park. At 1.3 miles, the trail hooks around the southernmost extent of the Smith Rock formation as the Crooked River makes a hairpin turn to the north. Continue following the river along the backside of Phoenix Buttress to a fork in the trail below Asterisk Pass, at 1.9 miles.

Take the right fork onto the Mesa Verde Trail, making a wide, switchbacking ascent under the shadow of Monkey Face. This 350-foot-tall pinnacle of rock offers some of the most challenging climbing routes in the park. As you reach the top of your ascent, at 2.5 miles, veer right at a fork in the trail and walk about fifty yards to a viewpoint, where you'll come nearly face-to-face with the simian-looking rock formation.

Here, you can also take in a sweeping view of Oregon's central and northern peaks, from the Three Sisters to Mount Hood. After your look, double back to the fork and proceed east across the summit plateau, where wildflowers are prolific in the spring.

Now it's time to pay the piper and begin your plunge down the Misery Ridge Trail. Watch your footing on the loose rock and steep switchbacks. The trail traverses the base of Red Wall, which is favored by climbers on hot summer days for its shady, east-facing direction. Descend through another series of steep switchbacks and find yourself back at the trail junction where you started the loop, at 3.3 miles. Cross back over the Crooked River, bypassing The Chute, and opting instead to return to the parking area via an easier stroll up the Canyon Trail.

79 *Steins Pillar*

Distance: 3.7-mile roundtrip
Difficulty: easy
Hiking time: short day hike
Elevation gain: 730 feet
High point: 4570 feet
Season: May–Nov
Management: Ochoco National Forest
Protection status: none
Map: USGS Quad: Steins Pillar, OR
GPS coordinates: N 44 39.494, W 120 62.389

Getting there: From Prineville, northeast of Bend, drive east on US Highway 26 for about 9 miles. At the east end of Ochoco Reservoir, turn left (north) on Mill Creek Road and proceed for 4.7 miles on good gravel. Watch for Forest Road 500 on the right, signed for Steins Pillar. Cross Mill Creek and take this steep, bumpy road for 2 miles to the trailhead on the left (north) side of the road.

Thanks in part to its largely volcanic makeup, Oregon is speckled with geologic curiosities. One of these is a 350-foot-high rock pinnacle called Steins Pillar. Named (and misspelled) for Major Enoch Steen, who explored the area in the mid-1900s, this towering monolith juts right out of the forested hillside in a semi-remote corner of the Ochoco Mountains. Many daring rock climbers attempt to scale the sheer, crumbly walls of Steins Pillar, which is composed of welded volcanic tuff. Hikers, however, can marvel at this natural wonder via a relatively easy hike along a flowery ridgeline.

From the trailhead turnout on the side of the road, the path immediately plunges into shady woods, crossing a seasonal creek and snaking through mountain roses under tall conifers. This lush ramble does not last for long, however, as the trail soon starts switchbacking up the

Steins Pillar is one of Oregon's more unusual sights.

ridgeline, becoming more and more exposed. In summer, look for pretty little pinkfairies carpeting the hillsides. Partway up the hill, at 0.4 mile, views start to open over the surrounding Ochoco hills and valleys, with a westward glimpse of the snowy cap of Mount Jefferson. Continue ascending until the trail tops out on the ridgeline at around 0.8 mile, where it passes through a wide, sloping meadow dotted with prairie flax, offering more views.

Opposite the meadow, the trail descends into the trees, curving around a drainage and then heading downward again. You'll soon see an impressive volcanic outcrop to the west of the trail, but this is not the pillar. Continue down to the next outcrop, at 1.8 miles, where you're presented with a sweeping view over the Mill Creek valley. Here, Steins Pillar vaults skyward, right out of the forest. It's an odd and impressive sight. The trail continues steeply down to the base of the pillar, but the best views are from above. Once you've taken in the scene, retrace your steps back to the trailhead.

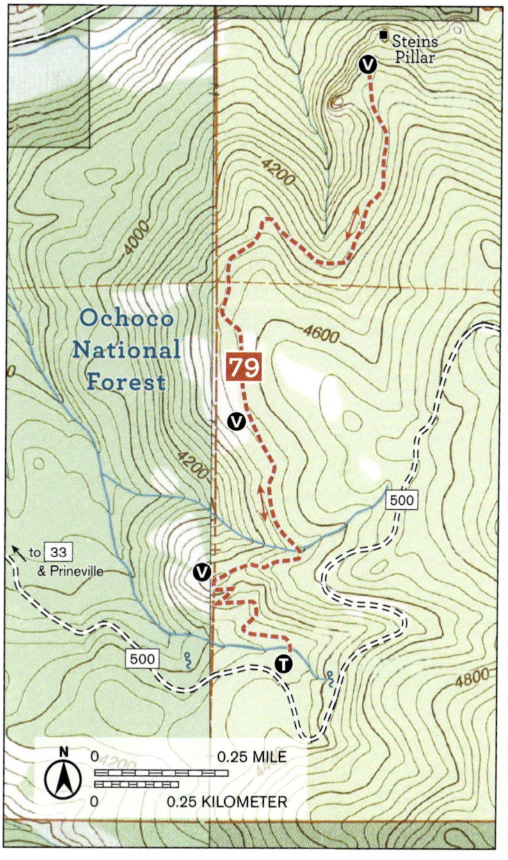

80 *Lookout Mountain*

Distance: 6.9-mile loop
Difficulty: moderate
Hiking time: day hike
Elevation gain: 1320 feet
High point: 6930 feet

Season: Jun–Oct
Management: Ochoco NF
Protection status: none
Map: USGS Quad: Lookout Mountain, OR
GPS coordinates: N 44 33.968, W 120 35.945

Getting there: From Prineville, head east on US Highway 26 for about 15 miles. At a fork signed for Walton Lake and Big Summit Prairie, veer right (east) on Ochoco Creek Road (Forest Road 42). Follow this good, paved road for 15 miles, keeping right at a fork shortly past the Ochoco Creek Campground. At a bend signed for the Independent Mine, turn onto rough gravel Lookout Mountain Road (FR 4205) and proceed 1 mile to the upper trailhead. ***Notes:*** If you're driving a low-clearance vehicle, you can park at the lower parking area and hike the 1-mile Round Mountain Trail (#805) up to the main loop. Never closely approach or enter any abandoned mine buildings or tunnels; they could be unstable and/or contain toxic or hazardous materials. Appreciate their historical significance from a distance. Avoid drinking water from streams near mines, even if filtered; it may be polluted with toxic mine waste.

Oregon's Ochoco Mountains, while picturesque, are not especially known for an abundance of hiking trails. However, this loop trail that visits an old mine site and fire lookout location is a true gem that should not be missed. You'll get a little bit of everything on this loop: from verdant, mixed woods to high desert prairie, with a summit plateau where you can trace almost three hundred miles of the Cascade Crest—one of the widest panoramas you're likely to find in Oregon.

From the trailhead at the top of the rough and difficult entrance road, start by heading west on the Lookout Mountain Trail (#804). Immediately veer left (southwest), bypassing the Round Mountain Trail (coming up from the lower parking area), and head into mixed woods brimming with lupine and cow parsnip. Looking upslope, you'll see the remains of the old Independent Mine, one of the many cinnabar operations in effect in the early 1900s. (Cinnabar was mined for its mercury content, which in turn was used in silver and gold mining.) Just beyond, the trail crosses a pretty creek, where the drainage is choked with monkey flower and larkspur.

Proceed up a moderate grade under pleasant, mostly shady woods. Although there are few views to be enjoyed along the way here, you're

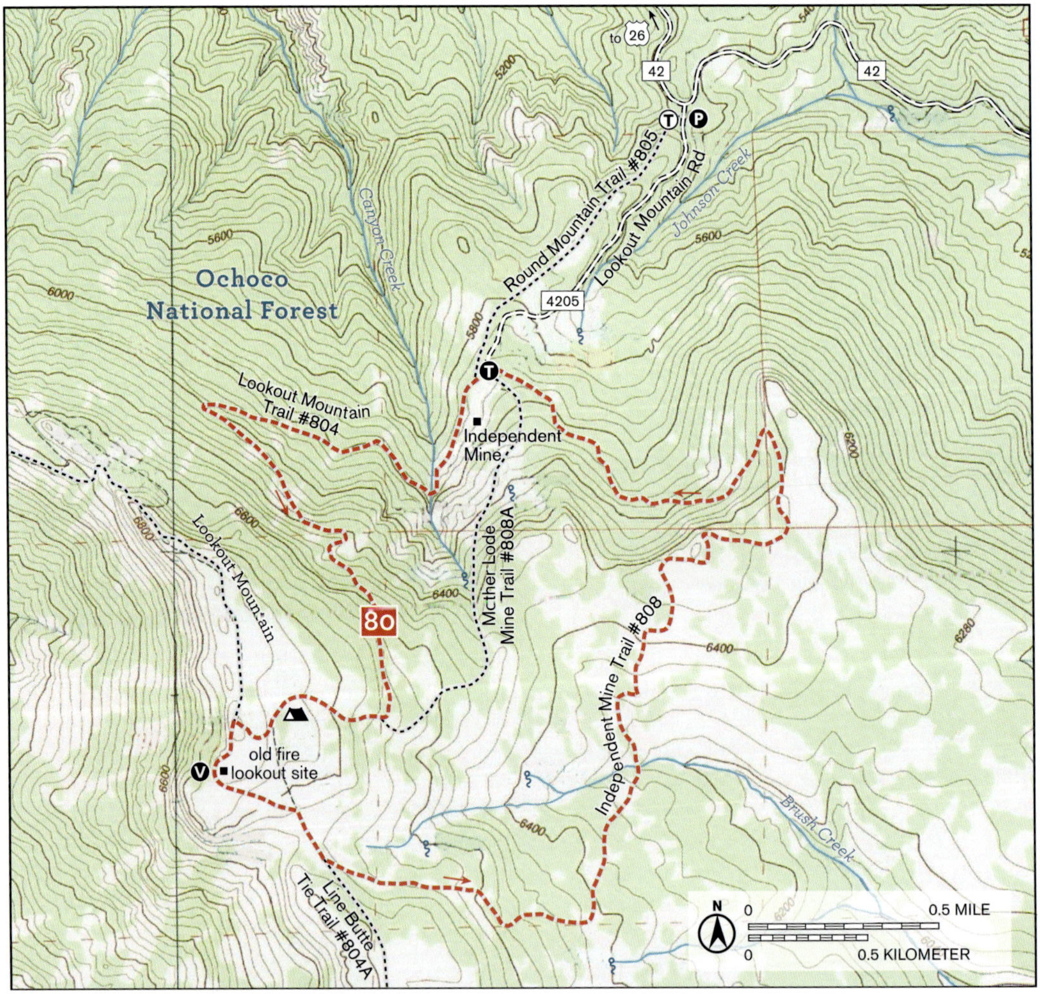

Enjoy sweeping views from Lookout Mountain.

likely to see an abundance of wildflowers and butterflies. The trail emerges from the trees at around 2.3 miles to meet the upper junction of the Mother Lode Mine Trail (#808A; this is the shorter, steeper route straight up the mountain from the parking area). Veer right (west) to stay on the Lookout Mountain Trail, crossing an open plain of sagebrush dotted with skyrocket and coyote mint. You'll soon pass a shelter tucked away in a grove of trees; this sturdy hut has a woodstove for warming up in the winter season. Just a little farther on, at 2.8 miles, burst out onto the summit plateau. There's nothing left of the old fire lookout, save a few rusty and crumbling remnants of its foundation, but the expansive view remains the same. Looking south to north on a bluebird day, you can pick out Mount Thielsen, Diamond Peak, the Three Sisters, Mount Jefferson, Mount Hood, and everything in between. That's a big view!

Once you've torn yourself away from the summit view, continue south on the Independent Mine Trail (#808) through open meadows of sagebrush, balsamroot, and aster, veering left (east) at a junction with the Line Butte Tie Trail (#804A). From here, the trail starts descending back into viewless woods, and it very much starts to feel like you're going the wrong way. Keep going a little farther as the trail makes an abrupt left (north) turn; a weathered trail sign posted on a lodgepole pine reassures you that you're on the right track. The trail dips through the Brush Creek drainage, then exits the trees once more to traverse a wide-open plain of rock and gravel. Among the tufts of buckwheat, hyacinth, and wild onion dotting the otherwise barren hillside, you're afforded some wide views over the Ochoco Mountains. Once you're back in the trees, the trail makes a quick descent under shady trees back to the trailhead parking area.

81 Blue Basin

Distance: 4-mile loop
Difficulty: moderate
Hiking time: short day hike
Elevation gain: 1010 feet
High point: 2900 feet
Season: trails Mar–Nov; visitor centers variable
Management: National Park Service
Protection status: John Day Fossil Beds National Monument
Map: NPS John Day Fossil Beds NM brochure
GPS coordinates: N 44 59.552, W 119 63.087

Getting there: From Prineville, northeast of Bend, take US Highway 26 east for about 77 miles toward Mitchell and John Day. When the highway forks in Sheep Rock Canyon, turn left (north) on the John Day Highway (Oregon Route 19). Proceed 5.5 miles to the trailhead parking area on the right (east) side of the road. ***Notes:*** This trail can be brutally hot in midsummer—not to mention populated with rattlesnakes. Plan your visit for spring or fall for a more enjoyable outing. Carry plenty of water to stay hydrated. Do not venture off trails or collect any fossils.

For a truly otherworldly Oregon experience, head to the John Day Fossil Beds National Monument. Consisting of three distinct units (Painted Hills, Sheep Rock, and Clarno), the park showcases unusual and vibrant landscapes—the result of volcanic activity that inundated central Oregon more than seven million years ago.

There are two good hiking trails at the Sheep Rock Unit. If you're short on time, consider walking the **Island in Time Trail**, a 1.3-mile out-and-back that heads up into the cerulean heart of the Blue Basin formation. Several fossil displays line the mixed trail, which consists of paths, bridges, and boardwalks. If you have more time,

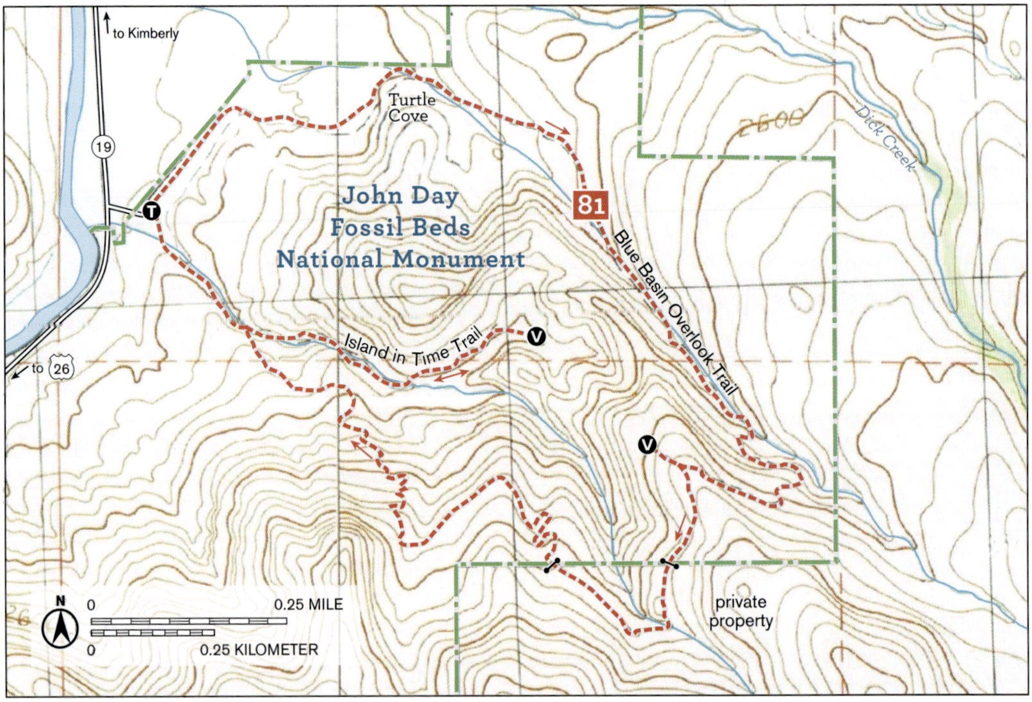

Go back in time at Blue Basin.

the **Blue Basin Overlook Trail** is a great choice. This 3.3-mile loop circuits the high slopes of the basin, offering impressive views over the area. Or combine the two trails for a 4-mile roundtrip that gives you both up-close and bird's-eye views over a prehistoric landscape that looks distinctly out of place in the Pacific Northwest.

For the full tour, go clockwise on the Blue Basin Overlook Trail by taking the left fork at the trailhead. Head up a dry drainage filled with rabbitbrush, chicory, and toadflax. Keep an eye out for rattlesnakes sunning themselves on and around the trail during warmer months. The trail hops over the creek bed about a mile up, then proceeds through a few switchbacks to gain the ridge at the back of the basin. When the trail forks at 1.5 miles, take the right (west) path and descend a few hundred yards to a viewpoint overlooking the basin. It almost appears as though you're peering down a portal into another world.

When you're sufficiently gobsmacked, return to the fork and continue the loop southward. The trail temporarily leaves the monument lands at 1.7 miles, when it passes through a gate to cross a parcel of private property—stay on the trail through here. The open, view-packed slope is dotted with mariposa lilies and pinkfairies. At 2 miles, pass through another gate back onto monument lands, continuing on a pleasant stroll with plenty of views. At 2.4 miles, the trail makes a steady, switchbacking descent toward the mouth of the basin. When you reach the next fork, at 3 miles, turn right (east) onto the Island in Time Trail.

Head up into the vibrant canyon. Depending on the time of day, sunlight illuminates the canyon walls in various shades of blue, green, and teal. Several interpretive sites along the way highlight some of the local fossil finds, including ancient cats and tortoises. The narrow, closed-in canyon traps heat and can be quite sweltering on hot summer days, so stay hydrated. The trail ends at the head of the canyon, where you're surrounded by an amphitheater of vibrant blue, green, and gray spires that were sculpted by millions of years of wind, water, and time. After you've taken it all in, head back down the canyon and veer right (west) at the fork, then walk 0.2 mile back to the trailhead.

Extend Your Trip: Learn more about the John Day Fossil Beds and surrounding area by visiting the nearby Thomas Condon Visitor Center and historic Cant Ranch. The paleontology-oriented visitor center features fossil displays and views of the working lab, with its collection of more than sixty thousand fossil specimens. The Cant Ranch is a restored 1917 farmhouse that serves as the monument's headquarters. Here, you can view photos and interpretive displays detailing farming practices of the early twentieth century. Both of these locations are just a few miles south of the Blue Basin trailhead. For more information, visit the monument's website (see Resources).

82 *Strawberry Loop*

Distance: 15.7-mile loop
Difficulty: strenuous
Hiking time: long day hike or overnight
Elevation gain: 3700 feet
High point: 8290 feet
Season: Jul–Oct
Management: Malheur National Forest
Protection status: Strawberry Mountain Wilderness
Map: USFS Strawberry Mountain Wilderness
GPS coordinates: N 44 31.924, W 118 67.442

Getting there: From the town of John Day, 150 miles east of Bend and 125 miles south of Pendleton, take US Highway 26 east to Prairie City. Turn right (south) on SW Bridge Street and follow it for 0.5 mile, then turn right (south) on S. Bridge Street, which becomes Strawberry Road. Continue on good gravel for 8 miles, watching out for cattle on the road. The road then becomes Forest Road 6001 and is rough and rocky for the last 2 miles, so take it slow. At the road's end, trailhead parking is on the right (south) and the small Strawberry Campground on the left (north). ***Notes:*** NW Forest Pass or Interagency Pass required for trailhead parking. Wilderness rules apply.

The Strawberry Wilderness is a unique little subalpine anomaly in the high desert regions of central Oregon. This remote area boasts numerous picturesque lakes, cascading waterfalls, flowery meadows, and more than a handful of impressive panoramic views from lofty peaks and ridges. And since it's nowhere near any of Oregon's larger population centers, you're sure to find some solitude. This loop hike around the central portion of the wilderness can be done as a long, full-day hike or as a multiday backpack. If you want to bag 9838-foot Strawberry Mountain as an additional side trip, plan for the latter.

Begin your journey on the Strawberry Basin Trail (#375), which sets out into shady woods. You'll immediately find abundant ferns, huckleberry, larkspur, and pipsissewa lining the trailside. The path climbs on a steady grade to a junction with the Slide Basin Trail (#372) at the 1-mile mark. This is the route you'll return by, so veer right (southwest), following signs to Strawberry Lake. In another 0.3 mile, come to the foot of sprawling Strawberry Lake in a wide, forested basin. Veer left (south) to stay on the Strawberry Basin Trail, bypassing the Strawberry Lake Trail (#375B) and contouring along the eastern shoreline. Pass the upper junction of the lake trail, staying left again, and continue climbing into the upper basin.

At 2.5 miles, the trail makes a switchback at the base of Strawberry Falls. This pretty cascade spills more than fifty feet over the bluff above and is a pleasant spot for cooling off on warmer days. Climb through a couple of switchbacks and cross over the brink of the falls at 2.7 miles. Just beyond the bridged crossing, a 0.6-mile side trail veers left (south) to Little Strawberry Lake. This smaller lake is nestled under the towering, rocky walls of 8300-foot Rabbit Ears, one of several prominent peaks that this loop circuits. Along the lake's brushy north shore are several small campsites, making it an ideal location for bedding down if you had a late start.

From this junction, it's time to get your climb on. Over the next 2.4 miles, you'll ascend more than fifteen hundred feet to the saddle between Strawberry Mountain and Peak 8452. Along the way, enjoy several wide wildflower meadows and increasingly bigger and wider views. At 4.2 miles, a nice campsite can be found to the right (north) of the trail, in a grove of trees at the edge of another meadow. A small creek meanders through the meadow,

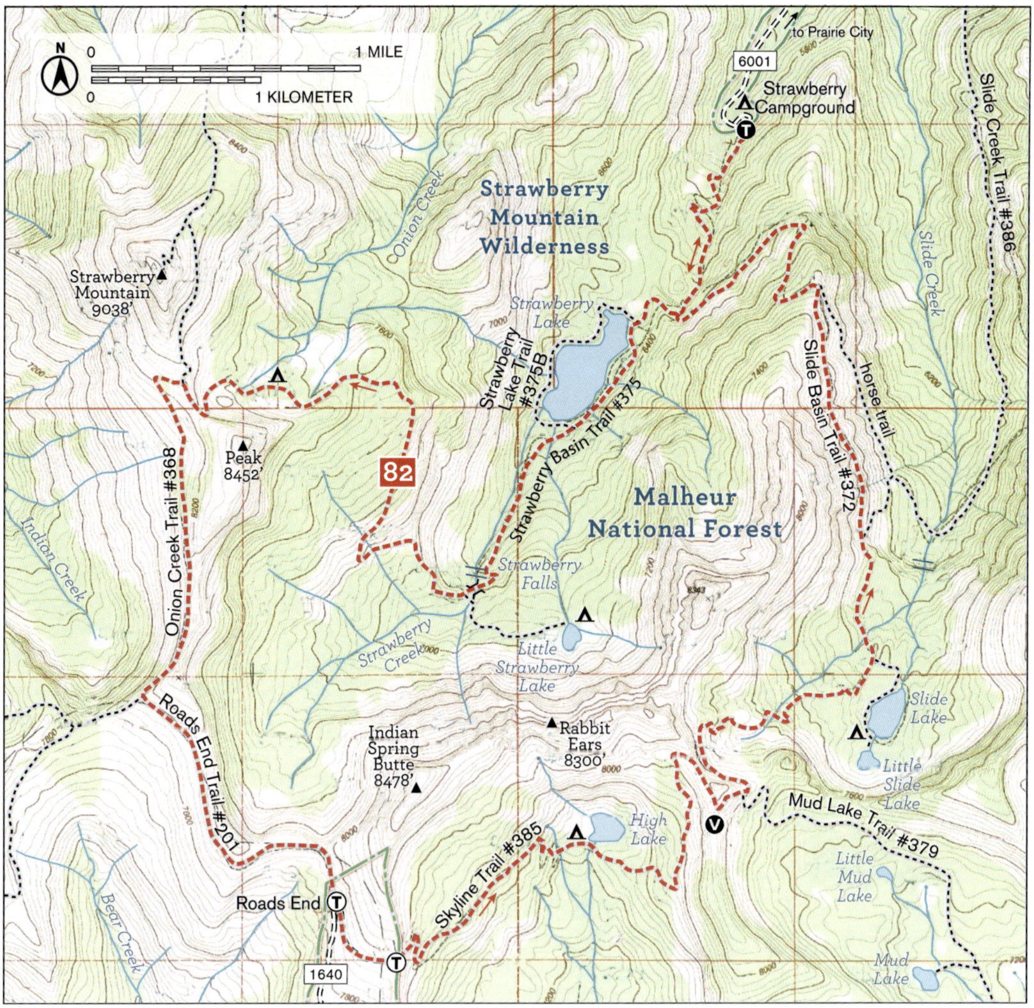

Get away from it all in the Strawberry Mountain Wilderness

providing water access. Nearing the saddle, the trail crosses the head of Onion Creek at 4.7 miles, then makes a contouring ascent up a rocky wall to the saddle ridge, at 5 miles. Just 0.1 mile farther, reach a junction with the Onion Creek Trail (#368). From here, you have the option of veering right (north) for a 1-mile ascent to the 9038-foot summit of Strawberry Mountain (see Extend Your Trip).

To continue the loop, veer left (west) on the Onion Creek Trail and traverse a wide-open slope along the backside of Peak 8452. Along the way, you'll be treated to sweeping views over the Indian Creek basin. As you reach the head of the basin, at 6.5 miles, veer left (southeast) onto the Road's End Trail (#201). This brushy old jeep road contours the ridge for 1.2 miles to a remote trailhead on gravel FR 1640. Walk the forest road uphill (southeast) to the end of the line at 8 miles. Find the trailhead for the Skyline Trail (#385) and begin descending the east flank of 8478-foot Indian Spring Butte, reaching the south shore of High Lake at 9.3 miles. A few campsites can be found on the west side of the lake.

After enjoying a break at the lake, begin the big climb out of the basin. The trail snakes through portions of burned forest on rough and rocky tread, contouring steadily upward. Between the huffing and puffing, take a little joy in the carpets of wildflowers that adorn the open, exposed slope. At 10.5 miles, reach the crest of the ridge and pause to appreciate the bird's-eye view of Rabbit Ears (to the northwest) and Mud Lake basin (to the southeast). Then descend through a series of switchbacks to a faint junction with the top of Mud Lake Trail (#379). Veer left (northwest), continuing on the Skyline Trail as it makes a wide, contouring descent into a sprawling, rocky basin. Watch your footing on the loose, narrow path.

Shorter Strawberry Wilderness Hikes

Don't have time to hike the full Strawberry Loop? Consider one of these shorter hikes to some of the area's highlights. All of these options start at the Strawberry Basin trailhead.

- Strawberry Lake: 4-mile lollipop loop; 640 feet elevation gain
- Strawberry Falls: 5-mile roundtrip; 940 feet elevation gain
- Slide Lake: 7.7-mile roundtrip; 1880 feet elevation gain
- Strawberry Mountain: 12.2-mile roundtrip; 3370 feet elevation gain

When the trail descends back under the cover of trees, continue for a mile to another junction, at 12 miles. This optional side trail veers off right (southeast) to Slide Lake and Little Slide Lake, with more backcountry campsites. Head north to continue your loop, now on the Slide Basin Trail (#372), and traverse a high, steep slope adorned by gobs of wildflowers and unusual lava formations. If you're acrophobic, you can opt for the lower horse trail, which parallels the main route and reconnects with it at 13.5 miles. From here, the path crosses over the ridge and descends back into the Strawberry basin, meeting up with the Strawberry Basin Trail at 14.7 miles. Veer right (north) here and retrace your steps for the last mile back to your starting point.

Extend Your Trip: Bagging Strawberry Mountain adds another 2 miles (roundtrip) and 740 feet of elevation gain to an already long hike. If you want to go for the big view from the top, consider camping at Little Strawberry Lake or the meadow below the saddle junction. Then you can make your summit the following morning, during the cooler part of the day.

83 *Arch Rock*

Distance: 0.5-mile lollipop loop
Difficulty: easy
Hiking time: short day hike
Elevation gain: 130 feet
High point: 4140 feet
Season: May–Nov
Management: Malheur National Forest
Protection status: none
Map: USGS Quad: Susanville, OR
GPS coordinates: N 44 63.289, W 118 84.353

Getting there: From Pendleton, drive south on US Highway 395 for approximately 76 scenic miles. Turn left (southeast) on Upper Middle Fork Road (County Road 20) and continue another 22 miles. Turn right (south) on Forest Road 36 and drive 5.2 miles on good gravel to a fork. Bear left (south) on FR 478, crossing over Camp Creek and driving 0.3 mile to a three-way fork. Park on the shoulder here; the signed trailhead is on the left (east) side of the fork.

Looking at the trail overview above, you may be asking, "Is it really worth the long drive for such a short, remote trail?" The short answer is a resounding "YES!" While you will probably complete the trail in less than an hour, the drive through Oregon's Blue Mountains to get here is half of the enjoyment. This scenic and picturesque corridor passes over the Battle Mountain

Arch Rock presents a window into ancient Oregon.

summit, through the Bridge Creek Wildlife Area, and along portions of the North and Middle Forks of the John Day River. By the time you reach the trailhead, you'll be ready for a nice stretch, and after your hike, you'll still have a portion of your day left to explore the surrounding area.

From the signed trailhead at the three-way fork in the road, head up the grassy slope under mixed fir, larch, and ponderosa pine, with corn lily and mountain strawberry adorning the hillside. Along the way, you will encounter several interpretive signs providing information about the geologic history of the surrounding landscape, where a tropical paradise once existed. In late spring and early summer, be on the lookout for a plethora of unique and colorful wildflowers along the trail. The most notable blossoms include clusters of pink prairie smoke and spreading phlox, balls of white clover, delicate woodland stars, and vivid-blue larkspur and wild hyacinth.

After a short distance, the path skirts along the base of the first of several rock outcrops. Part of the Clarno Formation, these pocked and weathered tuff deposits are the resistant remains of ancient volcanic lava flows and ash deposits that inundated the area millions of years ago. As the surrounding landscape eroded away, these rocks were eventually exposed, giving some insight into the lush environment that once existed here.

A little farther along, the path crosses a small spring and comes to a fork. Turn right and proceed to the next outcrop, which is Arch Rock. Here, time and weather has worn away the softer interior of the rock, resulting in a dramatic arch. Eventually, over many more centuries, the arch will collapse—and perhaps a new one will form in one of the other outcrops. For now, however, you can admire a scenic view of the Blue Mountains framed in a thirty-five-million-year-old window of volcanic tuff. Pass straight through the arch and take in another view from the other side. Then proceed across an open meadow of balsamroot before looping back over the top of the arch's exposed ridge. Drop back down into the trees and arrive back at a familiar fork. From here, retrace your steps back to the trailhead.

84 *Crawfish Lake*

Distance: 2.8-mile roundtrip
Difficulty: easy
Hiking time: short day hike
Elevation gain: 490 feet
High point: 7170 feet
Season: Jul–Nov
Management: Wallowa–Whitman NF (Whitman)
Protection status: North Fork John Day Wilderness
Map: USGS Quad: Crawfish Lake
GPS coordinates: N 44 95.064, W 118 26.507

Getting there: From Interstate 84 at North Powder (exit 285), drive west on River Lane for 4 miles, then turn left on Ellis Road. Drive for 0.7 mile, then turn right on Anthony Lakes Highway and continue west for 6.8 miles. The road then becomes Anthony Lake Road for 1.4 miles, then Elkhorn Drive Scenic Byway (Forest Road 73). Continue for 11.8 winding miles, passing the Anthony Lakes ski area, to a gravel road on the left. Turn left onto FR 216 and proceed a bumpy 0.2 mile to the upper trailhead.

Oregon's Blue Mountains, south of La Grande and west of Baker City, don't possess the glacier-carved grandeur of the nearby Wallowa Mountains, but they make a pleasant destination

Crawfish Lake in Oregon's Blue Mountains

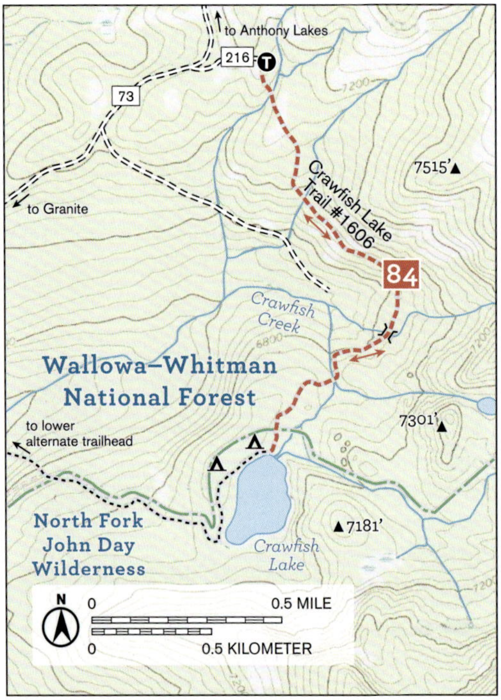

for finding solitude among long, rugged ridges and quiet, forested lakes. This short jaunt to a secluded pool is perfect for a family-friendly day trip or easy overnight, where you can relax outdoors, cast a line, or just watch the clouds float by. You can access the lake from trailheads to the north or south; the following description highlights the northern approach.

From the quiet upper trailhead, begin the Crawfish Lake Trail (#1606) with a pleasant descent into fir and lodgepole pine woods, quickly crossing a shallow spring gully. The forest thins as you lose elevation, reaching a small cascade at 0.4 mile. Hop across and begin an easy traverse of an open slope, with views looking southwest toward 6985-foot Badger Butte. Abundant wildflowers add splashes of color to the grassy slope. The trail then ducks back into the trees and makes a curving descent into the Crawfish Creek valley.

Cross several additional small creeks, using an old bridge at 0.8 mile and a small logjam at 1.1 miles. Near here, you may see a faint user path that heads east into the trees to Crawfish Meadow. Mount a small rise and, at 1.2 miles, enter the North Fork John Day Wilderness. Proceed just 0.2 mile farther to come to the shore of quiet Crawfish Lake, which lies in a tree-ringed basin. Several campsites can be found in the trees nearby. The trail continues around the lake and then heads southwest for another 1.6 miles to a lower trailhead, but this makes a good destination for an easy outing. When you're ready, retrace your steps to return to the upper trailhead.

Opposite, top: Long view over Nine Mile Ridge

Opposite, bottom: Backpacker heading into the Eagle Cap Wilderness

Wallowa Mountains

85. Nine Mile Ridge 236

86. Wenaha River Trail 238

87. Imnaha River Trail 240

88. Tenderfoot Loop 242

89. Mount Howard (Tram) 244

90. Ice Lake 246

91. Glacier Lake Loop 249

92. Francis Lake 252

93. Chimney Lake 254

94. Steamboat Loop 257

95. Echo Lake 260

96. Eagle Lake Loop 263

97. Lookingglass Lake 266

Tucked away in the quiet northeast corner of Oregon, the Wallowa Mountains are justifiably known as one of the Seven Wonders of Oregon. Here, sparkling granite peaks mingle with colorful volcanic ridges, all soaring over sprawling wildflower meadows and countless brilliant alpine lakes. Give yourself plenty of time to explore these mountains and valleys that were sculpted by time and ancient glaciers, as they are sure to leave you breathless—in more than one way!

85 *Nine Mile Ridge*

Distance: 7.4-mile roundtrip
Difficulty: strenuous
Hiking time: day hike
Elevation gain: 2190 feet
High point: 4560 feet
Season: May–Nov
Management: Umatilla NF (Walla Walla)
Protection status: North Fork Umatilla Wilderness
Map: USGS Quad: Bingham Springs, OR
GPS coordinates: N 45 71.856, W 118 18.740

Getting there: From downtown Pendleton, drive east on Court Avenue (Oregon Route 30) for about a mile. Veer right (southeast) on Pendleton Highway and continue east on Mission Road for 4.5 miles. Veer left (east) on Cayuse Road (County Road 900) and drive 10.9 miles, then jog right (south) across the train tracks. Make an immediate left (east) on Bingham Road and drive along the Umatilla River for 12 miles. Veer left (northeast) onto Forest Road 32 and follow this good gravel road for 3.6 miles. Just beyond the Umatilla Forks Campground, veer left onto FR 3200-045 and slowly take this rough road 0.2 mile to the small Buck Creek trailhead. Do not park in front of the locked gate. ***Notes:*** Wilderness rules apply. Do not rely on springs for water; pack in all you need. This trail is steep, with a sustained climb and a lot of exposure. Bring sun protection and consider skipping this trail on hot days to avoid overexertion. Be aware of the fall hunting season. Disregard older maps that show the trail switchbacking straight up the hillside; these are no longer accurate.

Wildflowers abound on Nine Mile Ridge.

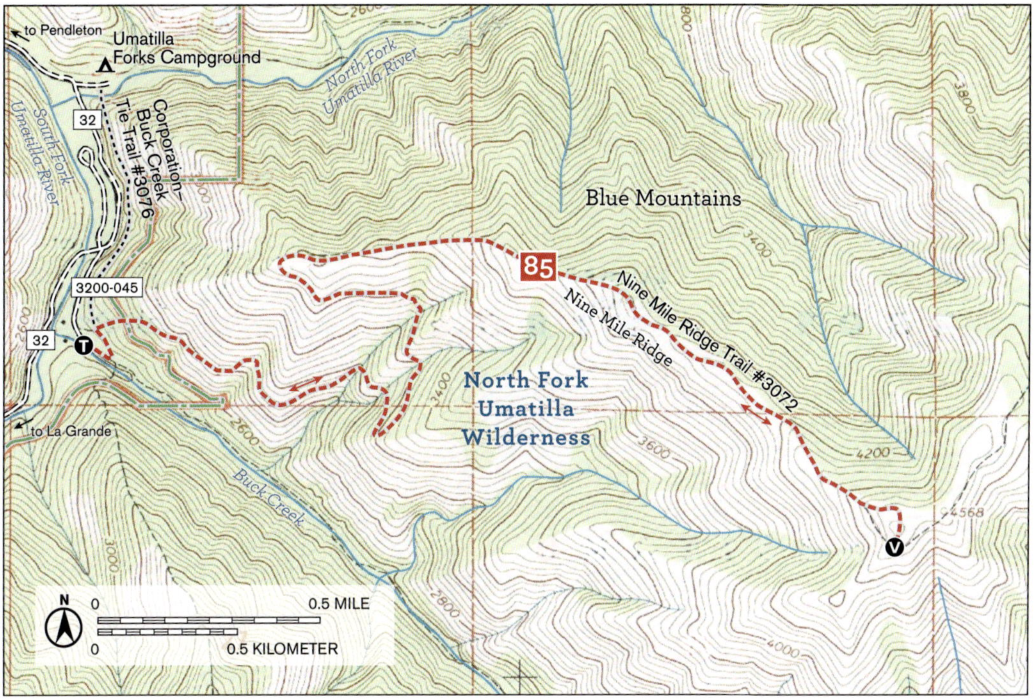

The North Fork Umatilla Wilderness, situated in a remote corner of the Blue Mountains, is an easy hour's drive east of Pendleton. One of Oregon's smaller wilderness areas, it encompasses just over twenty thousand acres and is characterized by wide-open slopes and deep, wooded canyons. Wildlife abounds here, including a population of Rocky Mountain elk. In springtime, the hills are painted with a variety of vibrant wildflowers, making this an ideal excursion in May and June, when the higher-elevation trails are still buried in snow.

Starting at the Buck Creek trailhead, head into dense mixed woods, where sword fern, Oregon grape, thimbleberry, huckleberry, and oceanspray are abundant. Just a few hundred yards up, make a sharp left (north) turn onto the Nine Mile Ridge Trail (#3072) and get your climb on. As you start to ascend, look for blooms of red clover, queen's cups, honeysuckle, and Nootka rose along the trailside. At 0.2 mile, turn right (east) at a junction, passing the Corporation–Buck Creek Tie Trail (#3076), and enter the North Fork Umatilla Wilderness. As you keep climbing, you'll get your first glimpses of 3620-foot Graves Butte to the west.

At 0.3 mile, the trail breaks out onto the open, grassy mountainside, where the slope is blanketed with knapweed, pinkfairies, buckwheat, and penstemon. Continue ascending on a moderate grade as the trail contours eastward, climbing ever higher over the wooded Buck Creek canyon. To the south, 4385-foot Buck Mountain soars skyward. At the 1-mile mark, curve through a wooded drainage, where a small, seasonal spring trickles across the trail. Enjoy the shady reprieve as the trail contours south through overgrown thimbleberry and ninebark, crosses another small drainage, and then switches back north to continue heading upward.

At 1.7 miles, the trail bursts out into the open again to traverse the slope westward, now much higher on the hillside. The views become more expansive, with more wildflowers joining the show, including Douglas's brodiaea, larkspur and lupine. Your next shady reprieve comes at

2 miles, where the trail reaches the lower end of the ridgeline in a grove of mixed woods. From here, the trail hooks eastward again and begins ascending, steeply at times, right along the ridgeline. Keep an eye on the trail as you ascend, as it gets thin and overgrown in places—and it's easy to get distracted by the increasingly wider views. When in doubt, stick to the tree line along the north side of the ridge. As you keep ascending, you get a breather when the trail dips through a couple of shallow saddles along the ridgeline. Then ramble past some delightful rock gardens brimming with paintbrush, penstemon, and wild onion.

At 3.3 miles, start the final push toward the top, zigzagging up through balsamroot and arrowleaf clover. Push through a brushy glen to crest the ridge at 3.6 miles. Take note of where you exited the brush, as the trail fades out on the summit plateau. For the best views, turn south and walk 0.1 mile to a large cairn at the edge of the summit. From here, take in a wide panorama south and east over the wilderness area. Observe the sharp relief of the summit plateau and the surrounding slopes and valleys. The Nine Mile Ridge Trail continues along the ridgeline for many more miles, eventually descending to another trailhead, but the route gets narrower and harder to follow. After you've enjoyed the view for a while, make this your turnaround spot and start the steep descent back to where you started.

86 *Wenaha River Trail*

Distance: 7.5-mile roundtrip
Difficulty: moderate
Hiking time: day hike
Elevation gain: 1160 feet
High point: 1900 feet
Season: Apr–Nov
Management: Umatilla NF (Pomeroy)
Protection status: none
Map: USGS Quad: Troy, OR-WA
GPS coordinates: N 45 94.749, W 117 45.438

Getting there: From Oregon Route 82 in Enterprise, drive north on NW 1st Street. After 0.9 mile, this becomes OR 3; continue another 32.8 miles. Turn left (west) on Flora Lane and drive for 3.2 miles, then go left (west) on Lost Prairie Road and proceed for 0.6 mile. Continue onto Flora Lane again, driving another 2.2 miles, then turn left (west) on Redmond Grade Lane. Slowly drive down this good but steep gravel road for 8 miles, then cross the Grande Ronde River. Turn left (south) on the paved Troy River Road and continue for 1.6 miles into town, then turn right (north) on the gravel Bartlett Road and proceed for 0.3 mile. Trailhead parking is at the first hairpin bend. ***Notes:*** Beware of ticks, rattlesnakes, and abundant poison ivy. Summer temperatures can be sweltering, so stay hydrated.

The entire length of the Wenaha River Trail (#3106) stretches for thirty miles, from Troy to Timothy Springs. However, since the 2015 Grizzly Bear Complex Fire burned much of the canyon, it is not as scenic as it used to be. The first few miles of trail are still enjoyable, but venturing farther up the river gets more challenging, with deteriorating trail conditions.

From the roadside trailhead, head out along a grassy slope dotted with ponderosa pines. Down below, the Wenaha River flows eastward to its nearby confluence with the Grande Ronde. In early summer, the open hillsides showcase a variety of colorful chicory, mock orange, dogbane, geranium, sumac, and blanketflower. The tall, spiky-looking stalks you may see are a variety of teasel. After a short while, the path descends to cross an open meadow before climbing again to continue contouring the slope above the river. At 1 mile, pass through a stock control gate (closing

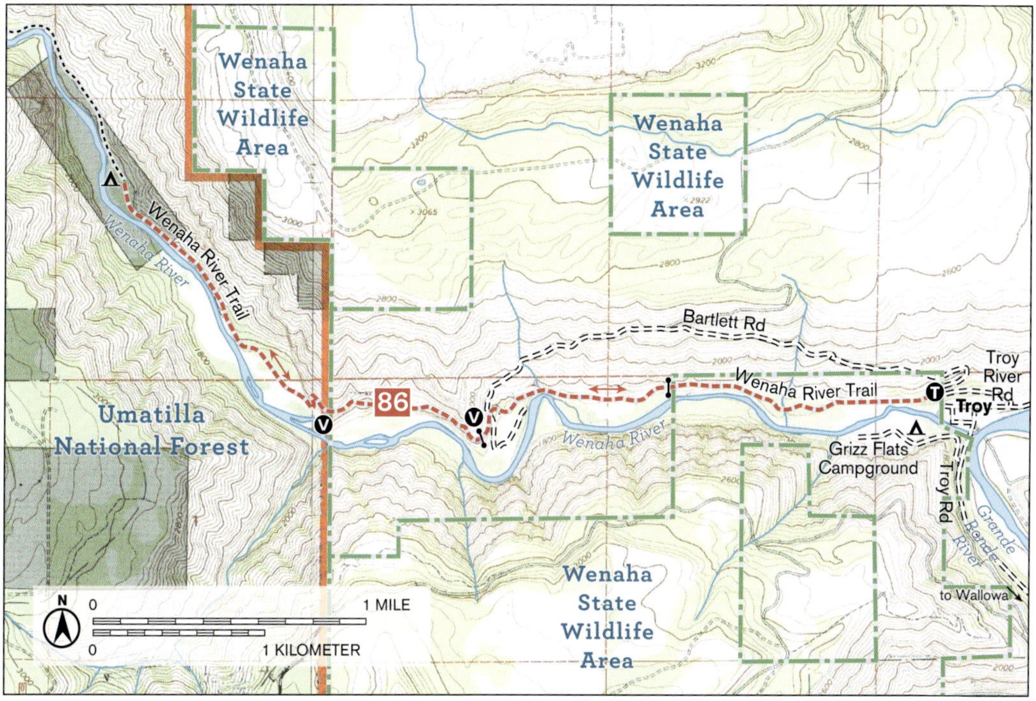

it behind you) and keep hiking. Look upslope for an outcrop of twisted volcanic rock that resembles a castle ruin.

As the trail rolls along, with pleasant views up and down the canyon, cross a small spring at 1.5 miles, then make a steady ascent to cross an old jeep road. The trail curves around a ridge extension, passing through another gate at 1.9 miles. Just beyond and around the bend, take in an impressive view of the Wenaha River canyon. The path then narrows and hugs the sheer canyon wall as it contours high above the river. Watch your footing on the loose trail surface—a slip here would be treacherous. Once you're past the narrow catwalk, the trail widens out again and continues ascending on a gentle grade to the next big view, at 2.5 miles.

The scene here takes in more of the charred canyon, though new growth along the river provides a lively contrast to the blackened trees. From this high perch, the trail descends quickly through a few switchbacks to the canyon floor and proceeds through overgrown locust and

Rock outcrops resembling castle ruins along the Wenaha River

rose thickets. Watch out for poison ivy through here, as it is abundant. Once out of the shrubbery, follow the faint trail as it parallels the river. The canyon floor widens again as the trail enters a meadow at 3.7 miles, where a campsite sits in a cluster of small pines. Scan the ridges above for bighorn sheep, as they are known to inhabit the area.

While anticlimactic, this location makes an ideal turnaround point for a moderate day trip. The trail forward gets more overgrown, heading through more poison ivy and into increasingly burned woods. If you do feel like venturing a little farther, you can proceed another 2.5 miles up the canyon to Crooked Creek, with a few campsites available near the crossing.

87 *Imnaha River Trail*

Distance: 9-mile roundtrip
Difficulty: moderate
Hiking time: day hike or overnight
Elevation gain: 1420 feet
High point: 1220 feet
Season: Apr–Nov
Management: Wallowa–Whitman NF (Clarkston)
Protection status: Hells Canyon NRA
Map: USGS Quad: Deadhorse Ridge, OR-ID
GPS coordinates: N 45 76.393, W 116 74.833

Getting there: From Oregon Route 82 in Joseph, head east on E. Wallowa Avenue (OR 350) for 29.4 miles to the tiny town of Imnaha. Turn left (north) on Lower Imnaha Road and continue 6.3 miles. Immediately after crossing Fence Line Creek Road, continue north on Dug Bar Road (Forest Road 4260) for 13.3 miles. This bumpy, narrow, winding gravel road clings to the steep hillsides for the first 7 miles, then drops down and eases out along the river for the final stretch. Turn left (north) on a short spur just before crossing the river to find the trailhead. High-clearance vehicles are recommended. ***Notes:*** This trail can get brutally hot in midsummer; wear sun protection and stay hydrated. Beware of ticks, rattlesnakes, and poison ivy.

Follow the Imnaha River to an abandoned mining town.

If you're looking for remote, this is it. Located in the far northeast corner of Oregon, the Imnaha River flows from the high, snowy peaks of the Wallowa Mountains to the border of Idaho, where it spills into the Wild and Scenic Snake River. The Imnaha River Trail (#1713) follows the last few miles of the river's journey. This trail is a mostly effortless stroll down a spectacularly scenic canyon, where birds of prey drift overhead and the river sings over whitewater cascades. Bring your lunch, your sunscreen, and your spirit of adventure for a secluded day on the river that culminates with a visit to an abandoned mining site.

Start at the Cow Creek trailhead on the west side of the Imnaha River. Nearby, there may be a fish trap station used for monitoring salmon populations. The trail starts off across a brushy slope adorned with chicory, fleabane, and moth mullein before passing through a stock control gate. (Be sure to close and latch the gate behind you.) Follow the trail downstream on a gentle, downward grade as it rolls alongside the riverbank, which is lined with alder and blackberry. In places, the trail hugs the rocky walls as the canyon narrows and rocky spires soar overhead. At about 1.3 miles, look upslope to the left (west) for an unusually balanced rock. It's easier to spot after you pass it, looking back over your shoulder.

Continue following the river as it snakes down the canyon. Watch for any brush encroaching on the trail, as it may be poison ivy—it is plentiful here. At around 2.8 miles, cross a small creek draining out of Hilliker Gulch, where numerous abandoned mines dot the hillside. You may see discarded relics from these olden days in the form of rusted cans and barrels strewn by the trailside. As you approach 4 miles, the canyon narrows again and the trail climbs high on the wall, giving you a nice view up- and downstream. Quickly drop to the opposite side and pass an old campsite and mine tunnel. Then spill out onto a gravelly bar along the Snake River, right next to the Imnaha River's terminus.

From here, you can head down to the shore of the Snake River and find a little shade to enjoy your lunch while watching eagles and osprey soar overhead. For a little more exploring, follow

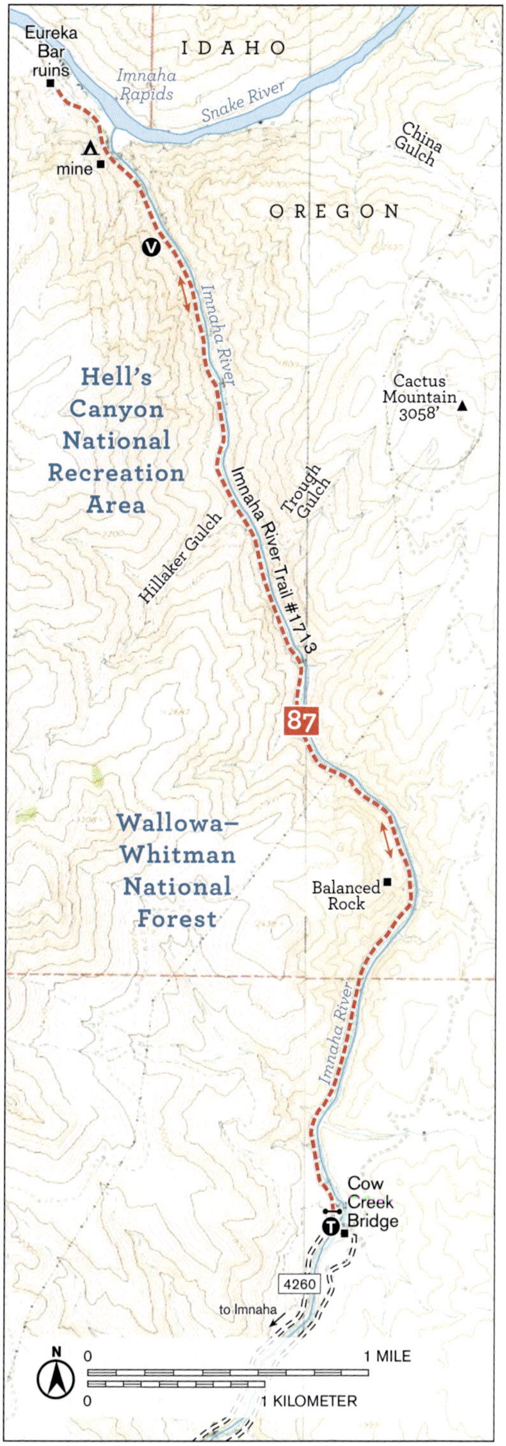

the path another 0.2 mile along the river to the old mining townsite of Eureka Bar. In the late 1890s, copper was discovered here, and the area quickly turned into a booming town of more than two thousand miners—all seeking their fortunes. Unfortunately, no fortunes were to be had, and the town was abandoned just a few years later. According to local legend, Eureka Bar's first official mail delivery arrived at a ghost town. Now all that remains are the foundations of the smelter, hotel, and warehouse. After your river explorations, return to the trailhead by the same route.

88 Tenderfoot Loop

Distance: 14.8-mile loop
Difficulty: strenuous
Hiking time: overnight
Elevation gain: 3380 feet
High point: 8470 feet
Season: Jul–Oct
Management: Wallowa–Whitman NF (Wallowa Mountains)
Protection status: Eagle Cap Wilderness
Map: Green Trails 475SX: Wallowa Mountains
GPS coordinates: N 45.17745, W 117.10324

Getting there: From US Highway 84 in La Grande, take exit 261 for OR 82 to Joseph and Wallowa Lake. Follow this road for 67 miles to the town of Joseph. Halfway through town, turn left (east) onto E. Wallowa Avenue (Imnaha Highway) and proceed 8.1 miles, then make a sharp right turn onto Wallowa Mountain Loop (Forest Road 39). Take this road 12.7 winding miles south, cross Big Sheep Creek, then make a sharp right

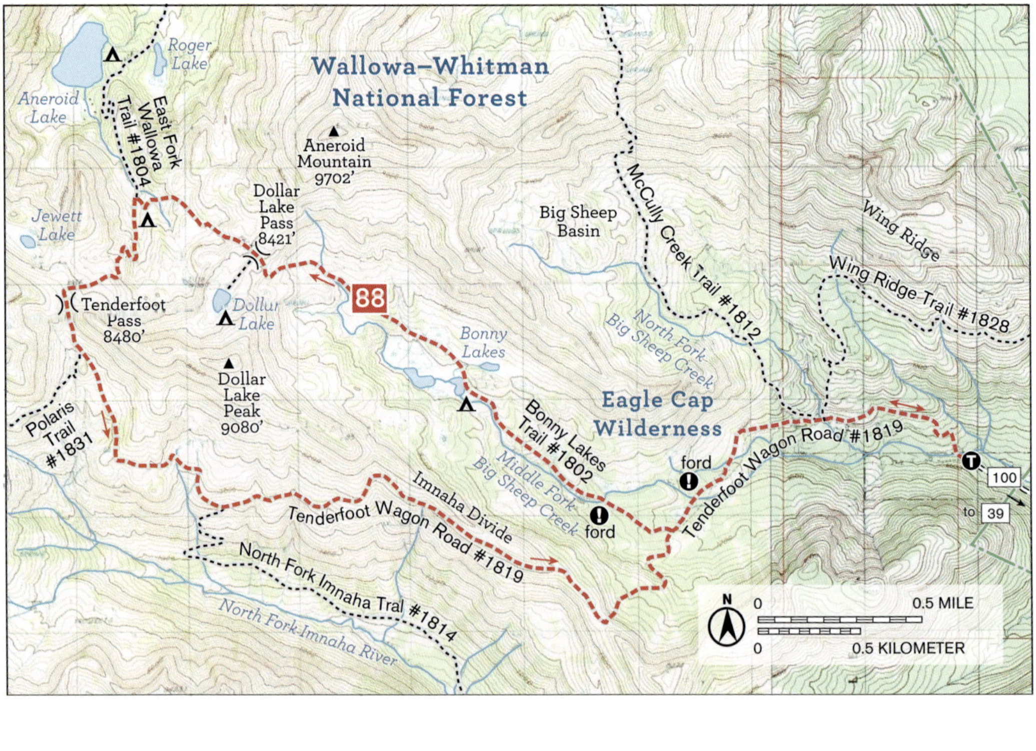

Looking toward Tenderfoot Pass and Pete's Point

(southwest) turn on FR 100. Take this bumpy gravel road 3.2 miles to the trailhead at the end. ***Notes:*** Wilderness rules apply. Complete a self-issue wilderness permit at the trailhead kiosk. Some routefinding may be necessary in recently burned areas.

This remote hike passes through a portion of forest that was burned in the 2022 Nebo Fire, making the start and finish a bit lackluster. But once you get through the burned area, you will be immersed in the glorious splendor of the Wallowa's high backcountry, replete with sprawling meadows, sparkling lakes, and an alpine pass with a sweeping view that is sure to take your breath away.

Begin your journey into the Eagle Cap Wilderness on the old Tenderfoot Wagon Road. The route immediately meets unbridged Big Sheep Creek, where you'll need to find a safe passage across. On the other side of the creek, the route turns west and proceeds into charred forest. A few islands of green trees amid flowery slopes offer a little shade and respite from the desolation. As the route contours up the canyon, it crosses the Middle Fork Big Sheep Creek at 1.9 miles, then comes to a junction at 2.2 miles. Head right (west) onto the Bonny Lakes Trail (#1802) and continue another 0.5 mile to hop across Big Sheep Creek one more time. These crossings can be tricky, especially during early summer runoff. Look for the safest place to cross and continue onward.

At a little past the 3-mile mark, the trail finally leaves the burn area behind, heading into the big, wide open. Climb above the creek into a resplendent meadow dotted with wildflowers and rocky mounds, with the long ridge of 9080-foot Dollar Lake Peak filling the southern skyline. At 3.7 miles, the trail arrives at the first of the Bonny Lakes in a wide, grassy basin, where it skirts around the western shoreline. A few dispersed campsites can be found in the trees around the south side. The views get bigger and wider as the route continues upward into sweeping wildflower meadows, finally reaching the Dollar Lake Pass at 5.3 miles. A faint spur trail here breaks off left (south) to the lake.

From the pass, traipse through more meadows and rock gardens until the trail dips over the west side of the pass. Steeply descend to a creek crossing and a well-signed junction with the East Fork Wallowa Trail (#1804), at 6.2 miles. To the right (north) the trail proceeds 1 mile to Aneroid Lake, with several campsites above its eastern shore. Continue left (south), following the creek upstream for a spell before climbing out of the basin toward Tenderfoot Pass. Several campsites are hidden in the trees along the creek, good options if you're seeking more solitude than what you'll likely find around Aneroid Lake.

The trail ascends high above the tree line into alpine tundra, where sweeping views can be had in every direction. To the northeast is 9702-foot Aneroid Mountain; to the southeast is the familiar site of Dollar Lake Peak. To the west, you can spy several high basins and glacial cirques; the most prominent and impressive is 9675-foot Petes Point. For the truly adventurous, a narrow path winds up the ridgeline to Petes' precipitous summit. At what appears to be an unsigned junction, veer left (south) to reach 8480-foot Tenderfoot Pass at 7.2 miles. Here, looking south into the Imnaha River valley, a whole new impressive scene unfolds, including 8887-foot Polaris Pass and 9360-foot Sentinel Peak to the southwest.

Contour downward into the upper valley, veering left (southeast) at a junction with the Polaris Trail (#1831). The route now continues on the North Fork Imnaha Trail (#1814) for the next 1.5 miles, crossing sprawling wildflower meadows and bubbling creeks along the southern slope of Dollar Lake Peak. At the 9-mile mark, veer left at the next junction to join the old Tenderfoot Wagon Road once again. The way contours upward along the slope, with more sweeping views high over the Imnaha River valley. At 10 miles, reach the ridge crest. Traipse along the ridge and spend some time enjoying the views, because the scenery will quickly and dramatically change just ahead.

For the final stretch, the trail dips over the north side of the crest at 11.6 miles, steeply dropping back into the Nebo Fire burn area. Carefully pick your way down the blackened slope, keeping your eyes peeled for the proper route over the next mile as you snake down through several charred drainages. At 12.6 miles, the routefinding tension eases when you reach a familiar junction with the Bonny Lakes Trail. Turn right (east) and hike the last few miles back to your starting point.

89 *Mount Howard (Tram)*

Distance: 2.5-mile loop
Difficulty: easy
Hiking time: short day hike
Elevation gain: 370 feet
High point: 8241 feet
Season: Jul–Oct
Management: Wallowa–Whitman NF (Wallowa Mountains)
Protection status: none
Map: Mount Howard trail brochure
GPS coordinates: N 45 27.727, W 117 20.724

Getting there: From La Grande, take Oregon Route 82 northeast for about 67 miles to Joseph and Wallowa Lake. Proceed through town onto OR 351, going another 6 miles to Wallowa Lake State Park. Near the Wallowa Lake Lodge, bear left at the fork onto Power House Road and proceed 0.2 mile to the tramway station on the left (east) side of the road, opposite Matterhorn Village. ***Notes:*** Requires a Wallowa Lake Tramway pass, available online or in person. High-elevation trail with full exposure; bring sun and wind protection. Stay on trails to avoid trampling rare and fragile alpine tundra.

Mount Howard looms large over the head of Wallowa Lake, vaulting nearly a vertical mile from the glacial valley floor to its windswept alpine summit. A quick gondola ride to the top gives you access to 2.5 miles of easy, view-packed trails. The hike is easy enough to complete in about an hour, but you may find yourself lingering for much longer, as the sweeping panoramas get bigger and more dramatic at each successive viewpoint. And if you have the time, prolong your viewing experience with a tasty bite or beverage at the Summit Grill before catching your ride back down to the bottom.

Your journey begins by letting the Wallowa Lake Tramway do the hard part for you—whisking you more than 3700 vertical feet up the forested slope of Mount Howard. As you gain elevation over the fifteen-minute ride, the views become ever more expansive and impressive. Peer out over the glacial valley of Wallowa Lake and up the deep canyons of the two Wallowa River forks. If you look down, you may spot the remnants of the old roads and trails that once zigzagged up the steep mountainside; you'll probably feel thankful for your luxurious air coach, which effortlessly carries you aloft. When you disembark at the summit terminal, turn left (north) to reach a road/trail junction, where the walking part of your journey begins.

Take the left (north) fork onto the summit loop for a gentle descent. Grouse whortleberry and heather carpet the ground as spots of yarrow, aster, and lupine add splashes of cheerful color. When all that whortleberry is fruiting in late summer, the mountain takes on the scent of fresh-baked blueberry muffins. When you reach a junction at 0.5 mile, take the left (north) fork and proceed another 0.1 mile across an open meadow of goldenrod and cinquefoil to the first of five major viewpoints. From the Valley Overlook, you can take in a sweeping view of Wallowa Lake and Wallowa Valley. To the northeast, you can look for Imnaha Canyon (see Hike 87) and Hells Canyon.

Return to the junction and veer left (southeast) to continue the loop, making quick tracks to the next viewpoint, at 1.2 miles. From here, you can spy the Snake River and the Seven Devils in

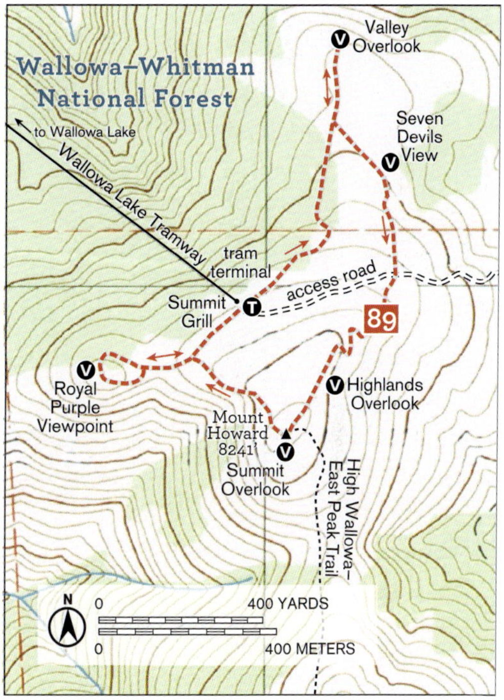

Idaho. Continue winding southward, crossing a gravel access road, then make a short ascent to traverse the next open slope, with a breathtaking view over The Highlands at 1.5 miles. The scene here follows 9838-foot East Peak and 9702-foot Aneroid Mountain along the ridgeline, as well as numerous peaks to the south and east. Push on just a little farther to the Summit Overlook, at 1.7 miles and 8241 feet of elevation, and cast your gaze over the heart of the Eagle Cap Wilderness. Across the valley, immense cirques sculpt the peaks and ridgeline. Look for a lacy cascade spilling down the mountainside to help you spot the high glacial valley containing Ice Lake (see Hike 90).

After you tear yourself away from the summit view, descend a couple of switchbacks and proceed onto a ridgeline extension populated by scrubby whitebark pines, coyote mint, and buckwheat. At 2 miles, reach a junction and continue straight onto the Royal Purple Viewpoint loop. Veer left and ascend a series of wooden steps to the viewpoint, taking in another look at the captivating Eagle Cap mountains. Several benches

Hiking the viewpoint loop on Mount Howard

here allow you to take a seat and really soak in the view. When you're ready, pick your jaw up off the ground and return to the previous junction, either by going back down the stairs or by taking the trail loop around the other side. Then turn left (northeast) and saunter down the last 0.1 mile to the tram terminal and Summit Grill, completing your trek.

Extend Your Trip: For a skyscraping ridge walk that's not for the faint of heart, you can hike the **High Wallowas–East Peak Trail** south from the Mount Howard summit to bag three big peaks: 9838-foot East Peak, 9430-foot Aneroid Mountain North, and 9702-foot Aneroid Mountain. It's a 10-mile roundtrip, with a whopping 3460 feet of elevation gain, so get an early start to enjoy these unparalleled views of the "Oregon Alps."

90 *Ice Lake*

Distance: 14.7-mile roundtrip
Difficulty: strenuous
Hiking time: day hike or overnight
Elevation gain: 3440 feet
High point: 7870 feet
Season: Jul–Oct
Management: Wallowa–Whitman NF (Wallowa Mountains)
Protection status: Eagle Cap Wilderness
Map: Green Trails 475SX: Wallowa Mountains
GPS coordinates: N 45 26727, W 117 21282

Getting there: From US Highway 84 in La Grande, take exit 261 for Oregon Route 82 to Joseph and Wallowa Lake. Follow this road for 67 miles to the town of Joseph. Proceed through town onto OR 351, going another 6 miles to Wallowa Lake State Park. Near the Wallowa Lake Lodge, bear left at the fork onto Power House Road and continue 1 mile to the trailhead at road's end. ***Notes:*** Wilderness rules apply. Complete a self-issue wilderness permit at the trailhead kiosk. Campfires prohibited within 0.25 mile of Ice Lake.

If there's one hike that epitomizes the rugged beauty of Oregon's Eagle Cap Wilderness, it's Ice Lake. Nestled in a high alpine cirque surrounded by sparkling granitic peaks, Ice Lake is the idyllic setting you dream about when you imagine the perfect mountain getaway. Make a big day of it with a long day hike or pack your gear and really immerse yourself in the wilderness with an overnight by the lake under a canopy of stars. You will have to work for this reward, as the trail gains a ton of elevation, but the payoff at the end makes every grunt and groan worth it.

Begin your hike on the West Fork Wallowa Trail (#1820). The path sets out from the trailhead under tall, shady firs and hemlocks, skirting around a fenced hydroelectric station. At junctions with the Chief Joseph Trail (#1803), at 0.3 mile, and the East Fork Cutoff (#1804), at 0.5 mile, veer left (south), then right (south), respectively, to stay on the West Fork Trail. The way then heads up the West Fork Wallowa River canyon, mostly staying high on the slope. Views are sparse along the way as the trail gradually ascends, crossing numerous small creeks and springs. A variety of wildflowers, including

An enchanting evening at Ice Lake

penstemon, honeysuckle, and mock orange keep the scenery pleasant.

When the trail bends around a large rock outcrop, at 2.5 miles, get your first decent look up and down the valley. Pause a moment to enjoy the view, then proceed another 0.25 mile to a junction with the Ice Lake Trail (#1808). Veer right and descend toward the river. Just before you reach the log-stringer bridge that spans the wide river, find a good campsite just to the right (north) of the trail. If needed, top off your water before crossing the bridge, as river access is easier here. Once across the river, the only way to go is up. Wind your way through pocket meadows of hyssop and mariposa lilies as you start ascending, getting brief glimpses of 9204-foot Craig Mountain as you go.

Continue zigging and zagging up the wall of the canyon, crossing a dry drainage several times. When you reach the top of the first series of switchbacks, at 3.6 miles, the trail makes a long contour of the hillside. At 4.3 miles, arrive at the edge of Adam Creek and peer down into the narrow gorge where the creek tumbles down the valley wall. Then proceed through a series of shorter switchbacks, climbing alongside the gorge. Use caution near the sheer edges. Just past the 5-mile mark, enjoy a view of an impressive waterfall pouring down the mountainside. Continue a little farther to reach the middle basin, at 5.3 miles.

Get a short reprieve from the ascent as you cross a seasonal creek and push your way through overgrown brush to head up the basin. A decent campsite is located to the right (north) of the trail at around 5.4 miles. Proceed through idyllic meadows of yellow columbine and white death camas while admiring the impressively high walls of the Hurwal Divide (to the north) and Craig Mountain (to the south) rising above you. Looking toward the upper basin (west), you can see Adam Creek pouring down the wall in a fanlike waterfall. Cross a small tributary at the head of the basin, then proceed upward through the final series of switchbacks. At 7 miles, the trail finally levels out for an easy stroll into the upper lake basin.

Approaching the lake, the sharp spire of the 9826-foot Matterhorn looms directly ahead (west). Proceed alongside the creek to the lake's outlet. If you're just out for the day, a large granite outcrop here offers a nice lunch spot with a primo view. If you're spending the night, carefully cross the outlet and proceed to any of the enticing campsites located near the lakeshore. If you're a peakbagger, you'll find the rough trail to the top of the Matterhorn along the north shoreline. This route heads straight up the basin's west wall, then up a narrow ridge to reach the summit. Once you've enjoyed your stay at Ice Lake, return by the same route you came.

91 *Glacier Lake Loop*

Distance: 26.5-mile lollipop loop
Difficulty: strenuous
Hiking time: overnight
Elevation gain: 4620 feet
High point: 8490 feet
Season: Jul–Oct
Management: Wallowa–Whitman NF (Wallowa Mountains)
Protection status: Eagle Cap Wilderness
Map: Green Trails 475SX: Wallowa Mountains
GPS coordinates: N 45 26727, W 117 21282

Getting there: From US Highway 84 in La Grande, take exit 261 for Oregon Route 82 to Joseph and Wallowa Lake. Follow this road for 67 miles to the town of Joseph. Proceed through town onto OR 351, going another 6 miles to Wallowa Lake State Park. Near the Wallowa Lake Lodge, bear left at the fork onto Power House Road and continue 1 mile to the trailhead at road's end. ***Notes:*** Wilderness rules apply. Complete a self-issue wilderness permit at the trailhead kiosk. This hike requires a river ford. Campfires prohibited within 0.25 mile of most of these lakes.

This hike may be the ultimate Eagle Cap Wilderness backcountry experience. Over the course of a multiday trek, you will see more wildflower meadows, pristine lakes, and glistening, glacier-carved peaks than you can shake a trekking pole at. All this gloriousness comes at a cost, however—you will have company. But with a little diligence and thoughtful timing, you can still find some peace and solitude in this deservedly popular portion of Oregon's spectacular Wallowa Mountains.

Begin your journey by heading up the West Fork Wallowa Trail (#1820). (For the first 3 miles, you'll follow the same route as the hike to Ice Lake; see Hike 90). When you reach the junction with the Ice Lake Trail (#1808), continue straight, keeping the river and 9204-foot Craig Mountain to your right (west). The route continues its gentle ascent of the river canyon, passing through more meadows and crossing multiple seasonal creeks and springs before reaching the next junction at 6-Mile Meadow. Here, the Lakes Basin Trail (#1810) branches off to the right (west). Several nice campsites sit in the trees surrounding the meadow, making this a nice place to stop if you had a late start; you can access water at the river nearby.

From the meadow, continue up the West Fork Wallowa Trail, saving the Lakes Basin Trail for the return trip. Proceed up the ever-widening glacial valley as the views start getting more and more impressive. Vaulting skyward to the east is 9675-foot Petes Point (see Hike 88). Continue to a junction with the Polaris Trail (#1831), at 8.3 miles, staying right (south) and ascending more earnestly toward the head of the valley. At 9.8 miles, the trail passes pleasant Frazier Lake, with a few campsites nearby. From here, fork right (west) onto the Glacier Lake Trail (#1806) and contour up a wide and ridiculously scenic glacial basin until you crest the ridge at 12 miles, right beside Glacier Lake's cascading outlet. A side trail left proceeds to several campsites near the lake's east and south shores. The lake is backed by 9495-foot Glacier Peak (south) and 9572-foot Eagle Cap (west).

Once you've spent some time absorbing the stunning scene (overnight recommended),

Get way up into the alpine at Glacier Lake.

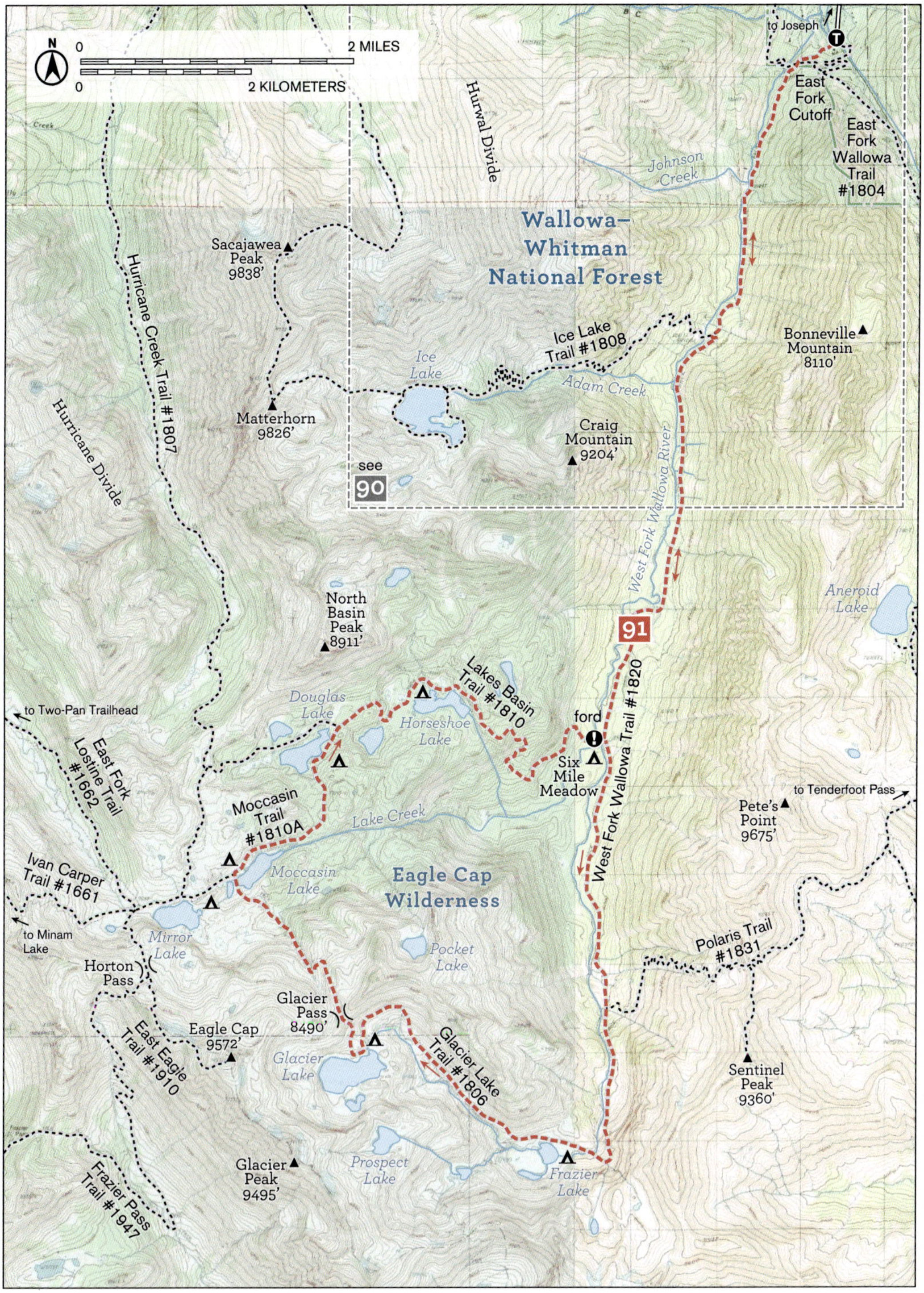

0 2 MILES
0 2 KILOMETERS
to Joseph
East Fork Cutoff
East Fork Wallowa Trail #1804
Hurwal Divide
Johnson Creek
Wallowa–Whitman National Forest
Sacajawea Peak 9838'
Hurricane Creek Trail #1807
Ice Lake Trail #1808
Bonneville Mountain 8110'
Ice Lake
Adam Creek
Matterhorn 9826'
Craig Mountain 9204'
Hurricane Divide
see 90
West Fork Wallowa River
Aneroid Lake
North Basin Peak 8911'
91
Lakes Basin Trail #1810
Douglas Lake
to Two-Pan Trailhead
Horseshoe Lake
ford
Six Mile Meadow
West Fork Wallowa Trail #1820
East Fork Lostine Trail #1662
to Tenderfoot Pass
Pete's Point 9675'
Moccasin Trail #1810A
Lake Creek
Ivan Carper Trail #1661
Moccasin Lake
Eagle Cap Wilderness
to Minam Lake
Mirror Lake
Polaris Trail #1831
Pocket Lake
Horton Pass
Glacier Pass 8490'
Eagle Cap 9572'
Glacier Lake
Glacier Lake Trail #1806
East Eagle Trail #1910
Sentinel Peak 9360'
Glacier Peak 9495'
Prospect Lake
Frazier Lake
Frazier Pass Trail #1947

switchback up to 8490-foot Glacier Pass, at 12.5 miles, where the next spectacular view smacks you in the face. The big pyramidal peak directly north is 8911-foot North Basin Peak. Make a steady descent through more idyllic meadows and across more bubbling creeks to the narrow spit of land at the head of Moccasin Lake, at 14.4 miles. Just beyond, come to a wide, well-traveled trail junction in the heart of the lakes basin. The route to the left (west) proceeds 0.6 mile to Mirror Lake, then another 0.4 mile to the East Fork Lostine Trail (#1807). This 7-mile trail to the Two Pan trailhead can be used as an alternative route into the lakes basin. To continue on the main loop, turn right (northeast) on the Moccasin Trail (#1810A) and proceed along the lake's north shore. Several nice campsites can be found along the way, most with fantastic views looking straight up the north face of Eagle Cap.

Continue through the lakes basin to the forest-ringed Douglas Lake, at 16 miles. Cross its outlet and find a few nice campsites on the peninsula on the lake's east side. Just beyond, at 16.3 miles, come to a junction with the Lakes Basin Trail and veer right (east) to continue. Cruise through pleasant woods and pocket meadows to the next junction, at 16.6 miles, veering right (east) to stay on the Lakes Basin Trail. At 17.6 miles, reach Horseshoe Lake, with a few campsites near the lake's northern shore. From here, the views scale back as the trail plunges into dense woods and steadily descends back into the wide Wallowa River valley. As the trail bottoms out, come to an unbridged crossing of the Wallowa River at 20.4 miles. Find a shallow spot and wade across. Just beyond, arrive at the 6-Mile Meadow junction and turn left (north) onto the West Fork Trail. To complete your lakes loop journey, turn left (north) and return to the Wallowa Lake trailhead.

92 *Francis Lake*

Distance: 17.5-mile roundtrip
Difficulty: strenuous
Hiking time: day hike or overnight
Elevation gain: 4520 feet
High point: 8610 feet
Season: Jul–Oct
Management: Wallowa–Whitman NF (Wallowa Mountains)
Protection status: Eagle Cap Wilderness
Map: Green Trails 475SX: Wallowa Mountains
GPS coordinates: N 45 29336, W 117 39486

Getting there: From US Highway 84 in La Grande, take exit 261 for Oregon Route 82 to Elgin. Follow this road for 53 miles to the town of Lostine. When the road turns left (east), continue straight on Lostine River Road for 14.7 miles; this road becomes gravel Upper Lostine Road, then rougher gravel Forest Road 8210. Park at the Bowman Francis trailhead, 0.3 mile past the Irondyke Forest Camp. ***Notes:*** NW Forest Pass or Interagency Pass required for trailhead parking. Wilderness rules apply. Complete a self-issue wilderness permit at the trailhead kiosk. There is no water along the way; pack all you need to stay hydrated.

Is it Frances, or is it Francis? You will find information and listings spelled both ways, even on the Forest Service website. Either way, don't let the large elevation gain steer you away from this little-used trail. After a little perseverance, you'll be rewarded with a fantastically lofty viewpoint looking out over the western Wallowa Mountains, and then you can head onward to a remote alpine lake nestled in a vibrant glacial basin.

Start at the Francis Lake trailhead on the south side of the parking area entrance road. Directly across the road is the Bowman trailhead,

It's a long hike up to Francis Lake in its high, glacial valley.

which heads off to Chimney Lake (see Hike 93) and beyond. The path starts out flat, paralleling the forest road as it crosses a small creek (the only water you'll see until the lake) and then passes a small picnic site. The trail then turns into the trees and starts a moderate ascent, snaking uphill under shady firs and hemlocks.

About 0.6 mile up the hill, the trail enters the Eagle Cap Wilderness. At this point, where the trail bends left (north), the first switchback begins. There are twenty-five switchbacks in total, so you can start counting from here. Fortunately, the trail maintains a gentle grade almost the entire way up, so it never gets steep or challenging—it's just long. Complete the first few switchbacks without much effort, quickly gaining elevation, with little to see except for the surrounding woods. Once you reach the fifth switchback, you'll start getting views out over the wide Lostine Canyon. The big peak directly across the valley is 8675-foot Chimney Lake North. Keep an eye on this peak as you climb.

The switchbacks start to shorten as you gain more elevation, making the back-and-forth pass quickly. When you get to the fifteenth switchback, the trail eases a bit and contours the hillside, passing through pretty rock gardens of subalpine wildflowers. At 3.6 miles, after another turn, the seventeenth switchback contours through a wide avalanche chute. With plenty of large rocks for sitting and a nice view over the canyon, this makes an ideal spot to break for a snack or lunch. You'll need the recharge, as most of the switchbacks from here are longer and more drawn out—but the views keep getting better and better.

Push through the next few switchbacks. The trail surface begins to transition to more rock and scree as you begin climbing out of the dense woods. As you trudge to the top of the twenty-fourth switchback, at 5.9 miles, you'll come face-to-face with the sheer north side of 8888-foot Marble Point. Make a U-turn and slog into the home stretch—the twenty-fifth switchback. Before you reach the crest of the ridge, look for a boot path heading right (east) at 6.2 miles. Take this short path to a stellar viewpoint atop the ridge. From here, you can peer down into the wide, colorful basin that holds Francis Lake. In addition to Marble Point, the string of high peaks ringing the basin include The Troll, Hinterstoisser, Francis Point, and The Undertaker.

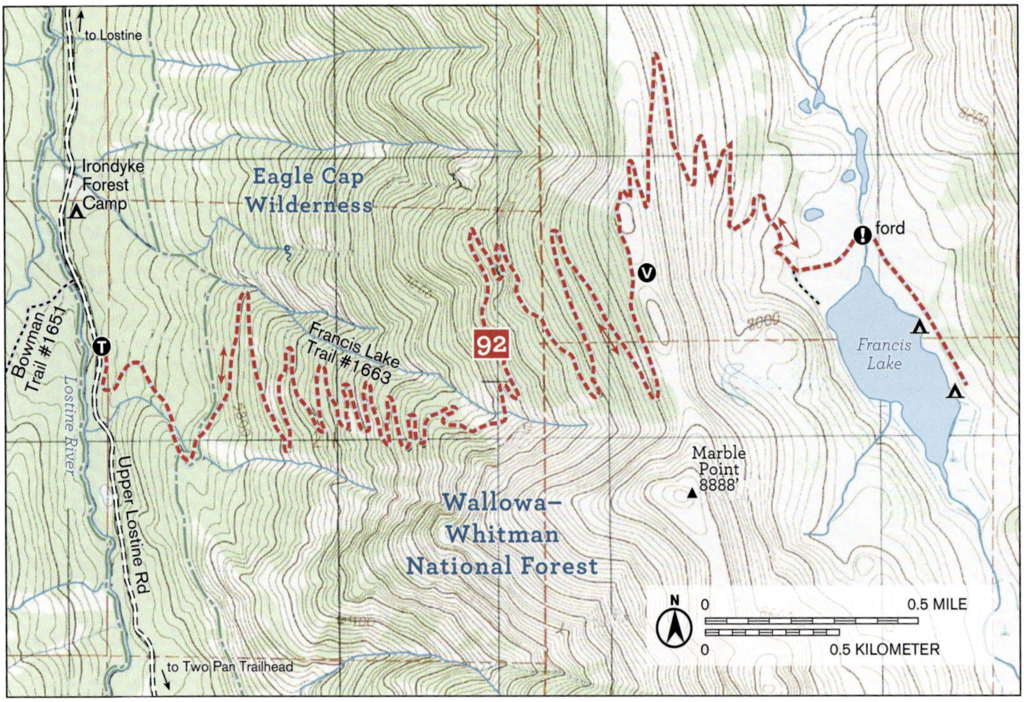

If you're day hiking, this spot makes an ideal turnaround point. If you're continuing to the lake for an overnight adventure, hike another 0.1 mile to crest the ridge. Here, atop a steep chute, enjoy an expansive view north over the Lostine Canyon and out to the Wallowa River valley. Then cross over the ridge and proceed down through a series of switchbacks (ten, to be precise) into the lake basin. As you go lower, the trail winds through meadows of pasque flower and around outcrops of glacier-polished granite. When the trail bottoms out in a grassy clearing, at nearly 8.2 miles, look left (east) for the trail as it continues across an expanse of lava rock. Follow this path northeastward to cross the lake's outlet at 8.3 miles, then turn southeast to continue along the lake's east side, ending at either of the two serviceable campsites.

93 *Chimney Lake*

Distance: 10-mile roundtrip
Difficulty: moderate
Hiking time: day hike or overnight
Elevation gain: 2690 feet
High point: 7610 feet
Season: Jul–Oct
Management: Wallowa–Whitman NF (Wallowa Mountains)
Protection status: Eagle Cap Wilderness
Map: Green Trails 475SX: Wallowa Mountains
GPS coordinates: N 45 29348, W 117 39486

Getting there: From US Highway 84 in La Grande, take exit 261 for Oregon Route 82 to Elgin. Follow this road for 53 miles to the town of Lostine. When the road turns left

Sunset paints Chimney Lake in vivid colors.

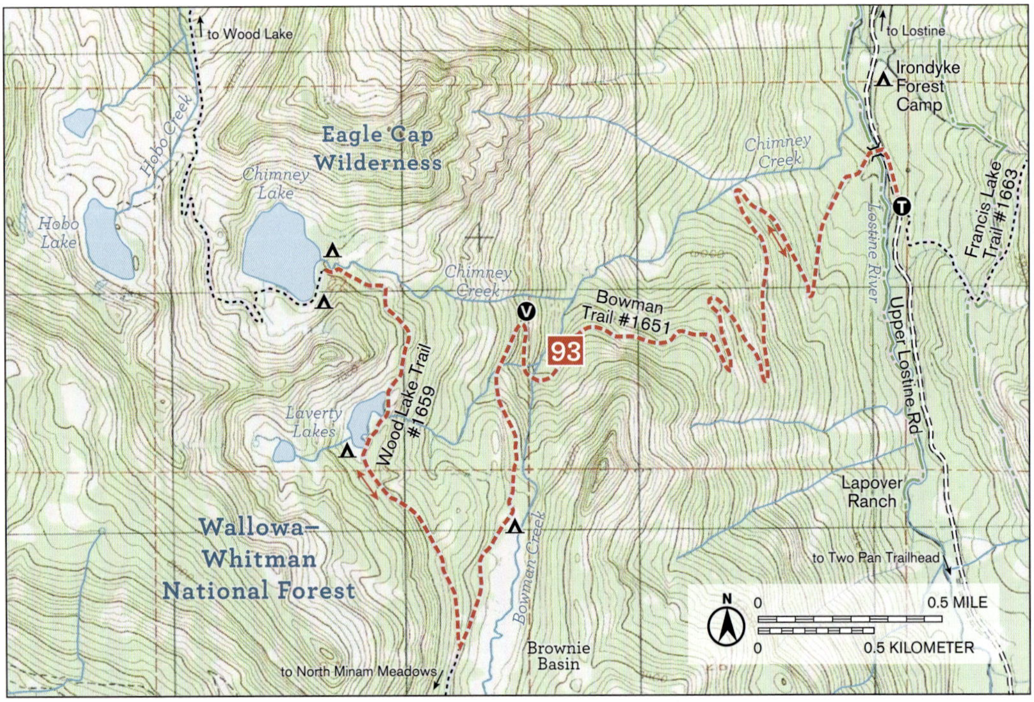

(east), continue straight on Lostine River Road for 14.7 miles; this road becomes gravel Upper Lostine Road, then rougher gravel Forest Road 8210. Park at the Bowman Francis trailhead, 0.3 mile past the Irondyke Forest Camp. ***Notes:*** NW Forest Pass or Interagency Pass required for trailhead parking. Wilderness rules apply. Complete a self-issue wilderness permit at the trailhead kiosk. Campfires prohibited within 0.25 mile of Chimney Lake.

When you think of the Eagle Cap Wilderness, the first landmarks that come to mind are probably the central lakes basin (see Hike 91) and 9572-foot Eagle Cap peak. Rightfully so. But there's so much more to explore in this vast backcountry wonderland. While everyone else is heading for the overcrowded Two Pan Trailhead at the end of the road, stop a few miles north of there instead, where you can find two trailheads that invite adventure into less traveled—but just as stunning—high lake country.

Start at the Bowman trailhead (#1651), on the north side of the parking area entrance road. Directly across is the Francis Lake trailhead (see Hike 92). Walk a short stretch on a flat path under shady evergreens, crossing Upper Lostine Road (FR 8210) after just 0.1 mile. Jog right (northwest) to pick up the trail on the other side, and immediately cross a footbridge over the Lostine River. The trail then starts ascending at a moderate grade, often on rough and rocky tread. Tall, mossy hemlocks and firs keep the route mostly shady as you climb. Along the trailside, you'll see an assortment of berry shrubs and wildflowers. As you gain elevation through several sweeping switchbacks, windows in the tree cover offer views over the Lostine Canyon. The high peak directly to the east is 8888-foot Marble Point.

After ascending for a while, the trail turns west along the base of a high ridge and eases to a more comfortable grade as it comes alongside Bowman Creek. Just ahead, as the trail curves through the lush drainage, it crosses the main branch of the creek at 2.6 miles. Then start climbing again, crossing a few small creeks. A fantastic viewpoint awaits at 2.8 miles, which offers panoramas up and down the Lostine River valley from an impressive perch. The trail continues ascending until it eventually flattens out to a comfortable walk into Brownie Basin. At 3.3 miles, a path veers off to the left (south) to a nice, large camp area.

Continue into the basin on the main trail as it starts contouring up the west side of the valley wall. Reach a junction at 3.7 miles and make a U-turn onto the Wood Lake Trail (#1659), then continue ascending to Laverty Lakes. At 4.4 miles, reach the larger of the two lakes, a shallow body of water resting at the base of a high wall of rocky talus. Several campsites lie on the south and east sides of the lake; the north side is too marshy for good camping. The trail continues around the base of the rocky ridge, curving west through overgrown berry shrubs. At 5 miles, finally reach Chimney Lake; a large campsite sits near the lake's outlet.

Several more secluded campsites are located around the lakeshore, so cross the outlet stream and continue around the northeast side of the lake. Once you've found your ideal spot, enjoy the view of this lovely pool nestled in an amphitheater of glacier-carved granite. Directly west is 8810-foot Lookout Mountain. When you're ready to return, after lunch or maybe an overnight stay, backtrack down by the same route.

Extend Your Trip: If you've got more juice in the tank, you can continue to Wood Lake. From the Chimney Lake outlet, the trail snakes up and out of the basin for 1.1 miles to a high pass on the shoulder of 8675-foot Chimney Lake North. From here, descend into the next basin, following Hobo Creek for another mile to Wood Lake. Find a few campsites on the southwest side of the lake.

94 *Steamboat Loop*

Distance: 26.2 miles one-way (plus a 3-mile road walk or shuttle)
Difficulty: strenuous
Hiking time: multiday
Elevation gain: 5890 feet
High point: 8580 feet
Season: Jul–Oct
Management: Wallowa–Whitman NF (Wallowa Mountains)
Protection status: Eagle Cap Wilderness
Map: Green Trails 475SX: Wallowa Mountains
GPS coordinates: N 45 25.008, W 117 37.649

Getting there: From US Highway 84 in La Grande, take exit 261 for Oregon Route 82 to Elgin. Follow this road for 53 miles to the town of Lostine. When the road turns left (east), continue straight on Lostine River Road (which eventually becomes Upper Lostine Road, then Forest Road 8210) for 17.7 miles to the Two Pan trailhead at the end of the road. The paved road eventually becomes good gravel, then rougher gravel, so take it slow.
Notes: NW Forest Pass or Interagency Pass required for trailhead parking. Wilderness rules apply. Complete a self-issue wilderness permit at the trailhead kiosk. Campfires prohibited within 0.25 mile of Swamp and Steamboat Lakes.

There is no shortage of stunning backcountry scenery in the Wallowa Mountains' Eagle Cap Wilderness. While most visitors head for the main lakes basin, consider this alternative multiday route that boasts equally impressive scenery—sans the trail traffic and crowded campsites. And if you really want to make an epic journey out of it, five additional lakes are accessible via connecting trails, giving you plenty of opportunities to fully immerse yourself in backcountry grandeur.

Vivid skies over the sprawling Elkhorn Meadows

The best way to conquer this hike is to leave a shuttle vehicle at the ending trailhead (Bowman–Francis). If you have only one vehicle, you can drop your gear and companions at the Two Pan trailhead, then drive to the Bowman–Francis trailhead to park; from there, it's a quick, gear-free, 3-mile walk up the road to join your party.

From the Two Pan trailhead, set out on the Minam Lake Trail (#1670) as it begins its journey up the Lostine River canyon. After a short 0.2 mile, veer right (south) at a junction with the East Fork Lostine Trail (#1662) to continue heading toward Minam Lake. The trail climbs steadily as it heads up the west fork of the Lostine River. After gaining a quick 900 feet of elevation in the first 2.6 miles, veer right (southwest) onto the Copper Creek Trail (#1656) and continue ascending, crossing the creek at 3.7 and 4.4 miles. The trail then levels out, giving you a brief reprieve as it crosses a pleasant meadow.

At the top of the meadow, begin ascending again, making a contouring circuit of a high, unnamed peak. At 5.6 miles, the trail levels out again at the foot of the sprawling Elkhorn Creek meadow. Several campsites can be found on the fringes of the meadow, not far from the creek that meanders through this spectacularly scenic setting. Climb out of the meadow into higher alpine country, passing little Sky Lake and proceeding across another wide-open meadow. Now high above the tree line, the terrain becomes barren and rocky, with little puffs of buckwheat adding splashes of vibrant color. At 7.3 miles, the trail reaches its high point.

Take in a wide view of the North Minam River valley as the trail traverses an open slope. At around 7.6 miles, reach a junction with the North Minam Trail (#1675). From here, you'll veer right to begin a long downhill jog, losing all the elevation you just gained. Descend through a series of switchbacks into the upper head of the valley, arriving alongside pretty (despite its name) Swamp Lake at 9.3 miles. After the lake, at 9.5 miles, the Long Lake Trail (#1669) splits off to the left (west), leading 1.4 miles to a secluded, pretty pool nestled under 7999-foot Minam Peak. This is another good option for exploring and camping opportunities. To continue on the main trail, drop down another steep series of switchbacks into the Steamboat Lake basin, reaching the lakeside and more camping at 11.1 miles.

Leaving Steamboat Lake behind, the trail mounts a small rise, then begins an extremely long, twisting, turning, switchbacking descent to the floor of the river valley, finally leveling out at around 15.5 miles. Enjoy a pleasant romp along the edge of the North Minam Meadows, finding a few campsites near the foot of the meadows with access to water. At 16.8 miles, it's time to get your climb on again. Turn right (east) onto the Bowman Trail (#1651) and begin a long, switchbacking ascent of the mountainside and drainage.

When you reach a junction with the Bear Creek Trail (#1653) at 19.1 miles, you're halfway up. Veer right (northeast) at the junction and continue ascending into Wilson Basin. At 20.3 miles, a 0.4-mile side trail leads to marshy John Henry Lake, where you can find a couple of campsites.

After another 1.1 miles, ascend to the saddle between 8079-foot Bailey Butte to the south and an unnamed peak to the north, where you're presented with a gobsmacking view over Brownie Basin. From here, the descent is quick and steady, heading into the meadowy basin. The Wood Lake Trail (#1659) branches off to the left (northwest) at 22.6 miles (see Hike 93). Veer right (northeast) to continue descending into increasingly dense woods, crossing Bowman Creek at 23.7 miles. The home stretch contours around the flank of a wooded ridge, then drops through a handful of switchbacks to cross the Lostine River on a sturdy footbridge beside the road. Jog right (south) to proceed to the Bowman-Francis trailhead and complete your epic journey.

95 *Echo Lake*

Distance: 9.8-mile roundtrip
Difficulty: moderate
Hiking time: day hike or overnight
Elevation gain: 1890 feet
High point: 7230 feet
Season: Aug–Oct
Management: Wallowa–Whitman NF (La Grande)
Protection status: Eagle Cap Wilderness
Map: Green Trails 475SX: Wallowa Mountains
GPS coordinates: N 45 08002, W 117 47683

Getting there: From US Highway 84 in La Grande, take Medical Springs Highway (Oregon Route 203) about 11 miles to the town of Union. Turn left (south) to continue on OR 203 and proceed another 14 miles to the Catherine Summit Sno-Park. Turn left (south) on Eagle Creek Road (Forest Road 77) and drive this good but occasionally bumpy gravel road for 15 miles to the West Eagle trailhead and campground. ***Notes:*** NW Forest Pass or Interagency Pass required for trailhead parking. Wilderness rules apply. Complete a self-issue wilderness permit at the trailhead kiosk. This trail requires several river fords, which can be challenging during high water seasons. Campfires prohibited within 0.25 mile of Traverse and Tombstone Lakes.

The Wallowa Mountains and Eagle Cap Wilderness draw—justifiably—gads of hikers and backpackers to their scenic peaks and sparkling lakes every summer. Most of these visitors flock to the popular trailheads on the north side of the range, making many of the more remote locations on the south side ideal for finding a little wilderness solitude. One of these quiet places is the stunning trail to Echo Lake. This picturesque pool lies in a high glaciated basin, looking as though someone plucked it straight out of the High Sierra and plopped it down in this quiet corner of Oregon.

From the West Eagle trailhead (#1934), start out on an old jeep road that skirts the West Eagle Meadow. Keep watch for deer and elk in the meadow. A few walk-in campsites can be found along the way. At 0.3 mile, pass a spur trail that returns to the West Eagle Meadow Campground. The route transitions into duff-covered trail and proceeds into shady spruce and fir forest. An assortment of huckleberry, whortleberry, and pipsissewa carpet the forest floor. Near the crossing of Fake Creek at 0.6 mile, the unsigned and easy-to-miss Fake Creek Trail (#1914) climbs off to the east (see Extend Your Trip).

Continue another 0.5 mile to the Eagle Cap Wilderness boundary and your first crossing of West Eagle Creek. This can be a challenging crossing during early summer and other high

Day hike or backpack to Echo Lake

runoff periods. Later in the summer, it's usually an easy rock-hop. Proceed across at the safest location you can find, then continue into greener and lusher woods. Approaching the 2-mile mark, the trail crosses a couple of small slopeside meadows, which are prolific with deer fern, aster, pearly everlasting, and thimbleberry. There are even a few aspen trees through here, their silvery leaves shimmering in even the slightest breeze. Peer skyward at a towering yet unnamed granite peak to the southeast.

The trail continues ascending on an easy grade, skirting alongside West Eagle Creek at times, then crosses it again at 2.3 miles. This is another crossing that may require scouting for the safest crossing location. Just beyond the creek crossing, an obvious boot path veers right (east) off the main trail to a large campsite in a grove of lofty evergreens. Check out the shattered remains of a huge Douglas-fir that was struck by lightning here. From this point, the trail gets down to business and starts switchbacking up the glacial valley. But the ascent never gets steep or challenging, and along the way, you'll enjoy increasingly wider valley views, with slopes decorated with paintbrush, skyrocket, penstemon, and currant.

At the top of the first series of switchbacks, at 2.8 miles, arrive at a junction with the Tombstone Lake Trail (#1943). This trail veers off to the north, where it proceeds over a high pass before dropping into Tombstone Lake's remote basin. To continue toward Echo Lake, keep switchbacking upward, gradually climbing out of the forest and ascending a wide talus field on a high, exposed slope. Notice the rocks here, which are mostly granite. These igneous rocks are a unique anomaly in Oregon's mostly volcanic landscape. Keep your eyes and ears alert for the furry residents among these rocks: cute little pikas.

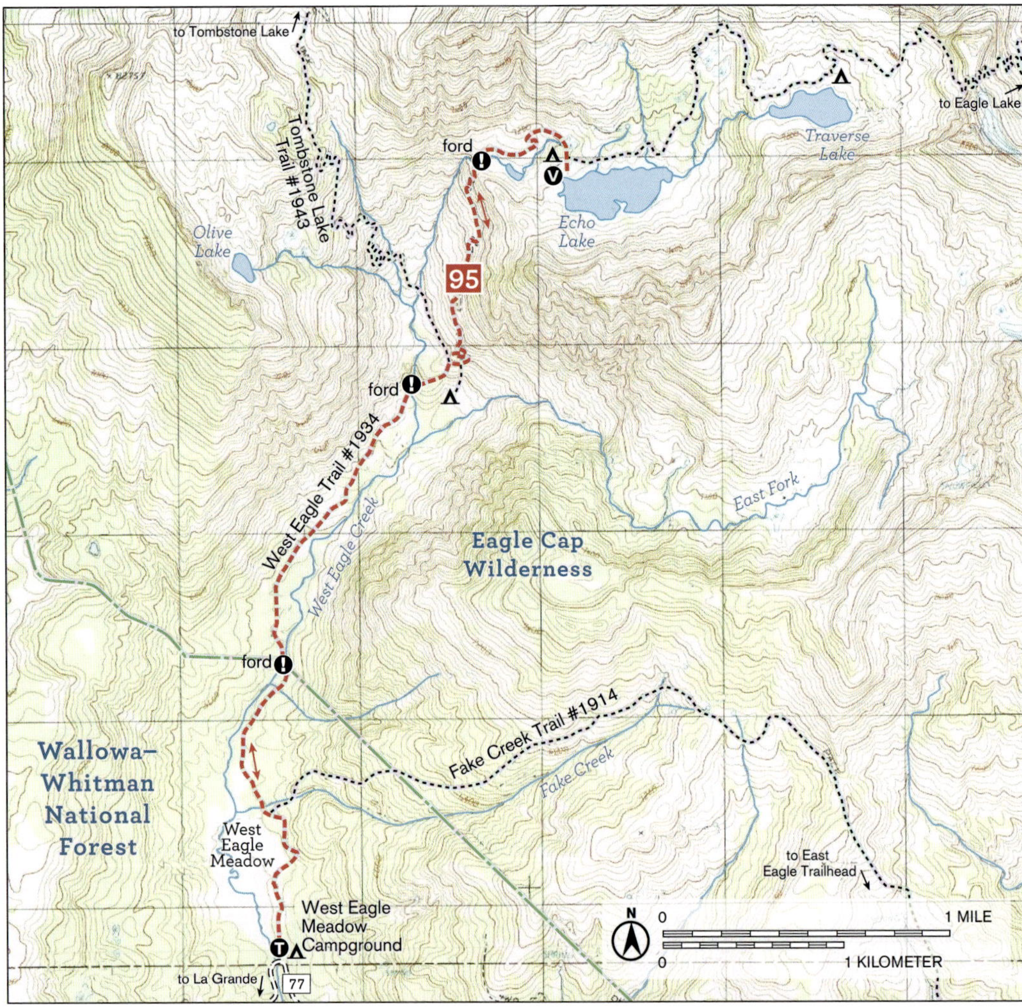

The views of the valley and surrounding walls and peaks become more and more impressive the higher you go. At 4 miles, where the trail switchbacks near an old, mangled tree, look for a dark cave extending under the granite talus. Peer in as closely as you dare, keeping in mind Gandalf's warning that "there are older and fouler things . . . in the deep places of the world." Continue up through another dozen switchbacks until the trail crests a saddle just above seven thousand feet. Here, come alongside one of the upper branches of West Eagle Creek. The creek crossing is just ahead. Use the log crossing if possible, or scout for another crossing if it looks unsafe.

Once across, proceed through a wide-open basin of waist-high brush. At 4.5 miles, where a river of rock and gravel cuts across the trail, jog slightly left (north) to find the continuation of the trail on the other side. Hike into the basin and through a grove of alders, where a few small springs spill across the trail. Just beyond, the path enters shady woods and crosses a couple of creek culverts; a nice campsite lies just right (west) of the trail. When the trail comes to an unsigned fork, at 4.9 miles, choose your path forward: left (east), to continue on the lake trail to more dispersed campsites and beyond; or right (south), heading across the lake's dam to a stunning viewpoint that takes in the whole scene. When you're ready, return by the same route.

Extend Your Trip: For another idyllic alpine lake and more high-country views, continue 1.6 miles past Echo Lake into the upper basin. Here, you'll find Traverse Lake surrounded by open meadows of summer wildflowers as ragged, granitic peaks rise overhead. A few campsites are situated around the lake basin. For an even longer journey, you can combine the trail to Echo Lake with the Eagle Lake Loop (see Hike 96) for an epic, 33-mile journey.

For the latter, continue over the 8500-foot pass east of Traverse Lake and drop steeply down the Main Eagle Trail (#1922) to Trail Creek. Cross the creek and climb to a wooded bench north of Arrow Lake, then climb some more to a view-packed ridgeline. Make a winding descent into the next valley, where you'll find good camping around Cached Lake. Continue past the Eagle Lake Trail (#1931; a worthwhile 2-mile roundtrip), turning south to head down the wide, glaciated valley. When you reach the trailhead at FR 7755, walk the gravel road southwest 0.3 mile to the Boulder Park Campground, where you'll find the Fake Creek trailhead (#1914). Hike this trail up and over several high drainages until it drops to meet the West Eagle Trail (#1934) near West Eagle Meadow. From here, turn left to return to your waiting vehicle. ***Note:*** Some of the trails in this loop are not regularly maintained and may be difficult to navigate. Only experienced hikers should attempt this route.

96 *Eagle Lake Loop*

Distance: 17.5-mile lollipop loop
Difficulty: strenuous
Hiking time: overnight or multiday
Elevation gain: 4510 feet
High point: 8190 feet
Season: Jul–Oct
Management: Wallowa–Whitman NF (La Grande)
Protection status: Eagle Cap Wilderness
Map: Green Trails 475SX: Wallowa Mountains
GPS coordinates: N 45 06796, W 117 40684

Getting there: From US Highway 84 in La Grande, take Medical Springs Highway (Oregon Route 203) about 11 miles to the town of Union. Turn left (south) to continue on OR 203 and proceed another 14 miles to the Catherine Summit Sno-Park. Turn left (south) on Eagle Creek Road (Forest Road 77) and drive this good but occasionally bumpy gravel road for 19.5 miles. Turn left (north) on FR 7755 and proceed 3.6 miles to the Main Eagle trailhead at the end of the road. ***Notes:*** NW Forest Pass or Interagency Pass required for trailhead parking. Wilderness rules apply. Complete a self-issue wilderness permit at the trailhead kiosk. Portions of this route are not regularly maintained; some routefinding may be required.

The Main Eagle trailhead is a less-used back-door into the Eagle Cap Wilderness. The road to get here is long and occasionally bumpy, but the splendid backcountry solitude you can find here makes it well worth the extra effort. You'll hike along empty trails to a plethora of view-packed ridges and remote lakes. This multi-day lollipop loop employs some trails that see little maintenance, making for some rough passage. But you'll be rewarded for your efforts with sweeping views of a remote, rugged wilderness, with little company, in one of the most scenic corners of Oregon's stunning Wallowa Mountains.

Big view over the southern Eagle Cap Wilderness

From the road's end trailhead, start heading up the Main Eagle Trail (#1922), quickly crossing Boulder Creek on a small bridge. The trail meanders upstream under partially shady woods for about 0.5 mile, then crosses Eagle Creek on a good footbridge and continues up the canyon on the east side of the creek. At 1.8 miles, hop across another small tributary. Cross Eagle Creek again at 2.3 miles on a good log-stringer bridge, then hop across Copper Creek at 2.6 miles; this latter crossing has no bridge and can be wide during high water seasons. Scout for the safest passage. At 2.8 miles, reach a junction with the Bench Canyon Trail (#1937).

Veer left (northwest) and climb this rough, unmaintained trail for 1.6 miles to the Heart Lake junction. Along the way, the slope opens, showcasing meadows and rock gardens brimming with wildflowers, and the route hops across the outlet creek for Arrow Lake a couple of times. For a short scenic detour, follow the 0.3-mile spur trail to picturesque Heart Lake. Otherwise, continue on the main trail, reaching Arrow Lake at 5 miles; directly behind the lake, 8448-foot Arrow Lake Peak vaults skyward. A few nice campsites are scattered around the benches surrounding the lake, making this an ideal spot to break for the day if you had a late start.

From Arrow Lake, slide over the back side of the ridge and start descending northward into the remote Trail Creek drainage. The high peaks to the west are 8858-foot Savage Peak and 8949-foot Traverse Lake East Peak. A little past 5.6 miles, the Bench Canyon Trail ends at its north junction with the Main Eagle Trail. Turn right (east) and start ascending again, now on nicer, well-maintained trail. The route zigs and zags upward through dense woods to crest the ridge at 7.2 miles. Here is the view you came for. To the east is a spectacularly colorful scene that showcases a combination of volcanic and granitic peaks, cones, and ridges. Tucked behind the ridge directly ahead is your next destination: Cached Lake.

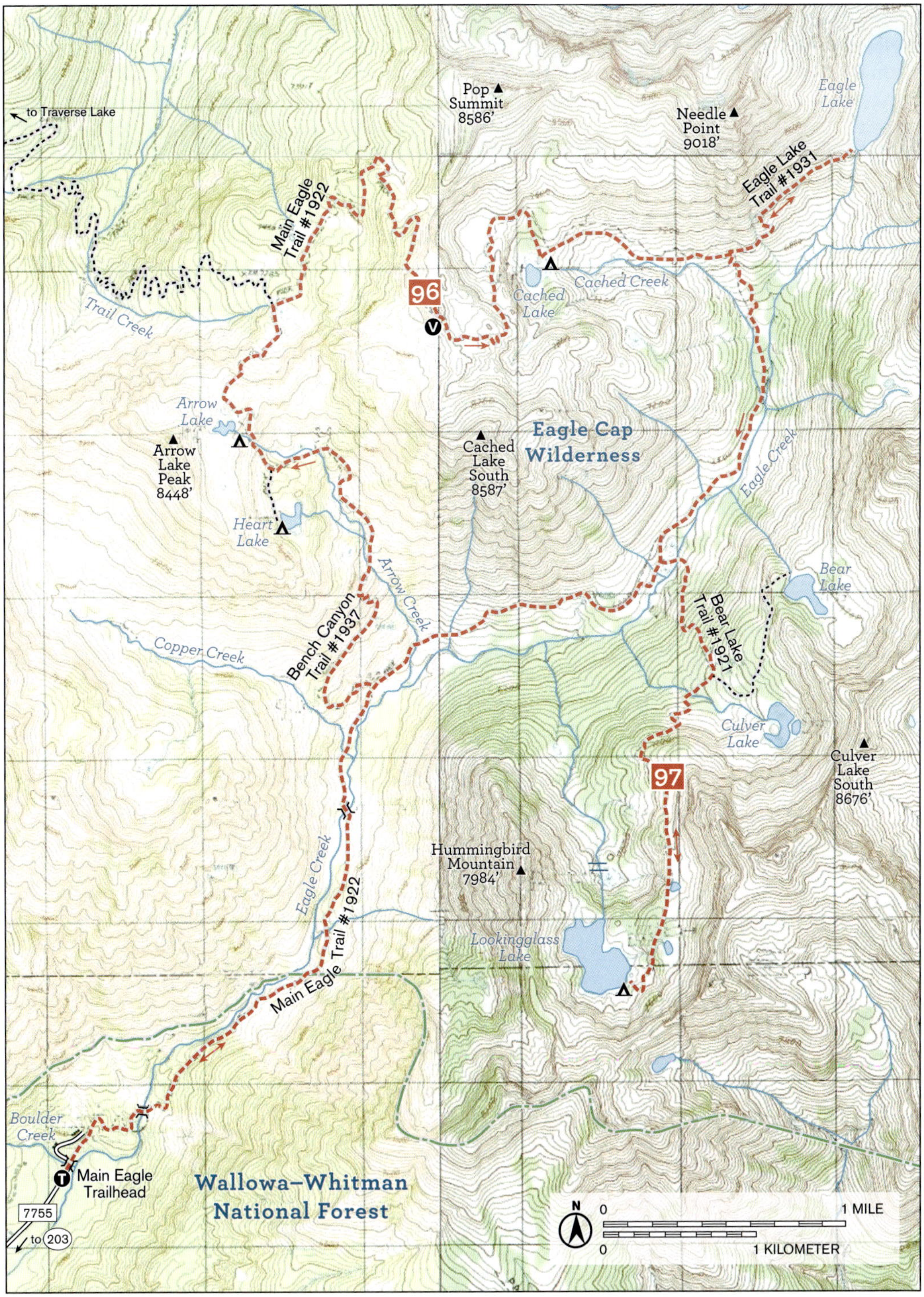
to Traverse Lake
Pop Summit 8586'
Needle Point 9018'
Eagle Lake
Eagle Lake Trail #1931
Main Eagle Trail #1922
96
Cached Lake
Cached Creek
Trail Creek
Arrow Lake
Arrow Lake Peak 8448'
Heart Lake
Cached Lake South 8587'
Eagle Cap Wilderness
Eagle Creek
Arrow Creek
Bear Lake
Bear Lake Trail #1921
Copper Creek
Bench Canyon Trail #1937
Culver Lake
Culver Lake South 8676'
97
Hummingbird Mountain 7984'
Eagle Creek
Main Eagle Trail #1922
Lookingglass Lake
Boulder Creek
Main Eagle Trailhead
7755
to 203
Wallowa–Whitman National Forest
N
0
1 MILE
0
1 KILOMETER

Start heading down into the basin, snaking and switchbacking to the next plateau. The high, pyramidal peak to the north is 8586-foot Pop Summit. The trail meanders through scenic meadows choked with bog stars, skirting wide talus slopes and crossing several small creeks. At 8.9 miles, arrive at Cached Lake. If you're camping, consider staying here instead of at Eagle Lake. There are more sites here, and most offer some shelter in the surrounding trees. Since the lakeshore is largely inaccessible due to its grassy, marshy shoreline, obtain your water from nearby streams. The high, rocky ridgeline behind the lake that lights up with evening alpenglow is an extension of 8587-foot Cached Lake South.

From Cached Lake, descend another mile to the Eagle Lake Trail (#1931), at 9.9 miles. Veer left (northeast) and take this 0.9-mile spur that contours up the rocky flank of 9018-foot Needle Point to Eagle Lake. This secluded pool sits in a rocky amphitheater surrounded by six distinct peaks. Camping here is not ideal due to its rugged shoreline and full exposure, but if you're determined, it is possible to find a few flat spots to fit a small tent. After your lake visit, return to the Main Eagle Trail and turn left (southeast) to follow Eagle Creek down through more rock gardens and meadows. At 13.4 miles, reach a junction with the Bear Lake Trail (#1921; see Hike 97). Now on the home stretch, stay right and continue following Eagle Creek downstream for 2.4 miles to the Bench Canyon Trail junction where you started your loop. From here, retrace your steps back down the canyon on familiar trail to return to the trailhead.

97 *Lookingglass Lake*

Distance: 12.9-mile roundtrip
Difficulty: strenuous
Hiking time: long day hike or overnight
Elevation gain: 3050 feet
High point: 7510 feet
Season: Jul–Oct
Management: Wallowa–Whitman NF (La Grande)
Protection status: Eagle Cap Wilderness
Map: Green Trails 475SX: Wallowa Mountains
GPS coordinates: N 45 06796, W 117 40684

Getting there: From US Highway 84 in La Grande, take Medical Springs Highway (Oregon Route 203) about 11 miles to the town of Union. Turn left (south) to continue on OR 203 and proceed another 14 miles to the Catherine Summit Sno-Park. Turn left (south) on Eagle Creek Road (Forest Road 77) and drive this good but occasionally bumpy gravel road for 19.5 miles. Turn left (north) on FR 7755 and proceed 3.6 miles to the Main Eagle trailhead at the end of the road. ***Notes:*** NW Forest Pass or Interagency Pass required for trailhead parking. Wilderness rules apply. Complete a self-issue wilderness permit at the trailhead kiosk.

Lookingglass Lake is a stunningly scenic pool of water that rests in a high glacial cirque, surrounded by five skyscraping alpine peaks. It's the kind of place where you can just sit and stare, letting your mind drift as lazily as the clouds as you channel your inner John Muir. It's the quiet, special places like this that make hiking and backcountry travel so inspiring and rewarding.

The trail begins in the same fashion as the Eagle Lake Loop (see Hike 96), which presents you with additional exploring opportunities if the urge arises. Enjoy your journey heading up Eagle Creek, crossing several times and traversing pleasant meadows. After crossing Copper Creek, shake the water off your boots, meet the Bench Canyon Trail (#1937) at 2.8 miles. Stay

A quiet dusk at Lookingglass Lake

right at this junction and cross Arrow Creek at 3.1 miles.

With most of your water crossings now behind you, the trail begins traversing the lower south flank of 8587-foot Cached Lake South on a contouring incline. When you reach the Bear Lake Trail (#1921) junction, at 4.1 miles, turn right (east) and begin a steady ascent to the next junction. Then veer right (south) and climb another 0.8 mile until the trail finally levels out for a pleasant amble around the edge of a high basin. The thundering waterfall across the basin, below 7984-foot Hummingbird Mountain, is the outlet of Lookingglass Lake. Proceed upward through more meadows and past small lakelets as you skirt the west flank of 8676-foot Culver Lake South. The trail eventually tips over the edge and dips into the Lookingglass basin. Descend this dusty path to the lakeshore, where several idyllic campsites await.

Now all you have to do is pick your perfect spot to sit and enjoy. The scene looks as if it were plucked right out of John Muir's "Range of Light"—a pristine alpine lake nestled in a glacier-carved basin, surrounded by sparkling granitic peaks. What more could you ask for—besides a taco and a margarita? (Maybe you should pack some along!) Enjoy your time here for as long as you can. On your way back down, consider taking the 0.9-mile spur trail to visit Bear Lake, a pretty pool in another glacial cirque. When you reach the Main Eagle Trail, turn left (southwest) and retrace your steps back to your starting point.

Opposite, top: The trail up Big Indian Gorge

Opposite, bottom: Bird's-eye view over Wildhorse Lake from the Steens Mountain summit

Southeast Oregon

98. Juniper Gulch **270**

99. Big Indian Gorge **272**

100. Wildhorse Basin **274**

Oregon's remote southeast section is rich in natural beauty, birding, and wildlife watching. Among the lonely mountain ranges and seemingly endless rolling prairies of high desert sagebrush, Steens Mountain and the Owyhee Canyonlands offer some surprisingly stunning scenery, making a trip to this region worth the extra effort.

98 *Juniper Gulch*

Distance: 1.9-mile roundtrip
Difficulty: easy
Hiking time: short day hike
Elevation gain: 360 feet
High point: 3760 feet
Season: Apr–Oct
Management: Oregon BLM
Protection status: Area of Critical Environmental Concern
Map: USGS Quad: Rooster Comb, OR
GPS coordinates: N 43 29.870, W 117 27.051

Getting there: From Ontario, take Interstate 84 east into Idaho for about 4 miles. Take exit 3 and merge onto US Highway 95 South. Continue for 57 miles, eventually reentering Oregon. Immediately after crossing the bridge over Succor Creek, turn right (west) onto washboard gravel Succor Creek Road. Take this bumpy but manageable road for 3 miles to a fork and veer right. Continue another 5 miles to a T-junction at the Rockville schoolhouse; turn left (west), proceed 0.3 mile, then go right (north) to stay on Succor Creek Road for another 1.5 miles. At the next fork, turn left (west) on Leslie Gulch Road and drive 6.6 miles to the canyon entrance. Go another 3.7 miles, with the last mile becoming a bumpy jeep road, to the Juniper Gulch trailhead on the right (north) side of the road. High-clearance vehicles recommended. ***Notes:*** Day use only. Not recommended during rain and thunderstorms; roads and canyons are susceptible to flash flooding. The trail is very brushy and overgrown; wear long pants. Summer temperatures can be extreme, and there is no water in the gulch; use sun protection and pack all the water you'll need. Beware of ticks and rattlesnakes.

When you're ready to leave Oregon behind to visit a distant alien desert—sans hyperdrive engine—all you have to do is point your car east and head for Leslie Gulch in the Owyhee Canyonlands. Here, you will find towering spires and unearthly formations of volcanic rhyolite tuff that have been sculped by nature for the last fifteen million years, following the eruption of ancient Mahogany Mountain. And while it may appear barren and desolate, this area is home to an abundance of flora and fauna, including bighorn sheep, pronghorn antelope, coyotes, prey birds, and several rare plants and wildflowers. It takes some effort to get here, but the scenic rewards for your efforts are nothing short of stunning—and unlike anything you would ever expect to see in Oregon.

From the roadside trailhead, plunge through thickets of sagebrush and rabbitbrush, immediately crossing a dry creek bed. Find the path marked with a rusty post and head into the canyon, where the trail is lined with a variety of clematis, serviceberry, wooly mullein, and the gulch's namesake juniper. Springtime brings a plethora of colorful little blooms to this otherwise dry environment. As the path starts to follow the sandy creek bed upcanyon, you may be hard-pressed to look down for flowers, as your gaze will doubtless

Otherworldly rock formations in Juniper Gulch

be drawn upward to the incredible rock formations towering overhead. Use your imagination to anthropomorphize some of the shapes you see in the rocks. Among other figures, you might spot a castle, a dragon, a train of turtles, a falcon, an ice-cream cone, and the Infinity Gauntlet.

About 0.6 mile up the gorge, where the trail splits around a rocky mound, veer left (west). Continue about ten yards, then veer right (east) to ascend the mound, forgoing the scramble up into a steep slot on the left. From the top of this ridge, you're presented with an impressive view back down the canyon. Continue up the canyon along the ridgetop for another 0.3 mile, following a well-trodden path dotted with mountain mahogany to the base of a honeycombed headwall. From here, the panorama of spires, columns, and sculptures of mind-bending rock formations are countless—and just slightly surreal. Numerous footpaths branch off from this location, but most are challenging and require scrambling, so this makes a good turnaround point. Soak in the scene, then enjoy the journey all over again on your way back down.

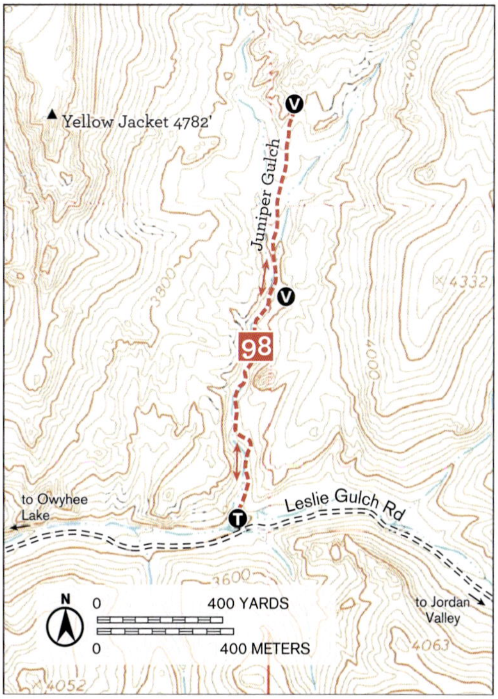

99 Big Indian Gorge

Distance: 16-mile roundtrip
Difficulty: moderate
Hiking time: long day hike or overnight
Elevation gain: 1990 feet
High point: 6940 feet
Season: Jul–Oct
Management: Oregon BLM (Burns)
Protection status: Steens Mountain Wilderness
Maps: USGS Quads: Fish Lake, OR; Wildhorse Lake, OR
GPS coordinates: N 42 65.622, W 118 72.417

Getting there: From Burns, take Oregon Route 205 south for 58 miles to the small town of Frenchglen. Continue another 10 miles south on OR 205, then turn left (east) on Steens Mountain Loop Road (BLM 8244). Drive this washboard gravel road for 19 miles to South Steens Campground. Enter the campground and drive around to the back of the loop to find the trailhead. Park on the shoulder; don't block campsite access.
Notes: Wilderness rules apply. Requires several potentially challenging river crossings. If water is running high or fast, consider turning around and visiting later in the season. Not recommended during rain and thunderstorms; rivers are susceptible to flash flooding. Beware of ticks, bees, hornets, and rattlesnakes.

Steens Mountain, located in the remote southeast corner of Oregon's high desert country, is a bit of a geologic anomaly. Stretching for more than forty miles and vaulting nearly a vertical mile above the valley floor, Steens is a "fault-block" mountain. This type of mountain results when layer upon layer of basalt lava cools, bulges, and fractures into massive blocks, which then slide and tilt into each other. During the last ice age, Steens's elevation made it susceptible to

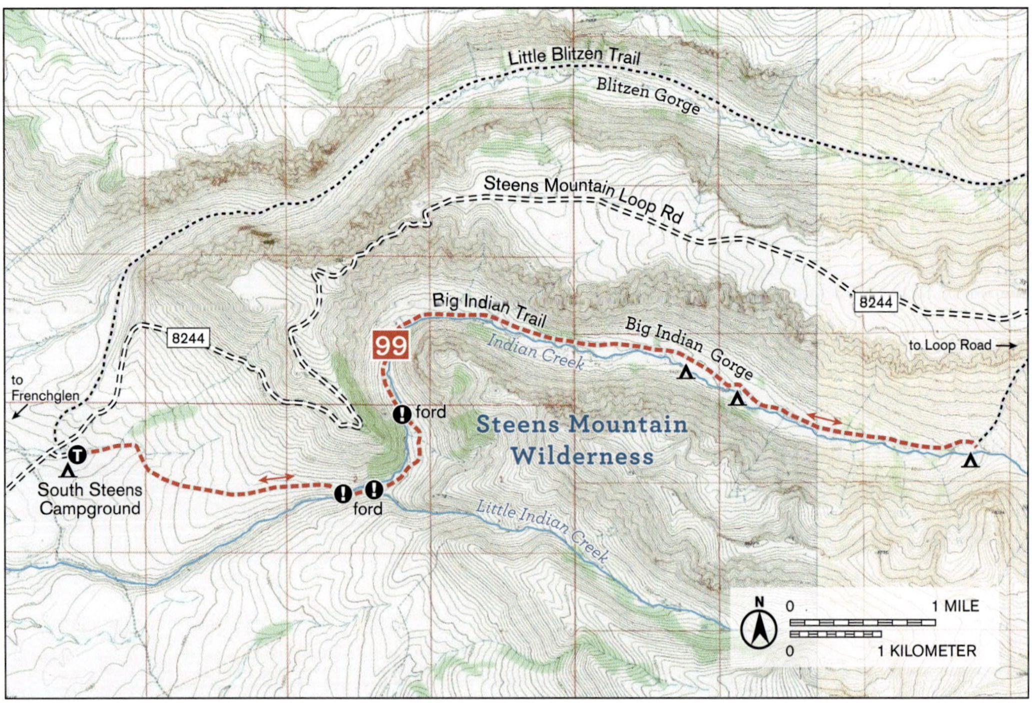

Big Indian Gorge on Steens Mountain

glaciation, which carved massive valleys out of the flanks of the mountain, creating the dramatic landscape that you see today.

Start out on an old wagon road, heading into sparse juniper woods. About 0.2 mile up the trail, stop at the metal box and sign the trail register. Then continue following the old road as it ascends a high prairie dotted with volcanic boulders, where the views are expansive in all directions. The trail then quickly drops to the first crossing of Indian Creek, at 1.9 miles. Ford the river and proceed to the next crossing, this one of Little Indian Creek at 2.1 miles. (See Safety in the Introduction for more information about fording rivers.) As you head farther up the canyon, you'll notice the terrain and landscape transitioning from dry juniper woods to lush aspen and alder. Cross Indian Creek again at 3 miles, following the river around a wide bend, and enter the heart of Big Indian Gorge.

From here, the trail heads easily up the floor of the valley, only intermittently coming alongside the river. Traipse through open meadows of sagebrush, rabbitbrush, bull thistle, goldenrod, and lupine while marveling at the skyscraping walls of the river valley. Then enjoy the shade breaks provided by aspen groves adorned with wild rose, sticky geranium, and elderberry. Despite the trail being narrow and brushy in places, the hiking is pleasant and mostly effortless, allowing you to spend more time admiring your surroundings than watching your step. As you pass the 4-mile mark, cast your gaze up the north valley wall to a cluster of sculpted outcrops that resemble the ruins of an ancient fortress—it looks like something plucked straight out of Middle Earth.

At around 6 miles, the first serviceable campsites begin to appear as the trail approaches the river through a grove of tall, shady cottonwoods. The views here are good, but they are limited to the north valley wall, so keep heading up the trail. The route passes through the biggest aspen grove yet—some of which have been flattened—and emerges into a higher meadow with sweeping views of the valley headwall. The grade increases notably as you begin ascending the lower slope of the headwall. If it's flowing, hop across a seasonal cascade at 7.9 miles. Then round a bend and carefully cross the slickrock at the top of a bigger cascade. If this one is flowing fast and heavy, look for a safer crossing upstream. Just beyond the cascade, you can find a few dispersed campsites with stellar views in all directions.

From this point, 8 miles from the trailhead, the only way forward is to hike very steeply up the headwall on loose, narrow tread, so this location makes a good turnaround point. It's also a stunning destination for a night in the valley. Thanks to its remote location, far from the light pollution of cities and developed areas, it has some of the darkest skies in Oregon—perfect for stargazing and meteor showers. Before the sun goes down, keep a sharp eye out for deer, elk, pronghorn, and bighorn sheep in the valley below and on the slopes above. Also look for a variety of song and prey birds flitting between the trees and in the skies overhead. When you've had your fill, return to the trailhead by the same route.

100 *Wildhorse Lake*

Distance: 2.4-mile roundtrip
Difficulty: strenuous
Hiking time: day hike or overnight
Elevation gain: 1120 feet
High point: 9540 feet
Season: Aug–Oct
Management: Oregon BLM (Burns)
Protection status: Steens Mountain Wilderness
Map: USGS Quad: Wildhorse Lake, OR
GPS coordinates: N 42 64.136, W 118 58.000

Getting there: From Burns, take Oregon Route 205 south for 58 miles to the small town of Frenchglen. Turn left (east) on Steens Mountain Loop Road (BLM 8244) and drive

The high, remote Wildhorse Lake on Steens Mountain

this washboard gravel road for 25.2 miles to a three-way fork. Take the middle fork for Wildhorse Lake and continue 2 miles to the trailhead at road's end. ***Notes:*** Wilderness rules apply. High-elevation trail with full exposure; bring sun and wind protection. Campfires prohibited in the lake basin. Dispersed camping is limited to two groups per night. Not recommended if there is snow on the trail. Do not cut switchbacks.

At the end of the highest drivable road in Oregon, an unassuming little trailhead marks one of the highest non-mountaineering, developed trails you can hike in the state. The view from the trailhead, just below the summit of 9733-foot Steens Mountain, is impressive enough—but once you reach the tipping point above Wildhorse Lake, prepare to be utterly gobsmacked. Nestled in a wide glacial basin, the scene is immense and surreal, and you can practically imagine the massive sheet of ice that once filled this canyon a mere ten thousand years ago. Even more mind-boggling is the fact that the tilted and fractured blocks of Steens Mountain are composed of layer upon layer of volcanic basalt—more than four thousand feet deep—which once formed the slopes of a prehistoric volcano.

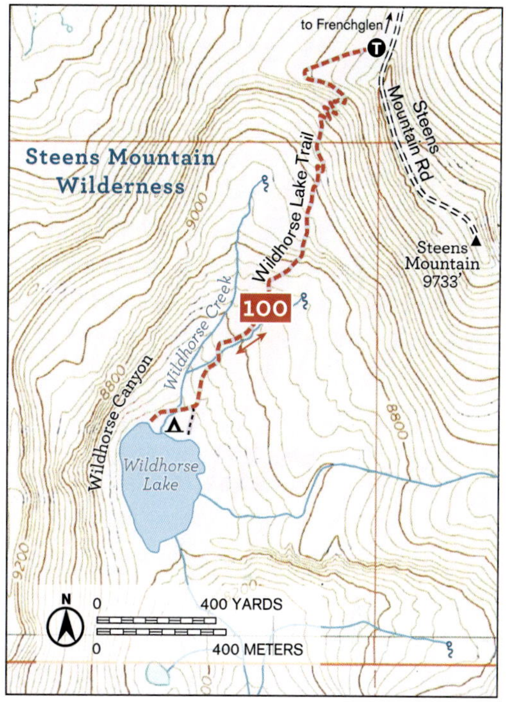

From the trailhead, hike down an old, rocky road for 0.2 mile to a trail fork and registration box. Along the way, stalks of desert thistle and clusters of dwarf lupine and yarrow paint the trailside in purple and white. Peer westward over the summit plateau and down into the head of Big Indian Gorge (see Hike 99). Tear your gaze away from the lake basin in front of you for just a minute to sign the register, then veer left (south) onto the lake trail. The way into the basin starts with a slightly harrowing traverse along the side of a sharp cliff on loose, rocky tread. The slope eventually widens and quickly descends along a series of switchbacks into the upper basin.

Due to the high elevation, wildflowers tend to linger longer into the summer here, with carpets of aster, monkey flower, and cinquefoil painting swaths of pink and yellow across the slopes. Cross a small spring that dribbles across the trail, then descend into the lower lake basin on a series of tight, steep switchbacks. The trail then follows the spring channel down toward the lake. Soon the lake basin becomes all-encompassing. Near the lakeshore, the trail breaks out into various user paths that lead to campsites and viewpoints. Head right (west) toward the head of the lake and a small, gravelly beach. The view across the lake from here mimics an infinity pool, with the walls of the basin rising high on either side. Enjoy the captivating serenity of the lake for as long as you can while giving yourself extra time for the long, steep hike back up to the trailhead.

Acknowledgments

Early in the development of this guidebook, I suffered a sudden and unexpected heart attack. Thankfully, I was not on a trail at the time (I was actually on a break between trails), and I was able to get swift and exceptional medical attention. After six months of rehab, I was back on the trails, diligently—albeit a little slowly at first—working to get back into my hiking and writing groove.

First and foremost, I need to thank my amazing wife, Mitzi Sugar, for being by my side—and occasionally on the trails with me—through every step of my recovery and return to "normal." I couldn't have done it without you, babe. My sincerest thanks also go to my uncle and aunt, Dale and Marilyn Boschetto, who—even from half a world away—were able to coordinate assistance and provide support through one of the scariest moments of my life.

Thanks to my ICU nurse, Chad Johnson, who inspired me to keep going and not give up over a pesky little heart attack, and to my therapist, Allie Corcoran, who has been instrumental in helping me deal with the emotional roller coaster of being a trauma survivor. Thanks also to my dearest friends, Ricky and Christina Lam and Catie Tharp, for their unwavering support and encouragement.

Props to all my PortLUG and LEGO community cohorts for their friendship, inspiration, and encouragement: Hunter, JJ, Kelly, TOG, Grant, John, John, Drew, Drew, Jesika, Larry, Rick, Cody, and Bryan. And to my fellow outdoor author friends—Tami, Lisa, Cassandra, Rachel, and Brandon—thanks for your continued support.

Thank you, too, to Kate Rogers, Janet Kimball, and Lori Hobkirk at Mountaineers Books, who were more than willing to move deadlines and push back schedules, allowing me to fully recover and return to the trails on my own time so I could develop this guidebook as fully and completely as possible. And thanks to my editor, Emily Estes, who helped polish my sometimes rambling and verbose editorial.

Opposite, clockwise from top left: elephants head, fairybells, monkey flower, larkspur, trillium, mariposa lily

Resources and Land Managers

Central Cascades Wilderness Permits

Day use:
www.recreation.gov/ticket/facility/300009
Overnight:
www.recreation.gov/permits/4675311

Columbia River Gorge National Scenic Area

www.fs.usda.gov/crgnsa
(541) 308-1700

Crater Lake Boat and Trolley Tours

https://explorecraterlake.com
(866) 292-6720

Crater Lake National Park

www.nps.gov/crla
(541) 594-3000

Deschutes National Forest

www.fs.usda.gov/deschutes

Bend–Fort Rock Ranger District
(541) 383-5300

Sisters Ranger District
(541) 549-7700

Fremont–Winema National Forest

www.fs.usda.gov/r06/fremont-winema
(541) 947-2151

Chemult Ranger District
(541) 365-7001

Klamath Ranger District
(541) 883-6714

Hoyt Arboretum

www.hoytarboretum.org
(503) 865-8733

John Day Fossil Beds National Monument

www.nps.gov/joda
(541) 987-2333

Lewis and Clark National Historical Park

www.nps.gov/lewi
(503) 861-2471

Malheur National Forest

www.fs.usda.gov/malheur
(541) 575-3000

Emigrant Creek Ranger District
(541) 573-4300

Prairie City Ranger District
(541) 820-3800

Mount Hood National Forest

www.fs.usda.gov/mthood
(503) 668-1700

Clackamas River Ranger District
(971) 333-4100

Hood River Ranger District
(541) 352-6002

Zigzag Ranger District
(503) 622-3191

Newberry National Volcanic Monument

www.fs.usda.gov/visit/destination/newberry-national-volcanic-monument-0
(541) 383-5300

Northwest Forest Pass

www.discovernw.org

Ochoco National Forest

www.fs.usda.gov/ochoco
(541) 416-6500

Opposite, clockwise from top left: bull thistle, bunchberry, prairie smoke, swamp onion, moth mullien, honeysuckle

Oregon Bureau of Land Management (BLM)

www.blm.gov/oregon-washington
(503) 808-6001

Burns District Office
(541) 573-4400

Medford District Office
(541) 618-2200

Oregon State Parks

https://stateparks.oregon.gov
(503) 986-0707

Portland Parks and Recreation

www.portland.gov/parks
(503) 823-2525

Rogue River–Siskiyou National Forest

www.fs.usda.gov/rogue-siskiyou
(541) 618-2200

Gold Beach Ranger District
(541) 247-3600

High Cascades Ranger District
(541) 560-3400

Siuslaw National Forest

www.fs.usda.gov/siuslaw
(541) 750-7000

Tillamook Rock Lighthouse

www.oregonencyclopedia.org/articles/tillamook_rock_lighthouse

Tillamook State Forest

www.tillamookforestcenter.org
(503) 815-6800

Umatilla National Forest

www.fs.usda.gov/umatilla
(541) 278-3716

North Fork John Day Ranger District
(541) 427-3231

Pomeroy Ranger District
(509) 843-1891

Walla Walla Ranger District
(509) 522-6290

Umpqua National Forest

www.fs.usda.gov/umpqua
(541) 440-4930

Diamond Lake Visitor Center
(541) 793-3310

North Umpqua Ranger District
(541) 496-3532

Wallowa–Whitman National Forest

www.fs.usda.gov/r06/wallowa-whitman
(541) 523-6391

La Grande Ranger District
(541) 962-8500

Wallowa Mountains Office
(541) 426-5546

Willamette National Forest

www.fs.usda.gov/willamette
(541) 225-6300

Detroit Ranger District
(503) 854-3366

McKenzie River Ranger District
(541) 822-3381

Middle Fork Ranger District
(541) 782-2283

References and Recommended Reading

Asars, Tami. *Hiking the Pacific Crest Trail: Washington*. Seattle: Mountaineers Books, 2016.

Boschetto, Eli. *Day Hiking Mount Hood*. Seattle: Mountaineers Books, 2020.

——. *Hiking the Pacific Crest Trail: Oregon*. Seattle: Mountaineers Books, 2016.

——. *Urban Trails: Portland*. Seattle: Mountaineers Books, 2018.

Fralic, Brandon, and Rachel Wood. *Beer Hiking Pacific Northwest*, 2nd ed. Switzerland: Helvetiq, 2022.

Henderson, Bonnie. *Hiking the Oregon Coast Trail*. Seattle: Mountaineers Books, 2021.

Holmes, Lisa. *I Heart Oregon's Seven Wonders*. Portland: Yulan Studio, 2016.

——. *Memorable Backcountry Meals*. Portland: Yulan Studio, 2021.

Manwill, Brittany. *Day Hiking Bend*. Seattle: Mountaineers Books, 2016.

McArthur, Lewis. *Oregon Geographic Names*, 6th ed. Portland: Oregon Historical Society, 1991.

Orr, Elizabeth, and William Orr. *Oregon Geology*, 6th ed. Corvallis: OSU Press, 2012.

Romano, Craig. *100 Classic Hikes in Washington*. Seattle: Mountaineers Books, 2016.

Sullivan, William. *Atlas of Oregon Wilderness*. Eugene: Navillus Press, 2009.

Tolkien, J. R. R. *The Lord of the Rings*. New York: William Morrow, 2013. Originally published 1965.

Zangle, Libby. *Rabid: The Pacific Crest Trail. 'Cause Therapy Ain't Working*. Lulu.com, 2014.

Index

A

a'a 165, 213
Alta Lake Trail 201
Ancient Juniper Forest 212
Aneroid Lake 244
Aneroid Mountain 244, 245
Angels Rest 102
Arch Rock 231
Arrow Lake 263
Aspen Butte 203

B

Badger Butte 234
Badger Creek Wilderness 142
Badlands Rock Trail 214
Bailey Butte 260
Balch Creek 94
Bald Mountain 123, 140
Barrett Spur 122, 141
Battle Mountain Summit 231
bears 27
Bear Lake Trail 266, 267
Beaver Creek Falls 60
Belknap Crater 164
Bench Canyon Trail 264
Bend Parks and Recreation 218
Big Indian Gorge 272, 272
Big Obsidian Flow 211
Bird Alliance of Oregon 93, 95
Bird Butte 149
Blacklock Point 65
Blow Lake 175
Blue Basin 226
Blue Mountains 233, 237
Bluegrass Ridge Trail 137
Bonny Lakes 243
Boulder Park Campground 263
Bowman Trail 256, 259
Bridge Creek Falls 171
Bridge Creek Wildlife Area 232
Broken Top 170, 173
Brownie Basin 257, 260
Buck Creek Trail 237
Buck Mountain 237
Burnt Lake 127

C

Cairn Basin 140
Cached Lake 263, 265
Cant Ranch 228
Cape Falcon 45
Cape Ferrelo 73
Cape Lookout 48
Cape Perpetua Scenic Area 57
Cape Sebastian State Park 70
Captain Cook Trail 58
Cascade Lakes 175
Cascade–Siskiyou National Monument 204
Cathedral Rocks 155
Cascade Head 50
Central Cascades Wilderness Permit 17
Chambers Lakes 169
Chief Josepy Trail 247
Chimney Lake 253, 254
Chimney Lake North 253
Chinidere Mountain 118
Cinder Hill 212
cinnabar 224
cirque 183, 184, 244, 247, 266, 267
Civilian Conservation Corps (CCC) 123, 133, 135
Clarno Formation 232
Clatsop Loop 43
Cleetwood Cove 195
Cliff Lake (Cascade Lakes) 177
Cliff Lake (Sky Lakes) 200
Cloud Cap Inn 132
Coe Glacier 122, 141
Collier Glacier 170
Columbia River Gorge NSA 100, 102, 104, 105, 107, 114
Cone Peak Trail 159
cooking 25
Cooper Mountain Nature Park 84
Cooper Spur 132, 141
Cooper Spur Shelter 133
Copper Creek Trail 258
cougars 27
Cow Creek Trailhead 241
Coyote Lake 156
Crater Butte Trail 183
Crater Lake Lodge 197
Crater Lake National Park 194, 196
Crater Lake Rim Village 196
Crater Rim Trail 211
Craig Mountain 248
Crawfish Lake Trail 233
Crescent Lake 183
Crooked River 220
Culver Lake South 267

D

Dellenback Dunes 61
Devil's Backbone 195
Devils Lake 168
Devils Peak 200
Diamond Peak 177, 180
Diamond Peak Loop 181
Diamond Peak Wilderness 180, 183
Diamond View Lake 183
dike 221
Divide Trail 143
dogs
Dollar Lake (Mount Hood) 141
Dollar Lake (Wallowas) 243
Dollar Lake Peak 243
Doris Lake 175
Douglas Lake 252
Drift Creek Falls 54
Duffy Lake 156

E

Eagle Cap 249, 256
Eagle Cap Wilderness 242, 245, 247, 249, 253, 256, 257, 260, 263
Eagle Creek (Wallowas) 264

Eagle Creek Trail (Columbia Gorge NSA) 108
Eagle Lake 2 63
East Eliot Moraine Trail 132
East Fork Lostine Trail 252
East Fork Wallowa Trail 244
East Lake 210
Eb and Zeb Lakes 202
Echo Lake 260
Ecola State Park 43
Ecola Falls 106
Eliot Branch 141
Eliot Glacier 133, 142
Elk Cove 141
Elk Devils Trail 168
Elk Meadows Trail 135
Elk Mountain 48
Elkhorn Meadows 258
Emigrant Pass 184

F

Fairy Falls 105
Fake Creek Trail 260
fault-block mountain 272
Flatiron Rock Trail 214
Flora Dell Falls 68
Floras Lake SNA 65
food storage 25
Forest Park 89, 94
Fort Rock State Natural Area 2 08
Fort to Sea Trail 38
Francis (Frances) Lake 252
Frazier Lake 249
Frog Lake Butte Trail 149

G

Garfield Peak 195, 196
Giant Spruce 57
Glacier Creek 169
Glacier Lake 249
Gnarl Ridge Trail 137
Gods Thumb 51, 53
Golden Lake 170
Gone Creek Campground 151
Goose Lake 177
granite 236, 248, 254, 257, 261
Grass Lake 199
Graves Butte 237
Green Lakes 170
Guy W. Talbot State Park 100

H

Hanks Lake 155
Heart Lake 264
Heather Canyon 137, 142
Hells Canyon NRA 240, 245
Hidden Lake Trail 129
High Lake 230
High Prairie 142
High Wallowas-East Peak Trail 246
Homestead Trail 214
Hood River Mountain 111
Hood View Campground 151
Horseshoe Lake (Cascade Lakes) 177
Horseshoe Lake (Wallowas) 252
Howlock Mountain 191, 192
Howlock Mountain Trail 192
Hoyt Arboretum 87
Humbug Mountain 67
Hummingbird Mountain 267
Hunters Cove 70
Hunts Cove 154
Hunts Lake 155
hunting 26
Hurwal Divide 248

I

Ice Cap Campground 162
Ice Lake 245, 246
Imnaha River Trail 240
Independent Mine Trail 225
Indian Spring Butte 230
Iron Mountain Lookout 158
Island in Time Trail 226
Island Lake 201

J

John Day Fossil Beds NM 226
John Day River 232
John Henry Lake 259
Jupiter 201

K

Kaleetan Butte 168
Kings Mountain 47
kipuka 164
Koosah Falls 161

L

Ladd Glacier 122, 141
Lake Alta 201
Lake Como 203
Lake Harriette 203
Lake Ivern 201
Lakes Basin Trail 249
Lakeside Trail 177
Lamberson Butte 142
Latourell Falls 100
Lava Butte Lookout 216
Lava Lands Visitor Center 216
Lava River Cave 75
lava tube 58, 164, 213, 214
Laverty Lakes 257
Leave No Trace 19
Le Conte Crater Trail 168
Lemolo Falls 187
Leslie Gulch 270
Lewis and Clark National Historical Park 38
lightning 24
Little Belknap 164
Little Crater Lake 150
Little Crater Meadow 150
Little Strawberry Lake 229
Llao Rock 195
Long Lake Trail 258
Lookingglass Lake 266
Lookout Mountain (Badger Creek) 142
Lookout Mountain (Ochocos) 223
Lookout Mountain (Wallowas) 257
Loowit Falls 109
Lostine River 256, 258
Lower Table Rock 76
Lucifer 201

M

maar volcano 208
Mac Lake 177
Mahogany Mountain 270
Maidu Lake 187
Main Eagle Trail 264
Marble Point 253, 256
Matterhorn 248
Matthieu Lakes 170
Mayer State Park 114
Mazama Trail 124, 140
McCall Point 113
McDowell Creek Falls 79
McGee Creek Trail 123

McKenzie River National Scenic Trail 160, 163
McNeil Point 122, 140
Meditation Point 150
Merrill Lake 177
Mesa Creek Meadows 169
Mesa Verde Trail 221
Middle Lake 200
Middle Sister 169
Miller Lake Campground 189
Minam Lake Trail 258
Mink Lake 174
Mirror Lake (Mount Hood) 144
Mirror Lake (Wallowas) 252
Misery Ridge Trail 220
Mississippi Head 129, 140
Moccasin Lake 252
Monkey Face 221
Moraine Lake Trail 168, 170
Morning Glory Wall 221
Mother Lode Mine Trail 225
Mountain Lakes Loop 201
Mountain Lakes Wilderness 202
Mountaineer Trail 129
Mount Bachelor 174
Mount Harriman 202
Mount Hood Wilderness 122, 124, 126, 128, 129, 132, 135, 140, 148
Mount Howard 244
Mount Jefferson Wilderness 154, 157
Mount Mazama 193, 194, 196
Mount McLoughlin 202
Mount Scott Lookout 198
Mount Shasta 205, 211
Mount Theilsen 191, 192
Mount Thielsen Wilderness 191
Mount Washington Wilderness 164
Mount Yoran Trail 180, 184
Mowich Lake 158
Muddy Fork 124
Multnomah Falls 104

N

Needle Point 266
Newberry Caldera 209
Newberry Crater Trail 212
Newberry National Volcanic Monument 209, 214, 216
Newton Clark Glacier 134, 142
Newton Creek Trail 136
Nine Mile Ridge 236
North Arm Campground 150
North Basin Peak 252
North Fork John Day Wilderness 233
North Fork Trail 171
North Lake 201
North Fork Imnaha Trail 244
North Fork Umatilla Wilderness 236
North Minam Meadows 259
North Minam Trail 258
North Umpqua Trail 187
Northwest Forest Pass 17
Notch Lake 180

O

Oak Fork Campground 151
Obsidian Falls 169
Old 1916 Trail 151
Old Salmon River Trail 146
Old Vista Ridge Trail 121
Onion Creek Trail 230
Opie Dildock Pass 170
Oregon Badlands Wilderness 212
Oregon BLM 76, 204, 212, 270, 272, 274
Oregon Coast Trail (OCT) 43, 49, 72
Oregon Dunes NRA 61
Oswald West State Park 45
Owl Point 120
Owyhee Canyonlands 270

P

Pacific Crest Trail (PCT) 123, 126, 129, 140, 148, 150, 155, 164, 169, 177, 178, 184, 189, 190, 192, 199, 204
Packsaddle Mountain 177
pahoehoe 163, 165, 213, 214
Palmateer Trail 149
Pamelia Lake 154
Paradise Park 129, 140
Paradise Park Loop 131, 140
Paulina Lake 210
Paulina Lake Campground 212
Paulina Lakeshore Trail 212
Paulina Peak Trail 211
Permits 17
Petes Point 244, 249
Phantom Ship 197
Pilot Rock 204
Pine Point Campground 151
Pinnacle Ridge Trail 141
Polaris Pass 244, 249
Pop Summit 266
Porky Lake 177
Powell Butte Nature Park 95
Pulpit Rock 179
Punchbowl Falls 109

R

Rabbit Ears 229
Ramona Falls 125, 140
Reese Lake 169
river fords
Road's End Trail 230
Rogue River Trail 68
Rosary Lakes 178
Round Mountain Trail 223
Rowena Plateau 113

S

S Lake 177
Saddle Mountain 40
safety 23
Sahale Falls Trail 136
Saint Perpetua Trail 58
Sahalie Falls 160
Salmon-Huckleberry Wilderness 146
Samuel H. Boardman State Scenic Corridor 72
Sandy Glacier 124
Sandy River Trail 126
Santiam Lake 156
Santiam Wagon Road Trail 160
Savage Peak 264
Seven Lakes Basin 198
Seven Lakes Trail 199
Sevenmile Trail 199
Shale Lake 156
Shelter Cove Resort 181
Shevlin Park 218
Shore Acres State Park 63
Silver Falls State Park 81

Siuslaw National Forest 50, 54, 57, 61
Six Lakes Trail 175
Six-Mile Meadow 249
Sky Lake (Wallowas) 258
Sky Lakes Wilderness 199
Skyline Trail 230
Slide Basin Trail 228
Slide Lake 230
Smith Rock State Park 220
Snake River, Wild & Scenic 241, 245
Soda Mountain Wilderness 204
Southshore Trail 151
South Sister 169, 177
South Sister Climber Trail 170
Spencer Butte 77
Spruce Ridge Trail 193
Steamboat Lake 257
Steens Mountain 272, 274
Steens Mountain Wilderness 272, 274
Steins Pillar 222
Strawberry Basin Trail 228
Strawberry Falls 229
Strawberry Lake 228
Strawberry Mountain 231
Strawberry Mountain Wilderness 228
Summit Lake 184
Sunset Bay State Park 62
Swamp Lake (Wallowas) 258
Swampy Lakes Trail (Deschutes NF) 171
Sweet Creek Falls 59

T

Tamolitch Falls (Blue Pool) 162
Ten Essentials 30
Tenderfoot Pass 244
Tenderfoot Wagon Road 243
The Castle 214
The Knoll Open Space 53
The Watchman 195, 198
Thielsen Creek Trail 192
Thomas Condon Visitor Center 228
Thor's Well 58
Three Sisters Loop 165
Three Sisters Wilderness 166, 168, 175
Tillamook Head 43
Tillamook State Forest 47
Tilly Jane Trail 132
Timberline Lodge 129, 140
Timberline Trail 123, 126, 129, 132, 137
Timothy Lake 149
Tipsoo Pass 191, 194
Tipsoo Peak 189
Todd Lake Loop 172
Toketee Falls 186
Tom Dick and Harry Mountain 145
Tom McCall Preserve 113
Tombstone Lake Trail 261
Top Spur Trail 123
trail etiquette 21
Trail of Molten Land 218
Trail of Ten Falls 81
Trailkeepers of Oregon 121
Trapper Creek Trail 183
Traverse Lake 263
Traverse Lake East Peak 264
Tryon Creek SNA 85
tuff 221, 222, 232, 270
Tumalo Creek 218
Tumalo Falls 170
Tunnel Falls 109
Twin Lakes 148
Two Pan Trailhead 252, 256

U

Umatilla Forks Campground 236
Umbrella Falls Trail 137, 142

V

Varney Creek Trail 202
Venus 201
Vista Ridge Trail 121, 141
Vivian Lake Trail 180

W

Wahclella Falls 107
Wahkeena Falls 105
Wallowa Lake State Park 244
Wallowa Lake Tramway 245
Wallowa Mountains 236, 241, 249, 252, 260, 263
Waterfalls Loop Trail 161
weather 23
Wenaha River Trail 238
Wenaha State Wildlife Area 239
West Eagle Campground 260
West Eagle Trail 260
West Fork Wallowa Trail 247, 249
Whaleshead Beach 73
Whispering Pines Trail 218
White River Canyon 142
Whiteface Peak 202
Whitefish Creek Trail 183
Wickiup Plains Trail 168
Wilderness Act 18
wilderness permits 17
Wildhorse Lake 274
wildlife 27
Wildwood Trail 89, 95
Wisendanger Falls 106
Witch's Castle 94
Wizard Island 194
Wood Lake Trail 257, 260
Wy'east Basin 141

Y

Yapoah Crater 170
Yocum Ridge Trail 138
Yoran Lake Trail 184

Z

Zigzag East Lookout 129
Zigzag Glacier 129
Zigzag Mountain Trail 129
Zigzag River 129, 140

About the Author

Eli Boschetto grew up hiking the alpine backcountry of California's Sierra Nevada mountains. He and his wife, Mitzi, moved to Portland, Oregon, in 2005 and continued their outdoor adventures throughout the Northwest, British Columbia, and several European countries. Eli's favorite place to hike in Oregon is the Eagle Cap Wilderness.

Eli is the author of *Hiking the Pacific Crest Trail: Oregon, Day Hiking Mount Hood* and *Urban Trails: Portland*. Prior to writing for Mountaineers Books, Eli wrote for *Backpacker* and served as the editor of *Washington Trails*. He was instrumental in planning Adidas's 2023 United by Summits Pacific Crest Trail Adventure, and has served on the advisory council of the Oregon Trails Coalition.

When not on the trails, Eli enjoys building custom LEGO creations and serves on the board of PortLUG, Portland's adult LEGO-building community. You might find him riding his bike around town or sitting at one of his favorite coffee shops planning his next adventures.